P9-CLD-526

# Unix and Linux

## FIFTH EDITION

DEBORAH RAY • ERIC RAY

Peachpit Press

Visual QuickStart Guide
**Unix and Linux, Fifth Edition**
Deborah Ray and Eric Ray

Peachpit Press
www.peachpit.com

To report errors, please send a note to errata@peachpit.com.
Peachit Press is a dvision of Pearson Education.

Copyright © 2015 by Deborah Ray and Eric Ray

Editor: Clifford Colby
Development editor: Robyn G. Thomas
Senior production editor: Lisa Brazieal
Copyeditor: Scout Festa
Technical editor: Bruce Byfield
Compositor: Danielle Foster
Indexer: James Minkin
Cover design: RHDG / Riezebos Holzbaur Design Group, Peachpit Press
Interior design: Peachpit Press
Logo design: MINE™ www.minesf.com

ISBN 13:  978-0-321-99754-8
ISBN 10:   0-321-99754-9

4 2021

Printed and bound in the United States of America

## Dedication

To Simon Hayes, who helped develop this book's first edition—the foundation for this book's long-term success.

## Acknowledgments

This book came together with the invaluable assistance of a number of very talented and supportive people. Thanks to Clifford Colby for his continued confidence and support; it's always a treat to work with you! Our thanks to Robyn Thomas as well, who was a delight to work with and helped tremendously in pulling the various pieces together. Scout Festa was really helpful as copyeditor and was a great proofreader. Lisa Brazieal did a great job in production, even with our special needs. And our special thanks to Bruce Byfield, whose careful attention to detail and deep knowledge of the idiosyncrasies of Unix and Linux helped iron out technical rough spots. Thanks, all!

# Table of Contents

NC 03.31.2021 1452

# Introduction

Greetings, and welcome to Unix and Linux!

In this book, you'll find the information you need to get started with the operating system, advance your skills, and make Linux or Unix do the hard work for you. This book focuses on the most common Unix and Linux commands, but it also gives you ideas for working smartly and efficiently.

For the purposes of this book, Unix and Linux are pretty much interchangeable—the commands and usages are the same. You may find small differences among Unix versions or between specific Unix or Linux versions, but they'll be small indeed.

## How Do You Use This Book?

We designed this book to be used as both a tutorial and a reference. If you're a Unix newbie, you should start at the beginning and work forward through the first several chapters. As you progress through the chapters, you'll build on concepts and commands you learned in previous chapters. Then, as you become more proficient, you

can start choosing topics, depending on what you want to do. Be sure to reference the table of contents, the index, and the appendixes to find information at a glance.

The commands used throughout this book apply to any version of Unix (or Linux) you might be using, including Solaris, OpenIndiana, BSD, Linux (any or all), AIX or HP-UX, your OS X or Linux system at home, or any other *flavor* (that's the technical term) you can find. Heck, you can even run something very Unix-like from your Windows system with Cygwin. Or you can run the Unix or Linux of your choice under VirtualBox, VMWare, or other virtualization programs. You'll find more about flavors and getting access to Unix or Linux in Chapter 1.

By the way, if you're looking around on the Internet for information, you'll find that a number of people sidestep the awkward discussion of various flavors of Unix and Linux by using the term *Un*x*. That seems a little too geeky, even for us, so we opted out of that one. (*Un*x* sidesteps a perceived issue of trademark enforcement with the specific name Unix and manages to convey the "and Linux too, when it's like

Unix" concept as well. Useful, but geeky. In this book, we'll stick to *Unix* and *Linux*.)

Each chapter covers several topics, each of which is presented in its own section. Each section begins with a brief overview of the topic, often including examples or descriptions of how or when you'd use a command.

Next, you'll find a step-by-step list (or a couple of them) to show you how to complete a process. Note that the code you type appears as the numbered step, and a description follows it, like this:

1. **The code you type will appear like**
   **→ this, in a blocky font.**

   An explanation will appear like this, in a regular font. Here, we often describe what you're typing, give alternatives, or provide cross-references to related information.

If a line of code in a numbered step is particularly long, the code might wrap to a second line. Just type the characters shown, without pressing Enter until the end of the command. Also, in code listings throughout the book, a single line of code onscreen might wrap to two lines in the book. If this happens, the continued line will start with an arrow, so it might look like this:

**The beginning of the code starts here,**
**→ but it continues on this line.**

Sometimes you'll have to press a special key or key combination—like Ctrl+C, which means to hold down the Ctrl key and press C. We'll use this special keyboard font for these keys, but not for letters or numbers or symbols you might type.

Finally, most sections end with a couple of handy tips. Look here for ways to combine Unix and Linux commands, suggestions for using commands more efficiently, and ideas for finding out more information.

# Who Are You?

We assume that you've picked up this book because you already have a need for or an interest in learning to use Unix or any Unix-like operating system, such as Linux, OpenIndiana, OS X, BSD, HP-UX, AIX, Solaris, or others.

Reasons and places to use Unix or Linux abound. Have an Android phone? Linux inside. How about a Kindle Fire tablet? Linux inside. Neighbors experimenting with a Raspberry Pi device? Yup, Linux. Your home Wi-Fi router probably contains Linux, as does your digital cable box. Unix and Linux are everywhere (even if they're hidden sometimes).

Many techie tasks are easier if you have some knowledge of Unix or Linux. For example, if you're installing Minecraft mods, knowing how your shell prompt works makes the process smoother. If you...or someone you know, that is...are rooting or flashing an Android device, knowing Linux can help there, too. And you get SuperGeek points for being able to watch movies and know that the villain is using Unix when writing that fatally flawed program to conquer the world.

We assume that

- You want to know how to use Unix or Linux to do things at work, school, or home.

- You may or may not already have experience with Unix or Linux.

- You don't necessarily have other geeky—er, techie—computer skills or experience.

- You want to learn to use Unix or Linux but probably do not want to delve into all the arcane details about the system.

In short, we assume you want to use Unix or Linux to achieve your computing goals. You want to know what you can do, get an idea of the potential that a command offers, and learn how to work smart. Very smart.

You can do all these things using this book. Basically, all you need is access to an account or system and a goal (or goals) that you want to achieve.

## What Do You Need Computer-Wise?

You can learn or experiment with Unix using virtually any computer you might have available. If you're using a Mac with OS X, you're all set; it's all Unix under the hood. If you have an extra computer sitting around, even something as old as a Pentium III, you can install several different flavors of Unix or Linux, including Solaris, OpenIndiana, Ubuntu, Red Hat, or SuSE. Certainly you can install Unix or Linux on an extra hard drive (or empty space on your current hard drive) on your regular desktop computer, and generally without affecting your existing Windows configuration.

Alternatively, you can dabble in Unix less invasively by using an account on a system at work or through an Internet service provider. If you have a reasonably new computer and are concerned about not messing up what you have, though, the easiest options are to

- Use Cygwin to run Unix as part of your Windows environment

- Use VirtualBox or a similar program to run Unix in a "virtual machine" as an application in your Windows environment

- Use a bootable Unix (Linux will be the easiest) CD to experiment on without having to install anything at all on your computer (and save files to a flash drive as needed)

## What Do You Need to Know to Get Started?

As you get started learning Unix or Linux, keep in mind the following Unix and Linux conventions for typing commands:

- The terminology and commands are typically arcane, cryptic, and funny-looking. For example, the command to list files or directories is just ls—short and cryptic. (The command ls is also short for list, as in "list the files." Many commands have these logical derivations.) We'll walk you through the commands one step at a time so that you know how to read them and apply them to your own uses. Just follow the steps in the order provided.

- Unix and Linux are case sensitive, so type commands following the capitalization used in the book.

- Whenever you type a command, you also have to press [Enter]. For example, if we say

1. **funny-looking command goes here**

   you'll type the code, then press [Enter], which sends the command along to the Unix system.

   Often, we'll tell you to press a combination of keys on the keyboard, as in [Ctrl]+[V]. Here, all you do is press the [Ctrl] key plus the (lowercase) [V] key, both at the same time. Even though the keyboard uses capital letters (and, thus, the little key icons also do in this book), you would not take the extra step to capitalize the V (or whatever) in applying key combinations. If you really need to press [Shift], we'll show you that.

   Some commands have flags or arguments (also called options) associated with them (you might think of flags as modifiers for the command) that give you additional control. For example, you might see the **ls** command used in variations like **ls -la** or **ls -l -a**. In either case, **ls** lists the files in a directory, the optional **-l** flag specifies that you want the long format, and the optional **-a** flag specifies all files, including hidden ones (don't worry, we'll go over this again!). Just keep in mind that flags and arguments are essentially options you can use with a given command.

- You can also put multiple commands on the same line. All you have to do is separate the commands with a semicolon (;), like this:

  `ls ; pwd`

  which would list the files in the current directory (**ls**) and find out what directory you're in (**pwd**)—all in one step!

So, with these things in mind, see you in Chapter 1!

# Anything Else You Should Know?

Yup! Please feel free to send us a message at **unixvqs@raycomm.com**. We welcome your input, suggestions, and questions related to this book. Thanks, and we look forward to hearing from you!

## Note to Mac Users

For simplicity, we consistently write [Enter] (not [Return]), [Ctrl] (not [Control]), and [Alt] (not [Option]), and we refer (not very often, though) to a Recycle Bin (not a Trash Can). No slight intended to those who do not use PCs or Windows—we just tried to keep the complexity of the instructions to a minimum.

# Getting Started with Unix and Linux

To start you on your journey through Unix and Linux, we'll take a quick look at a few basic concepts and commands. In this chapter, we'll get you started with basic Unix and Linux skills, such as accessing an account, logging in, and listing and viewing files and directories, among other things. We'll also show you how to explore Unix and Linux, see its capabilities, and discover just what you can do with it.

This chapter is essential for all Unix or Linux guru-wannabes. If you're a Unix or Linux novice, you should start at the beginning of this chapter and work through each section in sequence. With these basic skills mastered, you can then skip through this book and learn new skills that look useful or interesting to you. If you've used Unix or Linux before, you might skim this chapter to review the basics and dust off any cobwebs you might have.

The skills covered in this chapter apply to any version of Unix you might be using, including Linux, Solaris, or BSD; AIX or HP-UX at work; your OS X or Linux system at home; Cygwin on your Windows system; any number of options through VirtualBox or VMware—or even Linux or Unix from a bootable CD—on your home system; or any other *flavor* (that's the technical term) you can find. Whew. Keep in mind, though, that the exact output and prompts you see on the screen might differ slightly from what is illustrated in this book. The differences probably won't affect the steps you're completing, although you should be aware that differences could exist. (As much as possible, our examples will give you a sample of the diversity of Unix systems.)

# Accessing a Unix System

Using a shared Unix or Linux system is different from working on a personal computer. When you're using a personal computer, in general, the computer's hard drive is your personal space, and—generally—you don't have access to what's on someone else's system. With Unix or Linux, you have your own personal space that's located within a much bigger system.

You might think of Unix as an apartment building, with lots of individual apartment spaces, a central office, and perhaps other general spaces, like a maintenance office. With Unix, you have the entire system, which houses dozens, hundreds, or even thousands of personal spaces, as well as private spaces for, say, the system administrator, bosses, or IT (Information Technology) department staff. You can access only your apartment, but the system administrator (or designated people with authorization) can access any apartment.

Of course, if your Unix or Linux system is just installed in a virtual machine (under VirtualBox or VMWare) on your computer, then you still have full run of the system because you are your own system administrator. This book will sharpen those *sysadmin* skills!

People choose to use Unix or Linux for a number of reasons:

- **Control:** Unix and Linux offer users more control and customization on the legal and licensing side as well as on the "getting stuff done" side.

- **Economy:** Many flavors of Unix and Linux offer very friendly licensing terms, in which the operating system is free to use, or even free to use and for programmers to take and modify.

- **Power:** Experienced geeks can do more with less effort on Unix or Linux than on Windows—for many things, at least.

In the final analysis, though, most Unix or Linux people end up sticking with it because they tried it, slogged through the initial learning curve, and then decided they like it.

## Different types of Unix and Linux access

So, the first question is how you might access a system to get started with all of this. Given that this is Unix, you have many options:

- Connect to a shell account.

- Access your company's (or school's or organization's) Unix or Linux system.

- Use it on your Mac.

- Use a live CD, such as an Ubuntu or OpenIndiana CD.

- Do a Unix or Linux installation in a virtual machine on your computer.

- Do a Unix-only installation on an old or spare computer.

- Do a Unix/Windows installation on your everyday computer.

## Accessing a shell account

The traditional approach (back in the olden days, when we wrote the first version of this book) was to connect to a "shell account" provided by your dial-up ISP. That's still an option, if you have certain ISPs (and even with some broadband connections). If your ISP offers a shell account, go ahead and use it; it's still a good option. Try an online search for "Unix shell account" as well.

## Accessing your company's system

If your ISP does not offer a shell account (if you have a cable modem, DSL connection, or dial-up connection through any of the huge companies that provide Internet access, your ISP does not offer a shell account), you still have a ton of options. Check at work; many companies use Unix and Linux in a number of ways, and if you can provide the system administrator with appropriate quantities of cookies or other goodies, you may be able to get system access.

## Installing Unix or Linux on an old or spare computer

Alternatively, if you'd rather keep your Unix or Linux explorations closer to home, you can manage that as well. If you have an older computer sitting around (say, anything that's a Pentium III or later), you can just install Unix or Linux on that, and likely without hassles or problems. You could make it work on even older computers, but given how cheap new and used computers are, it's likely not worth the trouble. Either way, you'll download a CD or DVD from the web, burn it onto a disc or copy it to a USB flash drive, and boot your system from that device. The installation will start, and a few questions and a few minutes later, you'll be all set.

## Installing Unix and Windows side by side

You can also download the CD or DVD and install on your everyday desktop computer. Most of the time (actually virtually all the time, but we're making no promises here), you can install Unix or Linux onto your desktop right alongside your Windows environment without breaking anything (although we don't promise that you won't have to read the instructions on the particular operating system in the process). You'll get it installed, reboot your system, and choose Unix (Linux, OpenIndiana, whatever) or Windows when you boot up. This option isn't bad, but it does require you to stop what you're doing in Windows or Unix to change to the other. If your desktop computer is relatively old, this might be better than the following options, though.

If you have a beefy desktop computer (relatively new with ample memory and disk space), you could try using VirtualBox, VMWare, VirtualPC, or other virtualization environments, which gives you *computer emulation* (think "picture in picture" for your computer, but with one operating system within the other operating system).

Many of the examples and screenshots for this book were taken from Unix or Linux systems running under VirtualBox on one of our desktop computers (a Mac, technically).

Cygwin provides you with a Unix-like environment that's actually part of your Windows system. It takes a bit of getting used to, but Cygwin is stable and reliable. The hardest part about using Cygwin is that it can be confusing to know whether you're dealing with Unix or Windows concepts at any given moment.

## Choosing a Unix or Linux flavor

So, given all of those options for getting access to Unix and Linux, the choice of which kind of Unix or Linux (called a *flavor*) must be clear and straightforward, right? Of course not.

If you're just getting started, we recommend you choose the flavor that your most techie friends or the folks at work use. This will give you potential built-in tech support options.

If you're starting purely from scratch, look into the most popular and highly rated Linux distributions. (Currently, the website **www.distrowatch.com** provides a great set of recommendations, but as you know, websites change, so you might want to also do some web searching for recommended Linux distributions.)

Another interesting option is OpenIndiana, which is an open source offspring of Solaris, from Sun Microsystems and Oracle. For a while Solaris was a bit tricky (well, a lot tricky) to get installed and functional on a regular desktop system; however, OpenIndiana is now as easy as the easier Linux systems, and it offers a tremendous amount of power and flexibility, in addition to some cutting-edge technologies.

That said, any option you choose will be pretty similar for the purposes of this book. Differences among the options primarily show up in more advanced applications.

**TIP** If you're using OS X, you're already using Unix—you just need to bring up a terminal window to be able to follow right along with the book.

# Connecting to the Unix or Linux System

Your first step in using Unix or Linux is to connect to the system. Exactly how you connect will vary depending on what kind of Internet connection you use, but the following steps should get you started.

## To connect to the Unix system:

1. If you're using your Mac or Linux system at home, you're already connected. (Go ahead and open your terminal program.)

2. If you're connecting to a remote system, start your **ssh** program and connect to the Unix or Linux system.

   Using **ssh** you can connect to a remote computer (such as your ISP's computer) and work as if the remote computer were sitting on your desk. Essentially, **ssh** brings a remote computer's capabilities to your fingertips, regardless of where you're physically located. (See the "About Connecting" sidebar for more information about connection technologies.)

   Exactly how you connect depends on the particular program you're using. For Windows users, we recommend PuTTY, which is a free **ssh** client available at **www.chiark.greenend.org. uk/~sgtatham/putty/**. For pre–OS X Macintosh users, we recommend the predictably named **MacSSH**, also free, available at **http://sourceforge.net/ projects/macssh**.

## About Connecting

Once upon a time, when dinosaurs roamed the earth, Unix users connected to their systems using **telnet**. With **telnet**, your password and everything else you do is sent straight across the wire and can be easily read by anyone on the same part of the network. Yikes is right! That's why most ISPs and system administrators require something called **ssh** (Secure SHell) to connect to their systems. With **ssh**, everything is encrypted, precisely the way your web connection is encrypted when you use an e-commerce site and see that the little padlock in your web browser is closed.

Yes, we know, you don't have any secrets, but if a hacker logs in to your ISP's system as you, that same hacker has won 50 percent of the battle for taking over that system for any number of illegal activities. And if your neighbor's 19-year-old son *sniffs* (that's the technical term) your user identification (often called the userid or user ID) and password over your cable modem connection (and that's entirely possible), he can probably guess that your bank password or broker password (or whatever) is the same or at least similar.

Throughout this book, we'll show examples using an **ssh** connection. If, for whatever reason, your system administrators don't require **ssh**, we recommend using it anyway; there is absolutely no reason not to, because there are no disadvantages to **ssh** compared to **telnet**. If your systems don't support **ssh**, you can use the **telnet** (a poor choice) or **rlogin/rsh** program (a slightly better choice) as alternatives. And consider purchasing some extra wood for the steam engine that powers your antique.

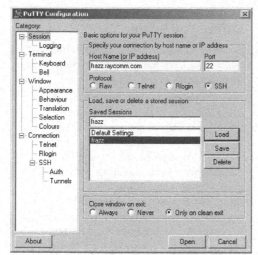

**(A)** Here we're connecting to `frazz.raycomm.com` using PuTTY. Other **ssh** programs might look slightly different, but this shows the general idea.

**(B)** For a quick start, fill in these fields, and then click Open.

**(C)** PuTTY shows a login as: prompt from `frazz.raycomm.com`.

And of course, after you're logged into your Unix-like system, you can use the **ssh** command to access other computers. Each program works a bit differently, and you'll have to refer to the specific documentation for details about using them.

In this example, we're connecting to a Unix system using PuTTY. **(A)** shows the Configuration dialog box, in which we've specified Host Name (frazz.raycomm.com), Port (22), and Protocol (**ssh**).

If you're looking for a quick start, just fill in the fields shown in **(B)** and click Open.

**3.** Check out the Categories (or the Preferences dialog box in many other programs) and become familiar with your options. You will not need to change anything initially, but you might later want to customize colors or other settings. Generally, though, PuTTY provides usable settings.

**4.** Marvel at the **login:** prompt, which is what you should see if you've connected properly **(C)**, and move along to the next section. (PuTTY displays "login as:", while most other programs will just show you "login:". Don't worry about this difference; it's just this program's idiosyncrasy.)

**TIP** If you modify the connection settings, you may need to disconnect from the session, then reconnect again for the new settings to take effect. See your documentation for specifics about disconnecting from your session.

**TIP** In addition to viewing the buffer to see commands you've used, as mentioned in the "The SSH Preferences Dialog Box" sidebar (later in this chapter), you can also use a command to let you review commands that you've issued. For more information, see the appropriate "Viewing Session History" section in Chapter 3.

## Before You Begin

Before you begin, have your connection information, such as your login name and password, handy.

Contact your system administrator if you don't yet have these. Throughout this book, we'll use "system administrator" to refer to your help desk, ISP technical support line, spouse, or anyone else you can call on who runs your Unix system and can help you. Sometimes that geeky daughter, brother, or otherwise Unix-y person can help you out with Unix, too; however, in many cases you'll find that you need to troubleshoot a problem with the person who can manage *your* account information.

## Write Down Details About Your Specific Login Procedure

As you go through your login procedure, take a minute to write down some details for future reference.

Your userid or login name (but not your password):

_____

The name of the program you use (or the icon you click) to connect to your Unix system and the process you use to get connected:

_____

_____

_____

_____

The name of your Unix system (such as **frazz.example.com** or **example.com**):

_____

The IP (Internet Protocol) address of your Unix system (such as **198.168.11.36** or **10.10.22.2**):

_____

**A** Our Unix system (**frazz.raycomm.com**) greets us with a quote of the day, called a "fortune."

**B** Some systems might greet you with system information or helpful tips.

# Logging In

After you've connected to the Unix or Linux system, your next step is to *log in*, or identify yourself to the Unix system. Logging in serves a few purposes, including giving you access to your email, files, and configurations. It also keeps you from inadvertently accessing someone else's files and settings, and it keeps you from making changes to the system itself.

## To log in:

1. Have your userid (user identification) and password ready.

   Contact your system administrator if you don't have these yet.

2. Type your userid at the login prompt, then press ⌈Enter⌋.

   Your userid is case sensitive, so be sure you type it exactly as your system administrator instructed.

3. Type your password at the password prompt (keeping in mind that you probably won't see anything being typed on the screen), then press ⌈Enter⌋.

   Yup. Your password is case sensitive too.

4. Read the information and messages that come up on the screen.

   The information that pops up—the message of the day—might be funny or lighthearted **A**, or it might contain information about system policies, warnings about scheduled downtime, or useful tips **B**. It may also contain both—or possibly neither, if your system administrators have nothing to say to you.

After you've logged in, you'll see a *shell prompt*, which is where you type in commands. Also, note that you'll be located in your *home directory*, which is where your personal files and settings are stored. Your "location" in the Unix or Linux system is a slightly unwieldy concept that we'll help you understand throughout this chapter.

**TIP** If you get an error message after attempting to log in, just try again. You likely just mistyped your userid or password. Remember, your ID and password are case sensitive.

**TIP** Contact your system administrator if you get warnings about having exceeded the permitted number of failed logins. Your account would need special attention in this case.

**TIP** When you log in, you might see a message about failed login attempts. If you unsuccessfully tried to log in, then don't worry about it; the message just confirms that you attempted to log in but failed. If, however, all your login attempts (with you sitting at the keyboard) have been successful or if the number of failed login attempts seems high—say, five or more—then you might also mention the message to your system administrator, who can check security and login attempts. This could be a warning that someone unauthorized is trying to log in as you.

## The SSH Preferences Dialog Box

In the SSH Preferences dialog box, you can fix some of the idiosyncrasies that are caused by how your **ssh** program talks to the Unix system. You can't identify these idiosyncrasies until you actually start using your Unix system, but you should remember that you can fix most problems here. For example:

- If your Backspace and Delete keys don't work, look for an option in your **ssh** or `telnet` program that defines these keyboard functions.

- If you start typing and nothing shows up onscreen, set local echo to on.

- If you start typing and everything shows up twice, set local echo to off.

- If you want to be able to scroll up onscreen to see what's happened during your Unix session, change the buffer size to a larger number.

Exactly which options you'll have will vary from program to program, but these are ones that are commonly available. Click OK when you're finished playing with the settings.

**Code Listing 1.1** Change your password regularly using the **passwd** command.

```
$ passwd
Changing password for ejr
(current) Unix password:
New UNIX password:
Retype new UNIX password:
passwd: all authentication tokens updated
→ successfully
$
```

# Changing Your Password with passwd

Virtually all Unix and Linux systems require passwords to help ensure that your files and data remain your own and that the system itself is secure from hackers and *crackers* (malicious hackers). **Code Listing 1.1** shows how you change your password.

Throughout your adventure, you'll likely change your password often:

- You'll probably want to change the password provided by your system administrator after you log in for the first time. Hint, hint.

- You'll probably change your password at regular intervals. Many systems require that you change your password every so often—every 30 or 60 days is common.

- You might also change your password voluntarily if you think that someone might have learned it or if you tell anyone your password (although you really shouldn't do that anyway).

## To change your password:

1. **passwd**

   To start, type **passwd**.

2. **youroldpassword**

   Enter your old password—the one you're currently using. (Of course, type in your old password, not the sample one we've used here!) Note that the password doesn't show up onscreen when you type it, in case someone is lurking over your shoulder, watching you type, and asking, "Whatcha doing?"

3. **yournewpassword**

   Type your new password. Check out the "Lowdown on Passwords" sidebar for specifics about choosing a password.

4. **yournewpassword**

   Here, you're verifying the password by typing it again.

   The system will report that your password was successfully changed (specific terminology depends on the system) after the changes take effect. This is also shown in Code Listing 1.1.

**TIP** Double-check your new password before you log out of the system by typing su - yourid at the prompt. Of course, substitute your real username (or login name) for yourid here. This command (switch user) lets you log in again without having to log out, so if you made a mistake when changing your password and now get a failed login message, you can find out before you actually disconnect from the system. If you have problems, contact your system administrator before you log out so you can get the problem resolved.

**TIP** In some environments, you will use yppasswd, not passwd, to change your password, or even use a webpage or other means. When in doubt, defer to what your system administrator told you to do. ("The Rays said to use this other command" is likely to get all of us in trouble.)

## The Lowdown on Passwords

In addition to following any password guidelines your system administrator mandates, you should choose a password that is

- At least eight characters long
- Easy for you to remember
- Not a single word or name in any dictionary in any language
- A combination of capital and lower-case letters, numbers, and symbols
- Not similar to your username
- Not identical or similar to one you've used recently
- Not your telephone number, birth date, kid's birth date, anniversary (even if you can remember it), mother's maiden name, pet's name, or anything else that someone might associate with you

Bluntly, most passwords are pretty easily crackable with current technology. Search online for "xkcd password" and follow the instructions in the resulting cartoon for a very good way to construct passwords. Or pick a phrase from a favorite song, and make your password the first letter of each word in the phrase.

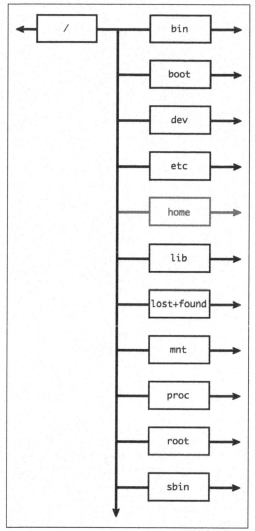

**A** All files and directories are nested within the root directory, which serves to contain everything in the system.

# Listing Directories and Files with ls

Your Unix or Linux system is made up of directories and files that store a variety of information, including setup information, configuration settings, programs, and options, as well as other files and directories. You might think of your system as a tree (tree roots, actually), with subdirectories stemming from higher-level directories. As shown in **A**, all these files and directories reside within the root directory, which contains everything in the system.

Using the **ls** command, you can find out exactly what's in your system and thereby find out what's available to you. You can list the files and directories of a directory that you're currently in or of a directory that you specify.

## To list the files and directories of the directory you're in:

**ls**

At the shell prompt, type **ls** to list the files and directories in the current directory, which in this case is our home directory (**Code Listing 1.2**).

**Code Listing 1.2** Use **ls** by itself to list the files and subdirectories of the directory you're in.

```
[jdoe@frazz jdoe]$ ls
limerick mail/ Project/ public_html/ testfile
→ testlink@ tmp/
[jdoe@frazz jdoe]$
```

## To list the files and directories of a specified directory:

`ls /bin`

Here, you type the **ls** command plus the name of a directory. As shown in **Code Listing 1.3**, this command lists the files and directories in the **/bin** directory, in which you'll find system commands and programs.

**TIP** You can list the files and directories of the *root directory* at any time and in any place by typing **ls /**. The root directory is the highest-level directory in a Unix system; all other directories are below the root directory.

**TIP** Can't remember that pesky filename? Just use **ls** to jog your memory. Or, refer to "Finding Forgotten Files with **find**" in Chapter 2, which can also help you remember filenames.

**TIP** Many other **ls** options are available to control the amount of information about your files that you see and the format in which they appear onscreen. See the section "Listing Directories and Files with **ls** (More Goodies)" in Chapter 2 for details.

**Code Listing 1.3** Use **ls** with the name of a directory to list the contents of that directory (**/bin**, in this case).

```
[jdoe@frazz jdoe]$ ls /bin
arch*           domainname@    ipcalc*        open*    tar*
awk@            echo*          ip6c           eys*     red@      unlink*
chmod*          fbresolution*  login*         rm*      usleep*
chown*          fgrep@         ls*            rmdir*   vi@
consolechars*   find*          lsb_release*   rpm*     view@
cp*             gawk*          mail*          rvi@     vim@
cpio*           gawk-3.1.1@    mkdir*         rview@
date*           gtar@          more*          sleep*   zcat*
dd*             gunzip*        mount*         sort*    zsh*
df*             gzip*          mv*            stat*
dmesg*          hostname*      netstat*       stty*
dnsdomainname@  id*            nice*          su*
doexec*         igawk*         nisdomainname@ sync*
[jdoe@frazz jdoe]$
```

Code Listing 1.4 Using cd, you can change directories and move around in the system. Note that the prompt in this code listing shows the name of the current directory, which can be handy.

```
[jdoe@frazz jdoe]$ cd /
[jdoe@frazz /]$ cd
[jdoe@frazz jdoe]$ cd /home/jdoe/Project/
[jdoe@frazz Project]$ cd /etc
[jdoe@frazz etc]$ cd /home/jdoe/
[jdoe@frazz etc]$ cd /home/jdoe/mail/
[jdoe@frazz mail]$ cd ..
[jdoe@frazz jdoe]$
```

# Changing Directories with cd

To explore Unix or Linux and its capabilities, you'll need to move around among the directories. You do so using the **cd** command, which takes you from the directory you're currently in to one that you specify. **Code Listing 1.4** illustrates how you use **cd** to change directories.

## To change directories:

1. **cd Projects**

   To move to a specific directory, type **cd** plus the name of the directory. In this example, we move down in the directory tree to a subdirectory named **Projects**. (See the "Moving Up and Down" sidebar for an explanation of what "up" and "down" mean in Unix terms.)

2. **cd ..**

   Type **cd ..** to move up one level in the directory tree.

3. **cd /etc**

   Here, **/etc** tells the system to look for the **etc** directory located at the system root.

**TIP** Keep in mind that your home directory isn't the same as the system root directory. You might think of your home directory as "the very small section of the Unix or Linux system that I can call my own." Every person using the system has his or her own little personal section.

**TIP** The current directory is always indicated with a **.**, while the next higher directory (the one that contains the current directory) is indicated with **..** (two dots). That is why you use **cd ..** to move up a directory. In Chapter 10, you will see a specific use for **.** to specify the current directory when running scripts or programs.

**TIP** Visit Chapter 2 for much more about directories and files.

**TIP** If you don't remember the name of the directory you want to change to, you can use **ls** to list the directories and files in your current directory, then use **cd** as shown earlier. See the previous section, "Listing Directories and Files with **ls**," for more information.

**TIP** You can return to your home directory from anywhere in the Unix or Linux system by entering **cd** without specifying a directory.

**TIP** You can often use a tilde (~) as a handy shortcut to your home directory. For example, if you want to change to the **Urgent** directory within the **Projects** directory in your home directory, you could use something like **cd /home/users/y/yourid/Projects/Urgent** or just use the shortcut **cd ~/Projects/Urgent**.

# Finding Yourself with pwd

As you begin using Unix or Linux and start moving around in directories and files, you're likely to get a bit lost—that is, forget which directory or subdirectory you're in. You can use the **pwd** (print working directory, if an acronym helps) command to get a reminder of where you are, as shown in **Code Listing 1.5**.

You can request just the directory name, or you can get fancy and request the directory's name and its contents, courtesy of **ls**.

### To find out the name of the current directory:

pwd

This command displays the path and name of the directory you are currently in. The path names each of the directories "above" the current directory, giving you the full picture of where you are in relationship to the system root.

### To find out the name of the current directory and its contents:

ls ; pwd

By combining the **ls** and **pwd** commands, you can request the directory's contents and name, as shown in Code Listing 1.5.

**TIP** Type pwd immediately after you log in. You'll see where your home directory is in the overall system (aka the full path name for your home directory).

**Code Listing 1.5 pwd** displays the name of the current directory, which is particularly handy if you've been exploring the system. By combining commands, you can request the directory's name and contents at one time.

```
[jdoe@frazz jdoe]$ pwd
/home/jdoe
[jdoe@frazz jdoe]$ ls ; pwd
codelisting1.2 codelisting1.4 mail/
→ public_html/ testlink@
codelisting1.3 limerick Project/
→ testfile tmp/
/home/jdoe
[jdoe@frazz jdoe]$ cd
[jdoe@frazz jdoe]$ cd /
[jdoe@frazz /]$ pwd
/
[jdoe@frazz /]$
```

**TIP** On some Unix or Linux systems, you won't need to use pwd to find out where you are. Some systems display the current directory at the shell prompt by default—something like /home/ejr>. If you'd like to add or get rid of this, or if you want more information about shells and customizing your shell prompt, see Chapter 8.

**A** To execute multiple commands in sequence, pipe them together using the pipe symbol ( | ).

# Piping Input and Output

In general, you can think of each Unix command (**ls**, **cd**, and so on) as an individual program that Unix executes. For example, if you type **cat /etc/motd** at the prompt, Unix will display the contents of **motd** in the **/etc** directory. Each program requires input (in this example, **cat**, the program, takes the contents of **/etc/motd** as input) and produces output (that is, the displayed results).

Frequently, you'll want to run programs in sequence. For example, you could tell Unix to read your résumé and then spell-check it. In doing this, you connect two commands and have them run in sequence. This process, in which you connect the output of one program to the input of another, is called *piping*. Depending on what you want to do, you can pipe together as many commands as you want—with the output of each command acting as the input of the next.

As **A** shows, you pipe commands together using the pipe symbol, which is the | character. In the following example, we'll pipe the output of the **ls** command (which lists the contents of a directory) to the **more** command (which lets you read results one screen at a time). For details about **more**, see "Viewing File Contents with **more**," later in this chapter.

## To pipe commands:

`ls | more`

Here, all you do is include a pipe symbol between the two commands, with or without a space on both sides of the pipe. This code produces a list of the files in the current directory, then pipes the results to **more**, which then lists the results one screen at a time Ⓐ.

**TIP** If you want to pipe more than two commands, you can. Just keep adding the commands (with a pipe symbol in between each, `like | this`) in the order you want them executed.

**TIP** Remember that the output of each command is piped to the next command. So a piped command, such as `ls | spell | sort`, could list files within a directory, then spell-check the list, then sort the misspelled words and display them onscreen. The filenames that are found in the system dictionary would not appear.

**TIP** Venture to Chapter 14 to find out more about running a spell checker and to Chapter 6 to find out more about sorting.

# Redirecting Output

Suppose you've developed your résumé and spell-checked it. As you learned in the previous section, the results you see onscreen will be the output of the last command—in this case, a list of misspelled words. A lot of times, you'll want to redirect the final output to another location, such as to a file or a printer (if a printer is an option for you), rather than view it onscreen. You can do this using *redirection*, which sends the final output to somewhere other than your screen.

As shown in **Code Listing 1.6**, you will often redirect output results to a file. Notice the greater-than symbol (**>**), which indicates that the output of the program is to be redirected to the location (or filename) you specify after the symbol.

In the following examples, we'll show you how to redirect output to a new file and how to redirect output to append it to an existing file.

**Code Listing 1.6** In this case, the output of `ls` gets redirected to **local.programs.txt**, as indicated by the greater-than (**>**) symbol. The asterisk wildcard (*) acts as a placeholder for letters or numbers. Finally, the listing of **/usr/bin** gets appended to the **other.programs.txt** file.

```
[jdoe@frazz jdoe]$ ls /usr/local/bin > local.programs.txt
[jdoe@frazz jdoe]$ ls local*
localize localono local.programs.txt localyokel
[jdoe@frazz jdoe]$ ls /usr/bin >> other.programs.txt
[jdoe@frazz jdoe]$
```

## To redirect output to a new file:

1. `ls /usr/local/bin >`
   `→ local.programs.txt`

   In this case, we start with the `ls` command and a specific directory, add a greater-than symbol (`>`), and then specify a filename. This will redirect the output of `ls` to a file named `local.programs.txt`.

   Be careful with this command! If the file already exists, it could be replaced with the output of the `ls` program here.

2. `ls local*`

   Here, we're just checking to see that the new `local.programs.txt` file has been created successfully. The asterisk wildcard (`*`) specifies that we want a list of all files that begin with the word `local`, such as `localize`, `localyokel`, or `localono` (see Code Listing 1.6). See the next section, "Using Wildcards," for handy wildcard information.

## To append output to an existing file:

`ls /usr/bin >> all.programs.txt`

Appending output to an existing file is similar to redirecting it to a new file; however, instead of creating a new file to hold the output (or replacing the contents of an existing file), you add content to the end of an existing file. Notice that you use two greater-than symbols here, rather than one.

> **TIP** You can pipe and redirect at the same time. For example, you might list a directory, pipe it to wc to count the entries, then append the results to a `directoryinfo` file, like this: `ls | wc -l >> directoryinfo`. You can learn more about counting files and their contents with wc in Chapter 6.

# Using Wildcards

You might think of wildcards as placeholders for omitted letters or numbers. For example, you could list the files of a directory with **ls kid\*** (Code Listing 1.7), which would list all files starting with the characters *kid*. In the resulting list, you'd find a file named **kid** if there were one, as well as files that begin with **kid** but have varying endings, such as **kidnews**, **kiddo**, or **kidneypie**.

You can use wildcards for just about any purpose in Unix, although listing files and directories will likely be the most common use. Just follow these guidelines:

- You use **?** as a placeholder for one character or number.

- You use **\*** as a placeholder for zero or more characters or numbers. Zero characters, in case you're curious, specifies that the search results include all variants of **kid**, including the word itself with no suffix.

- You can include a wildcard at any place in a name: at the beginning (**\*kid**), somewhere in the middle (**k\*d**), at the end (**ki\***), or even in multiple places (**\*kid\***).

**Code Listing 1.7** You use wildcards (**?** or **\***) to act as placeholders for missing characters.

```
[jdoe@frazz Project]$ ls
Keep          keeper.jpg     kept     kidder.txt   kiddo   kidnews    kidneypie   kids    kidupdate
[jdoe@frazz Project]$ ls ki*
kidder.txt   kiddo   kidnews    kidneypie    kids    kidupdate
[jdoe@frazz Project]$ ls kid*
kidder.txt   kiddo   kidnews    kidneypie    kids    kidupdate
[jdoe@frazz Project]$ ls k???
Keep         kept            kids
[jdoe@frazz Project]$ ls *date
kidupdate
[jdoe@frazz Project]$ ls *up*
kidupdate
[jdoe@frazz Project]$ ls k?d*
kidder.txt   kiddo   kidnews    kidneypie    kids    kidupdate
[jdoe@frazz Project]$
```

# Viewing File Contents with more

As you become more familiar with Unix, you'll want to start exploring the contents of files, including some program files and scripts as well as files you eventually create. One of the easiest ways to view file contents is to use the **more** command, which tells Unix or Linux to display files onscreen, a page at a time. As shown in **Ⓐ**, long files are displayed with "More" at the bottom of each screen so that you can move through the file one screen at a time using the spacebar.

## To view a file with more:

1. **more fortunes**

   At the prompt, type **more** plus the name of the file you want to view. You'll see the contents of the file you requested, starting at the top **Ⓐ**.

2. (Spacebar)

   Press (Spacebar) to see the next screen of information. As you move through the file, you can press Ⓑ to move back through previous screens.

3. Ⓠ

   When you're finished, press Ⓠ to go back to the shell prompt.

> **TIP** If you want to view just an additional line (rather than an entire screen) when using more, press (Backspace) instead of the (Spacebar).

> **TIP** You can also use less to view files. less is similar to more, but it's more powerful and flexible. How can less be more and more be less? As you'll see in Appendix C, the more command has 10 options or so; the less command has about 40.

> **TIP** You can also view files using the cat command. See the next section for the full scoop.

**Ⓐ** The **more** command lets you move through a file one screen at a time, providing a "More" indicator at the bottom of each screen.

Code Listing 1.8 With **cat**, long files whirl by, and all you'll see is the bottom of the file. You can also redirect **cat** output to a file, as shown at the end of the listing.

```
[jdoe@frazz jdoe]$ cat newest.programs.txt
...
xpmtoppm*
xpp*
xpstat*
xrfbviewer*
xscreensaver.kss*
xvminitoppm*
xwdtopnm*
xxd*
yaf-cdda*
yaf-mpgplay*
yaf-splay*
yaf-tplay*
yaf-vorbis*
yaf-yuv*
ybmtophm*
yelp*
yes*
ypcat*
ypchfn*
ypchsh*
ypmatch*
yppasswd*
ypwhich*
yuvsplittoppm*
yuvtoppm*
z42_cmyk*
z42tool*
zcmp*
zdiff*
zeisstopnm*
zforce*
zgrep*
zipgrep*
zipinfo*
zless*
zmore*
znew*
[jdoe@frazz jdoe]$ cat newer.programs.txt
→ newest.programs.txt > all.programs
[jdoe@frazz jdoe]$
```

# Displaying File Contents with cat

Instead of using **more** to display files, you can use **cat** (as in "con*cat*enate"), which displays files but does not pause so you can read the information. Instead, it displays the file or files—which whiz by onscreen—and leaves you looking at the last several lines of the file (**Code Listing 1.8**).

The **cat** command also lets you redirect one or more files, offering a function that some versions of **more** do not.

## To display file contents with cat:

- **cat newest.programs.txt**

  To begin, type **cat** plus the filename (probably not **newest.programs.txt** unless you're naming your files just like we are).

  The file contents will appear onscreen; however, if the file is longer than a single screen, the contents will whirl by, and all you'll see is the bottom lines of the file—the 24 or so that fit on a single screen.

  *or*

- **cat newer.programs.txt newest.**
  **→ programs.txt**

  You can also specify multiple files for **cat**, with each file displayed in the order specified. In this example the contents of **newer.programs** will zip by, then the contents of **newest.programs** will zip by.

  *or*

*continues on next page*

- `cat newer.programs.txt newest.`
  `→ programs.txt > all.programs`

  In this example, we've added a redirection symbol (**>**) plus a new filename. This tells Unix to print out both files; however, instead of displaying the files onscreen, it redirects them to the file named **all.programs**. Aha! Here's where **cat** does something better than **more**. See "Redirecting Output," earlier, for more information about redirecting commands.

**TIP** If you inadvertently use **cat** with a *binary file* (a nontext file), you might end up with a whole screen of garbage. On some systems, you might try **stty sane** or reset to fix it—more on this in "Fixing Terminal Settings with **stty**" in Chapter 3. You could also just close your terminal window and log in again to fix it.

**TIP** The **tac** command is just like **cat**, but backward. Try it! Oddly handy, eh?

**TIP** You can also view file contents using the **more** command. See the previous section for details.

**TABLE 1.1 Common Unix Directories and Their Contents**

| Directory | Contents |
| --- | --- |
| /bin | Essential programs and commands for use by all users |
| /etc | System configuration files and global settings |
| /home | Home directories for users |
| /sbin | Programs and commands needed for system boot |
| /tmp | Temporary files |
| /usr/bin | Commands and programs that are less central to basic Unix system functionality than those in /bin but still useful and often important |
| /usr/local | Most files and data that were developed or customized on the system |
| /usr/local/bin | Locally developed or installed programs |
| /usr/local/man | Manual (help) pages for local programs |
| /usr/share/man | Manual (help) pages |
| /var | Changeable data, including system logs, temporary data from programs, and user mail storage |

**TIP** You can type man followed by a command name to learn more about Unix programs. See the next section for information about Unix help.

# Exploring the System

With these few key skills in hand, you're ready to start exploring your Unix system. In doing so, you can quickly get an idea of what's available and gain some useful experience in entering commands.

Think of your Unix system as a thoroughly kid-proofed house: You can look around and touch some stuff, but you can't do anything to hurt yourself or the system (as long as you are not logged in as root, that is, but that's another topic in another chapter). So don't worry! You can't hurt anything by looking around, and even if you tried to break something, most Unix systems are configured well enough that you couldn't.

Table 1.1 shows some of the directories you're likely to find most interesting or useful (Appendix B of this book provides a more comprehensive list of directories). You can use the following steps to get started exploring.

## To explore locally installed programs:

1. **cd /usr/bin**

   Change to **/usr/bin**, which is where most installed programs are.

2. **ls | more**

   List the files (which will be programs, in this example) and pipe the output to **more** so you can read the names one screen at a time.

3. **ssh**

   Type the name of any program you want to run; **ssh**, in this case, allows you to connect to another system and use it just as you're using your Unix system now.

# Getting Help with man

Occasionally, you may need a bit of help remembering what a particular command does. Using **man** (which is short for "manual"), you can look up information about commands and get pointers for using them efficiently. **A** shows a Unix help page (also called a **man** page, for obvious reasons) for passwords. In the following steps, we'll show you how to look up specific Unix commands and find related topics.

## To access a man page:

man passwd

At the prompt, type **man** plus the name of the command you want help with (in this case, **passwd**). You'll get the **man** page for that command. Use the (Spacebar) and the (B) key (for Back) to navigate through the file, just as you do with **more**.

## To find a specific man page:

1. man -k passwd

   Type **man -k** plus the name of the command or the topic you want help with (in this case, **passwd**). As **Code Listing 1.9** shows, you'll see a list of possible **man** pages: command names, **man** page names, and a description. Note the **man** page name (and number if more than one page with the same name exists) so you can reference it in the next step.

**A** Using **man passwd**, you can access the standard **man** file about the **passwd** program.

**2.** `man 1 passwd`

Here, you type **man**, the **man** page you want to view (indicated by 1 in this case to specify section 1—this is necessary because more than one **man** page with the name **passwd** was listed in the last step), and the command name (**passwd**). Ⓐ shows the resulting **man** page.

**TIP** You can make a copy of a man page so you can edit it or comment on it, adding additional notes for your information or deleting irrelevant (to you) stuff. Just type man commandname | col -b -x > somefilename. For example, use man passwd | col -b -x > ~/my.password.command.notes to make a copy of the passwd man page, sans formatting, in your home directory, under the name my.password.command.notes. Then you'll use an editor (from Chapter 4) to edit, add to, and tweak the important points. (The col -b -x command fixes some formatting oddities; without it, all the underlined words might show up as _u_n_d_e_r_l_i_n_e, depending on the system.)

**TIP** You can use apropos instead of the man -k flag. For example, you might use this: apropos passwd.

**TIP** Some Unix systems might require a -s before the section number, as in man -s 1 passwd.

**Code Listing 1.9** man -k passwd gives you these results, showing specific password-related man pages.

```
$ man -k passwd
chpasswd (8)     - update password file in batch
gpasswd (1)      - administer the /etc/group file
mkpasswd (1)     - generate new password, optionally apply it to a user
mkpasswd (8)     - Update passwd and group database files
passwd (1)       - update a user's authentication tokens(s)
passwd (5)       - password file
userpasswd (1)   - A graphical tool to allow users to change their passwords
```

# Logging Out

When you finish your session, you need to log out of the system to ensure that nobody else accesses your files while masquerading as you.

## To log out:

```
logout
```

That's it! Just type **logout**, and the system will clean up everything and break the connection, and the **ssh** program window might very well just vanish completely.

**TIP** On some Unix systems, you can type exit or quit instead of logout, or press ⌈Ctrl⌋+⌈D⌋ on your keyboard.

## Moving Up and Down

Throughout this book, we'll talk about moving "up" and "down" through the Unix file system. Moving "up" means moving into the directory that contains the current directory—that is, closer to the root directory. Moving "down" means moving into subdirectories that are contained by the current directory—that is, further from the root directory.

# Using Directories and Files

As you learned in Chapter 1, directories and files are the heart of Unix and Linux; they contain things like setup information, configuration settings, programs, and options, as well as anything that you create. You access directories and files every time you type in a Unix or Linux command, and for this reason, you need to become familiar with the various things you can do with them.

Again in this chapter, the skills and commands we'll cover apply to any Unix or Linux flavor. What you see onscreen (particularly system prompts and responses) may differ slightly from what's illustrated in this book. The general ideas and specific commands, however, will be the same on all systems.

# Creating Directories with `mkdir`

You might think of directories as being drawers in a file cabinet; each drawer contains a bunch of files that are somehow related. For example, you might have a couple of file drawers for your unread magazines, one for your to-do lists, and maybe a drawer for your work projects.

Similarly, directories in your Unix system act as containers for other directories and files; each subdirectory contains yet more related directories or files, and so on. You'll probably create a new directory each time you start a project or have related files you want to store at a single location. You create new directories using the **mkdir** command, as shown in **Code Listing 2.1**.

**Code Listing 2.1** Typing **mkdir** plus a directory name creates a new directory. Listing the files, in long format, shows the new directory. The "d" at the beginning of the line shows that it's a directory.

```
$ ls
Projects      all.programs.txt  local.programs.txt  schedule
Xrootenv.0    files             newer.programs      short.fortunes
all.programs  fortunes          newest.programs     temp
$ mkdir Newdirectory
$ ls -l
total 159
drwxrwxr-x   2 ejr    users     1024   Jun 29 11:40 Newdirectory
drwxrwxr-x   2 ejr    users     1024   Jun 28 12:48 Projects
-rw-rw-r-    1 ejr    users     7976   Jun 28 14:15 all.programs
-rw-rw-r-    1 ejr    users     7479   Jun 28 14:05 all.programs.txt
-rw-rw-r-    1 ejr    users      858   Jun 28 12:45 files
-rw-rw-r-    1 ejr    ejr     128886   Jun 27 09:05 fortunes
-rw-rw-r-    1 ejr    users        0   Jun 28 14:05 local.programs.txt
-rw-rw-r-    1 ejr    users      497   Jun 28 14:13 newer.programs
-rw-rw-r-    1 ejr    users     7479   Jun 28 14:13 newest.programs
Lrwxrwxrwx   1 ejr    users       27   Jun 26 11:03 schedule -> /home/deb/Pre
-rw-rw-r-    1 ejr    ejr       1475   Jun 27 09:31 short.fortunes
drwxrwxr-x   2 ejr    users     1024   Jun 26 06:39 temp
$
```

## Naming Directories (and Files)

As you start creating directories (and files), keep in mind the following guidelines:

- Directories and files must have unique names. For example, you cannot name a directory **Golf** and a file **Golf**. You can, however, have a directory named **Golf** and a file named **golf**. The difference in capitalization makes each name unique. By the way, directories are often named with an initial cap, and filenames are often all lowercase.

- Directory and filenames can, but should generally *not* include the following characters: angle brackets (**< >**), braces (**{ }**), brackets (**[ ]**), parentheses (**( )**), double quotes (**" "**), single quotes (**' '**), asterisks (**\***), question marks (**?**), pipe symbols (**|**), slashes (**/ \**), carets (**^**), exclamation points (**!**), pound signs (**#**), dollar signs (**$**), ampersands (**&**), tildes (**~**), and spaces.

  Different shells handle special characters differently, and some will have no problems at all with these characters. Generally, though, special characters are more trouble than they're worth.

- Generally, avoid names that include spaces. Some programs don't deal with them correctly, so to use spaces you have to use odd workarounds; for example, surrounding a filename with quotation marks. Instead, consider using periods (**.**) and underscores (**_**) to separate words, characters, or numbers.

- Use names that describe the directory's or file's contents so you easily remember them.

## To create a directory:

1. **ls**

   Start by listing existing directories to make sure that the planned name doesn't conflict with an existing directory or filename.

2. **mkdir Newdirectory**

   Type the **mkdir** command to make a new directory; in this case, it's named **Newdirectory**. Refer to the sidebar "Naming Directories (and Files)" for guidelines.

3. **ls –l**

   Now you can use **ls -l** (the **-l** flag specifies a long format) to look at the listing for your new directory (Code Listing 2.1). The **d** at the far left of the listing for **Newdirectory** indicates that it's a directory and not a file. Of course, after you trust Unix or Linux to do as you say, you can skip this verification step.

**TIP** If you attempt to create a directory with a file or directory name that already exists, the system will not overwrite the existing directory. Instead, you'll be told that a file by that name already exists. Try again with a different name.

**TIP** You can create several directories and subdirectories at once with the **–p** flag. For example, if you want to create a new subdirectory named **Projects** with a subdirectory named **Cooking** within that and a subdirectory named **Desserts** within that, you can use **mkdir –p Projects/Cooking/Desserts** and get it all done at once. Without the **–p** flag, you have to create **Projects**, **Cooking**, then **Desserts** in order, which is a longer recipe to make the same tree structure.

# Creating Files
# with touch

Another skill you'll use frequently is creating files. You might think of creating files
as getting an empty bucket that you can
later fill with water...or sand...or rocks...
or whatever. When you create a file, you
designate an empty space that you can fill
with programs, activity logs, your résumé,
or configurations—practically anything you
want, or nothing at all.

Of course, you can always create a file by
writing something in an editor and saving it,
as described in Chapter 4, but you will sometimes encounter situations where you just
need an empty file as a placeholder for later
use. You create empty files using the **touch**
command, as shown in **Code Listing 2.2**.

**Code Listing 2.2** Use the **touch** command to create files, update their modification times, or both.

```
$ ls
$ touch file.to.create
$ ls -l file*
-rw-rw-r-    1 ejr    users    0 Jun 29 11:53  file.to.create
$ touch -t 12312359 oldfile
$ ls -l
total 0
-rw-rw-r-    1 ejr    users    0 Jun 29 11:53  file.to.create
-rw-rw-r-    1 ejr    users    0 Dec 31 2009  oldfile
$ touch -t 201612312359 new.years.eve
$ ls -l
total 0
-rw-rw-r-    1 ejr    users    0 Jun 29 11:53  file.to.create
-rw-rw-r-    1 ejr    users    0 Dec 31 2016  new.years.eve
-rw-rw-r-    1 ejr    users    0 Dec 31 2009  oldfile
$
```

## To create a file:

1. **touch file.to.create**

   To create a file, type **touch** followed by the name of the file. This creates an empty file.

2. **ls -l file***

   Optionally, verify that the file was created by typing **ls –l file***. As shown in Code Listing 2.2, you'll see the name of the new file as well as its length (0) and the date and time of its creation (likely seconds before the current time, if you're following along).

   **TIP** You can also use **touch** to update an existing file's date and time. For example, typing **touch -t 12312359** oldfile at the prompt would update oldfile with a date of December 31, 23 hours, and 59 minutes in the current year. Or, typing **touch -t 201612312359** new.years.eve would update the file named new.years.eve to the same time in the year 2016.

   **TIP** Each time you save changes in a file, the system automatically updates the date and time. See Chapter 4 for details about editing and saving files.

   **TIP** Refer to the sidebar "Naming Directories (and Files)" in this chapter for file-naming guidelines.

# Copying Directories and Files with cp

When working in Unix, you'll frequently want to make copies of directories and files. For example, you may want to copy a file you're working on to keep an original, unscathed version handy. Or you might want to maintain duplicate copies of important directories and files in case you inadvertently delete them or save something over them. Accidents do happen, according to Murphy.

Whatever your reason, you copy directories and files using the **cp** command, as shown in **Code Listing 2.3**. When you copy directories and files, all you're doing is putting a duplicate in another location; you leave the original untouched.

## To copy a directory:

1. **cp -r /home/ejr/Projects**
   **→ /home/shared/deb/Projects**

   At the shell prompt, type **cp -r**, followed by the old and new (to be created) directory names, to copy a complete directory. The **r** stands for "recursive," if that'll help you remember it.

2. **ls /home/shared/deb/Projects**

   You can use **ls** plus the new directory name to verify that the duplicate directory and its contents are in the intended location (Code Listing 2.3).

**Code Listing 2.3** Use **cp -r** to copy directories.

```
$ cp -r /home/ejr/Projects /home/shared/deb/Projects
$ ls /home/shared/deb/Projects
Current  new.ideas  schedule
$
```

## To copy a file:

**1. cp existingfile newfile**

At the prompt, type **cp**, followed by the old and new (to be created) filename.

**2. ls -l**

Optionally, check out the results with **ls -l**. The **-l** (for long format) flag displays the file sizes and dates so you can see that the copied file is exactly the same as the new one (**Code Listing 2.4**).

**3. cp -i existingfile oldfile**

If you use **cp** with the **-i** flag, it prompts you before overwriting an existing file, also shown in Code Listing 2.4.

**TIP** You can compare the contents of two files or two directories using cmp and dircmp, respectively. For example, typing cmp filename1 filename2 would compare the contents of the specified files. Use diff or sdiff to see the differences between files. See Chapter 6 for more information.

**TIP** You can copy directories and files to or from someone else's directory. Skip to Chapter 5 to find out how to get access, then use the copying procedure described here.

**TIP** Use cp with a -i flag to force the system to ask you before overwriting files. Then, if you like that, visit Chapter 8 to find out about using aliases with cp so that the system always prompts you before overwriting files.

**TIP** When copying directories and files, you can use either *absolute* (complete) names, which are measured from the root directory (/home/ejr/Projects), or *relative* (partial) names, which specify files or directories in relation to the current directory (ejr/Projects) and aren't necessarily valid from elsewhere in the Unix file system. Using absolute names, you can manipulate directories and files with certainty anywhere in the Unix system. Using relative names, you can manipulate files only with reference to your current location.

**Code Listing 2.4** Just use **cp** to copy files and add **-i** to insist that the system prompt you before you overwrite an existing file.

```
$ cp existingfile newfile
$ ls -l
total 7
-rw-rw-r-    1 ejr    users    1475 Jun 29 12:18 existingfile
-rw-rw-r-    1 ejr    users    1475 Jun 29 12:37 newfile
-rw-rw-r-    1 ejr    users    2876 Jun 29 12:17 oldfile
$ cp -i existingfile oldfile
cp: overwrite 'oldfile'? n
$
```

# Listing Directories and Files with ls (More Goodies)

If you've been following along, you're probably an expert at using **ls** to list directory contents and to verify that files and directories were copied as you intended. **ls**, though, has a couple of other handy uses. In particular, you can also use it to

- List filenames and information, which is handy for differentiating similar files as shown in .

- List all files in a directory, including hidden ones, such as **.profile** and **.login** configuration files (**Code Listing 2.5**). See Chapter 8 for more about configuration files. (Files might be hidden to minimize the chances of having them accidentally changed, to keep them out of the casual user's way, or to provide minimal security to keep them from being noticed.)

Ⓐ Use **ls -l** to get extra information about the directories and files in a specific directory.

**Code Listing 2.5** If you want to see hidden files, use **ls -a**.

```
$ ls -a
.    .stats   deb.schedule   other
..   current  new.ideas      schedule
```

## To list filenames and information:

**•ls -l**

At the shell prompt, type **ls -l** (that's a lowercase "L," not a one). You'll see the list of files in your directory fly by with the following information about each file (**Code Listing 2.6**):

- Filename.

- File size.

- Date of last modification.

- Permissions information (find out more about permissions in Chapter 5).

- Ownership and group membership (also covered in Chapter 5).

- Time of last modification (if the file's been modified recently) or year of last modification (if the file was last modified more than six months previously). Check out **touch** earlier in this chapter to see how files might have modification dates in the future.

**Code Listing 2.6** Use **ls -l** to see a listing of the contents of a directory in long format.

```
$ ls -l
total 13
-rw-rw-r-   1 ejr    users    2151 Jun 29 12:26 current
-rw-rw-r-   2 ejr    users    1475 Jun 29 12:35 deb.schedule
-rw-rw-r-   1 ejr    users    4567 Jun 29 12:26 new.ideas
drwxrwxr-x  2 ejr    users    1024 Jun 29 13:06 other
-rw-rw-r-   1 ejr    users    1475 Jun 29 12:22 schedule
```

## To list all files in a directory:

ls -la

Enter **ls -la** at the shell prompt to list all the files in the directory, including hidden files, with full information, as shown in **Code Listing 2.7**.

**TIP** You can hide (well, sort of hide) files by giving them a name that starts with a dot (.). That is, profile would not be hidden, but .profile would be.

**TIP** Remember that you can combine any flags to specify multiple options. For example, if you want to list all files (-a) in the long format (-l) you would use ls -la.

**TIP** Try ls –ltR to get the complete listing of your current directory, the directories it contains, and so forth until you run out of subdirectories to descend into.

**Code Listing 2.7** If you want to see everything, use **ls -la**.

```
$ ls -la
total 22
drwxrwxr-x   3 ejr     users      1024 Jun 29 13:07 .
drwxrwx--    7 ejr     users      1024 Jun 29 12:16 ..
-rw-rw-r-    1 ejr     users      6718 Jun 29 13:00 .stats
-rw-rw-r-    1 ejr     users      2151 Jun 29 12:26 current
-rw-rw-r-    2 ejr     users      1475 Jun 29 12:35 deb.schedule
-rw-rw-r-    1 ejr     users      4567 Jun 29 12:26 new.ideas
drwxrwxr-x   2 ejr     users      1024 Jun 29 13:06 other
-rw-rw-r-    1 ejr     users      1475 Jun 29 12:22 schedule
$
```

**Code Listing 2.8** List files to see the current files, then use **mv** to rename one of the files.

```
$ ls
afile     existingfile     oldfile
$ mv existingfile newfile
$ ls
afile     newfile          oldfile
$
```

**TIP** You can also use **mv** to move files into or out of directories. For example, **mv Projects/temp/testfile/home/ deb/testfile** moves testfile from the Projects and temp subdirectories of the current directory to Deb's home directory, also using the name **testfile**.

**TIP** Use **mv -i oldfilename newfilename** to require the system to prompt you before overwriting (destroying) existing files. The **-i** is for "interactive," and it also works with the cp command.

**TIP** Check out Chapter 8 to learn how to use aliases with **mv** so that the system always prompts you before overwriting files and you don't have to remember the **-i** flag.

**TIP** If you use **mv** and specify an existing directory as the target (as in, **mv something ExistingDirectory**), "something," in this case, will be placed into **ExistingDirectory**. "Something" can be either a file or a directory.

# Moving Files with mv

Moving directories and files means moving them from one location (think of *location* as an absolute file path, like **/home/ejr/aFile**) in your system to another location (say, **/tmp/File** or **/home/ejr/AnotherFile**). Essentially, you have only one version of a file, and you change the location of that version. For example, you might move a directory when you're reorganizing your directories and files. Or, you might move a file to rename it—that is, move a file from one name to another name but still within the same directory.

You move directories and files using **mv**, as shown in **Code Listing 2.8**.

## To move a file or directory:

**1.** **ls**

To begin, use **ls** to verify the name of the file you want to move. If you're changing the name of the file, you'll want to ensure that the new filename isn't yet in use. If you move a file to an existing filename, the contents of the old file will be replaced with the contents of the new file.

**2.** **mv existingfile newfile**

Type **mv** plus the existing filename and the new filename. Say goodbye to the old file and hello to the new one (Code Listing 2.8).

You use the same process—exactly—to move directories; just specify the directory names, as in **mv ExistingDirectory NewDirectory**.

**3.** **ls**

Verify that the file is now located in the location you intended.

# Removing Files with rm

You can easily—perhaps too easily—remove (delete) files from your Unix system. As Murphy will tell you, it's a good idea to think twice before doing this; once you remove a file, it's gone (unless, of course, you plead with your system administrator to restore it from a backup—but that's another story). At any rate, it's permanent, unlike deletions in Windows or in the Mac OS GUI (but not the Mac Unix command line), or even in many Unix desktop environments like GNOME or KDE, where the Recycle Bin or Trash gives you a second chance.

You remove files using **rm**, as shown in **Code Listing 2.9**. And, as you'll see in the following steps, you can remove files one at a time or several at a time.

## To remove a file:

1. **ls -l**

   List the files in the current folder to verify the name of the file you want to remove.

2. **rm -i soon.to.be.gone.file**

   At your shell prompt, type **rm -i** followed by the name of the file you want to remove. The **-i** tells the system to prompt you before removing the files (Code Listing 2.9).

3. **ls**

   It is gone, isn't it?

**Code Listing 2.9** Use **rm -i** to safely and carefully remove directories and files.

```
$ ls
afile          oldfile
newfile        soon.to.be.gone.file
$ rm -i soon.to.be.gone.file
rm: remove 'soon.to.be.gone.file'? y
$ ls
afile          newfile  oldfile
$
```

**TIP** If you have system administrator rights (or are logged in as `root` rather than with your userid), be extremely careful when using `rm`. Rather than remove merely your personal directories or files, you could potentially remove system directories and files. Scope out the sidebar "Can You Really Screw Up the System?"

**TIP** This is a good time to remind you to use the handy `cp` command to make backup copies of anything you value—before you experiment too much with `rm`. Even if the system administrator keeps good backups, it's ever so much easier if you keep an extra copy of your goodies sitting around. Try `cp -r . backup_files` for a space-hogging—but effective—means of making a quick backup of everything in the current directory into the `backup-files` directory. (Just ignore the error message about not copying a directory into itself; the system will do the right thing for you, and you don't have to worry about it.)

**TIP** We suggest using `rm -i`, at least until you're sure you're comfortable with irrevocable deletions. The `-i` flag prompts you to verify your command before it's executed.

**TIP** Check out Chapter 8 to find out about using aliases with `rm` so that the system always prompts you before removing the directories or files even if you forget the `-i` flag.

**TIP** If you accidentally end up with a file that has a problematic filename (like one that starts with -, which looks to Unix like a command flag, not a filename), you can delete it (with a trick). Use `rm -i -- bad-filename` to get rid of it.

## To remove multiple files:

1. `ls -l *.html`

   List the files to make sure you know which files you want to remove (and not remove).

2. `rm -i *.html`

   Using the asterisk wildcard (*), you can remove multiple files at one time. In this example, we remove all files in the current directory that end with `.html`. (Refer to Chapter 1, specifically the section called "Using Wildcards," for details about using wildcards.)

   *or*

1. `rm -i dangerous`

   Here, `-i` specifies that you'll be prompted to verify the removal of a directory or file named **dangerous** before it's removed.

2. `rm -ir dan*`

   This risky command removes all the directories or files that start with **dan** in the current directory and all the files and subdirectories in the subdirectories starting with **dan**. If you're sure, don't use the `-i` flag to just have the files removed without prompting you for confirmation. (Remember that the flag `-ir` could also be written as `-i -r` or `-ri` or `-r -i`. Unix is rather flexible.)

# Removing Directories with `rmdir`

Another handy thing you can do is remove directories using **`rmdir`**. Think of removing directories as trimming branches on a tree. That is, you can't be sitting on the branch you want to trim off. You have to sit on the next closest branch; otherwise, you'll fall to the ground along with the branch you trim off. Ouch! Similarly, when you remove a directory, you must not be located in the directory you want to remove.

You must remove a directory's contents (all subdirectories and files) before you remove the directory itself. In doing so, you can verify what you're removing and avoid accidentally removing important stuff. In the following steps (illustrated in **Code Listing 2.10**), we'll show you how to remove a directory's contents, and then remove the directory itself.

## Can You Really Screw Up the System?

In general, no. When you log in to a Unix or Linux system and use your personal userid, the worst you can do is remove your own directories and files. As long as you're logged in as yourself, commands you type won't affect anything critical to the system, only your own personal directories and files. Score one for Unix—as an average user, you cannot really break the system. With Windows, though, it can be a different story.

If you have system administrator rights, meaning that you can log in as **root** (giving you access to all the system directories and files), you can do a lot of damage if you're not extremely careful. For this reason, don't log in as **root** unless you absolutely have to. See Chapter 15 for more about being **root**.

Many newer systems won't even let you log in as **root**. Instead, you need to use **su** or an equivalent, as discussed in Chapter 3. There, you'll also find more information about **su**, which can help reduce the risk of being logged in as **root**.

**Code Listing 2.10** Removing directories with **`rmdir`** can be a little tedious—but better safe than sorry.

```
$ cd /home/ejr/Yourdirectory
$ ls -la
total 7
drwxrwxr-x  2 ejr    users    1024 Jun 29 20:59 .
drwxrwx--   8 ejr    users    1024 Jun 29 20:59 ..
-rw-rw-r--  1 ejr    users    1475 Jun 29 20:59 cancelled.project.notes
-rw-rw-r--  1 ejr    users    2876 Jun 29 20:59 outdated.contact.info
$ rm *
$ cd ..
$ rmdir Yourdirectory
$ ls
Newdirectory   all.programs.txt   newer.programs    short.fortunes
Projects       files              newest.programs   temp
Xrootenv.0     fortunes           newstuff          touching
all.programs   local.programs.txt schedule
$
```

## To remove a directory:

1. `cd /home/ejr/Yourdirectory`

   To begin, change to that directory by typing **cd** plus the name of the directory you want to remove.

2. `ls -a`

   List all (**-a**) the files, including any hidden files that might be present, in the directory, and make sure you don't need any of them. If you see only **.** and **..** (which indicate the current directory and its parent directory, respectively), you can skip ahead to step 4.

3. Do one or both of these:

   ▶ If you have hidden files in the directory, type `rm .* *` to delete those files plus all the rest of the files.

   ▶ If you have subdirectories in the directory, type **cd** and the subdirectory name, essentially repeating the process starting with step 1. Repeat this process until you remove all subdirectories.

   When you finish this step, you should have a completely empty directory, ready to be removed.

4. `cd ..`

   Use the change directory command again to move up one level, to the parent of the directory that you want to remove.

5. `rmdir Yourdirectory`

   There it goes—wave goodbye to the directory! See Code Listing 2.10 for the whole sequence.

**TIP** You can remove multiple directories at one time. Assuming you're starting with empty directories, just list them like this: `rmdir Yourdirectory Yourotherdirectory OtherDirectory`.

**TIP** As an alternative to `rmdir`, you can remove a directory and all its contents at once using `rm` with the **-r** flag; for example, `rm -r Directoryname`. Be careful, though! This method automatically removes the directory and everything in it, so you won't have the opportunity to examine everything you remove beforehand. If you're getting asked for confirmation before deleting each file and you're really, absolutely, positively, completely sure that you're doing the right thing, use `rm -rf Directoryname` to force immediate deletion.

**TIP** If you're getting comfortable with long command strings, you can specify commands with a complete directory path, as in `ls /home/ejr/DirectorytoGo` or `rm /home/ejr/DirectorytoGo/*`. This technique is particularly good if you want to be absolutely sure that you're deleting the right directory, and not a directory with the same name in a different place on the system.

# Finding Forgotten Files with find

Where, oh where, did that file go? Sometimes finding a file requires more than cursing at your computer or listing directory contents with **ls**. Instead, you can use the **find** command, which lets you search in dozens of ways, including through the entire directory tree (**Code Listing 2.11**) or through directories you specify (**Code Listing 2.12**).

## To find a file:

```
find . -name lostfile -print
```

Along with the **find** command, this specifies to start in the current directory with a dot (**.**), provide the filename (**-name lostfile**), and specify that the results be printed onscreen (**-print**). See Code Listing 2.11.

## To find files starting in a specific directory:

```
find /home/deb -name 'pending*' -print
```

This command finds all the files and directories with names starting with **pending** under Deb's home directory.

Or, you can find files under multiple directories at one time, like this:

```
find /home/deb /home/ejr -name
→ 'pending*' -print
```

This command finds files with names starting with **pending** in Deb's and Eric's home directories or any subdirectories under them (Code Listing 2.12).

**Code Listing 2.11** Use **find** to locate a missing file.

```
$ find . -name lostfile -print
./Projects/schedule/lostfile
$
```

**Code Listing 2.12** By using wildcards and specifying multiple directories, you can make **find** yet more powerful.

```
$ find /home/deb -name 'pending*' -print
/home/deb/Projects/schedule/pending.tasks
$ find /home/deb /home/ejr -name
→ 'pending*' -print
/home/deb/Projects/schedule/pending.tasks
/home/ejr/pending.jobs.to.do.today.to.do
$
```

## To find and act on files:

find ~ -name '*.backup' -ok rm { } \;

Type **find** with a wildcard expression, followed by **-ok** (to execute the following command, with confirmation), **rm** (the command to issue), and **{} \;** to fill in each file found as an *argument* (an additional piece of information) for the command. If you want to, say, compress matching files without confirmation, you might use find ~ -name '*.backup' -exec compress {} \; to do the work for you.

**TIP** On most Unix and Linux systems, you do not need the -print flag. Try entering find without the -print flag. If you see the results onscreen, then you don't need to add the -print flag.

**TIP** Avoid starting the find command with the root directory, as in find / -name the. missing.file -print. In starting with the root directory (indicated by the /), you'll likely encounter a pesky error message for each directory you don't have access to, and there will be a lot of those. Of course, if you're logged in as root, feel free to start with /.

**TIP** If you know only part of the filename, you can use quoted wildcards with find, as in find . -name '*info*' -print.

**TIP** find offers many chapters' worth of options. If you're looking for a specific file or files based on any characteristics, you can find them with find. For example, you can use find /home/shared -mtime -3 to find all files under the shared directory that were modified within the last three days. See Appendix C for a substantial (but not comprehensive) listing of options.

# Locating Lost Files with `locate`

If you're looking for a system file—that is, a program or file that is part of the Unix system itself, rather than one of your personal files in your home directory—try **locate** to find it. You may get more results than you can handle, but it's a quick and easy way to locate system files.

The **locate** command isn't available on all Unix and Linux systems, but it is worth a try at any rate. See **Code Listing 2.13** for **locate** in action.

## To locate a file:

`locate fortune`

If you try to locate **fortune**, you'll get a listing of all of the system files that contain "fortune" in them. This listing includes the **fortune** program, fortune data files for the **fortune** program to use, and related stuff. It's a huge list in most cases (Code Listing 2.13).

> **TIP** Use `locate` in combination with `grep` (see "Using Regular Expressions with `grep`" in Chapter 6) to narrow down your list, if possible.

> **TIP** Many people use `locate` to get a quick look at the directories that contain relevant files (`/usr/share/games/fortunes` contains a lot of files related to the `fortune` program), then use other tools to take a closer look.

> **TIP** Not all systems include `fortune`—it's certainly just a fun thing and not essential by any means. If you don't "locate" it, try looking for `bash` or `zsh` (known as shells) to see how `locate` works. (See Chapter 8 for more information about different shells and their benefits and drawbacks.)

**Code Listing 2.13** Use `locate` to find everything—everything—related to most system files.

```
[jdoe@frazz jdoe]$ locate fortune
/usr/share/man/man6/fortune.6.bz2
/usr/share/doc/fortune-mod-1.0
/usr/share/doc/fortune-mod-1.0/cs
/usr/share/doc/fortune-mod-1.0/cs/HISTORIE
/usr/share/doc/fortune-mod-1.0/cs/LICENSE
/usr/share/doc/fortune-mod-1.0/cs/README
/usr/share/doc/fortune-mod-1.0/fr
/usr/share/doc/fortune-mod-1.0/fr/
→ COPYING.linuxfr
/usr/share/doc/fortune-mod-1.0/fr/COPYING.glp
/usr/share/doc/fortune-mod-1.0/fr/ffr
...
/usr/share/games/fortunes/songs-poems
/usr/share/games/fortunes/sports.dat
/usr/share/games/fortunes/sports
/usr/share/games/fortunes/startrek.dat
/usr/share/games/fortunes/startrek
/usr/share/games/fortunes/translate-me.dat
/usr/share/games/fortunes/translate-me
/usr/share/games/fortunes/wisdom.dat
/usr/share/games/fortunes/wisdom
/usr/share/games/fortunes/work.dat
/usr/share/games/fortunes/work
/usr/share/games/fortunes/zippy.dat
/usr/share/games/fortunes/zippy
/usr/share/sol-games/fortunes.scm
/usr/games/fortune
[jdoe@frazz jdoe]$
```

# Linking with ln (Hard Links)

Suppose your boss just hired an assistant for you ('bout time, right?). You'll need to make sure your new helper can access your files so you can pawn off your work on him. And you'll need to access the revised files just so you can keep up with what your helper's been doing—and perhaps take credit for his work at the next staff meeting.

A great way to give your helper easy access to your files is to create a *hard link* from your home directory. In making a hard link, all you're doing is starting with an existing file and creating a link, which (sort of) places the existing file in your helper's home directory. The link does not create a copy of the file; instead, you're creating a second pointer to the same physical file on the disk. Rather than the additional pointer being secondary (like an alias or shortcut in Mac or Windows computers), both of the pointers reference the same actual file, so from the perspective of the Unix system, the file actually resides in two locations (**Code Listing 2.14**).

**Code Listing 2.14** Hard links let two users easily share files.

```
$ ls /home/deb/Projects/schedule/our* /home/helper/our*
ls: /home/helper/our*: No such file or directory
/home/deb/Projects/schedule/our.projects.latest
/home/deb/Projects/schedule/our.projects.other
$ ln /home/deb/Projects/schedule/our.projects.latest /home/helper/our.projects
$ ls -l /home/helper/o*
-rw-r-r-   3 ejr    users    1055 Jun 26 11:00 /home/helper/our.projects
$
```

Because using hard links often requires that you have access to another user's home directory, you might venture to Chapter 5 for details about using **chmod**, **chgrp**, and **chown** to access another user's directories and files.

## To make a hard link:

1. **ls -l /home/deb/Projects/schedule/**
   **→ our\* /home/helper/our\***

   To begin, list the files in both directories to make sure that the file to link exists and that there's no other file with the intended name in the target directory. Here, we list the files that start with **our** in both **/home/deb/Projects/schedule** and in **/home/helper**. In this example, we're verifying that the file does exist in Deb's directory and that no matching files were found in the helper's directory (Code Listing 2.14).

2. **ln /home/deb/Projects/schedule/**
   **→ our.projects.latest /home/helper/**
   **→ our.projects**

   Here, **ln** creates a new file with a similar name in the helper's home directory and links the two files together, essentially making the same file exist in two home directories.

3. **ls -l /home/helper/o\***

   With this code, your helper can verify that the file exists by listing files that begin with **o**.

   Now the file exists in two places with exactly the same content. Either user can modify the file, and the content in both locations will change.

**TIP** You can remove hard links just like you remove regular files, by using **rm** plus the filename. See the section "Removing Files with **rm**," earlier in this chapter.

**TIP** If one user removes the file, the other user can still access the file from his or her directory.

**TIP** Hard links work from file to file only within the same file system. To link directories or to link across different file systems, you'll have to use soft links, which are covered in the next section.

**TIP** If you're sneaky, you can use hard links to link directories, not just files. Make a new directory where you want the linked directory to be, and then use **ln /home/whoever/existingdirectory/\* /home/you/newdirectory/** to hard-link all the files in the old directory to the new directory. New files won't be linked automatically, but you could use a **cron** job to refresh the links periodically—say, daily. See Chapter 9 for **cron** details.

# Linking with ln -s (Soft Links)

Now suppose you want to pawn off your entire workload on your new helper. Rather than just give him access to a single file, you'll want to make it easy for him to access your entire project directory. You can do this using soft links (created with **ln -s**), which essentially provide other users with a shortcut to the file or directory you specify.

Like hard links, *soft links* allow a file to be in more than one place at a time; however, with soft links, there's only one copy of it, and with soft links, you can link directories as well. The linked file or directory is dependent on the original one—that is, if the original file or directory is deleted, the linked file or directory will no longer be available. With hard links, the file is not actually removed from disk until the last hard link is deleted.

Soft links are particularly handy because they work for directories as well as individual files, and they work across different file systems (that is, not just within **/home**, but anywhere on the Unix system).

Like hard links, soft links sometimes require that you have access to another user's directory and files. See Chapter 5 for more on file permissions and ownership and Chapter 7 for the lowdown on file systems.

## To make a soft link:

1. **ls /home/deb /home/helper**

   To begin, list the contents of both users' home directories. Here, we're verifying that the directory we want to link does exist in Deb's directory and that no matching directories or files exist in the helper's directory. See **Code Listing 2.15**.

2. **ln -s /home/deb/Projects**
   **→ /home/helper/Projects**

   This command creates a soft link so the contents of Deb's Projects directory can also be easily accessed from the helper's home directory.

3. **ls -la /home/helper**

   Listing the contents of **/home/helper** shows the existence of the soft link to the directory. Notice the arrow (**->**) showing the link in Code Listing 2.15.

**TIP** **If you only need to create a link between two files within the same file system, consider using hard links, as discussed in the previous section, "Linking with ln (Hard Links)."**

**Code Listing 2.15** Use **ln -s** to make soft links and connect directories.

```
$ ls /home/deb /home/helper
/home/deb:
Projects
/home/helper:
our.projects
$ ln -s /home/deb/Projects /home/helper/Projects
$ ls -la /home/helper/
total 11
d-wxrwx--    2 helper   users    1024 Jun 29 21:18 .
drwxr-xr-x  11 root     root     1024 Jun 29 21:03 ..
-rw-rwxr-    1 helper   users    3768 Jun 29 21:03 .Xdefaults
-rw-rwxr-    1 helper   users      24 Jun 29 21:03 .bash_logout
-rw-rwxr-    1 helper   users     220 Jun 29 21:03 .bash_profile
-rw-rwxr-    1 helper   users     124 Jun 29 21:03 .bashrc
lrwxrwxrwx   1 ejr      users      18 Jun 29 21:18 Projects -> /home/deb/Projects
-rw-rwxr-    3 ejr      users    1055 Jun 26 11:00 our.projects
```

# 3

# Working with Your Shell

When you access a Unix or Linux system, the first thing you see is the prompt, called the *shell prompt*, which is where you interact with Unix or Linux. The shell determines how easily you can enter and reenter commands and how you can control your environment. What's cool is that you're not stuck with one shell—that is, on most systems you can choose to use shells that have different features and capabilities, depending on your preferences and needs.

In this chapter, we'll look at your shell, show you how to change it, and get you started using a few of the more common shells.

## In This Chapter

# Discovering Which Shell You're Using

When you first log in to your Unix or Linux account, you'll be using the default shell on your system. The default shell, its features, and its options depend completely on what your system administrator specifies. **Code Listings 3.1** and **3.2** show examples of how default shell prompts differ on two different systems.

## To discover which shell you're using:

**echo $SHELL**

At your shell prompt, type **echo $SHELL** (capitalization counts!). This command tells Unix to display (echo) information about shell settings. This information, by the way, is contained in one of the environment variables, so the technical phrasing (which you might hear in Unix circles) is to "echo your shell environment variable."

The system's response will be the full path to your shell—something like **/bin/zsh**, **/bin/bash**, or **/bin/ksh**.

**TIP** You can also use finger *userid*, substituting your login name for *userid*, to find out more about your shell settings. You can substitute any other userid and see comparable information about the other account holders. See Chapter 7 for more about finger. (Most systems do not support finger, at least remotely, because finger can be a bit of a security hole.)

**TIP** You'll find more information about different shells and their capabilities throughout this chapter.

**Code Listing 3.1** This ISP account uses the **/bin/csh** shell by default.

```
example-isp> echo $SHELL
/bin/csh
example-isp> finger ejray
Login name: ejray In real life: "RayComm"
Directory: /home/users/e/ejray Shell:
→ /bin/csh
On since Jul 23 06:58:48 on pts/16 from
→ calvin.raycomm.com
1 minute 28 seconds Idle Time
No unread mail
No Plan.
example-isp>
```

**Code Listing 3.2** On hobbes, a Linux system, the default shell is **/bin/bash**.

```
[ejr@hobbes ejr]$ echo $SHELL
/bin/bash
[ejr@hobbes ejr]$ finger ejr
Login: ejr Name: Eric J. Ray
Directory: /home/ejr Shell: /bin/bash
On since Wed Jul 22 07:42 (MDT) on tty1
→ 3 hours 15 minutes idle
On since Thu Jul 23 08:17 (MDT) on ttyp0
→ from calvin
No mail.
Project:
Working on UNIX VQS.
Plan:
This is my plan–work all day, sleep
→ all night.
[ejr@hobbes ejr]$
```

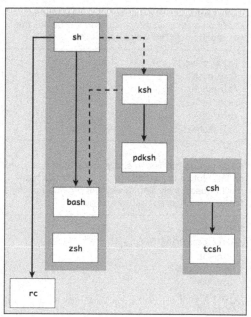

**A** Shells fit neatly into a few "families" with the exception of a few stragglers. Each shell in a family shares many characteristics with the others in the same family.

# Understanding Shells and Options

Depending on the particular Unix or Linux system you're using, you may have several shells available to you. **Table 3.1** describes a few of the more common ones. Each of these shells has slightly different capabilities and features. Keep in mind that the differences in shells do not affect what you can do; rather, they affect how easily and flexibly you can interact with the system.

You'll likely have **bash** as your shell, but you can change to one of many other shells fairly easily. As **Code Listings 3.3** and **3.4** show, you can start by finding out which shells are available to you. **A** shows some shells and how they relate to each other.

**TABLE 3.1 Common Unix and Linux Shells**

| Shell Name | Features |
|---|---|
| **sh** | This shell, which is the original Unix shell (often called the Bourne shell), is fine for scripting but lacks a lot of the flexibility and power for interactive use. For example, it doesn't have features like command completion, email checking, history, or aliasing. |
| **csh** and **tcsh** | This family of shells adds great interactive uses but discards the popular scripting support that **sh**-related shells offer in favor of a C programming-like syntax. Because of the C syntax, this shell is often just called the C shell. Unless you're a C programmer, these are not likely to be your best choices. |
| **ksh**, **bash**, and **zsh** | These provide a good blend of scripting and interactive capabilities, but they stem from different sources (**bash** is most similar to **sh**, hence the Bourne Again SHell name). |

## To see which shells are available to you:

### cat /etc/shells

At the shell prompt, type **cat /etc/shells** to find out which shells are available to you. Code Listings 3.3 and 3.4 show the results of this command on two different systems.

**TIP** Before you go leaping forward through the next sections and changing your shell, you might check with your system administrator or help desk to find out which shells they support and sanction.

**TIP** If all else is equal in terms of support from your system administrator or help desk, and you have no clear preference, we'd suggest zsh as a first choice, with bash as a close second. For most purposes, either will be fine. Power users will like zsh better in the long run.

**TIP** Not all systems use /etc/shells to list acceptable shells—you may have to just look for specific shells, as shown later in this chapter.

**Code Listing 3.3** A minimal listing of available shells on a Unix system, including the basics but not too much in the way of choices.

```
[ejr@hobbes]$ cat /etc/shells
/bin/bash
/bin/sh
/bin/tcsh
/bin/csh
[ejr@hobbes]$
```

**Code Listing 3.4** These shells are available through an ISP. Notice the additional, custom shells that this ISP uses, including shells that provide special features such as not allowing logins.

```
example-isp> cat /etc/shells
/usr/local/bin/tcsh
/bin/csh
/usr/bin/csh
/bin/ksh
/usr/bin/ksh
/sbin/sh
/usr/bin/sh
/usr/local/bin/zsh
/usr/local/bin/bash
/usr/local/bin/nologin
/usr/local/bin/terminated
/usr/local/bin/xmmenu.email
/usr/local/bin/xmmenu.noshell
/usr/lib/uucp/uucico
example-isp>
```

**Code Listing 3.5** You must remember the path to the shell to change shells on this system. Additionally, the password check helps ensure that only the account owner changes the shell.

```
[ejr@hobbes ejr]$ cat /etc/shells
/bin/bash
/bin/sh
/bin/tcsh
/bin/csh
/bin/zsh
[ejr@hobbes ejr]$ chsh
Changing shell for ejr.
Password:
New shell [/bin/bash]: /bin/zsh
Shell changed.
ejr@hobbes ~ $
ejr@hobbes ~ $ su - ejr
Password:
ejr@hobbes ~ $
```

# Changing Your Shell with chsh

If you decide that you want to change your shell, you probably can, depending on how your system administrator has set up things. As **Code Listing 3.5** shows, you would do so using **chsh**. We usually change to **bash**.

## To change your shell with chsh:

1. **cat /etc/shells**

   At the shell prompt, list the available shells on your system with **cat /etc/ shells**.

2. **chsh**

   Enter **chsh** (for "change shell"). Code Listing 3.5 shows the system response. Some systems prompt for a password, and some don't.

3. **/bin/zsh**

   Type the path and name of your new shell.

4. **su - *yourid***

   Type **su -** and your userid to log in again and verify that everything works correctly. If it doesn't, use **chsh** again and change back to the original shell or to a different one. If you can't change back, email your system administrator for help.

**TIP** After changing shells, you might have problems running some commands or have a prompt or display that's not as good as the original. That's likely a result of your default shell being carefully customized by your system administrator. You're probably on your own to set and configure your new shell, and Chapter 8 can help you do this.

**TIP** Some systems don't let users use chsh to change shells. If this is the case, you'll need to email your system administrator and ask for a change, or see if there are alternative methods, as shown in 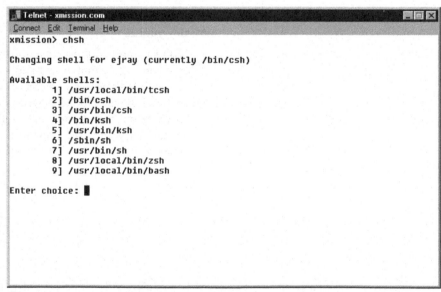. You could also change your shell temporarily, as described in the next section.

**TIP** See "Changing Your Identity with su," later in this chapter, for more about the su command.

**TIP** Some people prefer specific shells for specific purposes, and end up using several shells at the same time (in different terminal windows or tabs, of course). See "Changing Your Shell Temporarily" to learn how to start a specific shell without changing your default settings.

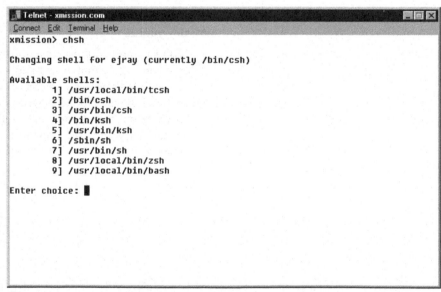

```
Telnet - xmission.com
Connect  Edit  Terminal  Help
xmission> chsh

Changing shell for ejray (currently /bin/csh)

Available shells:
        1] /usr/local/bin/tcsh
        2] /bin/csh
        3] /usr/bin/csh
        4] /bin/ksh
        5] /usr/bin/ksh
        6] /sbin/sh
        7] /usr/bin/sh
        8] /usr/local/bin/zsh
        9] /usr/local/bin/bash

Enter choice: █
```

Ⓐ Some ISPs provide a handy interface for changing shells that lets users pick their new shells from a menu, like this one.

**Code Listing 3.6** Checking the list of shells from **/etc/shells** and looking for other programs that end with **sh** is a good way to find all of the shells on the system.

```
[ejr@hobbes]$ cat /etc/shells
/bin/bash
/bin/sh
/bin/tcsh
/bin/csh
[ejr@hobbes]$ ls /usr/local/bin/*sh
/usr/local/bin/pdksh
[ejr@hobbes]$
```

# Changing Your Shell Temporarily

You can change your shell temporarily by creating a subshell and using that instead of the original shell. You can create a subshell using any shell available on your Unix or Linux system. This means that you can look in the **/etc/shells** file and use a shell listed there, or you can use a shell installed elsewhere on the system (**Code Listing 3.6**).

## To find out which temporary shells you can use:

1. **cat /etc/shells**

   At the shell prompt, type **cat /etc/shells** to find out which shells are listed in the shells file.

   If you don't find a shell you want to use in the shells file, look for other shells installed elsewhere on the system.

2. **ls /usr/local/bin/*sh /usr/bin/*sh**

   At the shell prompt, type **ls /usr/local/bin/*sh /usr/bin/*sh** to find additional shells in the **/usr/local/bin** or **/usr/bin** directories. Note that not all programs that end with **sh** are shells, but most shells end with **sh** (Code Listing 3.6).

## To create a temporary shell (subshell):

**/usr/bin/csh**

At the shell prompt, type the path and name of the temporary shell you want to use. In this case, we're using the **csh** shell, located at **/usr/bin/csh**. You might see a new prompt, perhaps something like the one shown in **Code Listing 3.7**.

## To exit a temporary shell (subshell):

**exit**

At the shell prompt, type **exit**. You'll be returned to the shell from which you started the subshell. If you created more than one subshell, you'll have to exit all of them.

**TIP** Using temporary shells is a great way to experiment with other shells and their options. We recommend using a temporary shell to experiment with the shells covered in this chapter.

**TIP** You can also often use Ctrl + Delete to exit from a subshell, but this depends on the system configuration. Try it out and see.

**TIP** See Chapter 1, specifically the listings of directories containing programs, for other places to look for shells.

**Code Listing 3.7** Type the shell name (which is really just another Unix command) to change shells.

```
[ejr@hobbes]$ /usr/bin/csh
ejr>
```

# Using Completion in the bash Shell

One of the cool features of the **bash** shell is *command argument completion*. With this feature, you can type just part of a command, press Tab, and have **bash** complete the command for you (**Code Listing 3.8**).

## To use completion in the bash shell:

1. ls

   Use **ls** to list the files in your current directory.

2. cd pub Tab

   Type a partial command, as shown here, and then press Tab to complete the command. In this example, we typed the **cd** command and part of the **public_html** directory (truncated to **pub** in the example), then pressed Tab to complete it (see Code Listing 3.8).

**TIP** Completion works only if there's just one possible match to the letters you type before you press Tab. For example, if you type **cd pu** (for **public_html**) and there's another subdirectory called **puppy**, the shell will beep and wait for you to type in enough letters to distinguish the two subdirectories. In many cases, if you persist and type Tab again, the shell will show you the options that match so far.

**TIP** You can use the completion feature to complete commands, directory names within commands, and nearly anything else you might enter that's sufficiently unambiguous.

Code Listing 3.8 In this example, we typed only the **ls** command followed by **cd pub** and pressed the Tab key; **bash** completed the command for us.

```
bash-2.00$ ls
Complete    NewProject  bogus2       ftp          puppy
Completed   News        dead.letter  mail         temp
Mail        access      files        public_html  testme
bash-2.00$ cd public_html/
bash-2.00$
```

# Viewing Session History in the bash Shell

Another cool feature of the **bash** shell is that it lets you easily reuse commands from your session history, which shows you the list of commands you've used during a session or in previous sessions (**Code Listing 3.9**). Viewing history is handy for reviewing your Unix or Linux session, using previous commands again (rather than retyping them), and modifying (rather than completely retyping) complex commands.

## To view session history in the bash shell:

**1.** Use the shell for a little while, changing directories, redirecting output, or doing other tasks.

Take your time. We'll wait.

**2.** Press the ⬆ key one time.

Note that the last (previous) command you used appears on the command line, as shown in Code Listing 3.9. To reissue the command, just press Enter.

**Code Listing 3.9** In this example, we typed the first command, then pressed the ⬆ key to reuse the previous **ls** command. **!40** recycled the 40th command from the listing.

```
[ejr@hobbes clean]$ ls
background.htm info.htm logo.gif
[ejr@hobbes clean]$ ls
background.htm info.htm logo.gif
[ejr@hobbes clean]$ history
   1  free
   2  id deb
   3  id ejr
   4  uname -a
   5  ls
...
  40  cd
  41  cp .bash_history oldhistory
  42  vi .bash_history
  43  elm
  44  ls -la
  45  ls -la .e*
  46  elm
  47  lynx
  48  history
  49  vi .bash*his*
  50  history
  51 cd clean
  52  ls
  53  ls
  54  history
[ejr@hobbes clean]$ !40
cd
[ejr@hobbes ejr]$
```

**3.** Continue to press ⬆ or ⬇ to scroll back or forward through your history. When you reach a command you want to use, press Enter.

If you see a command that's close but not exactly what you want to use, you can edit it. Just use the ⬅ and ➡ keys to move across the line, insert text by typing it, and use Backspace or Delete to delete text. When you've fixed the command, press Enter (you don't have to be at the end of the line to do so).

**4.** `history`

Type **history** at the shell prompt to see a numbered list of previous commands you've entered.

> **TIP** Commands from the current session are kept in memory to scroll through, while commands from previous sessions are kept in the ~/.bash_history file. You can edit ~/.bash_history with any editor to delete unneeded commands or simply delete the file to get rid of the whole history file, which will then be re-created with the next command you issue. (A history of commands is a great jumping-off point to write a script to do the commands automatically. Chapter 10 gives you the specifics.)

> **TIP** When you're viewing the history, you can recycle commands by typing an exclamation point (!) and the line number of the command you want to run again. You'd type !40, for example, to rerun command 40.

> **TIP** Use **history** followed by a number to specify the number of items to list. For example, **history** 10 shows the last 10 commands.

# Using Completion in the zsh Shell

The **zsh** shell (also known as the Z shell) also offers completion but with added twists over the **bash** shell for the power user. Basically, though, you can type just part of a command, press Tab, and have the Z shell complete the command for you (**Code Listing 3.10**).

## To use completion in the **zsh** shell:

**1.** **ls**

Use **ls** to list the files in your current directory.

**2.** **cd pub** Tab

Type a partial command, as shown here, and then press Tab to complete the command. In this example, we typed the **cd** command and part of the **public_html** directory (truncated to **pub** in the example), and then pressed the Tab key to complete it (see Code Listing 3.10).

**TIP** In the Z shell, command completion works even if multiple files might match the partial command that you type. For example, if you type **cd pu** (for **public_html**) and there's another subdirectory called **puppy**, when you press Tab to complete the name, the shell will show you the options that match (**public_html** and **puppy**) and then cycle through the options as you continue pressing Tab.

**TIP** You can use command completion to complete commands, directory names within commands, and nearly anything else you might enter.

**TIP** The Z shell is smart enough to show you only the subdirectories you could change to. **bash**, on the other hand, would show you files and directories and beep at you—not as helpful, for sure.

**Code Listing 3.10** In this example, we typed only the **ls** command followed by **cd pub** and pressed the Tab key; **zsh** completed the command for us.

```
$ ls
Complete  NewProject  bogus2  ftp  puppy
Completed  News  dead.letter  mail  temp
Mail  access  files  public_html  testme
$ cd public_html/
$
```

**Code Listing 3.11** In this example, we typed the first command, and then pressed the [↑] key to reuse the previous command. !40 recycled the 40th command from the listing.

```
[ejr@hobbes clean]$ ls
background.htm info.htm logo.gif
[ejr@hobbes clean]$ ls
background.htm info.htm logo.gif
[ejr@hobbes clean]$ history
 1 free
 2 id deb
 3 id ejr
 4 uname -a
 5 ls
...
40 cd
41 cp .bash_history oldhistory
42 vi .bash_history
43 elm
44 ls -la
45 ls -la .e*
46 elm
47 lynx
48 history
49 vi .bash*his*
50 history
51 cd clean
52 ls
53 ls
54 history
[ejr@hobbes clean]$ !40
cd
[ejr@hobbes ejr]$
```

# Viewing Session History in the zsh Shell

The Z shell also lets you easily reuse commands from your session history, which is the list of commands you've used during a session or in previous sessions (**Code Listing 3.11**). The history functions are handy for reviewing your Unix or Linux session, reusing previous commands (instead of retyping), and modifying (rather than completely redoing) long or complex commands.

## To view session history in the zsh shell:

1. Use **zsh** as you usually would, changing directories, redirecting output, or doing other tasks. For example, review the previous chapter and practice the commands you've learned so far.

2. Press [↑] one time.

   Note that the last (previous) command you used appears on the command line, as shown in Code Listing 3.11. To reissue the command, just press [Enter].

3. Continue to press [↑] or [↓] to scroll back or forward through your history. When you reach a command you want to use, press [Enter].

   If you see a command that's close but not exactly what you want to use, you can edit it. Just use the [←] and [→] keys to move across the line. Then, insert text by typing it or using [Backspace] or [Delete] to delete text. When you've modified the command, press [Enter] (you don't have to be at the end of the line to do so).

4. Type **history** at the shell prompt to see a numbered list of previous commands you've entered.

**TIP** If you have a minor change to a command, you can edit it quickly and easily. For example, if you just used `ls /home/unixvqs` and wanted to issue `cd /home/unixvqs` next, you could just type `^ls^cd` to tell the system to replace `ls` from the previous command with `cd` and then reissue the command.

**TIP** You can use Ctrl+A and Ctrl+E while editing a command line to move to the beginning and end of the line, respectively.

**TIP** Commands from the current session are kept in memory to scroll through, while commands from previous sessions are kept in the `~/.zsh_history` file. You can edit `.zsh_history` with any editor to delete unneeded commands or simply delete the file to get rid of the whole history file, which will then be re-created with the next command you issue.

**TIP** Reviewing session history is a great way to identify your work patterns and needs. If you find yourself repeatedly using the same series of commands, consider writing a script to do the commands automatically, as Chapter 10 describes.

**TIP** Most of the command completion options from `bash` also work in `zsh`. Give them a try!

# Changing Your Identity with su

Occasionally, you may need to log in with a userid other than your own or need to re-log in with your own userid. For example, you might want to check configuration settings that you've changed before logging out to make sure that they work. Or, if you change your shell, you might want to check it before you log out (and you should do that, by the way).

You can use the **su** (substitute user) command either to log in as another user (**Code Listing 3.12**) or to start a new login shell.

**Code Listing 3.12** Changing back and forth from one user to another (and exiting from multiple shells) can get a little confusing, but the prompt often tells you who you are and what directory you're in.

```
[ejr@hobbes asr]$ ls
Projects testing
[ejr@hobbes asr]$ su asr
Password:
[asr@hobbes asr]$ ls
Projects testing
[asr@hobbes asr]$ su - ejr
Password:
[ejr@hobbes ejr]$ ls
Mail            editme          script2.sed
Projects        fortunes.copy   scriptextra.sed
Xrootenv.0      fortunes1.txt   sedtest
above.htm       fortunes2.txt   sorted.address.temp
address.book    groups          temp.htm
address.temp    history.txt     tempsort
axhome          html.htm        test
bogus           html.html       test2
chmod.txt       mail            testing.gif
clean           manipulate      testing.wp
compression     nsmail          typescript
[ejr@hobbes ejr]$ exit
[asr@hobbes asr]$ exit
[ejr@hobbes ejr]$ exit
```

## To log in as a different user with su:

`su unixvqs`

At the shell prompt, type **su** plus the userid of the user you're logging in as. You'll be prompted for a password just as though you were logging in to the system for the first time (Code Listing 3.12).

If you do not specify a username, the system will assume you mean the **root** user.

If you're logged in as **root** to begin with, you won't be prompted to give a password.

You will now be logged in as the new user and be able to work just as if you were that user, though you'll be in the same directory with the same settings that you had before you issued the **su** command.

## To start a new login shell with su:

`su - yourid`

At the shell prompt, type **su - yourid** (of course, use your own userid or that of the user you want to change to). The addition of the hyphen (-) will force a new login shell and set all the environment variables and defaults according to the settings for the user you are switching to.

## To return to the previous shell:

`exit`

Type **exit** at the shell prompt to leave the current shell and return to the previous one. If you use **exit** from the original login shell, you'll log completely out of the Unix or Linux system.

**TIP** If you have root access and you **ssh** to the system to administer it, you should use **su** to provide a little extra security. Rather than log in directly as **root** and leave the remote possibility of having your password stolen (or sniffed) off your local system, log in as yourself, then use **su** (with no other information) to change to **root**.

**TIP** If you **su** to another user with **su user** (no hyphen) and the new user doesn't have read and execute permissions for the current directory, you will see shell error messages. You can disregard these. See Chapter 5 for more about read and execute permissions.

**Code Listing 3.13** You can often straighten out a confused **telnet** program or Unix system by using an **stty** command. This one fixes the errant Backspace key.

```
example-isp> ls ^?^?^?^?
: No such file or directory
example-isp> stty erase '^?'
example-isp> ls
```

**Code Listing 3.14** The **stty** command here fixes the Delete key to work like Backspace.

```
example-isp> jf^H^H
jf^H^H: Command not found
example-isp> ls ^H^H
: No such file or directory
example-isp> stty erase '^H'
example-isp>
```

**TIP** If **stty sane** doesn't fix a messed-up display, try **reset** or even logging out and logging back in or restarting your terminal program.

**TIP** You can fix Backspace oddities permanently by adding the appropriate **stty** command to your configuration files or by making changes in your terminal client. See Chapter 8 for details about your configuration files. Refer to Chapter 1 for more helpful details about terminal programs like **ssh** and **telnet**.

# Fixing Terminal Settings with stty

Another handy thing you can do with your shell is fix those annoying problems that occur with terminal programs. Back in Chapter 1, we mentioned that you might encounter oddities such as your Backspace and Delete keys not working properly. You can fix these problems using **stty** (see Code Listing 3.13).

## To fix Backspace and Delete key oddities with stty:

**stty erase '^?'**

If you're accustomed to using Backspace to erase characters to the left of the cursor and you just get a bunch of **^H** symbols on the screen when you try it, you need to educate the terminal about your preferences. Type **stty erase** and press Backspace to fix it (Code Listing 3.13).

In some cases, depending on your terminal program, you might need to set **stty erase '^H'** and then press Ctrl+H to backspace. To enter this command, type **stty erase** and press Ctrl+V, then Ctrl+H (Code Listing 3.14).

## To fix general terminal weirdness with stty:

**stty sane**

Typing **stty sane** at the shell prompt will fix a lot of oddities. For example, if you accidentally issue a bad command and all of a sudden nothing shows up on the screen or if you have general gibberish showing up on the screen, **stty sane** may return your terminal session to sanity.

The **reset** command is also often effective at fixing a messed-up terminal. Issue it like this:

**reset**

# Exiting the Shell

When you're finished with your Unix or Linux session, you need to exit the shell. If you've been playing with the **su** and shell commands, you might actually have shells within shells and need to exit from all of them. All you have to do is type **exit** once for each shell.

## To exit from the shell:

```
exit
```

At the shell prompt, type **exit**. Ta-da!

**TIP** If you're located at the login shell prompt, you could also type `logout` rather than `exit`. At all other shells, though, you need to type `exit`. In some cases, you could also press Ctrl+D, but that depends on your local system configuration.

**TIP** Be sure to log off rather than simply close your window or break your connection. It's possible, if the settings at your host are seriously incorrect, that your session could remain open and someone else could pick up right where you left off with your session under your `userid`.

# 4

# Creating and Editing Files

Creating and editing files are likely the most common tasks you'll perform in Unix or Linux. If you're programming, developing webpages, sending email (uh-huh, really), writing a letter, configuring your environment (see Chapter 8), or just exploring the system, you'll spend a lot of time in an editor.

In this chapter, we'll introduce you to two of the most common editors: **nano** and **vi**. We'll launch this chapter with a general overview of each, and then discuss some how-tos of using each one. With the information presented here, you'll be able to choose an editor based on your needs and get started using it (or using both of them).

## In This Chapter

# Choosing an Editor: nano/pico or vi/vim

Basically, all editors are designed to do the same things: enable you to create, modify, and save text files. These files could include configuration files, email messages, or shell scripts—essentially any text file you can create. Which editor you choose is up to you, depending on your specific needs and how much you're willing to learn.

In this book, we'll stick to the two biggies: **nano** and **vi**, which will likely give you all the capabilities you'll need. We chose these because **nano** is (arguably) the easiest Unix or Linux editor to use and **vi** is one of the most powerful and is available on almost every Unix or Linux system.

Which to choose? We recommend that you explore both. While you'll no doubt find **nano** easier to use, we highly recommend that you make a concerted effort to learn to get around in **vi**. You'll find that **vi**'s learning curve is steeper—much—but that being a skilled **vi** user will provide many benefits, not the least of which is that **vi** is really the only editor you can count on being on any Unix or Linux system you use.

**A** **nano** offers onscreen command reminders to make it easier to use.

## About nano or pico

**nano** is one of the more straightforward Unix editors and has become quite popular because it's extremely easy to use. In particular, as shown in **A**, it's menu-driven and intuitive. All the commands are visible, and you can open, modify, and close files with little effort. **nano** is a great choice if you're just getting started with Unix or Linux, or if you won't be needing an editor able to leap tall files in a single bound.

For a variety of reasons, mostly connected to open-source licensing issues, **nano** is a near-clone of **pico**, which in the past was included in a number of Linux/Unix distributions as well as on systems that you might be using today. The **nano** editor is command-for-command the same as **pico**, but it does offer some supplemental higher-end (yet still easy-to use) features.

For the purposes of this book, we're going to treat **pico** and **nano** as equivalent—if you have **pico**, just mentally write that in wherever you see **nano**.

**pico** is distributed with the **pine** email program, so if you have **pine** available to you, you likely also have **pico**. (See Chapter 1 for a reminder on how to find out if specific programs are available to you.) If **pico** is not available to you, and if you cannot find **nano** either, ask your system administrator to install one or the other.

## About `vi` or `vim`

Although **vi** is likely responsible for much of Unix's and Linux's reputation for being complicated and confusing, it offers enormous power and flexibility. Plus, **vi** is universally available (unlike **nano**), so for these two reasons, you should consider taking the time to learn it. You might find **vi** cryptic, counterintuitive, and nitpicky, and for this reason, you might want to choose a different editor if you won't require **vi**'s capabilities. As  shows, if you use **vi**, you won't have menus at your disposal—you'll have to get used to using commands like (Esc)**:q** or (Esc)**:%s/vi is arcane/vi is powerful/**.

Yes, continuing the theme from the previous section, there is an equivalent of **vi**, called **vim**, that's licensed differently and that's somewhat more powerful. For basic use—everything in this book and far more—the two are identical. In this case, though, you will always find **vi**, even if it's really **vim** (**vi** may actually be a *symlink*, or shortcut, to **vim**). If you find **vim**, though, it will assuredly be **vim**. All commands will be the same, so just dive in and enjoy.

**B** **vi** gives you a clean screen and makes you remember all of its cryptic commands.

## Editors Abound

In addition to **nano** and **vi** (covered in this chapter), dozens of other editors exist:

- **emacs** offers a reasonable middle ground between the user-friendliness of **nano** and the power of **vi** (or **vim**). Do note that it's fully as powerful as **vi** for the experienced user, but it is still far easier to get started with. It's not available on all systems, though, so you'll just have to type in the command to see if you have access to it.

- **joe**, **jed**, and **e3**, which are fairly simple editors and comparable to **nano** in many ways. These are certainly worth a look if you're interested.

- **ed**, **ex**, and **red**, which are simple (in functionality, but not necessarily usage) line-by-line editors. They're probably not recommended for the novice user. We haven't had to use them in years.

**A** **nano** offers an intuitive interface for editing text.

# Starting nano and Dabbling with It

You can start and dabble with **nano** using the following steps. Notice that the **nano** interface is intuitive and easy to navigate, as shown in **A**.

## To start nano and dabble with it:

**1.** nano

Type **nano** at the shell prompt. The program starts up, and you'll see something like **A**, with the text area up at the top of the window and the command hints at the bottom.

If you know the name of the file you want to edit, type **nano** at the shell prompt followed by the path and name of the file you want to edit (**hairyspiders**, for example).

**2.** hairyspiders

Go ahead. Type something—anything—just to try it out.

▸ Use Delete and Backspace to help edit text.

▸ Use the arrow keys to move up, down, right, or left.

**TIP** Start nano with the **-w** option (for example, nano **-w** filename) to disable word wrapping. You'll find this particularly useful when editing configuration files, as covered in Chapter 8.

**TIP** Throughout nano, you'll see ^C, ^J, and dozens of other ^*something* characters hanging out in the menu at the bottom. The ^ stands for Ctrl, so ^C is Ctrl+C, ^J is Ctrl+J, and so on.

# Saving in nano

You'll generally save your files frequently whenever you're editing them—and you should. Remember, Murphy is watching you!

## To save in nano:

1. Ctrl+O

   Use Ctrl+O periodically to save ("write out") the text you're editing.

2. **hairyspiders**

   Specify the filename for your file .

> **TIP** After you save a file for the first time and want to save new changes, just press Ctrl+O and then press Enter to confirm the current filename and save it.

> **TIP** When you exit nano, you'll get a last chance to save your changes. See "Exiting nano" in this chapter for the specifics.

> **TIP** If you try to save a new file over an existing one—which would obliterate the original—nano carefully asks you if you want to overwrite the file. Answer Yes, and you'll no longer have the original; No, and you'll get to choose a new filename.

**A** In **nano** lingo, "writing out" just means "saving."

**A** Marking, cutting, and pasting text in **nano** can be very handy.

**TIP** You can select and cut blocks of text without also pasting them back into a file. Just skip steps 6 and 7.

**TIP** You can paste text blocks as many times as you want. After you select and cut text, just press Ctrl+U at each place where you want to insert the cut text.

**TIP** If you don't select text, Ctrl+K just cuts a single line.

# Cutting and Pasting Text Blocks in nano

As you're typing along in **nano**, you'll probably need to cut and paste blocks of text, as shown in **A**.

## To cut and paste text in nano:

1. **nano hairyspiders**

   At the shell prompt, type **nano** followed by the name of the file to edit.

2. Move the cursor to the first line of the text you want to cut.

3. Ctrl+^

   Press Ctrl+^ to mark the beginning of the text you want to cut. (Note that Ctrl+^ is really Ctrl+Shift+6—it might work without Shift, but it might not, depending on your terminal program. Try it out and see what happens.)

4. Use the arrow keys to move the cursor to the end of the text you want to cut.

   Note that the text gets highlighted as you select it **A**.

5. Ctrl+K

   This "kuts" the text.

6. Using the arrow keys, move the cursor to where you want to insert the cut text.

7. Ctrl+U

   Use this key combination to paste the cut text into the file at the new location.

# Checking Spelling in nano

Another handy thing you can do in **nano** is chek yoor speling, as shown in  and .

## To spell-check in nano:

1. **nano hairyspiders**

   At the shell prompt, type **nano** and the filename of the file to edit.

2. ⌈Ctrl⌉+⌈T⌉

   Pressing these keys starts spell-checking the file. **nano** will stop at each misspelled word as shown in .

3. **correctspelling**

   Type in the correct spelling for any words flagged as misspelled, or press ⌈Enter⌉ to accept the current spelling and move along to the next word.

**TIP** You can press ⌈Ctrl⌉+⌈C⌉ to cancel spell-checking at any time.

**TIP** Because the spell-checker in nano isn't full-featured, consider using an alternate spell-check program by specifying it on the command line, like nano -s ispell hairyspiders, so you can get a little more assistance. See Chapter 14 for more information.

**TIP** When the entire document has been spell-checked, nano will tell you that it's finished, and you can continue editing the file .

**A** **nano** prompts you to correct the spelling of misspelled words.

**B** **nano** informs you when the procedure is complete.

**A** **nano** gives you all the information you need.

# Getting Help in nano

A great way to find out more about **nano** is to access **nano** help. In addition to finding answers to your questions, you can discover its features and capabilities as shown in **A**.

## To get help in nano:

1. Ctrl+G

   In **nano**, press Ctrl+G to access help.

2. Move through the help pages:

   ▸ Ctrl+V moves you down through the help page.

   ▸ Ctrl+Y moves you up through the help page.

3. Ctrl+X

   Use this combination to exit help.

## To get help with nano startup options:

**man nano**

At the shell prompt, type **man nano** to learn more about startup options, including a variety of options that control how **nano** works.

**TIP** Keep your eye on the nano status line for current information, error messages, and occasional hints about using nano. The status line is the third line from the bottom of the screen, just above the menu, as shown in **A**.

**TIP** Keep in mind that nano really is a basic program. And if you're using pico, it's even more basic. If you're looking for a command or function that isn't readily available, it's probably not there. You might check out vi or emacs instead if you want more power than nano offers you.

# Exiting nano

When you're finished editing in **nano**, you'll exit it using the following steps.

## To exit nano:

1. ⎡Ctrl⎤+⎡X⎤

   Within **nano**, press ⎡Ctrl⎤+⎡X⎤. If you haven't made any changes to the text since you last saved the file, you'll find yourself immediately back at the shell prompt. If you have made changes, you'll be prompted to "Save modified buffer" **A**.

2. At the "Save modified buffer" prompt:

   ▸ Press ⎡Y⎤ if you want to save your changes. Proceed to step 3.

   ▸ Press ⎡N⎤ if you don't want to save your changes. You'll end up back at the shell prompt.

3. `bighairyspiders`

   Specify the filename for your file if it's the first time you've saved it. If you've saved it before, press ⎡Enter⎤ to confirm the current filename or change the name to save a copy and not change the original file.

> **TIP** A *buffer* is what the computer uses to temporarily store information, and if it's modified, that means that it's temporarily storing something that you haven't saved to disk.

**A** **nano** gives you the opportunity to "Save modified buffer." Without the techno-babble, this means to save the text you just wrote or edited before you exit.

 The **vi** editor inundates you with tons of onscreen help and advice, as shown here. Well, documentation is available, but the **vi** interface itself isn't really helpful at all!

# Starting vi (or vim) and Dabbling with It

Before you go running off to use **vi**, understand that it has two modes (both of which look pretty much like ):

- *Insert mode* (sometimes called input mode), in which the keys you press actually show up in the file that you're editing. You use this mode to add or change text.

- *Normal mode* (sometimes called command mode), in which every keystroke is interpreted as a command. You use this mode to do everything except enter text.

What's confusing for many people about **vi** is that it starts you in command mode, meaning that if you just start typing, you may see some blank spaces, characters, and bits of words that you type—essentially, a bunch of garbage that does not exactly represent what you're typing—and you'll hear a lot of beeping. So, as we'll show you in the following steps, you'll need to access the insert mode as soon as you start **vi**.

## To start vi:

1. **vi**

   At the shell prompt, type **vi**. The program starts up, and you'll see something like Ⓐ. The ~ symbols show blank lines below the end of the file.

2. **i**

   Type **i** to get into insert mode. This itself is a command issued in command mode, so it won't show up on the screen.

3. **hairy spiders lurk**

   In insert mode, type anything you want.

   Everything you type will show up on the screen until you return to normal mode by pressing ⎋Esc⎦. When you are in normal mode, you can use the arrow keys to navigate up and down in the file line by line and use ⎡Ctrl⎦+⎡F⎦ and ⎡Ctrl⎦+⎡B⎦ to scroll one screen forward and backward, respectively.

   **TIP** To get help for **vi**, type **man vi**. See Chapter 1 for more about **man** pages.

   **TIP** If you're not sure what mode you're in, press ⎡Esc⎦ to go into normal mode. If you're already in normal mode, you'll hear a beep. If you're in insert mode, you'll change to normal mode.

   **TIP** Many Unix-like systems, including Linux and OS X, actually provide a program called **vim** in the place of **vi**. **vim** (for *VI iMproved*) is like **vi** but feature-rich and more flexible, and you can still start it with the command **vi**.

   **TIP** You can open specific files or even multiple files when you access **vi**. At the shell prompt, type **vi filetoedit** (or whatever) to open a specific file. Or, for example, type **vi *.html** to open all the HTML documents in a directory, then use ⎡Esc⎦**:n** (for "next") and then press ⎡Enter⎦ to move to each subsequent file.

   **TIP** See "Adding and Deleting Text in **vi**" later in this chapter for more details about editing in **vi**.

A Save early, save often. That's the safe rule for **vi**.

# Saving in vi

You'll want to save changes to your documents frequently, especially as you're learning to use **vi** Ⓐ. Until you're accustomed to switching between insert and normal mode, you may accidentally type in commands when you think you're typing text, with unpredictable results. To save files, just follow these steps.

## To save text in vi:

[Esc]**:w limerick**

Press [Esc] to get out of input mode and into command mode, then type **:w** (for "write," as in write to the disk) followed by a space and then the filename (**limerick**, in this example) you want to use for the file, then press [Enter]. If you've already saved the file once, just press [Esc] and type **:w**, then press [Enter].

> **TIP** If you've already saved your file at least once, you can save changes and exit **vi** in one fell swoop. In command mode, type **:wq** (for "write quit"). For more information about quitting **vi**, see the section "Exiting **vi**," later in this chapter.

> **TIP** If you want to save a file over an existing file (obliterating the original as you do), use **:w! existingfilename** in command mode. The **!** forces **vi** to overwrite the original.

# Adding and Deleting Text in vi

Adding and deleting text in **vi** is a bit more complicated than doing the same in **nano**. In **nano**, you basically just place your cursor where you want to make changes, whereas **vi** has a whole slew of commands that you use to specify where the changes should occur. (**Tables 4.1**, **4.2**, and **4.3** list only a very few of your options.) Plus, to issue the commands, you have to switch to normal mode.

## To add or delete text in vi:

1. **vi**

   To begin, type **vi** at the shell prompt.

2. **i**

   Change into insert mode.

3. **There once was a man from Nantucket**

   Type some text that you'll want to add to.

4. Esc

   Press Esc to enter normal mode before you issue the commands.

5. Choose a command, based on what you want to do to the text.

   ▸ Table 4.1 lists commands to add text.

   ▸ Table 4.2 lists commands to delete text.

   ▸ Table 4.3 lists miscellaneous editing commands.

6. **dd**

   Type the command. Here, we're deleting the current line of text.

**TABLE 4.1** vi Commands to Add Text

| Command | Function |
| --- | --- |
| a | Adds text after the cursor |
| A | Adds text at the end of the current line |
| i | Inserts text before the cursor |
| I | Inserts text at the beginning of the current line |
| o | Inserts a blank line after the current line |
| O | Inserts a blank line before the current line |

**TABLE 4.2** vi Commands to Delete Text

| Command | Function |
| --- | --- |
| x | Deletes one character (under the cursor) |
| X | Deletes one character (behind the cursor) |
| dd | Deletes the current line |
| 5dd | Deletes five lines starting with the current line (any number would work here) |
| dw | Deletes the current word |
| cw | Changes the current word (deletes it and enters input mode) |
| r | Replaces the character under the cursor with the next character you type |
| R | Replaces the existing text with the text you type (like overtype mode in most word processors) |

**TABLE 4.3** Other Handy vi Editing Commands

| Command | Function |
| --- | --- |
| yy | Copies the current line |
| p | Pastes any copied text after the cursor or line |
| J | Joins the current and following lines |
| u | Undoes the last change |
| U | Undoes all changes on the current line |
| . | Repeats the last command |

**A** Reading an additional file into the current one can make your editing tasks much easier.

# Importing Files into vi

You can also merge multiple files in **vi** by reading additional files into the current one, as shown in **A**. Basically, all this means is that you insert one file into the file you're currently editing.

## To import files in vi:

1. **vi hairyspider**

   At the shell prompt, type **vi** followed by the filename—in this case, the **hairyspider** file.

2. [Esc]**:r filename**

   At the point in the file where you want to import text, press [Esc], then type **:r** and the filename you want to read into the file.

> **TIP** **vi also lets you read the output of commands into the file. For example, if you want to read the list of files in a specific directory into the file, use** [Esc]**:r !ls in normal mode.**

# Searching and Replacing in vi

One of **vi**'s better features (and advantages over **nano**) is that it allows you to search and replace throughout entire files. As shown in the next sections, you can just find a specific string of text (a *regular expression*, in Unix lingo; see ), or you can find the text and replace it with other text, as in **B**.

## To find a string of text in vi:

**1. vi hairyspider**

For starters, access **vi** and a specific file.

**2.** Esc**/spider**

Enter command mode, then type / followed by the text you're looking for. Here, we're looking for "spider," but you may be looking for "the fly" or "wiggled and jiggled and tickled inside her." Or whatever.

**3.** Enter

Press Enter to find the first occurrence of the term. Type N to find the next one.

**A** Searching for text in **vi** is quick and reliable.

**B** Replacing text in **vi** requires a bit of arcane syntax, but you get used to it quickly.

## To search and replace in vi:

**1.** `vi hairyspider`

For starters, access **vi** and a specific file.

**2.** [Esc]**:%s/spider/horrible horrible awful spider/**

Enter [Esc]**:%s/** plus the text to find, another **/**, followed by the replacement text, as in ⑧. Here, we replace "swallowed a fly" with "swallowed a spider to catch the fly," but perhaps you might forgo the spider and simply go for some antacid.

**TIP** A great use for the search-and-replace feature is if you end up with DOS text files in your Unix account (by transferring a text file from a Windows machine as a binary file, most likely). If you view DOS files through a Unix shell, all the lines in the file will end with ^M. But if you try to type ^M when you're doing a search and replace, the ^M won't show up. What to do? Press [Ctrl]+[V], then [Ctrl]+[M]. Just search and replace with :%s/[Ctrl]+[V][Ctrl] ˈ[M]//g. The [Ctrl]+[V] command "escapes" the following character, so you can press it without actually doing what the command would otherwise do. If you don't escape the [Ctrl]+[M], vi thinks you just pressed [Enter] and tries to execute the unfinished command.

**TIP** See the section on `grep` in Chapter 6 for information about searching with regular expressions.

**TIP** Add a g at the end of the command to make it apply to all occurrences in the file. Otherwise, it applies only to the first occurrence on each line.

# Exiting vi

Whew! Time to exit **vi** .

## To exit vi:

[Esc]**:q**

Enter command mode by typing [Esc], then type **:q** to quit **vi**. If you haven't saved your latest changes, **vi** will not quit and will tell you to use **!** to override. To quit without saving your changes, use **:q!**, as shown in .

> **TIP** If you don't really want to quit but want to edit a different file instead, type :e `filename` to open a new file to edit.

> **TIP** We recommend that you take a few minutes to try out some of the commands that you'll use throughout your **vi** experience. If you don't think you'll need this range of commands, consider using `nano` rather than **vi**.

> **TIP** It takes some practice to get accustomed to **vi**, but the time spent is well worth it. With patience and practice, you'll quickly become proficient in using **vi**. Take your time, take deep breaths, and plow ahead.

This morning I got up, went downstairs, and found a HUMONGOUS horrible horrible awful spider in the bathroom where the little potty is. After I quietly composed myself from the shock (I didn't want to alert the kids), I looked around the house for something to put him in...the kids' bug catcher thing (nowhere to be found)...a jar...tupperware...a lidded cup...the salad spinner (BwaaaaHaaaHaaa !)....

I went back and checked on the horrible horrible awful spider and decided that I just couldn't face putting him in something.

I mean, what if he got close to me...or TOUCHED me?!?!

And, since I hate the crunching sound and feel of squashing bugs, I knew I couldn't just kill him. This horrible horrible awful spider had *bones*, I'm tellin' ya'. So, I hunted for bug spray. And hunted. But nothing.

:q!

**A** Use [Esc]**:q!** to quit **vi** without saving changes.

# 5

# Controlling Ownership and Permissions

Unix, Linux, and Unix-like operating systems are multiuser systems in which your files are separate from Jane's files, which are separate from Joe's files, and so on. Any file you create is separate from other users' files and usually cannot be directly accessed by Jane, Joe, or any other user. The file permissions determine what you can or cannot see, access or use.

Occasionally, though, you'll need to share files. For example, you might be collaborating with Jane on a project for which sharing files (rather than creating and maintaining separate ones) is essential.

This chapter provides an overview of Unix and Linux file permissions and ownership. For many systems, only the root user can make ownership changes, so you may have to ask for help from your system administrator to do this.

# Understanding File Ownership and Permissions

Unix and Linux provide three levels of file ownership:

- **User.** Refers to the single userid that's primarily in charge of the file. You have this level of ownership for the files you create.

- **Group.** Refers to the group (of users) associated with a specific file. All users within a group have the same permissions for interacting with a file.

- **Other.** Refers to any users not identified with either the group or user for a file.

Within these levels, you can specify permissions for file access and rights in three categories:

- **Read.** Users with read permission can view a file; they cannot make changes to it.

- **Write.** Users with write permission can make changes to or delete a file.

- **Execute.** Users with execute permission can run files (programs or scripts) and view directories.

In this chapter, we'll show you some of the commands that can be used (sometimes by you, usually by the root user) to set ownership and permissions. Keep in mind that you can set or change any permissions for files you create and possibly for files created by others; however, exactly which permissions and ownerships you can change depends on the system. Even if you don't currently need to change file ownerships or permissions, you should take a quick read through this chapter to see what options might be available to you.

**TIP** An interesting twist on this whole ownership issue is that not all "owners" are people. Programs or processes run as a specific user, and if they create files, those files have permissions reflecting the individual and group membership of the program. See Chapter 9 for more information.

**TIP** Some Linux and Unix-like operating systems have additional or supplementary means of controlling access to specific files. Usually, though, you'll know if such a system is in use. For now, just know that such things exist; the procedures in this chapter will handle 95 percent of your needs.

# Finding Out Who Owns What

Your first step in changing ownership and permissions is to find out who owns which files. You'll need this information to determine whether you can make changes to the permissions.

## To find out who owns what:

1. **cd**

   At the shell prompt, type **cd** to return to your home directory.

2. **ls -l**

   Enter **ls -l** to see the long listing of the files in the current directory. (See **Code Listing 5.1**.)

*continues on next page*

Code Listing 5.1 Many systems use only a few group names to allow easy file sharing and collaboration.

```
exampleisp> cd
/home/users/e/ejray
exampleisp> ls -l
total 60
drwx-x-x     2 ejray    users      512 Jul 21 13:32  Complete/
drwx-x-x     2 ejray    users      512 Jun 24 09:23  Completed/
drwx-x-x     2 ejray    users      512 Sep 15 2013   Mail/
drwx-x-x     2 ejray    users      512 Jun 24 09:35  NewProject/
drwx-x-x     2 ejray    users      512 Sep 15 2013   News/
drwx-x-x     2 ejray    users      512 Sep 15 2013   access/
-rw----      1 ejray    users      163 Jul 22 07:28  bogus2
drwxrwx-x    2 ejray    www        512 Jul 24 04:44  chat.conf/
-rw----      1 ejray    users      853 Sep 13 2007   dead.letter
-rw----      1 ejray    users    14286 Jun 28 12:40  files
lrwxrwxrwx   1 ejray    users       27 Sep 15 2013   ftp -> /home/ftp/pub/users
-rw----      1 ejray    users       36 Jul 24 12:09  limerick
drwx-x-x     2 ejray    users      512 Jun 8 13:32   mail/
drwxr-s-x   15 ejray    www       2560 Jul 10 10:30  public_html/
drwx-x-x     2 ejray    users      512 Jul 22 08:23  puppy/
drwx-x-x     2 ejray    users      512 Jul 24 04:44  temp/
-rw----      1 ejray    users        0 Jul 19 13:24  testme
```

The left column contains ten characters, the last nine of which specify permissions for each file:

▸ **r** means read permission, **w** means write permission, and **x** means execute permission.

▸ The first set of **rwx** is for the user, the second set is for the group, and the last set is for other.

▸ A dash (**-**) instead of a letter indicates that the user/group/other does not have that level of permission. For example, **rwx------** would mean that the user has read, write, and execute permission, while group and other have no permissions at all.

The two columns in the middle indicate the file's owner (in all likelihood your userid, for this example) and the group membership for the file. In Code Listing 5.1, **ejrays** is the owner of all the files. Most of the files are associated with the **users** group, while just a few directories are associated with the **www** group.

On this system, files that individual users create are associated with the **users** group, while files destined for the web have **www** group associations. On other systems, the default group for files might be a group with the same name as the userid, as shown in **Code Listing 5.2**.

**Code Listing 5.2** Sometimes the group name and username are the same, depending on how the system was set up.

```
[ejr@hobbes permissions]$ ls -l
total 152
-rw-rw-r-   1 ejr    ejr    128889 Jul 24 14:33   sage.sayings
-rw-rw-r-   1 ejr    ejr     23890 Jul 24 14:33   sayings
[ejr@hobbes permissions]$
```

Terminal
```
cmixxos@LinuxMint ~ $ cd /etc
cmixxos@LinuxMint /etc $ ls -l
total 1264
drwxr-xr-x 3 root  root    4096 Nov 26 09:56 acpi
-rw-r--r-- 1 root  root    2981 Nov 26 08:59 adduser.conf
-rw-r--r-- 1 root  root      10 Mar 14 06:32 adjtime
-rw-r--r-- 1 root  root      51 Mar 16 20:17 aliases
-rw-r--r-- 1 root  root   12288 Mar 16 20:17 aliases.db
drwxr-xr-x 2 root  root   12288 Mar 16 20:17 alternatives
-rw-r--r-- 1 root  root     401 Dec 20  2012 anacrontab
-rw-r--r-- 1 root  root     112 Oct  1  2012 apg.conf
drwxr-xr-x 6 root  root    4096 Nov 26 09:40 apm
drwxr-xr-x 3 root  root    4096 Nov 26 08:58 apparmor
drwxr-xr-x 6 root  root    4096 Nov 26 09:52 apparmor.d
drwxr-xr-x 5 root  root    4096 Nov 26 09:42 apport
drwxr-xr-x 6 root  root    4096 Mar 14 06:34 apt
drwxr-xr-x 2 root  root    4096 Nov 26 09:51 at-spi2
drwxr-xr-x 3 root  root    4096 Nov 26 09:51 avahi
-rw-r--r-- 1 root  root    3130 Oct 26 12:42 bash.bashrc
-rw-r--r-- 1 root  root      45 Jun 17  2012 bash_completion
drwxr-xr-x 2 root  root    4096 Nov 26 09:52 bash_completion.d
-rw-r--r-- 1 root  root     356 Jan  1  2012 bindresvport.blacklist
-rw-r--r-- 1 root  root     321 Jun 12  2013 blkid.conf
lrwxrwxrwx 1 root  root      15 Mar 14 06:31 bootlog  -> /var/log/boot.log
```

Ⓐ Most of the files in **/etc** are owned by **root**.

3. **ls -l /etc**

You can also use the **ls -l** command on a system directory, such as **/etc**. Here, you'll see that most of the files are owned by **root**, possibly with a variety of different group memberships Ⓐ.

**TIP** Sometimes you'll see references to world-readable, or world, permissions. This is the same as other. "Other" just refers to anyone who is not you or not in the group.

**TIP** You might also hear of s or SetUID permissions, which indicate that the program or file can run with the effective userid of the file's owner (usually root). For example, /usr/bin/passwd has s permissions because you can run passwd to change your password, but the command needs to run as root to actually modify the password database.

**TIP** You might also see a t at the end of the list of permissions, which indicates that the sticky bit is set. Setting the "sticky bit" means that, in a shared directory, you can delete only your own files (and not accidentally delete files belonging to others).

# Finding Out Which Group You're In

If you want to collaborate on a project and share files, you'll need to be in the same group with the other people on the team. Your first step is to find out which group you're in, as shown in **Code Listing 5.3**.

## To find out which group you're in:

1. **grep yourid /etc/passwd**

   Here, **grep yourid** pulls your userid out of the **/etc/passwd** file (which is where user information is stored) and displays it as shown in Code Listing 5.3. From left to right, you see

   ▸ Your username

   ▸ The encoded password (or nothing, or an **x** if the system is configured for "shadow" passwords)

   ▸ Your userid (each user has a unique number in the system)

2. Note the number of the group.

   You'll need the number to match it up with a group name in step 4. In this case, our group id is 500.

Code Listing 5.3 You'll find tons of information in **/etc/passwd**, including your default group number.

```
[ejr@hobbes permissions]$ grep ejr /etc/passwd
ejr:x:500:500:Eric J. Ray:/home/ejr:/bin/bash
[ejr@hobbes permissions]$
```

**Code Listing 5.4** The group file lists groups and additional members (as shown in the **users** group).

```
[ejr@hobbes permissions]$ more /etc/group
kmem::9:
wheel::10:root,ejr
mail::12:mail
news::13:news
uucp::14:uucp
man::15:
games::20:
gopher::30:
dip::40:
ftp::50:
nobody::99:
users::100:ejr,deb,asr,awr
floppy:x:19:
pppusers:x:230:
popusers:x:231:
slipusers:x:232:
postgres:x:233:
ejr:x:500:
bash:x:501:
csh:x:502:
asr:x:503:
awr:x:504:
deb:x:505:
[ejr@hobbes permissions]$
```

**3.** `more /etc/group`

Here, we're exploring the contents of the **/etc/group** file using **more** to see which groups are currently defined on the system. As shown in **Code Listing 5.4**, the first column contains the name of the group, the third contains the group number, and the last column contains extra names the system administrator added to the group. Users can belong to multiple additional groups, and this is how the additional group membership is indicated.

**4.** Match up the group number for your ID with the group name.

Our number was 500, which corresponds to the **unixvqs** group name here.

**TIP** If you're collaborating on a project, ask your system administrator to create a special group just for the project. That way, you and your teammates can easily share files.

**TIP** You can also use the `groups` or `id` commands, which offer a quicker way of finding out about group membership. These give you essential details about group membership (and userids, too), but they don't flood you with other interesting and potentially useful details about the system. Wander to Chapter 7 for more information.

**TIP** Check out Chapter 1 for more on `more`.

**TIP** See Chapter 6 for the full scoop on `grep`.

# Changing the Group Association of Files and Directories with chgrp

Suppose you have a file called **black** that is currently being used by the **pot** group and you want to change the file's permissions so that it can be accessed by the **kettle** group. To do this, you'll need to change which group the file is associated with—in this case, change the association from the **pot** group to the **kettle** group. You can change which group a file or directory is associated with using **chgrp**, as shown in **Code Listing 5.5**.

## To change group association with chgrp:

**1.** `ls -l`

Type `ls -l` at the shell prompt to verify the file's name and the group it's associated with. Remember that the second column—in the middle of the listing, just before the file sizes—lists the group membership.

Code Listing 5.5 Pots and kettles can both be black, but only one at a time.

```
[ejr@hobbes permissions]$ ls -l
total 178
-rw-rw-r--    1 ejr    pot      24850 Jul 24 14:59   black
-rw-rw-r--    1 ejr    ejr     128889 Jul 24 14:33   sage.sayings
-rw-rw-r--    1 ejr    ejr      23890 Jul 24 14:33   sayings
[ejr@hobbes permissions]$ chgrp kettle black
[ejr@hobbes permissions]$ ls -l
total 178
-rw-rw-r--    1 ejr    kettle   24850 Jul 24 14:59   black
-rw-rw-r--    1 ejr    ejr     128889 Jul 24 14:33   sage.sayings
-rw-rw-r--    1 ejr    ejr      23890 Jul 24 14:33   sayings
```

2. `chgrp kettle black`

   Type **chgrp** followed by the name of the existing group you want the file to be associated with and the filename. Here, the **chgrp** command changes the group association for the file called **black** to the **kettle** group.

   **TIP** If you try to change group ownership and get an error message like "Not owner" or something similarly obscure, your userid doesn't have the necessary authority to make the change. You'll have to ask your system administrator for help.

   **TIP** Change group association only if you have a specific need to do so; you don't want to make your files available to other people unnecessarily. Unless you are the system administrator, you won't be able to control exactly who belongs to the group to which you've given access to your files.

   **TIP** If you change the group association of a specific directory, you also need to check permissions for the directory containing it. Users will not be able to change into the specific directory (regardless of their group membership) unless they also have read and execute permission for the directory containing it.

   **TIP** If you need to make changes to group permissions and find you can't, consider looking at `sudo` to help out. Covered in Chapter 15, `sudo` provides some users with the ability to act with the power of a system administrator, in limited circumstances. Take a look.

   **TIP** Just as with the `cp` and `mv` commands, covered in Chapter 2, you can use the `-R` flag with `chgrp` to recursively apply changes to a directory and all the subdirectories and files in it. For example, to change the group association of the `LatestProject` directory and all its contents to the `project` group, use `chgrp -R project LatestProject` from the directory above `LatestProject`.

# Changing Ownership of Files and Directories with chown

Suppose you've been working on a file named **rowyourboat**, and your boss decides to let a coworker, Merrilee, take over the project. In this case, to fully pawn off the project to your coworker, you need to change ownership of the file from you to her. Depending on how your system administrator set up the system, you can often change ownership of files using **chown (Code Listing 5.6)**.

## To change ownership with chown:

**1. ls -l**

For starters, type **ls -l** at the shell prompt to verify the file's name and ownership, as in Code Listing 5.6. Remember that the ownership information is located after the permissions and linking information.

**Code Listing 5.6** Changing ownership of files transfers complete control.

```
[ejr@hobbes merrilee]$ ls -l
total 26
-rw-rw-r-    1 ejr    users    24850 Jul 24 15:17 rowyourboat
[ejr@hobbes merrilee]$ chown merrilee rowyourboat
[ejr@hobbes merrilee]$ ls -l
total 26
-rw-rw-r-    1 merrilee    users    24850 Jul 24 15:17 rowyourboat
[ejr@hobbes merrilee]$
```

**2. chown merrilee rowyourboat**

Type **chown** followed by the userid of the person you want to transfer ownership to and the filename. In this case, the **chown** command changes the ownership for **rowyourboat** to **merrilee**. **rowyourboat** and its associated problems will now be hers, and life will be but a dream.

**TIP** After you change a file's ownership, what you can do with the file depends on the group and other permissions and memberships. The new owner, however, will be able to do anything with the file.

**TIP** When changing the ownership of a directory, you can add the -R flag to chown to make it apply recursively to all files and directories below it.

**TIP** If the system does not allow you to use chown to give files away, consider using cp to make a copy of a file to accomplish the same thing. If you copy someone else's file (that you have permission to read) to another name or location, the copy is fully yours. (In this giving-the-file-away example, the recipient should use cp.)

**TIP** If you need to make changes to permissions and find you can't, take a glance at sudo to see if that might help you in your situation. As described in Chapter 15, sudo provides some users with the ability to act with the power of a system administrator, in limited circumstances. Of course, if that doesn't solve your problem, there's always the next tip.

**TIP** Even if you can't use chown, you are still able to request that the system administrator change file ownership for you: "Could you please change the ownership of my rowyourboat file to Merrilee, with chown merrilee /home/shared/ me/rowyourboat. Thanks!" (This could happen because many versions of Unix allow only root users to change file ownership.)

# Changing Permissions with chmod

Suppose you've been working on a file named **rowyourboat** and you want to have your coworkers down the stream review it. To do so, you'll need to give other people permission to access the document. You can either give people in specific groups access or give everybody on the Unix system access. In particular, you can specify permissions for **u**(ser—that's you), **g**(roup), **o**(thers), and **a**(ll).

In addition to specifying permissions, you can also specify how much access a person or group can have to your file. For example, you can specify **r**(ead), **w**(rite), and (e)**x**(ecute) access, depending on how much you trust them not to ruin your **rowyourboat** masterpiece.

As shown in **Code Listing 5.7**, your first step is to check out what the current permissions are. Then, you can set permissions, add to them, or remove them as necessary.

## To check current permissions:

**ls -l r***

To begin, type **ls -l r*** to get a long listing of **rowyourboat** in the current directory. Code Listing 5.7 shows that the permissions are **rwxr-x---**. This is actually three sets of permissions:

- For the user (**rwx**, in this example)
- For the group (**r-x**, in this example)
- For the world (**---**, in this example)

In this example, the user has read, write, and execute permissions; the group has only read and execute permissions; and all other users have no permissions.

**TIP** You can also use the -R flag with chmod to recursively apply the changes you make to permissions to all files and subdirectories in a directory. For example, chmod -R go-rwx * revokes all permissions from everyone except the user for all files in the current directory, all subdirectories in the current directory, and all files in all subdirectories.

**TIP** There are about a million and one ways to express permissions. For example, you could use chmod ugo= * (note the space before the *) or chmod u-rwx,g-rwx, o-rwx * to revoke all permissions from all files in the directory. (Note that if you try this out you'll have to add your own permissions back to the files before you can do anything with them.)

**TIP** If you want to change permissions for multiple files, use a wildcard expression.

## To set permissions:

chmod u=rwx,g=rx,o=r row*

Type **chmod** and specify who has access. In this case **u**sers have **r**ead, **w**rite, and execute permissions; the **g**roup has **r**ead and execute permissions; and **o**thers have **r**ead permission for all files in the directory that start with **row** (Code Listing 5.8).

The equals sign (=) specifies that the permissions granted in the command are the only permissions that apply. Any previous permissions will be removed.

The wildcard expression here (**row***) specifies that the command applies to all files and directories that start with "row" in the current directory.

**Code Listing 5.7** Use **ls -l** to see the permissions on files.

```
[ejr@hobbes permissions]$ ls -l r*
-rwxr-x---   1 ejr    users    152779 Jul 24 15:10 rowyourboat
[ejr@hobbes permissions]$
```

**Code Listing 5.8** You can set permissions to ensure that all files have specific permissions.

```
[ejr@hobbes permissions]$ ls -l
total 332
-rw-rw-r-   1 ejr    users     24850 Jul 24 14:59 black
-rwxr-x--   1 ejr    users    152779 Jul 24 15:10 rowyourboat
-rw-rw-r-   1 ejr    users    128889 Jul 24 14:33 sage.sayings
-rw-rw-r-   1 ejr    users     23890 Jul 24 14:33 sayings
[ejr@hobbes permissions]$ chmod u=rwx,g=rx,o=r row*
[ejr@hobbes permissions]$ ls -l
total 329
-rw-rw-r-   1 ejr    users     24850 Jul 24 14:59 black
-rwxr-xr-   1 ejr    users    152779 Jul 24 15:10 rowyourboat
-rw-rw-r-   1 ejr    users    128889 Jul 24 14:33 sage.sayings
-rw-rw-r-   1 ejr    users     23890 Jul 24 14:33 sayings
[ejr@hobbes permissions]$
```

## To add permissions:

**chmod g+w rowyourboat**

At the shell prompt, enter **chmod**, followed by

- The category. In this case, we've used **g**, for group, but you could also use **o** for others, or, of course, **u** for user, but you already have that access. You could also use **a** for all users (which includes **u**, **g**, and **o**).

- A plus sign indicates that you're adding the permission to the existing permissions, rather than setting absolute permissions.

- The permissions to grant. Here, we've used **w**, for write permission, but you could also use **r** for read or **x** for execute permissions, as your needs dictate.

- The filename (**rowyourboat**).

## To remove permissions:

**chmod go-w rowyourboat**

At the shell prompt, use **chmod go-w** plus the filename to remove write permissions for everyone except you, the file's owner. Note that we handled both **group** and **other** in a single command this time, although we could have used **chmod g-w rowyourboat** and **chmod o-w rowyourboat** to accomplish the same thing.

**TABLE 5.1** Numeric Equivalents for Mnemonic Permissions

| Mnemonic (rwx) Permissions | Binary Equivalent | Numeric Equivalent |
| --- | --- | --- |
| --- | 000 | 0 |
| --x | 001 | 1 |
| -w- | 010 | 2 |
| -wx | 011 | 3 |
| r- | 100 | 4 |
| r-x | 101 | 5 |
| rw- | 110 | 6 |
| rwx | 111 | 7 |

# Translating Mnemonic Permissions to Numeric Permissions

The permissions of a file, as you've seen throughout this chapter, come in sets of three—**rwx**, for **r**ead, **w**rite, and e**x**ecute permissions. And, as we showed you, you set these permissions by specifying that each one is either "on" or "off." For example, **ugo+rwx** sets **r**ead, **w**rite, and e**x**ecute permissions to "on" for **u**ser, **g**roup, and **o**ther, while **a+rw** sets read and write to "on" for everyone, and **a-x** sets execute to "off" (indicated in directory listings with the **-**).

Rather than set permissions with letters and hyphens, however, you can translate them into numeric values, using 1 for "on" and 0 for "off." So, **rw-**, with **r**ead and **w**rite "on" and execute "off," would translate into the numbers **110**. You could think of this as counting in binary—000, 001, 010, 011, 100, 101, 110, 111, with a 1 in each place that the permission is set to "on."

Each of these combinations of on/off permissions (or binary numbers) can be expressed as a unique decimal digit between 0 and 7, as shown in **Table 5.1**. It is these decimal digits that you use to set permissions.

## To set permissions using numeric equivalents:

`chmod 777 rowyourboat`

Type **chmod** followed by the desired permissions for the user, group, and other using the numeric equivalents listed in Table 5.1, followed by the filename. In this example, we've used **777** to set read, write, and execute permissions to "on" for the user, group, and other.

Or, for example, **724** would give the user full read, write, and execute permissions, the group only write permissions, and other only read permissions.

**TIP** Setting permissions with numeric equivalents sets permissions absolutely, rather than adding to or subtracting from existing permissions.

**TIP** You can use either numeric or mnemonic permissions—whichever format is easier for you. However, you will need to use the numeric system to set default permissions that apply when you create new files. See the next section for the full scoop.

# Changing Permission Defaults with umask

Every time you create a file, the Unix or Linux system applies default permissions for you. This is great because, for many uses, the default permissions will be just what you want. In other cases, though, you'll want to specify different default permissions.

Keep in mind that tighter (more restrictive) permissions increase security but make it harder to share and collaborate. Looser (less restrictive) permissions facilitate collaboration but at the cost of reduced security.

You can change the default permissions using **umask**. The **umask** command uses a numeric representation for permissions (as discussed in the previous section), but the numeric value you specify here is not the same as the one you'd use with **chmod**. (Don't ask why. We assume that Batman and Robin got together and made this command usable only by the Wonder Twins when their powers were activated.) So you have to figure out the **umask** value for the permissions you want, then use that value to set the new default permissions.

Note that you cannot set execute permissions by default, so you're really only figuring out the read and write permissions for **u**, **g**, and **o** categories.

## To figure the umask value:

**1.** 666

Start with 666. Again, don't ask why; it's just what you're supposed to start with.

**2.** Figure out which numeric values you'd use to set your desired permissions with the **chmod** command.

You might review the previous section, "Translating Mnemonic Permissions to Numeric Permissions," and peek at Table 5.1 in that section.

**3.** Subtract that numeric value from 666.

For example, if the numeric value you'd use with **chmod** is 644, subtract that value from 666: 666 − 644 = 022. So 022 is the number you'll use with **umask**.

## To set default file-creation permissions with umask:

umask 022

Enter **umask** plus the number you calculated in the previous steps in this section (**Code Listing 5.9**).

**TIP** Any changes made with **umask** apply only to the current shell session. If you want to revert to the default permissions but don't remember what they were, just log out and log back in, and you'll be back to normal.

**TIP** If you want to change permission defaults permanently—or at least beyond the current shell session—change them in the configuration files, as discussed in Chapter 8.

**TIP** You cannot set the default permissions to include execute permission; it's a security feature, not an omission in the system's capabilities. For example, suppose you make a new file and copy your favorite commands (or the ones you often forget) into it. If you accidentally type the filename and the file is executable, you'll run that list of commands and the consequences could be unfortunate. Therefore, you have to explicitly grant execute permission for all files.

**TIP** Yes, 666 is considered the Number of the Beast. We think that it's just a coincidence, but given the potential for confusion in this section, we're not sure.

**TIP** Use umask or umask -s (depending on your specific shell and environment settings) to display your current umask settings.

**Code Listing 5.9** Use **umask** to set default permissions for future files.

```
[ejr@hobbes permissions]$ umask 022
[ejr@hobbes permissions]$ touch tryit
[ejr@hobbes permissions]$ ls -l try*
-rw-r-r-   1 ejr    users    0 Jul 26 16:35 tryit
```

# 6

# Manipulating Files

As you learned back in Chapter 4, you can easily work with text by opening an editor and making the changes you want. But you can do more than just copy, paste, cut, or move text in files. As we'll discuss in this chapter, you can manipulate entire files and look at specific parts of them, get information about the files, find text in files, compare files, and sort files. All kinds of neat stuff!

Note that we are discussing only plain text files here, which are the most common files you'll encounter when using Unix or Linux. We are not addressing specialized files for word processing programs, image files, and other files associated with specific applications in this chapter.

In this chapter, we'll use a lot of options to augment commands. You'll find a full list of the most common commands and their options (or flags) in Appendix C if you need further explanation or a quick reminder later.

## In This Chapter

# Counting Files and Their Contents with wc

One of Unix's or Linux's handier capabilities lets you count files and their contents. For example, you can count the number of files in a directory, or you can count the number of words or lines in a file. You do this counting with the **wc** command, as shown in **Code Listing 6.1**.

## To count words using wc:

**wc -w honeydo**

At the shell prompt, type **wc -w** (for words) and the name of the file in which you want to count the words. **wc** will oblige, as shown in Code Listing 6.1.

## To count lines with wc:

**wc -l honeydo**

Use **wc -l** followed by the filename to count the lines in the file (**Code Listing 6.2**). This is useful for poetry or for things like lists (for example, our "honey-do" list always has a minimum of 73 items in it).

**TIP** You can find out how many files you have in a directory by using **ls | wc -l** to count the regular files and directories, or **ls -A | wc -l** to count all files and directories (except for the **.** and **..** directories).

**TIP** You can also find out how many bytes a specific file takes up using **wc -c**. Or, you can use **wc** with no flags at all to get the lines, words, and bytes.

**Code Listing 6.1** Use **wc -w** to count the words in a file. The "honey-do" list in this example is quite a way from being the length of a novel.

```
[unixvqs@linuxmint Examples]$ wc -w honeydo
    235 honeydo
```

**Code Listing 6.2** With 93 separate items in the list, however, it's plenty long enough.

```
[unixvqs@linuxmint Examples]$ wc -l honeydo
    93 honeydo
```

**Code Listing 6.3** Use **head** to look at just the top of a file, which gives you a manageable view of the file.

```
[unixvqs@linuxmint Examples]$ head honeydo
Take garbage out
Clean litter box
Clean diaper pails
Clean litter box
Mow lawn
Edge lawn
Clean litter box
Polish swamp cooler
Buff garage floor
Clean litter box
[unixvqs@linuxmint Examples]$
```

**Code Listing 6.4 head**, with the help of **more**, lets you see the beginnings of several files in sequence.

```
[unixvqs@linuxmint Examples]$
→ head honey* | more
= => honeyconsider <= =
Mother-in-law visits next week
Cat mess in hall to clean up
Cat mess in entry to clean up
Cat mess in living room to clean up
Toddler mess in family room to clean up
Cat and toddler mess in den to clean up
IRS called again today
Neighbors on both sides looking for
→ donations for the annual fund drive
Boss called last Friday and said
→ it's urgent
= => honeydo <= =
Take garbage out
Clean litter box
Clean diaper pails
Clean litter box
Mow lawn
Edge lawn
Clean litter box
Polish swamp cooler
Buff garage floor
```

# Viewing File Beginnings with head

Using **head**, as shown in **Code Listing 6.3**, you can find out in a jiffy what's in a file by viewing the top few lines. This is particularly handy when you're browsing file listings or trying to find a specific file among several others with similar content.

### To view file beginnings with head:

**head honeydo**

At the shell prompt, type **head** followed by the filename. As Code Listing 6.3 shows, you'll see the first ten lines on the screen. Notice that "lines" are defined by hard returns, so a line could, in some cases, wrap to many screen lines.

### To view a specified number of lines:

**head -20 honeydo**

Add **-20** (or whatever number of lines you want) to view a specific number of lines.

### To view the beginnings of multiple files:

**head honey\* | more**

You can view the tops of multiple files by piping **head** (plus the filenames) to **more**. Note that **head** conveniently tells you the filename of each file, as shown in **Code Listing 6.4**.

# Viewing File Endings with `tail`

Occasionally, you might also need to use **`tail`**, which displays the last lines of a file. **`tail`** is particularly handy for checking the latest records in a log file (more about this in Chapter 15, "Being Root") or for viewing information added to a file (see **Code Listing 6.5**). Just as with **head** (described in the previous pages), **`tail`** offers several options for viewing files.

### To view file endings with `tail`:

`tail honeydo`

At the shell prompt, type **tail** followed by the filename. As Code Listing 6.5 shows, you'll see the last ten lines on the screen.

### To view a specified number of lines:

`tail -15 honeydo`

Here, all you do is add a specific number of lines you want to view (**-15**).

### To view the endings of multiple files:

`tail honey* | more`

Pipe the **tail** command and the files (multiple files indicated with **\***) to **more** (**Code Listing 6.6**).

**TIP** head and its counterpart, `tail`, are great for splitting long files. Use `wc -l` to count the lines. If the file has 500 lines but you care about only the beginning and ending lines, then type head -25 filename > newfilename to put the first 25 lines of the file into a new file. Then do the same with `tail` to put the last 25 lines of the file into another new file.

**Code Listing 6.5 `tail`** lets you check out just the end of files.

```
[unixvqs@linuxmint Examples]$ tail honeydo
Empty diaper pails
Take garbage out.
-End of today's list-
Buy more garbage bags
Get cleaning supplies at store
Take cat to vet
Fix lawnmower
[unixvqs@linuxmint Examples]$
```

Code Listing 6.6 Use **tail** with **more** to see
→ the ends of multiple files.

```
[unixvqs@linuxmint Examples]$
→ tail honey* | more
= => honeyconsider <= =
Cat mess in entry to clean up
Cat mess in living room to clean up
Toddler mess in family room to clean up
Cat and toddler mess in den to clean up
IRS called again today
Neighbors on both sides looking for
→ donations for the annual fund drive
Boss called last Friday and said
→ it's urgent
-End of today's list-
= => honeydo <= =
Empty diaper pails
Take garbage out.
-End of today's list-
Buy more garbage bags
Get cleaning supplies at store
Take cat to vet
Fix lawnmower
-More-
```

**Code Listing 6.7** Use **grep** to see all occurrences of a specific string in a file.

```
[unixvqs@linuxmint Examples]$
→ grep bucket limericks
Who carried his lunch in a bucket,
[unixvqs@linuxmint Examples]$
```

**Code Listing 6.8 grep** can show the context around instances of the string as well.

```
[unixvqs@linuxmint Examples]$
→ grep -5 bucket limericks
he strummed and he hummed,
and sang dumdeedum,
But him a musician...whoda thunk it?
There once was a man from Nantucket,
Who carried his lunch in a bucket,
Said he with a sigh,
As he ate a whole pie,
If I just had a donut I'd dunk it.
A nice young lady named Debbie,
[unixvqs@linuxmint Examples]$
```

**TIP** Use the -n flag (for example, **grep -n string file**) to print each found line with a line number.

**TIP** You can use **grep** with multiple file-names, such as in **grep Nantucket lim\*** or **grep Nantucket lim\* poetry humor**.

**TIP** If you want to get creative, you can look for spaces as well, but you need to use quotes, like **grep "from Nantucket" limerick\***.

**TIP** Win nerdy bar bets by knowing the heritage of **grep**.

# Finding Text with grep

You can search through multiple files for specific strings of characters and then view the list of matching files onscreen. You do this using the **grep** command (which stands for "**g**lobal **r**egular **e**xpression **p**rint," a once useful and now rather arcane **ed** or **vi** command), as shown in **Code Listing 6.7**. As we'll show you, you can add several flags to **grep** to get slightly different results.

## To find text strings with grep:

- **grep bucket limericks**

  At the shell prompt, type **grep**, the text you're trying to locate (in this case, **bucket**), and the file you're searching in (in this case, **limericks**). **grep** will return all lines in the file that contain the specified string, as shown in Code Listing 6.7.

- **grep -5 bucket limericks**

  You can specify that a number of lines (say, **5**) on either side of the found text string should also be displayed. Sometimes you can't tell what you need to know with just the line that contains your search string, and adding lines around it can help give you a context (see **Code Listing 6.8**).

  Note that this option isn't available on all versions of **grep**, but it'll work for most.

- **grep -c Nantucket limericks**

  By adding the **-c** flag, you can find out how many times a text string appears in a file.

- **grep -v Nantucket limericks**

  Or, with the **-v** flag, you can find all the lines without the specified string.

- **grep -i nantucket limericks**

  With the **-i** flag, you can search without case-sensitivity. Here any line with **nantucket** or **Nantucket** or **nAntuCKet** would be found.

# Using Regular Expressions with grep

In addition to using **grep** to search for simple text strings, you can use **grep** to search using *regular expressions*. Regular expressions are like fancy wildcards, where you use a symbol to represent a character, number, or other symbol. With regular expressions, you can search for different parts of files, such as the end of a line or a text string next to another specified text string. (You might see this process described as "globbing" as well.) **Table 6.1** lists some of the more common regular expressions.

**TABLE 6.1** Regular Expressions, Examples, and Explanations

| Regular Expression | Function | Example | Explanation |
|---|---|---|---|
| . | Matches any character. | grep b.rry | This finds all instances of "berry" or "barry." |
| * | Matches zero or more instances of the preceding item, so a *b would find "b" as well as "ab" and "aaab," but not "acb." | grep 's*day'/home/ejr/schedule | Here, the * matches zero or more of the items that immediately precede the *; in this case, the letter 's'. |
| ^ | Matches only instances of the string at the beginning of a line. | grep '^Some' sayings | With the ^, you specify that the search string must appear at the beginning of a line. The example would find a line beginning with "Some" but not one beginning with "Read Some." |
| $ | Matches only instances of the string at the end of a line. | grep 'ach$' sayings | This example finds all lines in the file **sayings** that end with "ach." |
| \ | Escapes (quotes) the following character—so you can search for literal characters like * or $ that are also operators. | grep '\*' saying | **sgrep \* sayings** searches for all instances of * in the **sayings** file. The \ tells **grep** to interpret the* literally, as an asterisk character, rather than as a wildcard. |
| [ ] | Matches any member of the set, like [a-z], [0-6], or [321] (three or two or one). | grep 'number[0-9]' specifications | Use square brackets ([ ]) to enclose a set of options. Here, **number[0-9]** would match all instances of number1, number2, number3, and so forth in the file called **specifications**. |

**Code Listing 6.9** Use **grep** with regular expressions to create fancy wildcard commands.

```
[unixvqs@linuxmint Examples]$
→ grep .logan limerick
Worked hard all day on a slogan,
You see, the slogan's still brogan.
[unixvqs@linuxmint Examples]$
```

## To use regular expressions with grep:

**grep .logan limerick**

Type **grep** followed by the regular expression and the filename. Here, we've used the regular expression **.logan** to find all instances of "logan" that are preceded by a single character (**Code Listing 6.9**). Note that this usage of a **.** (period) to match a single character closely resembles the **?** wildcard.

You could also use multiple periods for specific numbers of characters. For example, to find "Dogbert" and "Dilbert," you might use **grep D..bert plagiarized.sayings**.

In some cases, you may need to structure the search string slightly differently, depending on the expression you're using and the information you're looking for. Check out the additional examples in Table 6.1 for more information.

**TIP** "Regular expression" is often abbreviated as "regexp" or "regex" in Unix or Linux documentation and Internet discussions.

**TIP** The command **egrep** is closely related to **grep**, adding a little more flexibility for extended regular expressions, but it fundamentally works the same. On many systems the **grep** command is really **egrep**—when you type in either one, you're really running **egrep**.

**TIP** If you're searching for whole words through large files, use **fgrep** for faster searching. It uses the same general syntax as **grep** but searches only for whole words (not regular expressions) and so goes much faster.

**TIP** See Chapter 1 for details about wildcards.

# Using Other Examples of Regular Expressions

In the previous section, we showed you how to use the **grep** command to search with regular expressions. You can do other neat finding tasks, as we'll discuss in this section.

## To find lines with specific characteristics:

- **grep '^Nantucket' limerick***

  Here, we use **grep** to find all the lines in the limericks that start with **Nantucket**, if there are any.

- **grep 'Nantucket$' limerick***

  Similarly, you can find the lines that end with **Nantucket**.

- **grep '^[A-Z]' limerick**

  Or, you can find the lines that start with a capital letter by including the **[A-Z]** regular expression.

- **grep '^[A-Za-z]' limerick**

  Here, you can find all the lines that start with any letter, but not a number or symbol. Fancy, huh?

**TIP** You can also use regular expressions with awk and sed. See "Making Global Changes with sed" and "Changing Files with awk" in this chapter for details.

```
[unixvqs@linuxmint Examples]$
→ sed 's/oldaddr@raycomm.com/
→ newaddr@raycomm.com/g'
→ address.htm > address-new.htm
[unixvqs@linuxmint Examples]$
→ head address-new.htm
<BODY>
<P>
Please send all comments to
→ <A HREF="mailto:newaddr@raycomm.com">
→ newaddr@raycomm.com</A>.
</P>
<TABLE BORDER=0>
<TR>
<TD WIDTH="150" VALIGN=TOP>
[unixvqs@linuxmint Examples]$
```

**TIP** You can have **sed** cruise through multiple documents. See Chapter 10 for information on how to make a shell script with a loop.

**TIP** Because **sed** commands can be long and unwieldy, it might be helpful to save the commands in a separate text file (so you don't have to retype them). For example, if you saved the command **s/oldaddr@ raycomm.com/newaddr@raycomm.com/g** in a file named **script.sed**, you could issue **sed -f script.sed address.htm > address-new.htm** to run the **sed** commands from the **script.sed** file. You can have as many commands as you want in your **script.sed** file.

# Making Global Changes with sed

Another handy command you can use is **sed**, which lets you make multiple changes to files without ever opening an editor. For example, as a new webmaster, you might use **sed** to change all occurrences of the previous webmaster's email address to your own. As we'll show in this section, you can use **sed** to make global changes within documents.

## To make global changes with sed:

**sed 's/oldaddr@raycomm.com**
→ **/newaddr@raycomm.com/g'**
→ **address.htm > address-new.htm**

Type **sed**, followed by

- A single quote (')
- A leading **s**
- A slash (/)
- The text you want to replace (**oldaddr@raycomm.com**)
- Another slash (/)
- The replacement text (**newaddr@raycomm.com**)
- Yet another slash (/)
- **g**, which tells **sed** to apply the change globally (If you omit the **g**, only the first occurrence on each line will be changed.)
- Another single quote (')
- The name of the file in which the changes should be made (**address.htm**)

You can redirect the output to a new filename (see **Code Listing 6.10**) or pipe it to another command entirely. You can't redirect to the same filename or you'll end up with no content in your file.

# Changing Files with awk

While **sed** is line oriented and lets you fiddle to your heart's content, **awk** is field oriented and is ideal for manipulating database or comma-delimited files. For example, if you have an address book file, you can use **awk** to find and change information in fields you specify, as in **Code Listing 6.11**. In the following steps, we'll show you a sampling of the things you can do using **awk** to modify; in this example, an address book file.

## To change files with awk:

1. **awk '{ print $1 }' address.book**

   At the shell prompt, use **awk '{ print $1 }' address.book** to look at the **address.book** file and select (and send to standard output) the first field in each record (line). More specifically, starting from the inside out

   ▸ **$1** references the first field in each line. Unless you specify otherwise, **awk** assumes that whitespace separates the fields, so the first field starts at the beginning of the line and continues to the first space.

   ▸ **{}** contain the **awk** command, and the quotes are necessary to tie the **awk** command together (so the first space within the command isn't interpreted by the shell as the end of the command). See Code Listing 6.11.

**Code Listing 6.11 awk** lets you access individual fields in a file.

```
[unixvqs@linuxmint Examples]$
→ awk '{ print $1 }' address.book
Schmidt,
Feldman,
Brown,
Smith,
Jones,
[unixvqs@linuxmint Examples]$
```

**Code Listing 6.12** With a little more tweaking, **awk** lets you do a lot of processing on the files to get just the information you need.

```
[unixvqs@linuxmint Examples]$
→ awk -F, '{print $2 " " $1 " " $7 }'
→ address.book> phone.list
[unixvqs@linuxmint Examples]$
→ more phone.list
    Sven Schmidt 555-555-8382
    Fester Feldman
    John Brown 918-555-1234
    Sally Smith 801-555-8982
    Kelly Jones 408-555-7253
[unixvqs@linuxmint Examples]$
```

## De-what?

A *delimited file* uses a specific character to show where one bit of information ends and another begins. Each piece of information is a separate field. For example, a file that contains "John, Doe, Thornton, Colorado" is comma-delimited, sporting a comma between fields. Other files, such as the **/etc/passwd** file, use a colon (**:**) to separate the fields. Just about any symbol that's not used in the content could be used as a delimiter.

**2.** `awk -F, '{ print $1 }' address.book`

The **-F** flag tells **awk** to use the character following it—in this case, a comma (**,**)—as the field separator. This change makes the output of the command a little cleaner and more accurate. If you were working with **/etc/passwd**, you'd use **-F:** to specify that the **:** is the field separator.

**3.** `awk -F, '{ print $2 " " $1 " " $7 }'`
`→ address.book > phone.list`

With this code, you can pull specific fields, in an arbitrary order, from your database. Although it looks complex, it's just one additional step from the previous example. Rather than printing a single field from the address book, we're printing field 2, then a space, then field 1, then a space, then field 7. The final bit just redirects the output into a new file. This example would produce a list of names and phone numbers, as shown in **Code Listing 6.12**.

**4.** `awk -F, '/CA/{ print $2 " " $1 " " $7 }'`
`→ address.book > phone.list`

You can also specify a matching pattern. Here, we added **/CA/** to search and act on only the lines that contain **CA**, so only those lines will be in the **phone.list** file.

**TIP** You can load awk scripts from a file with `awk -f script.awk filename`. Just as with sed, this keeps the retyping to a minimum, which is helpful with these long and convoluted commands. Refer to Chapter 10 for more details about scripting.

**TIP** Take a glance at "Sorting Files with `sort`" later in this chapter and consider piping your awk output to `sort`. Let Unix do the tedious work for you!

# Comparing Files with cmp

Suppose you've been working on the **dearliza** file and you want to know how it differs from the **dearhenry** file. Using **cmp**, you can compare the two files, as shown in **Code Listing 6.13**.

## To compare files with cmp:

### cmp dearliza dearhenry

At the shell prompt, type **cmp** followed by both filenames. As Code Listing 6.13 shows, these two files are not the same.

If the files are identical, you'll find yourself back at the shell prompt with no comment from **cmp**. If both files are identical until one of them ends—that is, say, the first 100 lines are the same, but one continues and the other ends—then you'll see an EOF (end of file) message, as in **Code Listing 6.14**.

> **TIP** You can find other ways that files differ by using diff, as described in the next section, "Finding Differences in Files with diff."

> **TIP** Unix and Linux provide an exit status message that you can use to get more information about how the program stopped and why. See "Using Advanced Redirection with stderr" in Chapter 16 for more information.

> **TIP** You can also use diff to find out which files are in one directory but not another. Just type diff followed by the names of the two directories; for example, diff /home/ejr/ Directory /home/ ejr/Newdirectory.

> **TIP** You might also check out the section "Finding Differences in Files with sdiff," later in this chapter, for yet another way to compare files.

**Code Listing 6.13 cmp** gives just the facts about the first difference between two files.

```
[unixvqs@linuxmint Examples]$
→ cmp dearliza dearhenry
dearliza dearhenry differ: char 20, line 2
[unixvqs@linuxmint Examples]$
```

**Code Listing 6.14 cmp** also tells you if the files matched until one ended (**EOF** stands for "end of file").

```
[unixvqs@linuxmint Examples]$
→ cmp limerick limericks
cmp: EOF on limerick
[unixvqs@linuxmint Examples]$
```

**Code Listing 6.15 diff** tells you all you ever wanted to know about the differences between two files but not in an easily readable manner.

```
[unixvqs@linuxmint Examples]$
 ↪ diff dearliza dearhenry
2,3c2,3
< Dear Liza,
< There's a hole in my bucket, dear Liza,
 ↪ dear Liza, dear Liza.
> Dear Henry,
> Please fix it dear Henry, dear Henry,
 ↪ dear Henry.
5,6c5,6
< Henry
<
> Liza
> PS, you forgot your toolbox last time.
[unixvqs@linuxmint Examples]$
```

# Finding Differences in Files with diff

In addition to using **cmp** to find out how files differ, you can use **diff**. This command tells you specifically where two files differ, line by line, not just that they differ and at which point the differences start (see **Code Listing 6.15**).

## To find differences with diff:

### diff dearliza dearhenry

Type **diff**, followed by both filenames. The **diff** output, as in Code Listing 6.15, shows lines that appear only in one file or the other. The lines from file 1 are indicated with **<**, while the lines from file 2 are indicated with **>**.

Above each line are the affected line numbers in the first file, then **d**, **a**, or **c**, then the corresponding line numbers from the second file:

- **d** means that the line would have to be deleted from file 1 to make it match file 2.

- **a** means that text would have to be added to file 1 to match file 2.

- **c** means that changes would have to be made to the line for the two files to match.

**TIP** If you're comparing email messages or other less-structured documents, you might consider adding the flags -i (case insensitive), -B (ignore blank lines), or even -w (ignore spaces and tabs) to avoid cluttering your results with unimportant differences. For example, you could use diff -ibw file1 file2 to find all differences between two files except those involving blank lines, spaces, tabs, or lowercase/uppercase letters.

# Finding Differences in Files with `sdiff`

Yet another—and often better—way to compare files is to use **sdiff**, which presents the two files onscreen so that you can visually compare them (see **Code Listing 6.16**).

## To compare files with `sdiff`:

`sdiff dearliza dearhenry`

At the shell prompt, type **sdiff** and the filenames to compare the two files. The output, as shown in Code Listing 6.16, presents each line of the two files side by side, separating them with

- **(Nothing)** if the lines are identical
- < if the line exists only in the first file
- > if the line exists only in the second file
- | if they are different

**TIP** If most of the lines are the same, consider using the `-s` flag so the identical lines are not shown. For example, type `sdiff -s dearliza dearhenry`.

**TIP** If the output scoots by too fast to read, remember that you can pipe the entire command to `more`, as in `sdiff dearliza dearhenry | more`.

**Code Listing 6.16** `sdiff` puts the files side by side, so you can easily see the differences.

```
[unixvqs@linuxmint Examples]$ sdiff dearliza dearhenry
March 16, 2014        March 16, 2014

Dear Liz             Dear Henry,

There's a hole in my bucket, dear Liza, dear Liza.  |  Please fix it, dear Henry, dear Henry.

Yours,               Yours,
Henry                | Liza
                     > PS, you forgot your toolbox last time.
 [unixvqs@linuxmint Examples]$
```

# Sorting Files with sort

If you want to be really lazy—er, um, smart—let Unix or Linux sort files or the contents of files for you. You can use **sort** to, for example, sort your address book alphabetically—as opposed to the random order in which you might have entered addresses (see **Code Listing 6.17**).

## To sort files with sort:

**sort address.book > sorted.address.book**

To begin, type **sort**, followed by the name of the file whose contents you want to sort. Unix will sort the lines in the file alphabetically and present the sorted results in the file you specify (here, **sorted.address.book**), as shown in Code Listing 6.17.

**TIP** You can sort fields in comma-delimited files by adding -t to the command. For example, **sort -t, +1 address.book** tells Unix and Linux to sort by the second field. The -t and following character (,) indicate what character separates the fields—the comma in this case. If a character isn't given, **sort** thinks that whitespace marks the boundaries between fields. The +1 says to skip the first field and sort on the second one.

**TIP** You can sort numerically, too, with **sort -n filename**. If you don't use the -n flag, the output will be ordered based on the leftmost digits in the numbers—for example "1, 203, 50"—because the alphabetic sort starts at the left of the field.

**TIP** If you have multiple files to sort, you can use **sort file1 file2 file3 > complete. sorted.file**, and the output will contain the contents of all three files—sorted, of course.

Code Listing 6.17 An unsorted address book springs to order with the help of **sort**.

```
[unixvqs@linuxmint Examples]$ more address.book
Schmidt, Sven, 1 Circle Drive, Denver, CO, 80221, 555-555-8382
Feldman, Fester, RR1, Billings, MT 62832, 285-555-0281
Brown, John, 1453 South Street, Tulsa, OK, 74114, 918-555-1234
Smith, Sally, 452 Center Ave., Salt Lake City, UT, 84000, 801-555-8982
Jones, Kelly, 14 Main Street, Santa Clara, CA, 95051, 408-555-7253
[unixvqs@linuxmint Examples]$ sort address.book
Brown, John, 1453 South Street, Tulsa, OK, 74114, 918-555-1234
Feldman, Fester, RR1, Billings, MT 62832, 285-555-0281
Jones, Kelly, 14 Main Street, Santa Clara, CA, 95051, 408-555-7253
Schmidt, Sven, 1 Circle Drive, Denver, CO, 80221, 555-555-8382
Smith, Sally, 452 Center Ave., Salt Lake City, UT, 84000, 801-555-8982
[unixvqs@linuxmint Examples]$ sort address.book > sorted.address.book
[unixvqs@linuxmint Examples]$ cat sorted.address.book
Brown, John, 1453 South Street, Tulsa, OK, 74114, 918-555-1234
Feldman, Fester, RR1, Billings, MT 62832, 285-555-0281
Jones, Kelly, 14 Main Street, Santa Clara, CA, 95051, 408-555-7253
Schmidt, Sven, 1 Circle Drive, Denver, CO, 80221, 555-555-8382
Smith, Sally, 452 Center Ave., Salt Lake City, UT, 84000, 801-555-8982
[unixvqs@linuxmint Examples]$
```

# Eliminating Duplicates with uniq

If you've sorted files using the handy-dandy **sort** command, you might end up with results that have duplicates in them. Heck, you might have files with duplicates. At any rate, here's how to find and work with them. As **Code Listing 6.18** shows, you can get rid of duplicate lines by using the **uniq** command (short for "unique") in conjunction with **sort**.

## To eliminate duplicates with uniq:

`sort long.address.book | uniq`

At the shell prompt, type **sort** and the filename, then type **| uniq** to pipe the output to **uniq**. The output of **uniq** will not contain any duplicated entries (Code Listing 6.18).

**TIP** uniq finds only identical, adjacent (sorted) lines. For example, if you have both Jones and jones in your address book, uniq won't identify either entry because they differ in capitalization.

**TIP** You can also use the -d flag to specify that you want to see only the duplicate lines. For example, say you want to see all the people who are in both your carpool file and your nightout file. You'd just use sort carpool nightout | uniq -d.

**TIP** You can sort and eliminate duplicates in one step with sort -u address.book.

**Code Listing 6.18** Use **sort** with **uniq** to eliminate duplicates.

```
[unixvqs@linuxmint Examples]$ more long.address.book
Schmidt, Sven, 1 Circle Drive, Denver, CO, 80221, 555-555-8382
Feldman, Fester, RR1, Billings, MT 62832, 285-555-0281
Brown, John, 1453 South Street, Tulsa, OK, 74114, 918-555-1234
Smith, Sally, 452 Center Ave., Salt Lake City, UT, 84000, 801-555-8982
Jones, Kelly, 14 Main Street, Santa Clara, CA, 95051, 408-555-7253
Schmidt, Swen, 1 Circle Drive, Denver, CO, 80221, 555-555-8382
Feldman, Fester, RR1, Billings, MT 62832, 285-555-0281
Brown, Jonathon, 1453 South Street, Tulsa, OK, 74114, 918-555-1234
Smith, Sally, 452 Center Ave., Salt Lake City, UT, 84000, 801-555-8982
Jones, Kelly, 14 Main Street, Santa Clara, CA, 95051, 408-555-7253
[unixvqs@linuxmint Examples]$ sort long.address.book | uniq
Brown, John, 1453 South Street, Tulsa, OK, 74114, 918-555-1234
Brown, Jonathon, 1453 South Street, Tulsa, OK, 74114, 918-555-1234
Feldman, Fester, RR1, Billings, MT 62832, 285-555-0281
Jones, Kelly, 14 Main Street, Santa Clara, CA, 95051, 408-555-7253
Schmidt, Sven, 1 Circle Drive, Denver, CO, 80221, 555-555-8382
Smith, Sally, 452 Center Ave., Salt Lake City, UT, 84000, 801-555-8982
[unixvqs@linuxmint Examples]$
```

## tee Time?

You might think of the **tee** command as similar to a plumber's pipe joint—that is, it takes stuff from one location and sends it out to two different places.

# Redirecting to Multiple Locations with tee

Suppose you just updated your address book file and want to send it to your boss in addition to putting it in your own files. You can do just that, using **tee**, which redirects output to two different places (see **Code Listing 6.19**).

## To redirect output to two locations with tee:

```
sort address.book new.addresses | tee
→ sorted.all | mail boss@raycomm.com
→ -s "Here's the address book, boss"
```

At the shell prompt, use the **tee** command plus a filename in the middle of the pipe line to send the sorted information to that filename as well as to the standard output (which could, of course, be redirected to another filename). Here, we send the results of the sort to the **sorted.all** file and to standard output, where **mail** will take over and send the file to the boss. See Chapter 11 for more on fancy mail tricks.

**Code Listing 6.19** Use **tee** to send output to two different places at once.

```
[unixvqs@linuxmint Examples]$ sort address.book new.addresses | tee sorted.all |
→ mail boss@raycomm.com -s "Here's the address book, boss"
[unixvqs@linuxmint Examples]$
```

# Changing with tr

Sometimes you just have to make changes to a file to change all occurrences of one term or character to another. For example, you might have reversed the case in a file (by accidentally typing with Caps Lock on... argh!) and need to change it back. Or you might want to turn a document into a list of words (one per line) that you can sort or count. The **tr** utility is just what you need (see **Code Listing 6.20**).

## To translate case with tr:

`cat limerick | tr a-zA-Z A-Za-z`

At the shell prompt, use the **cat** command and the pipe to send a file to **tr**, which will then translate lowercase to uppercase, and vice versa.

## To break lines with tr:

`cat limerick | tr -c a-zA-Z "\n"`

Change anything that's not a letter (upper- or lowercase) to a new line, thus breaking the limerick into a list of words. The **-c** indicates that anything that does not match the first set of characters (the complement of those characters) should be changed to the new character.

**TIP** Rather than use **cat** to send the file to **tr**, you can use spiffy Unix or Linux redirection tools (< in this case) to do it. An equivalent command to translate case would be `tr a-zA-Z A-Za-z < limerick`.

**TIP** With **tr**, you can accomplish all kinds of translations. For example, you could set up a bit of a code to keep secret information somewhat secret, by translating letters to garble your text, then retranslating when you want them. For example, use `cat limerick | tr a-mA-Mn-zN-Z n-zN-Za-mA-M > limerick.rot13` to encode and `cat limerick.rot13 | tr n-zN-Za-mA-M a-mA-Mn-zN-Z` to decode. This is the same as ROT13, discussed in Chapter 16, but far more flexible and spiffy if you use **tr** to do it.

**TIP** Check out the man page for **tr** (man tr) for details on the other cool translations and conversions it can do.

**Code Listing 6.20** Use **tr** to translate characters in files.

```
[jdoe@frazz jdoe]$ cat limerick
There once was a man from Nantucket,
Who carried his lunch in a bucket,
Said he with a sigh,
As he ate a whole pie,
If I just had a donut I'd dunk it.
[jdoe@frazz jdoe]$ cat limerick | tr a-zA-Z A-Za-z
tHERE ONCE WAS A MAN FROM nANTUCKET,
wHO CARRIED HIS LUNCH IN A BUCKET,
sAID HE WITH A SIGH,
aS HE ATE A WHOLE PIE,
iF i JUST HAD A DONUT i'D DUNK IT.
[jdoe@frazz jdoe]$ cat limerick | tr -c a-zA-Z "\n"
There
once
was
a
man
from
Nantucket
Who
carried
his
lunch
in
a
bucket
Said
he
with
a
sigh
As
he
ate
a
whole
pie
If
I
just
had
a
donut
I
d
dunk
it
```

# Formatting with fmt

After you've been typing away—writing the Great American Novel, perhaps—you might notice that you're suffering from creeping margin uglies, like those shown in **Code Listing 6.21**. Never fear, **fmt** can help. Just run your text through **fmt**, and all will be well.

## To format with fmt:

**fmt spiderstory.unformatted**

At the shell prompt, just tell **fmt** to do its thing, and you'll be in business.

**TIP** You can supplement **fmt** with handy flags to help make lines more readable. For example, you can often use **fmt -u** to make spacing uniform: one space between words, and two spaces between sentences. Or, try **fmt -w** to specify the width of the formatted text; for example, **-w 60** would specify a 60-character-wide line.

**Code Listing 6.21** With `fmt` you can clean up all kinds of idiosyncrasies in the format of your documents.

```
[jdoe@frazz jdoe]$ cat spiderstory.unformatted
This morning I
got up, went
downstairs, and found a HUMONGOUS spider
in the bathroom where the little potty is.
After I
quietly composed myself
from the shock (I didn't want
to alert the kids),

I looked around the
house for
something to put him in...the
kids' bug catcher thing
(nowhere to be found)...a jar...tupperware...a lidded
cup...the
salad spinner (BwaaaaHaaaHaaa !)....

I went back and checked on the spider and decided that I just couldn't face putting him in something.
I mean, what if he got close to me...or TOUCHED
me?!?!
And, since I hate the crunching sound and feel of
squashing bugs,
I knew I couldn't just kill him.
This spider had *bones*, I'm tellin' ya'. So, I
hunted for bug spray.
And hunted. But
nothing.
[jdoe@frazz jdoe]$ fmt spiderstory.unformatted
This morning I got up, went downstairs, and found a HUMONGOUS spider in the bathroom where the little
potty is. After I quietly composed myself from the shock (I didn't want to alert the kids),

I looked around the house for something to put him in...the kids' bug catcher thing (nowhere to be
found)...a jar...tupperware...a lidded cup...the salad spinner (BwaaaaHaaaHaaa!)....

I went back and checked on the spider and decided that I just couldn't face putting him in something.
I mean, what if he got close to me...or TOUCHED me?!?! And, since I hate the crunching sound and
feel of squashing bugs, I knew I couldn't just kill him. This spider had *bones*, I'm tellin' ya'.
So, I hunted for bug spray. And hunted. But nothing.
-
```

# Splitting Files with `split`

Suppose you're futzing with your new digital camera and you want to share a photo of your new computer (what else is cool enough to take pictures of?) via email with your friends and family. You access the file, attach it to an email message, and then—argh!—your ISP fails to send the file because it's too big. Although you could modify the file itself—reduce the physical size, reduce the number of colors used, or crop out nonessential parts, for example—you can also just split the file with `split`. For example, if the ISP tells you that no files larger than 0.51 GB will be accepted, you can use `split` to send the file in chunks—all using one easy command (Code Listing 6.22).

## To split files with `split`:

`split -b 500M mongopicture.jpg`

With that, `split` gives you three files (**xaa**, **xab**, **xac**) that are each 500 MB (the first two) or less (the last one, containing the leftovers). Mail each of those, and you've put one over on any restrictions about size.

**TIP** Control the names of the files by adding a prefix at the end. For example, try `split -b 500M mongopicture.jpg chunk` to get three pieces called chunkaa, chunkab, and chunkac.

**TIP** Use `cat` to restore the original; for example, `cat chunkaa chunkab chunkac > reconstitutedpicture.jpg`.

**TIP** If you're following the photo file example used here, note that the recipient of the emailed file pieces will have to assemble the pieces in order to view the photo. Even if the recipient isn't a Unix or Linux user, all systems have utilities to accomplish this task. Now, whether your recipient would want to take the time or would have the skill to do this is another question. You might check first.

**Code Listing 6.22** Use **split** to break files into smaller chunks.

```
[jdoe@frazz split]$ ls -lh
total 1.1M
-rwxrwxr-x   1 jdoe     jdoe     1.0G Jan 1 12:42 mongopicture.jpg*
[jdoe@frazz split]$ ls -l
total 1060
-rwxrwxr-x   1 jdoe     jdoe     1079300 Jan 1 12:42 mongopicture.jpg*
[jdoe@frazz split]$ split -b 500M mongopicture.jpg
[jdoe@frazz split]$ ls -lh
total 2.1M
-rwxrwxr-x   1 jdoe     jdoe     1.0G Jan 1 12:42 mongopicture.jpg*
-rw-rw-r-    1 jdoe     jdoe     500M Jan 1 13:03 xaa
-rw-rw-r-    1 jdoe     jdoe     500M Jan 1 13:03 xab
-rw-rw-r-    1 jdoe     jdoe     54M Jan 1 13:03 xac
[jdoe@frazz split]$ split -b 500k mongopicture.jpg chunk
[jdoe@frazz split]$ ls -lh
total 3.2M
-rw-rw-r-    1 jdoe     jdoe     500M Jan 1 13:03 chunkaa
-rw-rw-r-    1 jdoe     jdoe     500M Jan 1 13:03 chunkab
-rw-rw-r-    1 jdoe     jdoe     54M Jan 1 13:03 chunkac
-rwxrwxr-x   1 jdoe     jdoe     1.0G Jan 1 12:42 mongopicture.jpg*
-rw-rw-r-    1 jdoe     jdoe     500M Jan 1 13:03 xaa
-rw-rw-r-    1 jdoe     jdoe     500M Jan 1 13:03 xab
-rw-rw-r-    1 jdoe     jdoe     54M Jan 1 13:03 xac
[jdoe@frazz split]$ cat chunkaa chunkab chunkac > reconstitutedpicture.jpg
[jdoe@frazz split]$ cmp mongopicture.jpg reconstitutedpicture.jpg
[jdoe@frazz split]$
```

# Getting Information About the System

Now is your chance to nose around in everyone else's business! In this chapter, we'll show you how to get information about the system, about other users, and about your own userid.

## In This Chapter

# Getting System Information with uname

Information about your Unix or Linux system might come in handy if you are planning to try some new software or need to figure out system idiosyncrasies. Some systems tell you this information when you log in. Sometimes, however, especially if you're using an ISP, you may not have been told any particulars about the system. You can easily find out what kind of system you're using with **uname**, as shown in **Code Listings 7.1** and **7.2**.

## To find out about the system using uname:

1. **uname**

   Type **uname** to find out what kind of a system you're on. The Unix system in Code Listing 7.1 is Solaris (aka SunOS). Other common systems (not an exhaustive list, by any means) are Linux (obviously), AIX, BSD, and HP/UX.

2. **uname -sr**

   Add the **-sr** flags to the command, yielding **uname -sr**, to find out both the operating system type and the release level. This is useful to determine whether specific software is compatible with the operating system.

3. **uname -a**

   For the whole nine yards, use **uname -a** to print all information, including the operating system type, host name, version, and hardware. The specifics you get here will vary a bit from system to system.

**Code Listing 7.1** Variants on the **uname** command provide all kinds of interesting or useful information about the system.

```
ejray@home $ ssh frizz
Last login: Wed Oct 10 09:59:09 from frazz
Sun Microsystems Inc. SunOS 5.9 Generic
→ May 2002
ejray@frizz $ uname
SunOS
ejray@frizz $ uname -sr
SunOS 5.9
ejray@frizz $ uname -a
SunOS frizz 5.9 Generic_112233-01 sun4u
→ sparc SUNW,Ultra-5_10
```

**Code Listing 7.2** On a different system, the same commands provide slightly different details, although the basic information remains the same.

```
ejray@frazz $ uname
Linux
ejray@frazz $ uname -sr
Linux 2.4.19-16mdk
ejray@frazz $ uname -a
Linux frazz.raycomm.com 2.4.19-16mdk
→ #1 Fri Sep 20 18:15:05 CEST 2002 i686
→ unknown unknown GNU/Linux
ejray@frazz $
```

# Viewing File Systems with df

If you're used to Windows or Macintosh operating systems, you're probably accustomed to seeing separate hard drives (C:, D:, or E: for Windows users, or real names for Macs), which are just different storage spaces. In Unix and Linux systems, different storage spaces are grafted onto the overall tree structure—tacked onto what already exists without any clear distinction indicating where actual disk drives are located. For example, if you have a folder on a Windows computer, you know that all the subfolders and files within it are located on the same hard drive. In Unix and Linux, everything resides within the root directory, but any different directory could be located on a different physical hard drive, flash drive, DVD, or other storage system. You might think of it as tacking a new branch onto your artificial Christmas tree.

These tacked-on storage spaces are called *file systems*. Particularly if you're running a Unix system (as opposed to just using one), you might need to find out what file systems are in use (or *mounted* in the system, in technical terms), how much space they have, and where they attach to the Unix system (or where their mountpoints are). You can find out this information using **df**, as shown in **Code Listings 7.3** and **7.4**.

**Code Listing 7.3** This small Linux system has relatively simple file systems.

```
[ejr@hobbes ejr]$ df
Filesystem     1024-blocks    Used     Available  Capacity  Mounted on
/dev/hda1      515161         316297   172255     65%       /
/dev/hdb4      66365          4916     58022      8%        /home
/dev/hdb1      416656         324633   70504      82%       /usr/local
/dev/sbpcd     596704         596704   0          100%      /mnt/cdrom
[ejr@hobbes ejr]$
```

## To find out about file systems with df:

df

At the shell prompt, type **df**. You'll usually get output showing you the following:

- The name of the device, which refers to the physical part that stores the data, such as a hard drive, CD-ROM, or whatever. In Code Listing 7.3 the first one is **/dev/hda1**, indicating the first hard drive in the system.

- The number of blocks, which are 1-kilobyte-sized storage units (1-kilobyte-sized in this case, although some systems report them as 512 bytes).

- The number of used and available blocks on the device.

- The percentage of the space on the device that is being used.

- The name of the file system, which is the full path name from the Unix system. This is also known as the *mountpoint*.

Code Listings 7.3 and 7.4 show the output of **df** on two different systems.

**Code Listing 7.4** This large ISP's file systems are considerably more complex.

```
example> df
/                   (/dev/dsk/c0t3d0s0  ):  154632 blocks      71721 files
/usr                (/dev/dsk/c0t3d0s6  ):  225886 blocks      144820 files
/proc               (/proc              ):  0 blocks           7830 files
/dev/fd             (fd                 ):  0 blocks           0 files
/var                (/dev/dsk/c0t1d0s0  ):  1001142 blocks     962598 files
/tmp                (swap               ):  1236032 blocks     95277 files
/usr/local          (/dev/dsk/c0t1d0s5  ):  630636 blocks      457211 files
/archive            (/dev/dsk/c0t1d0s3  ):  1180362 blocks     1789487 files
/var/mail           (mail.example.com:/var/mail):  2776576 blocks  1438385 files
/home               (krunk1.example.com:/home):     20091072 blocks 13066932 files
/var/spool/newslib  (news.example.com:/var/spool/newslib):  19327664 blocks  1248s
/.web               (krunk1.example.com:/.web):        1019408 blocks   470095 files
/var/maillists      (lists.example.com:/var/maillists):    293744 blocks  89732s
example>
```

**TIP** You can use df with a specific directory to get a report on the status of the file system containing that directory. For example, you might use df /usr/local/src to find out where that directory is mounted and how much space is available on it.

**TIP** Use df -k to make sure that the usage is reported in 1-kilobyte blocks, not in 512-byte blocks. Adding the -k flag will also ensure that you get output like that shown in Code Listing 7.3.

**TIP** Use df -h to get human-readable output. This works with many commands (like ls, for example) that output marginally comprehensible file information, as Code Listing 7.5 shows.

If you're a system administrator, you can use this information to help diagnose problems occurring in the system. If you're an average user (of above-average curiosity), you can use this information to satisfy your inquisitive inclinations or to tip off a system administrator to problems. For example, if you're getting odd errors or unpredictable results with a specific program, using **df** might reveal that the **/home** file system is full or maybe that you don't have the **/dev/cdrom** file system that you thought was installed and mounted. Hmmm!

**Code Listing 7.5** Use df -h to get "human readable" output.

```
122 ejr@frazz $ df -h
Filesystem          size   used   avail   capacity   Mounted on
/dev/dsk/c0d0s0     19G    4.5G   15G     24%        /
/devices            0K     0K     0K      0%         /devices
/dev                0K     0K     0K      0%         /dev
ctfs                0K     0K     0K      0%         /system/contract
proc                0K     0K     0K      0%         /proc
mnttab              0K     0K     0K      0%         /etc/mnttab
swap                1.5G   856K   1.5G    1%         /etc/svc/volatile
objfs               0K     0K     0K      0%         /system/object
/usr/lib/libc/libc_hwcap1.so.1
                    19G    4.5G   15G     24%        /lib/libc.so.1
fd                  0K     0K     0K      0%         /dev/fd
swap                1.5G   164K   1.5G    1%         /tmp
swap                1.5G   32K    1.5G    1%         /var/run
/dev/dsk/c0d0s7     51G    18G    33G     36%        /export
pooldata            226G   106M   69G     1%         /pooldata
pooldata/family     226G   140G   69G     68%        /pooldata/family
pooldata/raycomm    226G   5.9G   69G     8%         /pooldata/raycomm
poolscratch         228G   46G    181G    21%        /poolscratch
123 ejr@frazz $
```

# Determining Disk Usage with du

Another piece of information that you can access is how much disk space within the Unix or Linux system is in use. You can do so using **du**, as shown in **Code Listing 7.6**.

## To determine disk usage with du:

du

At the shell prompt, enter **du**. As Code Listing 7.6 shows, you'll get information about disk usage in the current directory as well as in all subdirectories. The numbers are usually measured in 1-kilobyte blocks (as with **df**). You can actually read the output by using **du -h**.

**TIP** If you're on a system that enforces disk-space quotas (as many companies do), you can find out what your quota is and how close you are to reaching it. Just type `quota -v` at the shell prompt.

**TIP** You can use du with a path name to check the disk usage in just a single directory or subdirectory (see Code Listing 7.7). du summarizes the usage by subdirectory as it prints the results.

**TIP** Use du -s, optionally with a specific directory, to just print a summary of the amount of space used.

**Code Listing 7.6** The **du** command reports—exhaustively—about the disk usage in the current directory and in its subdirectories.

```
[ejr@hobbes ejr]$ du
2       ./Mail
1       ./nsmail
1       ./.datastore/cache/0F
3       ./.datastore/cache/1A
22      ./.datastore/cache
1       ./.datastore/archive
172     ./.datastore
1       ./Projects
28      ./.wprc
3       ./axhome
5       ./groups
1       ./manipulate/empty
154     ./manipulate
1       ./mail
1       ./unixvqs/ch6
2       ./unixvqs
6       ./dupgroups
255     ./compression/Folder
670     ./compression/temp/BackupFolder
1921    ./compression/temp
670     ./compression/BackupFolder
4657    ./compression
5       ./clean
1       ./.elm
15      ./editors
5619    .
[ejr@hobbes ejr]$
```

**Code Listing 7.7** Using **du** with a specific directory name gives you focused results.

```
[ejr@hobbes ejr]$ du /home/ejr/compression
255     /home/ejr/compression/Folder
670     /home/ejr/compression/temp/BackupFolder
1921    /home/ejr/compression/temp
670     /home/ejr/compression/BackupFolder
4657    /home/ejr/compression
[ejr@hobbes ejr]$
```

# Finding Out File Types with `file`

If you come from a Windows or Macintosh background, you're probably used to accessing files and being able to see what type of files they are—HTML files, JPEGs, documents, or whatever. In Unix and Linux, though, you often can't tell the file type just by listing files or displaying directory contents. That's where `file` comes in handy, as shown in **Code Listing 7.8**.

## To identify file types with `file`:

### file /bin/nano

At the shell prompt, type **file**, followed by the path (If necessary) and filename. You'll see output similar to that in Code Listing 7.8.

> **TIP** Not all files have the "magic" information associated with them that makes `file` work, but most do. Where they don't, you get a best-guess response, like the second response in Code Listing 7.8. Unfortunately, you can't tell by looking if it's definitive information or a guess, but if it's terse (as in the second response), take it with a grain of salt.

**Code Listing 7.8** The `file` command provides useful information about what kind of data is in specific files.

```
[ejr@hobbes ejr]$ file /bin/nano
/bin/nano: ELF 64-bit LSB executable, x86-64, version 1 (SYSV), dynamically linked (uses
→ shared libs), for GNU/Linux 2.6.24, BuildID[sha1]=0xcaba96a927ba6af0d5a2bdbb9c473e93310457ea,
 › stripped [ejr@hobbes ejr]$ file temp.htm
temp.htm: ASCII text
[ejr@hobbes ejr]$
```

# Finding Out About Users with `finger`

Using the **finger** command, you can find out who is currently logged in to the system as well as what they're doing, how long they've been logged in, and other snoopy, not-necessarily-your-business information (**Code Listing 7.9**).

**Code Listing 7.9** The **finger** command often provides interesting information about who is logged on to different systems.

```
[ejr@hobbes ejr]$ finger
Login     Name          Tty     Idle    Login Time   Office   Office Phone
asr                     *4      1       Jul 24 13:32
deb                     5       1       Jul 24 13:32
ejr       Eric J. Ray   1       3:20    Jul 22 07:42
ejr       Eric J. Ray   p1      1:12    Jul 24 12:14 (calvin)
ejr       Eric J. Ray   p0              Jul 24 13:02 (calvin)
root      root          *2      1d      Jul 22 15:13
[ejr@hobbes ejr]$ finger @example.com
[example.com]
No one logged on
[ejr@hobbes ejr]$ finger @osuunx.ucc.okstate.edu
[osuunx.ucc.okstate.edu]
finger: connect: Connection refused
[ejr@hobbes ejr]$
```

## To find out who is logged in using `finger`:

1. `finger`

   At the shell prompt, type **finger** to see who else is logged in to the system and to get a little information about them (Code Listing 7.9).

2. `finger @example.com`

   Type **finger**, **@**, and a host name (in this case, **example.com**) to find out who is logged in to another host.

   Fingering a different host usually doesn't work, unless you are probing a different system within a lab or company network. The reason it doesn't work is that security settings on the other host computer(s) usually preclude use of **finger**. If the host doesn't allow it, you'll get a message like the one in Code Listing 7.9.

## To find out about users using `finger`:

1. **`finger ejr`**

   At the shell prompt, type **finger** followed by the userid of the person you want to know about. You'll get a ton of information, including some or all of the following: the user's name, home directory, and default shell; when, from where, and for how long they've been logged on; and whatever other information they choose to provide. **Code Listing 7.10** shows two users with varying activity. **deb** has apparently been loafing, and **ejr** has been working his buns off.

2. **`finger ejray@example.com`**

   Using **finger** plus a specific user address, you can find out about users on other systems. As with generic **finger** requests, sometimes they're blocked for security reasons.

**TIP** You can also sniff out user information using who (see the next section).

**TIP** You can provide extra information to anyone who gets your user information with `finger` by creating files that describe your "plan" and "project" (as `ejr` has done in Code Listing 7.10). Use your favorite editor to create .plan and .project files in your home directory. Then, change the protection so that the files are both world readable (chmod go+r .plan ; chmod go+r .project) and so that the directory is accessible (chmod +rx .). See Chapter 5 for specifics about chmod.

**TIP** Information you obtain through `finger` can be handy when diagnosing connection difficulties. In particular, system administrators or help desk personnel are likely to ask where you're connected (pts/57, for ejray@ example.com) and what kind of software you're using.

**Code Listing 7.10** The **finger** command can also provide in-depth information about specific users.

```
[ejr@hobbes ejr]$ finger deb
Login: deb              Name:
Directory: /home/deb    Shell: /bin/bash
Never logged in.
No mail.
No Plan.
[ejr@hobbes ejr]$ finger ejr
Login: ejr              Name:
Directory: /home/ejr    Shell: /bin/bash
On since Wed Jul 22 07:42 (MDT) on tty1    2 hours 32 minutes idle
On since Wed Jul 22 06:58 (MDT) on ttyp1 from calvin
No mail.
Project:
Working on VQS.
Plan:
This is my plan---work all day, sleep all night.
[ejr@hobbes ejr]$ finger ejray@example.com
[example.com]
Login    Name     TTY     Idle    When      Where
ejray    "RayComm  pts/57  <Jul 22 09:39> calvin.raycomm.c
[ejr@hobbes ejr]$
```

# Learning Who Else Is Logged In with who

If you're not interested in all the gory details you get about users when you **finger** them, you can instead use **who** to get just the basics. With **who** you get just the users' names, connection information, login times, and host names, as shown in **Code Listing 7.11**.

## To snoop with who:

**who**

At the shell prompt, type **who**. You'll get user information like that shown in Code Listing 7.11. Optionally, you could pipe the output of **who** to **more**, as in **who | more**, which would give you a long list of results one screen at a time.

> **TIP** If you are a system administrator or use several different userids, you might occasionally need to use a special case of who, called **whoami**. Just type **whoami** at the shell prompt, and it'll tell you which userid you're currently logged in as.

> **TIP** See Chapter 1 for more on **more** and on piping commands.

Code Listing 7.11 Use **who** to find out who else is currently logged in to the system.

```
[ejr@hobbes ejr]$ who
ejr     tty1    Jul 22 07:42
root    tty2    Jul 22 15:13
asr     tty4    Jul 24 13:32
deb     tty5    Jul 24 13:32
ejr     ttyp1   Jul 24 12:14 (calvin.raycomm.com)
ejr     ttyp0   Jul 24 13:02 (calvin.raycomm.com)
[ejr@hobbes ejr]$
```

# Learning Who Else Is Logged In with w

Another way to find out about other people logged in to the system is to use **w**, which tells you who is logged in, what they're doing, and a few other details (**Code Listing 7.12**).

## To find out who is logged in with w:

**w**

At the shell prompt, type **w**. You'll usually see output much like that in Code Listing 7.12. The top line shows

- The time.

- System uptime in days, hours, and minutes (uptime is how long it's been since the system was restarted and is usually measured in weeks or months for Unix or Linux systems, as opposed to hours or days for personal computers).

- The number of users.

- System load averages (the numbers indicate jobs—programs or scripts to execute—lined up to run in the past 1, 5, and 15 minutes).

**Code Listing 7.12** The **w** command provides tons of information about the system and its users.

```
[ejr@hobbes ejr]$ w
 1:49pm  up 6 days,   4:21,     6 users, load average: 0.08, 0.02, 0.01
USER   TTY    FROM     LOGIN@   IDLE    JCPU   PCPU   WHAT
ejr    tty1            Wed 7am  3:36m   7.07s  6.01s  -bash
root   tty2            Wed 3pm  28:46m  1.22s  0.32s  -bash
asr    tty4            1:32pm   17:22   1.04s  0.30s  pine
deb    tty5            1:32pm   3.00s   1.22s  0.42s  lynx
ejr    ttyp1  calvin   12:14pm  1:28m   1.33s  0.57s  vi hairyspiders
ejr    ttyp0  calvin   1:02pm   1.00s   1.70s  0.24s  w
[ejr@hobbes ejr]$
```

The following lines, one per logged-in user, show

- The login name
- The **tty** name (the connection to the host)
- The remote host name
- The login time
- Current idle time (that is, the time since a key on the keyboard was touched)
- JCPU (job CPU time, or the total processing time for jobs on the current connection, which is the **tty**, for those into the jargon)
- PCPU (process CPU time, or the processing time for the current process)
- The command line of the current process

Whew! As you can see from Code Listing 7.12 and **Code Listing 7.13**, different systems' **w** commands produce slightly different (but similar) output.

**TIP** Use **w** with **grep** to find information (slightly more abbreviated) about a specific user. For example, **w | grep ejr** gives limited information, but just about a specific user. See Chapter 1 for more information about piping commands.

**Code Listing 7.13** w yields different information on different systems.

```
example> w
 1:47pm  up 38 day(s), 23:35, 36 users, load average: 1.58, 1.78, 1.75
...
ejray  pts/16  Thu 6am  1:14  -csh
...
```

# Getting Information About Your Userid with `id`

Occasionally, you may need to find out information about your userid, such as your userid's numeric value and to what groups you belong. This information is essential when you're sharing files (as discussed in Chapter 5) because you'll need it to let people access your files and to access theirs. You can easily get information about your userid with **id**, as shown in **Code Listing 7.14**.

## To check userid information using `id`:

`id`

At the shell prompt, type **id** to find the numeric value of your userid and to what groups (by name and numeric userid value) you belong (see Code Listing 7.14). See "Finding Out Which Group You're In," in Chapter 5, for more about the **/etc/group** file.

**TIP** You can also check someone else's status with **id** to find out what groups they're in. Just use **id userid** (substituting the other person's userid for **userid**, of course).

**TIP** Use **groups** to find out which groups—in human-readable terms—a specific userid is in. For example, **ejr** is in the **ejr**, **wheel**, and **users** groups, as shown in Code Listing 7.14.

Code Listing 7.14 Use **id** to get information about userids and group memberships.

```
[ejr@hobbes ejr]$ id
uid=500(ejr) gid=500(ejr) groups=500(ejr), 10(wheel),100(users)
[ejr@hobbes ejr]$ id deb
uid=505(deb) gid=505(deb) groups=100(users)
[ejr@hobbes ejr]$ groups ejr
ejr : ejr wheel users
```

# 8

# Configuring Your Unix or Linux Environment

Back in Chapter 3, we introduced you to shells—what they are and what you can do with them. In this chapter, we'll take you a bit further and look at configuring your environment using the **zsh** and **bash** shells, because they are two of the most common (popular) and useful shells. By configuring your environment, you can make the system adapt to your needs, rather than adapting to an existing environment that may not work for you. These configuration tips differ (slightly) for different shells, so make sure you're following along with the instructions appropriate for the shell you use.

## In This Chapter

# Understanding Your Unix or Linux Environment

Environment variables are settings in the system that specify how you, your shell, and the system interact. When you log in to the system, it sets up your environment variables—the shell you want to use, the default search path, and other information to help programs run, among other things. You might think of your environment variables as being similar to having a standing order with a deli to deliver the same thing to you every day. You set up your "standing environment variables" and the Unix system delivers them to you session after session unless you specify otherwise.

Technically, there is a distinction between "shell" variables, which exist in the particular shell you're using, and "environment" variables, which are in your environment and independent of your particular shell. The key difference is that shell variables retain their values only in the current shell, whereas environment variables are propagated to all child processes of the shell. For most purposes, though, including this book, you can do as we're doing and conveniently blur the distinction. As long as you know that they're not precisely synonymous, you'll be fine.

Basically, just like with the lunch deli, you can configure your environment in one of two ways:

- Changing the variables for the current session—kind of like calling in a special order for the day (as in ordering onion and extra cheese on today's sandwich). You do this from the shell prompt, as discussed in the "Adding or Changing Variables" section later in this chapter.

- Changing the variables for all subsequent sessions—kind of like changing your standard order (say, when the doctor tells you to cut back on mayonnaise and suggests mustard for your long-term deli order). You do this within the configuration files, as discussed in sections following "Adding or Changing Variables."

If you want to change your environment variables, you should first try changing them from the shell prompt for the current session. That way, you can try out the changes before you make them permanent (at least until you change them again) in your configuration files.

When you do change your environment in the configuration files, keep in mind that configuration files are generally run in a specific order:

- Systemwide configuration files (such as **/etc/profile**) run first upon login. These systemwide configuration files in **/etc** (if they exist) help set up your environment, but you cannot change them.

- Configuration files specific to your Unix account (such as **~/.profile** and **~/.bashrc**) run next if they're available. If you want to change environment variables originally set in the systemwide files, you can reset the values in your own personal files.

What this order means to you is that your own personal configurations override system ones. So, in making changes to your configuration files, be sure that you make changes to the configuration file that runs last. We'll tell you which specific files to look for in the relevant sections of this chapter.

Find out about discovering your current environment variables and adding or changing environment variables manually in the next two sections in this chapter.

**TIP** You can use echo $SHELL to remind yourself of what shell you're using. Visit Chapter 3 for more details.

**TIP** Find out about changing environment variables in your system configuration files in other sections of this chapter, according to which shell you're using.

# Discovering Your Current Environment

A good first step in changing your environment is determining what environment you have. Using the steps in this section, you can discover which environment and shell variables are set currently—including ones specified in the configuration files as well as ones you've set for the current session (**Code Listing 8.1**).

As you're going through these steps, you might check out the sidebar "Variables in Your Environment You Shouldn't Touch" in this section for a list of variables you should leave alone. Then, in the next section, check out "Variables You Can Mess With" to find ones you can change.

## To show your current environment in zsh or bash:

**env**

At the shell prompt, type **env**. You'll see a list of the current environment and shell variables, as shown in Code Listing 8.1.

Some of the variables may look familiar to you (such as the ones showing your shell or user name), while others are likely to be more cryptic (such as the line showing the last command you ran; in this case, **_=cd**).

**TIP** If you do as we often do and try to use **show** to show the environment variables ("showing" the variables seems logical, right?), you might get a weird question about the standard mail directories and the MH mailer. Most Linux distributions don't have a **show** command. Just press Ctrl+C to return to your shell prompt.

**TIP** If the list of environment variables is long, you can pipe **env** to **more** so that you can read the variables one screen at a time. Try **env | more**. See Chapter 1 for a reminder about piping commands.

Code Listing 8.1 You can find out which variables exist in the **zsh** or **bash** shells with **env**.

```
[ejr@hobbes ejr]$ env
BASH=/bin/bash
BASH_VERSION=1.14.7(1)
COLUMNS=80
ENV=/home/ejr/.bashrc
EUID=500
HISTFILE=/home/ejr/.bash_history
HISTFILESIZE=1000
HISTSIZE=1000
HOME=/home/ejr
HOSTNAME=hobbes.raycomm.com
HOSTTYPE=i386
IFS=
LINES=24
LOGNAME=ejr
MAIL=/var/spool/mail/ejr
MAILCHECK=60
OLDPWD=/home/ejr/src/rpm-2.5.1
OPTERR=1
OPTIND=1
OSTYPE=Linux
PATH=/usr/local/bin:/bin:/usr/bin:/usr/
→ X11R6/bin:/home/ejr/bin
PPID=1943
PS1=[\u@\h \W]\$
PS2=>
PS4=+
PWD=/home/ejr
SHELL=/bin/bash
SHLVL=3
TERM=vt220
UID=500
USER=ejr
USERNAME=
_=cd
[ejr@hobbes ejr]$
```

## Variables in Your Environment You Shouldn't Touch

Before you go running off and changing your environment, note that there are some things you should really leave alone. These variables that the shell automatically sets affect how your Unix or Linux system works (or doesn't work, if you try to change some of these variables!). Some of these cannot be changed, but some can, with unpredictable results. When in doubt, don't. See the sidebar "Variables You Can Mess With" in the following section for a list of variables you can change.

| zsh and bash | Description |
| --- | --- |
| HISTCMD | Keeps track of the number of the current command from the history. |
| HOSTTYPE | Holds a string describing the type of hardware on which the shell is running. |
| IFS | Specifies the characters that indicate the beginning or end of words. |
| LINENO | Contains the number of the current line within the shell or a shell script. |
| OLDPWD | Contains the previous working directory. |
| OSTYPE | Holds a string describing the operating system on which the shell is running. |
| PPID | Contains the process ID of the shell's parent. |
| PWD | Contains the current working directory. |
| RANDOM | Contains a special value to generate random numbers. |
| SECONDS | Contains the number of seconds since the shell was started. |
| SHELL | Contains the name of the current shell. |
| SHLVL | Contains a number indicating the sub-shell level (if SHLVL is 3, two parent shells exist and you'll have to exit from three total shells to completely log out). |
| UID | Contains the userid of the current user. |

# Adding or Changing Variables

After you've poked around in your environment, you might determine that you want to set a variable that's currently not available or change one to make it better meet your needs. In general, you won't randomly specify variables; you'll do it because a certain program requires a specific variable in order to run.

By following the steps in this section, you can add or change environment variables for the current session. As **Code Listing 8.2** shows, for example, you can specify a news server environment variable (called **NNTPSERVER**) that some Usenet news readers require to access the news (**nntp**) server.

## To add or change a variable in zsh or bash:

1. **NNTPSERVER=news.example.com**

   At the shell prompt, type the name of the variable (in this case, **NNTPSERVER**), followed by = and the value you want for the variable (here, **news.example.com**), as shown in Code Listing 8.2. In this step, you're setting up the variable and its value and making it available to all programs and scripts that run in the current shell session.

   If the value contains spaces or special characters, put the value in quotes.

2. **export NNTPSERVER**

   Type **export** followed by the name of the variable. By exporting the variable, you make it available to all programs and scripts that run in the current shell session (again, Code Listing 8.2).

   Until it is exported, it is a shell variable, which will not be available to other processes that this shell starts.

**Code Listing 8.2** In the **zsh** and **bash** shells, you can add a new environment variable by specifying the variable and its value, then exporting the variable to the system.

```
[ejr@hobbes ejr]$ NNTPSERVER=news.example.com
[ejr@hobbes ejr]$ export NNTPSERVER
[ejr@hobbes ejr]$ echo $NNTPSERVER
news.example.com
[ejr@hobbes ejr]$
```

**3. echo $NNTPSERVER**

Optionally, type **echo** followed by a **$** and the name of the variable to have the shell tell you what the variable is set to.

**TIP** In bash or zsh, save a step by typing **export NNTPSERVER=news.example.com.**

## Variables You Can Mess With

The following table includes some of the variables you can safely change. Keep in mind that the shell itself might not use a specific variable, like **NNTPSERVER**, whereas programs running under the shell might. Sometimes shells assign default variables, while in other cases you'll have to manually set the value.

| zsh and bash | Description |
| --- | --- |
| CDPATH | Specifies the search path for directories specified by **cd**. This is similar to **PATH**. |
| COLUMNS | Specifies the width of the edit window in characters. |
| EDITOR | Specifies the default editor. |
| ENV | Specifies where to look for configuration files. |
| HISTFILE | Specifies the name of the file containing the command history. |
| HISTFILESIZE | Specifies the maximum number of lines to keep in the history file. |
| HISTSIZE | Specifies the number of commands to keep in the command history. |
| HOSTFILE | Specifies the name of the file containing host name aliases for expansion. |
| IGNOREEOF | Specifies that Ctrl + D should not log out of the shell. Use **IGNOREEOF=**. |
| LINES | Specifies the number of lines on the screen. |
| MAIL | Specifies the location of incoming mail so **bash** can notify you of mail arrival. |
| MAILCHECK | Specifies how often (in seconds) **bash** checks for mail. |
| MAIL_WARNING | Specifies the message to be displayed if you have read mail but not unread mail. |
| noclobber | Specifies that the shell should not overwrite an existing file when redirecting output. |
| PATH | Specifies the search path for commands, including multiple paths separated by colons. |
| PROMPT_COMMAND | Specifies the command to be run before displaying each primary prompt. |
| PS1 | Specifies the primary prompt. |
| PS2 | Specifies the default second-level prompt. |
| PS3 | Specifies the prompt for the **select** command in scripts. |
| PS4 | Specifies the prompt used when tracing execution of a script. |
| TMOUT | Specifies time in seconds to wait for input before closing the shell. |
| VISUAL | Specifies the default visual editor—usually the same as **EDITOR**, but referenced by different programs. |

# Looking at Your zsh Configuration Files

Your first step in modifying or adding **zsh** environment variables in your configuration files is to look at the configuration files, which show you the variables that are explicitly defined. As **Code Listing 8.3** shows, you do this using **more** or the editor of your choice.

Remember that **zsh** configuration files exist in two places:

- Systemwide configuration files (such as **/etc/zprofile** or **/etc/zshenv** or **/etc/zsh/zshrc**)
- Configuration files specific to your Unix account (such as **~/.zprofile** or **~/.zshrc**)

## To look at your zsh configuration files:

1. **more ~/.z\* /etc/zl\* /etc/zprofile**
   **→ /etc/zsh/\***

   At the shell prompt, type **more** followed by each of the possible system configuration filenames to view your configuration files. If you don't have all (or any) of the files mentioned here, don't worry. Just make note of the ones you do have. Code Listing 8.3 shows an example of what you might see.

   *continues on page 155*

**Code Listing 8.3** Your **zsh** configuration files set up your environment variables and other features of your Unix or Linux experience.

```
jdoe@sulley ~ $ more ~/.z* /etc/zl* /etc/zprofile /etc/zsh/*
::::::::::::::::
/home/jdoe/.zprofile
::::::::::::::::
# /etc/zprofile and ~/.zprofile are run for login shells
#
::::::::::::::::
/home/jdoe/.zshenv
::::::::::::::::
export X11HOME=/usr/X11R6
if (( EUID == 0 )); then
 path=(/sbin /usr/sbin)
fi
typeset -U path
path=($path $X11HOME/bin /bin /usr/bin /usr/local/bin)
PATH=$PATH:/home/jdoe/scripts
::::::::::::::::
/home/jdoe/.zshrc
::::::::::::::::
# Reset prompts
PROMPT="%n@%m %3~ %(!.#.$) " # default prompt
#RPROMPT=' %~' # prompt for right side of screen
# bindkey -v    # vi key bindings
bindkey -e      # emacs key bindings
if [[ ! -r ${ZDOTDIR:-$HOME}/.zshrc ]];then
    if [[ -f /usr/share/zsh/$ZSH_VERSION/zshrc_default ]];then
        source /usr/share/zsh/$ZSH_VERSION/zshrc_default
    fi
fi
::::::::::::::::
/etc/zlogin
::::::::::::::::
# /etc/zlogin and .zlogin are sourced in login shells.
::::::::::::::::
/etc/zlogout
::::::::::::::::
# /etc/zlogout and ~/.zlogout are run when an interactive session ends
# clear
::::::::::::::::
/etc/zprofile
::::::::::::::::
#
::::::::::::::::
/etc/zshenv
::::::::::::::::
export X11HOME=/usr/X11R6
if (( EUID == 0 )); then
 path=(/sbin /usr/sbin)
```

*code listing continues on next page*

```
fi
typeset -U path
path=($path $X11HOME/bin /bin /usr/bin /usr/local/bin)
:::::::::::::::
/etc/zshrc
:::::::::::::::
if [[ $(id -gn) = $USERNAME && $EUID -gt 14 ]]; then
    umask 002
else
    umask 022
fi
# Get keys working
if [[ $TERM = "linux" ]];then
    bindkey "^[[2~" yank
    bindkey "^[[3~" delete-char
    bindkey "^[[5~" up-line-or-history
    bindkey "^[[6~" down-line-or-history
   bindkey "^[[1~" beginning-of-line
    bindkey "^[[4~" end-of-line
elif [[ $TERM = "xterm" || $TERM = "rxvt" ]];then
    bindkey "^[[2~" yank
    bindkey "^[[3~" delete-char
    bindkey "^[[5~" up-line-or-history
    bindkey "^[[6~" down-line-or-history
    bindkey "" beginning-of-line
    bindkey "" end-of-line
fi
# Set prompts
PROMPT="%n@%m %3~ %(!.#.$) "  # default prompt
#RPROMPT=' %~'  # prompt for right side of screen
# Some environment variables
path=($path $HOME/bin)
export HISTFILE=${HOME}/.bash_history
export HISTSIZE=1000
export SAVEHIST=1000
export USER=$USERNAME
export HOSTNAME=$HOST
# bindkey -v   # vi key bindings
bindkey -e    # emacs key bindings
for profile_func ( /etc/profile.d/*.sh ) source $profile_func
unset profile_func
# See comment at top.
if [[ ! -r ${ZDOTDIR:-$HOME}/.zshrc ]];then
    if [[ -f /usr/share/zsh/$ZSH_VERSION/zshrc_default ]];then
        source /usr/share/zsh/$ZSH_VERSION/zshrc_default
    fi
fi
jdoe@sulley ~ $
```

## Fill In Your zsh System Configuration Files

_____

_____

_____

_____

_____

_____

_____

2. Write down, for your reference, the system configuration files and the order in which they're run. (Remember, settings in the last file run override all previous ones.) Our system configuration files, all automatically called by the system, include

- **/etc/zshenv** (or **/etc/zsh/zshenv**) then **~/.zshenv**

- **/etc/zprofile** (or **/etc/zsh/zprofile**) then **~/.zprofile**

- **/etc/zshrc** (or **/etc/zsh/zshrc**) then **~/.zshrc**

- **/etc/zlogin** (or **/etc/zsh/zlogin**) then **~/.zlogin**

Keep in mind that the files you have may differ from the files that we have.

**TIP** Take special note of any lines in any of the files that end with a path and filename, or that reference other files directly, with something like **/etc/profile** on a line by itself. Each of those lines references another file that plays a role in getting you set up. Notice that some of the lines will reference others that don't directly configure your environment.

**TIP** Some zsh files include oddities—like export HISTFILE=${HOME}/.bash_history line—that reference the .bash_history file containing the list of commands you've run. (Looks like a goof by the Linux distributor. Good thing you're checking up on them, huh?)

**TIP** You can use grep to make it easy to find the configuration files that set your path. grep -i path ~/.z* is a good way to start.

**TIP** If you see something like path=($path $HOME/bin) in your configuration files, that's OK. Just go ahead and use the syntax shown in this section on the following line anyway. It's a feature of zsh that it understands about a bazillion different ways to express any single command.

# Adding to Your zsh Path

One of the most useful changes you can make to your environment is adding to the default path, which is determined by the path statement. The path statement tells the shell where to look for commands, scripts, and programs. That is, if you issue a command, the path statement tells the system to look for that command in each of the named directories in a specific order.

If a command is not in your path, you have to type out the whole path as part of the command, like **/home/unixvqs/myscripts/latest/test/command.sh**. If you put **/home/unixvqs/myscripts/latest/test** in your path, you can just run **command.sh**.

Be sure not to remove anything from your path unless you really know what you're doing, but feel free to add as many additional directories to it as you want. For example, if you get started writing scripts (as described in Chapter 10), you might put them in a **scripts** subdirectory and want to add that directory to your path.

As the following steps show, you change your **zsh** path by first identifying where your path statement is located, then editing the file that contains it (**Code Listing 8.4**).

Code Listing 8.4 You should find your path statement in your configuration files.

```
jdoe@sulley ~ $ tail .zshrc
# See comment at top.
if [[ ! -r ${ZDOTDIR:-$HOME}/ .zshrc ]];then
    if [[ -f /usr/share/zsh/$ZSH_VERSION/zshrc_default ]];then
        source /usr/share/zsh/$ZSH_VERSION/zshrc_default
    fi
fi
PATH=/bin:/usr/bin:/opt/bin
jdoe@sulley ~ $
```

**(A)** You add to or modify a **zsh** path statement in your editor.

**Code Listing 8.5** Test out your edits to the configuration files.

```
jdoe@sulley ~ $ su - jdoe
Password:
jdoe@sulley ~ $ echo $PATH
/bin:/usr/bin:/opt/bin:/home/jdoe/scripts/
jdoe@sulley ~ $
```

**TIP** If you look through the path statements in your various configuration files, you might find a path statement that includes just a . (dot). For example, you might see something like PATH=/usr/bin:/usr/local/bin:.:. The . adds your current directory, whatever it might be, to your path. Keep in mind, though, that it's often safer not to have the current directory in the path so you don't unintentionally run a different program from the one you expect.

## To change your zsh path:

1. **more ~/.zshenv ~/.zprofile ~/.zshrc**

   View your configuration files (just the ones you can edit) in the order they're executed.

   Look through your system configuration files for a path statement. As Code Listing 8.4 shows, it will look something like **PATH=/bin:/usr/bin:/opt/bin**. If you have more than one path statement, find the last one executed.

   Remember that different systems will have different configurations, so you might need to do a little digging to find your personal path statement(s).

2. **cp .zshrc .zshrc_backup**

   Make a backup of the file containing the path statement so that you can recover the file when problems or errors occur. See Chapter 2 if you need more information on copying files.

3. **vi .zshrc**

   Use your favorite editor to open the file whose path you want to change.

4. **PATH=$PATH:$HOME/scripts**

   Add a new path statement immediately below the last path statement. In this example, **PATH** is set to its current value (**$PATH**) plus the directory (**$HOME/scripts**) you wish to append to your path **(A)**.

5. Save the file and exit from your editor.

   Refer to Chapter 4 for help if you need it.

6. **su - yourid**

   As you learned back in Chapter 3, this command starts a new login shell so you can test your changes before logging out.

7. **echo $PATH**

   Display the current path environment variable. This should include the addition you just made. It's there, right? (See **Code Listing 8.5**.)

# Changing Your zsh Prompt

Your default prompt (the text on the screen in front of the place you type commands) may vary a bit, depending on your Unix system; you might see just a dollar sign (**$**), a dollar sign and date, or other information as outlined in the "Setting Your **zsh** Prompt Promptly" sidebar. You can set your prompt to include information that's handy for you.

You actually have multiple prompts:

- The main prompt that you usually think of as the shell prompt. This prompt is called **PS1** or just **PROMPT**.

- A secondary prompt that you see when the system requires additional information to complete a command. Logically, this prompt is called **PS2**.

You can change either of these prompts using the following steps. You start by finding your prompt statement (**Code Listing 8.6**), then modifying it in your editor Ⓐ.

Ⓑ Edit your **zsh** prompt statement in the editor of your choice.

**Code Listing 8.6** Use **grep** to search your configuration files for a **zsh** prompt statement.

```
jdoe@sulley ~ $ grep -i PROMPT ~/.z*;
→ grep -i PS1 ~/.z*
/home/jdoe/.zshrc:# configuration for keys
→ umask PROMPT and variable
/home/jdoe/.zshrc:# Set prompts
/home/jdoe/.zshrc:PROMPT="%n@%m %3~
→ %(!.#.$) "  # default prompt
jdoe@sulley ~ $
```

## Setting Your zsh Prompt Promptly

You can set your prompt to contain all sorts of information. The following list shows you what code to use to add certain kinds of information to your prompt (and it will help you translate the code in your existing prompt):

- **%n** shows the userid of the current user—that's you.

- **%~** shows the current working directory with a path, using a ~ notation within your home directory.

- **%c** shows the current directory without the path.

- **%t** shows the time.

- **%w** shows the date without the year.

- **%W** shows the date with the year.

- **\n** forces a new line, making the prompt appear split on two lines (you need single quotes around the prompt).

- **%m** shows the host name of the computer (like the LinuxMint and hobbes examples in this book).

- **%M** shows the complete host name of the computer, including the domain name.

## To change your zsh prompt:

1. **grep -i PROMPT ~/.z\*; grep -i PS1 ~/.z\***

   To begin, search through the configuration files located in your home directory and, if necessary, in the **/etc** directory to find your prompt statement. It may look something like **PROMPT="%n@%m %3~ %(!.#.$) "  # default prompt**, as shown in Code Listing 8.6.

   The "Setting Your **zsh** Prompt Promptly" sidebar will help translate these symbols.

2. **cp ~/.zshrc ~/.zshrc-backup; → vi ~/.zshrc**

   Make a backup copy. The **~/.zshrc** file is a likely place for your prompt to be set, as it is only read when your shell is interactive.

3. **PROMPT="%n %d $ "**

   For example, we often set our prompt to include two tidbits of information: the userid (as we have many different accounts, we can always use a reminder!) and the date (time flies when you're having fun, right?). We're adding these bits of information instead of the existing default prompt, but saving the default with a # sign at the beginning, just in case Ⓐ.

4. Save the file and exit from the editor.

5. **su - ejr**

   Log in again with your changed prompt to try it out.

**TIP** In some newer Linux distributions, the zsh prompt is configured through all kinds of interesting black magic. For the purposes of this example, we recommend editing `~/.zshrc`, and finding lines that look like this:

```
autoload -Uz promptinit
promptinit
prompt adam1
```

and putting a # sign in front of each, then saving the file. Those lines should look like this:

```
#autoload -Uz promptinit
#promptinit
#prompt adam1
```

**TIP** This will "comment out" those three lines, so your prompt customizations will take. If you want the black magic back, just edit the file again and remove the # at the beginning of each line.

**TIP** Note the trailing space in the prompt code: PROMPT="%n %d $ ". This space can help make it easier to use the prompt because it keeps your commands from bumping into your prompt.

**TIP** You can also set your prompt so that the information you set appears on one line and your actual prompt appears on the next (Code Listing 8.7). To do so, use single quotes ('') and a $ in the environment variable setting and then a \n for the new line, as in PROMPT=$'%n %W\n $'. This forces the shell to treat the \n as a new line, not just as random characters in the prompt string.

**Code Listing 8.7** Testing after you update your prompt is always a good idea.

```
jdoe /home/jdoe $ PROMPT=$'Top line
→ \nNext line $'
Top line
Next line $pwd
/home/jdoe
Top line
Next line $
```

# Looking at Your bash Configuration Files

Your first step in modifying or adding **bash** environment variables in your configuration files is to look at the configuration files, which show you the variables that have been defined. As **Code Listing 8.8** shows, you do this using **more** or the editor of your choice.

Remember that configuration files run in a specific order:

- Systemwide configuration files (such as **/etc/profile**) run first upon login.

- Configuration files specific to your Unix account (such as **~/.bash_profile** or **~/.profile**) run next if they're available.

## To look at your bash configuration files:

1. **more ~/.bash\* ~/.profile /etc/bash\***
   **→ /etc/profile**

   At the shell prompt, type **more** followed by each of the possible system configuration filenames to view your configuration files. If you don't have all the files mentioned here, don't worry. Just make note of the ones you do have. Code Listing 8.8 shows an example of what you might see. Notice that some of the lines will reference other files, like the **ENV=$HOME/.bashrc** line that references the **.bashrc** file, containing other configuration settings.

   *continues on page 163*

**Code Listing 8.8** Your configuration files set up your environment variables and other features of your Unix experience.

```
[ejr@hobbes ejr]$ more ~/.bash* ~/.profile /etc/bash* /etc/profile
::::::::::::::
/home/ejr/.bash_profile
::::::::::::::
# .bash_profile
# Get the aliases and functions
if [ -f ~/.bashrc ]; then
    . ~/.bashrc
fi
# User-specific environment and startup programs
PATH=$PATH:$HOME/bin
ENV=$HOME/.bashrc
USERNAME=""
export USERNAME ENV PATH
/home/ejr/.profile: No such file or directory
::::::::::::::
/etc/bashrc
::::::::::::::
# /etc/bashrc
# System-wide functions and aliases
# Environment stuff goes in /etc/profile
# Putting PS1 here ensures that it gets loaded every time.
PS1="[\u@\h \W]\\$ "
alias which="type -path"
::::::::::::::
/etc/profile
::::::::::::::
# /etc/profile
# Systemwide environment and startup programs
# Functions and aliases go in /etc/bashrc
PATH="$PATH:/usr/X11R6/bin"
PS1="[\u@\h \W]\\$ "
ulimit -c 1000000
if [ 'id -gn' = 'id -un' -a 'id -u' -gt 14 ]; then
    umask 002
else
    umask 022
fi
USER='id --un'
LOGNAME=$USER
MAIL="/var/spool/mail/$USER"
HOSTNAME='/bin/hostname'
HISTSIZE=1000
HISTFILESIZE=1000
export PATH PS1 HOSTNAME HISTSIZE HISTFILESIZE USER LOGNAME MAIL
for i in /etc/profile.d/*.sh ; do
    if [ -x $i ]; then
        . $i
    fi
done
unset i
[ejr@hobbes ejr]$
```

## Fill In Your bash System Configuration Files

_____

_____

_____

_____

_____

_____

_____

_____

**2.** Write down, for your reference, the system configuration files and the order in which they're run. (Remember, settings in the last file run override all previous ones.) Our system configuration files include

▸ **/etc/profile** (automatically called by the system if it exists)

▸ **~/.bash_profile** (automatically called by the system if it exists)

▸ **~/.bashrc** (automatically called by the system if it exists)

▸ **/etc/bashrc** (often called by ~/.bashrc)

Keep in mind that the files you have may differ from the files that we have.

**TIP** The bash shell sometimes daisychains configuration files together, referencing one from the previous one. Be careful to preserve the references and sequence as you edit your configuration files, or you might end up with unexpected results.

**TIP** All lines that start with # are comments, which contain notes to help you better understand the files. Comments don't actually do anything, but they help you see what each section in the file does. Any line with a # at the beginning is not executed and is considered non-existent by the system.

**TIP** The techie term (that you'll likely see in these files) for executing a configuration file or a script is to _source_ it. That is, when you log in, your .profile may source .bashrc.

# Adding to Your bash Path

One of the most useful changes you can make to your environment is adding to the default path, which is determined by the path statement. The path statement tells the shell where to look for commands, scripts, and programs. That is, if you issue a command, the path statement tells the system to look for that command in each of the named directories in a specific order.

If a command is not in your path, you have to type out the whole path as part of the command, like **/home/unixvqs/myscripts/latest/test/command.sh**. If you put **/home/unixvqs/myscripts/latest/test** in your path, you can just run **command.sh**.

Be sure not to remove anything from your path unless you really know what you're doing, but feel free to add as many additional directories as you want to it.

As the following steps show, you change your **bash** path by first identifying where your path statement is located, then editing the file that contains it (**Code Listing 8.9**).

Code Listing 8.9 Your first step is finding out the location of your path statement(s).

```
[ejr@hobbes ejr]$ more ~/.bash_profile ~/.bashrc
::::::::::::::::
/home/ejr/.bash_profile
::::::::::::::::
# .bash_profile
# Get the aliases and functions
if [ -f ~/.bashrc ]; then
    . ~/.bashrc
fi
PATH=/bin:/usr/bin:/usr/local/bin
# User-specific environment and startup programs
PATH=$PATH:/usr/local/games
ENV=$HOME/.bashrc
USERNAME=""
export USERNAME ENV PATH
-More-(Next file: /home/ejr/.bashrc)
```

```
# idoe@frazz.raycomm.com: /home/idoe          _ □ X
#
#ejray test
echo "~/.bash_profile"
# .bash_profile

# Get the aliases and functions
if [ -f ~/.bashrc ]; then
        . ~/.bashrc
fi

# User specific environment and startup programs

PATH=$PATH:/usr/local/bin
PATH=$PATH:$HOME/bi█

export PATH
unset USERNAME
~
~
~
~
~
~
".bash_profile" 17L, 254C                14,20      All
```

Ⓐ You add to or modify a **bash** path statement in your editor.

## To change your bash path:

1. `more ~/.bash_profile ~/.bashrc`

   View your configuration files (just the ones you can edit) in the order they're executed.

   Look through your system configuration files for a path statement. As Code Listing 8.9 shows, it'll look something like **PATH=/bin:/usr/bin:/usr/local/bin**. If you have more than one path statement, find the last one executed.

   Remember that different systems will have different configurations, so you might need to do a little digging to find your personal path statement(s).

2. `cp .bash_profile`
   `↪ .bash_profile_backup`

   Make a backup of the file containing the path statement so that you can recover if you make mistakes. See Chapter 2 if you need more information on copying files.

3. `vi .bash_profile`

   Use your favorite editor to open up the file in which you'll be changing the path.

4. `PATH=$PATH:$HOME/scripts`

   Add a new path statement immediately below the last path statement. In this example, **PATH** is set to its current value (**$PATH**) plus the directory (**$HOME/scripts**) you wish to append to your path Ⓐ.

5. Save the file and exit from your editor.

   Refer to Chapter 4 for help if you need it.

6. `su - yourid`

   As you learned back in Chapter 3, this command starts a new login shell so you can test your changes before logging out.

**7. echo $PATH**

Display the current path environment variable. This should include the addition you just made. It's there, right? (See **Code Listing 8.10**.)

**TIP** If you look through the path statements in your various configuration files, you might find a path statement that includes just a . (dot). For example, you might see something like PATH=/usr/bin:/usr/ local/bin:.:. The . adds your current directory, whatever it might be, to your path. Keep in mind, though, that it's often safer not to have the current directory in the path so you don't unintentionally run a program that isn't the one you expect to run (because there's an executable file by the same name in your current directory).

**TIP** You can use grep to make it easy to find the configuration files that set your path. grep PATH ~/.bash* ~/.profile is a good way to start, and grep PATH /etc/* is another goodie.

**TIP** Your system configuration files will be much less confusing later on if you keep all related changes together. Therefore, you should keep the path statements together rather than just plug an entirely random PATH statement into your configuration files.

**Code Listing 8.10** Using **echo**, you can verify that your new path statement exists.

```
[ejr@hobbes ejr]$ echo $PATH
/bin:/usr/bin:/usr/local/bin:/usr/bin/X11:
→ /usr/X11R6/bin:/usr/local/games:
→ /home/ejr/bin
[ejr@hobbes ejr]$
```

**A** Edit your **bash** prompt statement in the editor of your choice.

# Changing Your bash Prompt

Depending on your Unix system, by default you might see a dollar sign (**$**) as your prompt, or perhaps a dollar sign and date, or other information as outlined in the "Setting Your **bash** Prompt Promptly" sidebar. You can set your prompt to include information that's handy for you.

You have a couple of prompts in **bash**:

- The main prompt that you usually think of as the shell prompt. This prompt is called **PS1**.

- A secondary prompt that you see when the system requires additional information to complete a command. Logically, this prompt is called **PS2**.

You can change either of these prompts using the following steps. You start by finding your prompt statement (**Code Listing 8.11**), then modifying it in your editor **A**.

**Code Listing 8.11** Use **grep** to search your configuration files for a prompt statement.

```
[ejr@hobbes ejr]$ grep PS1 ~/.bash* ~/.bashrc /etc/bashrc
/home/ejr/.bashrc:PS1='\u \d $ '
/etc/bashrc:PS1='[\u@\h \W]$ '
[ejr@hobbes ejr]$
```

## To change your bash prompt:

1. **grep PS1 ~/.bash* ~/.bashrc**
   **→ /etc/bashrc**

   To begin, search through the configuration files located in your home directory and in the **/etc** directory to find your prompt statement. It'll look something like **PS1="$ " or PS1="[\u@\h \W]$ "**, as shown in Code Listing 8.11.

   The "Setting Your **bash** Prompt Promptly" sidebar will help translate these symbols.

2. **vi ~/.bashrc**

   Because the files with the prompt setting are in the systemwide **/etc** directory, we cannot change them directly, so we have to make the changes to **.bashrc** or a different configuration file in our home directory.

3. **PS1="\u \d $ "**

   For example, we often set our prompt to include the userid (because we have enough different accounts on different systems that we need a reminder) and the date (because we're scattered). We're adding this at the end of the file so it will take precedence over the **PS1** setting in the **/etc/bashrc** file that is referenced from the **~/.bashrc** file Ⓐ.

4. Save the file and exit from the editor.

5. **su - ejr**

   Log in again with your changed prompt to try it out.

## Setting Your bash Prompt Promptly

You can set your prompt to contain all sorts of information. The following list shows you what code to use to add certain kinds of information to your prompt (and it will help you translate the code in your existing prompt):

- **\u** shows the userid of the current user—that's you.

- **\w** shows the current working directory with a path, using a ~ notation within your home directory.

- **\W** shows the current directory without the path.

- **\t** shows the time.

- **\d** shows the date.

- **\n** forces a new line, making the prompt appear split on two lines.

- **\h** shows the host name of the computer.

**TIP** Note the trailing space in the prompt code: PS1="\u \d $ ". This space can help make it easier to use the prompt because it keeps your commands from bumping into your prompt.

**TIP** Consider changing your PS1 environment variable at the shell prompt, as discussed in Chapter 3, before you make changes in your configuration files. That way, you can try out a modified shell prompt before you change it in your configuration files.

**A** Setting aliases can keep you from typing long names and code.

## Good Aliases to Set

Here are a few aliases you might find worthwhile to set on your system:

- **alias rm="rm -i"** causes the system to prompt you about all deletions.
- **alias quit="logout"** lets you use **quit** as a synonym for **logout**.
- **alias homepage="links http:// www.raycomm.com/"** lets you use **homepage** to start the links browser and connect to the Raycomm home page (substitute your home page as necessary).

Or, if you're coming from a DOS background, you might find the following aliases handy:

- **alias dir="ls -l"** lets you use **dir** to list files.
- **alias copy="cp"** lets you use **copy** to copy files.
- **alias rename="mv"** lets you use **rename** to move or rename files.
- **alias md="mkdir"** lets you use **md** to make a directory.
- **alias rd="rmdir"** lets you use **rd** to remove a directory.

# Setting Aliases with alias

Aliases are nicknames of sorts that you use to enter commands more easily. For example, if you frequently use the command **mail -s "Lunch today?" deb < .signature**, you could set an alias for this command and call it **lunch**. Then, in the future, all you have to do is type in **lunch**, and the result is the same as if you had typed in the longer command.

## To set an alias with alias:

1. Choose the appropriate file to edit, depending on which shell you're using:
   - **zsh** users should use **~/.zshrc**
   - **bash** users should use **~/.bashrc**

   If you don't have the appropriate file, you're welcome to use a different configuration file. Many people store all their aliases in a separate **.alias** file and update their standard configurations with a line that references their new **.alias** file.

2. **vi .bashrc**

   Edit the configuration file you've selected.

3. **alias quit="logout"**

   Type **alias** followed by the term you want to use as the alias, =, and the command for which you're making an alias (in quotes). Here, we're setting the word **quit** as an alias for the system command **logout**, so we can type **quit** instead of **logout** **A**.

   *continues on next page*

4. Add as many other aliases as you want.

   See the sidebar "Good Aliases to Set" for more ideas.

5. Save the file and exit from the editor.

   See Chapter 4 for details about saving and exiting in **vi**, **pico**, and **nano**.

6. `su - yourid`

   Start a new login shell to test out the alias.

7. `alias`

   Type **alias** at the shell prompt for a listing of all the aliases you have defined (**Code Listing 8.12**).

**TIP** You can put aliases in other files, but it's customary to put them in the `.bashrc` file (for bash) or the `.zshrc` file (for zsh) so they'll be set automatically when you log in, rather than having to be manually set.

**TIP** You can also issue `alias` commands from the shell prompt to set aliases for the current session.

**TIP** Enter `alias` by itself to see the currently defined aliases.

**TIP** Be sure to make a backup copy of any configuration files you plan to change before you change them. That way, if you mess up, you still have the original file to work with.

**Code Listing 8.12** Type **alias** at the shell prompt to see a list of aliases you've set.

```
example> alias
clr      clear
cls      clear
copy     cp -i
del      rm -i
delete   rm -i
dir      ls -alg
home     cd ~
ls       ls -F
md       mkdir
move     mv -i
pwd      echo $cwd
type     more
example>
```

# 9

# Running Scripts and Programs

Throughout this book, you've been running scripts and programs by typing commands and pressing Enter. The commands zoom along to the Unix or Linux system, which responds by obediently doing whatever the command or script dictates. In doing this, you run the commands and scripts—called *jobs* in this context—right then and there.

You can also run jobs at specified times; run them on a schedule you set up; or start, stop, or delete them as you choose. Plus, you can find out when they are scheduled to run, time how long they take, or monitor them as they run. Sound cool? Great! Let's take a look.

## In This Chapter

# Running a Command

Throughout this book, you've been practicing running a single command. Unix and Linux don't really care if you're running a built-in command that came with the system, a program you installed later, or a script your best friend wrote—it's all the same to the system. **Code Listing 9.1** shows some options for running a command.

## To run a command:

`ls`

At the shell prompt, type the command and press ⎡Enter⎤.

## To run a specific command:

**/home/jdoe/scripts/ls**

It's certainly possible that you would want to write a script that would list the files in your directory in a special way—for example, a script to list the files and to save the listing into a new file for later reference. (You might name it something else but could certainly call it **ls** if you want to.) To run the specific script, enter the whole path to the script (so Unix or Linux doesn't just run the first one it finds in your path). See Chapter 8 for more about path statements.

**TIP** You can combine commands on the same line, as you've seen earlier in this book. Just use a ; to separate the commands, and you're set. For example, you could do `ls`; `pwd` to list files and show the current directory.

**TIP** If you use && to combine commands, the system will run both in sequence but run the second only if the first succeeds. For example, you could use `mv todolist todolist.done && touch todolist` to move your to-do list to a different file and create a new to-do list. If the first command fails (for example, because you don't have permission to create a new file), the second command won't run.

**Code Listing 9.1** To run a script, command, or program, just enter the name or the path and the name at the shell prompt.

```
[jdoe@frazz Project]$ ls
keep keeper.jpg kept kidder.txt kiddo kidnews kidneypie kids kidupdate
[jdoe@frazz Project]$ /bin/ls
keep keeper.jpg kept kidder.txt kiddo kidnews kidneypie kids kidupdate
[jdoe@frazz Project]$ /home/jdoe/scripts/ls
keep keeper.jpg kept kidder.txt kiddo kidnews kidneypie kids kidupdate
You listed these files.
[jdoe@frazz Project]$ ls ; pwd
keep keeper.jpg kept kidder.txt kiddo kidnews kidneypie kids kidupdate
/home/jdoe/Project
[jdoe@frazz Project]$
```

```
# minute (m), hour (h), day of month (dom), month (mon),
# and day of week (dow) or use '*' in these fields (for 'any').#
# Notice that tasks will be started based on the cron's system
# daemon's notion of time and timezones.
#
# Output of the crontab jobs (including errors) is sent through
# email to the user the crontab file belongs to (unless redirected).
#
# For example, you can run a backup of all your user accounts
# at 5 a.m every week with:
# 0 5 * * 1 tar -zcf /var/backups/home.tgz /home/
#
# For more information see the manual pages of crontab(5) and cron(8)
#


# m h  dom mon dow   command
0 0 * * * /home/unixvqs/bin/backup-script
0 0 1,15 * * mail ejray@raycomm.com -s "Take Backups to Offsite Archive < /home/
unixvqs/.signature

"crontab.SwpBX5/crontab" 29L, 1834C written
```

**A** To schedule a onetime job, all you have to do is specify the time and the job to run.

# Scheduling Onetime Jobs with at

Occasionally, you may need to schedule jobs to run one time, at a time you designate. For example, you could schedule an email message to yourself, reminding you to attend a staff meeting. Or, you could schedule a meeting reminder for your co-workers that includes a meeting agenda. You can schedule these and other onetime jobs using **at**, which lets you designate a time at which a job (or jobs) should run. **A** demonstrates scheduling an email about that all-important staff meeting.

## To schedule a onetime job with at:

1. **at 12:01 1 Jan 2015**

   To begin, specify when you want the job to run, using **at** plus a time statement **A**. In this example, we specify a time, date, month, and year, although you can create a variety of other time statements, like these:

   ▸ at noon tomorrow

   ▸ at 01/01/2015

   ▸ at 3:42am

   ▸ at now + 3 weeks

   ▸ at teatime

   Yes, teatime is a valid option. It's at 4 p.m., by the way.

2. **mail -s "Staff Meeting at 8:30am"**
   **→ ejr < ~/agenda**

   Specify the job. In this case, it sends an email to the user (**ejr**), specifies the subject "Staff Meeting at 8:30am," and sends the contents of the file named **agenda**. See Chapter 11 for the full scoop on using **mail**.

   *continues on next page*

**3.** `Ctrl`+`D`

Indicate that you've finished issuing commands.

## To schedule sequential onetime jobs with at:

**1.** `at midnight`

Specify when you want the sequential jobs to run, using **at** plus a time statement (**Code Listing 9.2**). You can use a variety of time statements, as shown in the previous example.

**2.** `tar -icf ~/bigdog.tar`
`→ ~/HereKittyKitty`

Enter the first job you want to run. This job collects all the files from the directory named **~/HereKittyKitty** into a single file named **~/bigdog.tar**. Chapter 13 will tell you more about archiving with **tar**.

**3.** `gzip ~/bigdog.tar`

Enter the next job to run. This compresses the **~/bigdog.tar** file, making it easier to store and email.

**4.** `mutt -a bigdog.tar.gz -s "Read this`
`→ by lunch time" deb < /dev/null`

Specify the next job in the sequence. Here, we're using **mutt**'s command-line mail options to attach a file, specify a subject, and mail the whole shebang to Deb. See Chapter 11 for more on emailing with **mutt**.

**5.** `Ctrl`+`D`

Ta-daaaa! Use this key combination to finish the sequence.

**Code Listing 9.2** To schedule sequential onetime jobs, just specify the time and the jobs in the order you want them to run.

```
[ejr@hobbes ejr]$ at midnight
at> tar -icf ~/bigdog.tar ~/HereKittyKitty
at> gzip ~/bigdog.tar
at> mutt -a bigdog.tar.gz -s "Read this
→ by lunch time" deb < /dev/null
at>
at> <EOT>
warning: commands will be executed using
→ /bin/sh
job 12 at 2015-08-28 00:00
[ejr@hobbes ejr]$
```

**Code Listing 9.3** Delete scheduled jobs by specifying the job number.

```
[ejr@hobbes ejr]$ atq
4       2015-08-28 12:01 a
9       2016-01-01 12:01 a
13      2015-08-27 16:00 a
12      2016-08-28 00:00 a
[ejr@hobbes ejr]$ atrm 12
[ejr@hobbes ejr]$ atq
4       2015-08-28 12:01 a
9       2016-01-01 12:01 a
13      2015-08-27 16:00 a
[ejr@hobbes ejr]$
```

## To delete a scheduled job:

1. **atq**

   For starters, show the list of jobs waiting in the **at** queue with **atq** (**Code Listing 9.3**). The second column, which shows the scheduled time, should jog your memory about which job is which. The first column, which specifies the job number for each job, lets you identify which job to delete in the next step.

2. **atrm 12**

   Remove the queued job by typing **atrm** and the job number—in this case, job number 12.

**TIP** **atq** is also handy for reviewing jobs that you've scheduled.

**TIP** Use **at** to send yourself reminders.

**TIP** If you have a long list of commands that you want to run periodically, consider making them into a brief shell script, then using **at** to run the shell script. It's less work in the long run, and you don't have to concentrate on getting the commands just right as you do when telling **at** what to do. See Chapter 10 for the full scoop on shell scripts.

**TIP** Different flavors of Unix and Linux sometimes present the information from **at** differently. You get all the information you need, but it may be arranged somewhat differently.

# Scheduling Regularly Occurring Jobs with cron

Suppose you want to send yourself a reminder message just before you go home at the end of each day—say, a reminder to turn off the coffeepot. Or, suppose you want to make a backup copy of specific files each week. You can do this by using the **crontab** command to schedule commands or scripts to run regularly at times you specify. In doing so, you can schedule tasks to occur on specific days at specific times and know that the jobs will happen unattended .

**A** The **cron** file, which is where you specify the **cron** job, opens in your default editor. If you've previously specified **cron** jobs, they'll show up in the editor.

## What Are Those Funky Numbers?

When entering a **cron** job, you specify

- Minutes (0–59)
- Hours (0–23)
- Day of the month (1–31)
- Month (1–12)
- Day of the week (0–6, with Sunday as 0)

If you replace the number with a **\***, **cron** will match all possible values, so, if a job is scheduled for

- **1 \* \* \* \***, it will happen at one minute after every hour
- **15 3 \* \* \***, it will happen at 3:15 a.m. every day
- **59 23 31 \* \***, it will happen at 11:59 p.m., seven times a year (once in each of the months with a 31st)
- **0 12 \* \* 0**, it will happen at noon on Sundays

You can use a comma to separate multiple values. For example, if you want something to happen on the hour and half-hour during December, you might use **0,30 \* \* 12 \***.

Use a hyphen (-) to indicate a range. For example, to schedule something for every hour from 9 a.m. to 5 p.m. every day, use **0 9-17 \* \* \***.

**Code Listing 9.4** This job reminds **ejray** to go home every day. The message toward the end indicates that the **cron** job has been successfully entered.

```
55 16 * * 1-5 mail -s "Go Home Now!"
→ ejray@raycomm.com < /dev/null
~
~
~
~
~
~
~
~
~
~
~
~
~
~
~
~
~
~
~
~
"/tmp/crontab.16206" 3 lines, 192 characters
→ written
crontab: installing new crontab
[ejr@hobbes ejr]$
```

**TIP** When scheduling **cron** jobs, you need to specify full and absolute paths to the files—that is, specify /home/ejray/file rather than file. Also, if you write a shell script and reference it in a **cron** job, you'll need to specify paths in the shell script as well. **cron** doesn't check out your personal environment variable settings when it runs, so the full path name is essential.

**TIP** Use **crontab -l** to display a listing of your **cron** jobs.

## To schedule a regularly occurring job with cron:

1. **crontab -e**

   At the shell prompt, type **crontab**, followed by the **-e** flag, which lets you edit your **cron** file. As shown in Ⓐ, your **cron** file will appear in your default editor. It's likely to be empty (if you haven't set up **cron** jobs before), but you might have some content in there.

2. **55 16 * * 1-5 mail -s "Go home now!"**
   **→ ejray@raycomm.com**

   On the first line of the **cron** file, enter values for minutes, hours, day of the month, month, and day of the week, then the command you want to run. See the "What Are Those Funky Numbers?" sidebar for more details about specifying times and days. In this example, we're sending an email to **ejray** every weekday at 4:55 p.m. reminding him to go home.

3. Save and close the file.

   Chapter 4 will give you a quick reminder about saving and closing with **pico** and **vi**.

   If you set the times and dates correctly (that is, if you didn't accidentally set them to happen in the 59th hour of the day or whatever), you'll see a message like the one near the end of **Code Listing 9.4**, confirming that you're all set. (You'll get an appropriate error message if you scheduled something to happen at 55 hours, 12 minutes, on the ninth day of the week.)

# Suspending Jobs

Suppose you've just started a job that requires no input from you—say, downloading multiple files with **ftp**—and you suddenly realize that you've got to finish something else right now. Instead of waiting for the files to download or stopping the job completely, you can instead just suspend the job and resume it later (**Code Listing 9.5**). In doing so, you can make the Unix system work your way—that is, you don't lose the progress you've made toward getting the job done, and you can do the other stuff you need to do as well.

## To suspend a job:

Ctrl + Z

While the job is running, press these keys to suspend the process (Code Listing 9.5). Ctrl + Z doesn't actually terminate the process; it pauses the job in much the same way that pressing the Pause button on your iPod pauses the song.

**TIP** After you've suspended a job, you can restart it in the background using bg, restart it in the foreground using fg, check on its status using jobs, or delete it completely using kill. Refer to the appropriate sections in this chapter for details on using these commands. (Note that if the suspended job requires input from you, as the FTP example above does, then it will be immediately re-suspended if you try to restart it in the background.)

**TIP** You can suspend as many jobs at a time as you want. Just use Ctrl + Z to do so, then use jobs to check the status of each suspended job if you need to.

**TIP** Because it's pretty easy to forget that you've suspended a job, most shells will remind you that "there are stopped jobs" when you try to log out of the system. You should either resume the job or kill it before you log out. Yes, the Unix system uses the terms "stopped jobs" and "suspended jobs" more or less interchangeably.

**Code Listing 9.5** Suspending jobs is just like pushing the Pause button on your favorite music device.

```
[ejr@hobbes ejr]$ ftp calvin.raycomm.com
Connected to calvin.raycomm.com.
220 calvin Microsoft FTP Service (Version 2.0).
Name (calvin.raycomm.com:ejr): anonymous
331 Anonymous access allowed, send identity (e-mail name) as password.
Password:
230 Anonymous user logged in.
Remote system type is Windows_NT.
ftp>
[1]+ Stopped     ftp calvin.raycomm.com
[ejr@hobbes ejr]$
```

# Checking Job Status with jobs

Occasionally, you may have multiple jobs running or suspended and need a quick update about the jobs' status. Using **jobs**, you can find out whether a job is running, stopped, or waiting for input, as shown in **Code Listing 9.6**.

## To check job status with jobs:

**jobs**

At the shell prompt, type **jobs**. You'll see a list of the current jobs (that is, processes that you've suspended or otherwise controlled) either running or stopped, as shown in Code Listing 9.6. Using the job numbers on the left, you can choose to run the jobs in the background or foreground, to resume them, or to kill the jobs, as described in the next few sections in this chapter.

**TIP** Depending on your shell, you can often kill jobs with kill followed by a % and the job number or command name—for example, you could kill the ftp job in Code Listing 9.6 with kill %ftp or kill %1. See "Deleting Processes with kill" later in this chapter for more on killing jobs.

Code Listing 9.6 Viewing jobs lets you know which jobs you have suspended and their statuses.

```
[ejr@hobbes ejr]$ jobs
[1]- Running    ftp calvin.raycomm.com &
[2]+ Stopped    (tty input)    sh
[3] Stopped     (signal)       links http://www.raycomm.com/
[ejr@hobbes ejr]$
```

# Running Jobs in the Background with bg

If you're running a job that doesn't require input from you, consider running it in the background using **bg** (Code Listing 9.7). In doing so, you can keep the program running while working on other Unix activities at the same time.

## To run jobs in the background with bg:

1. **jobs**

   At the shell prompt, type **jobs** to see the list of all jobs, running or stopped. Note the job numbers on the left.

2. **bg %3**

   Type **bg** followed by **%** and the number of the job you want to run in the background (Code Listing 9.7).

**TIP** If you want to put the most recently suspended job into the background, just type **bg** (without the number) at the prompt.

**TIP** You can also put jobs directly into the background without first suspending them. Just type the command to run and **&** (as in **bigdog &**). The **&** moves the job directly into the background.

Code Listing 9.7 Restarting suspended jobs in the background lets you do two things—or more—at once. To move a job to the background, just type **bg** followed by **%** and the job number.

```
[ejr@hobbes ejr]$ jobs
[3]- lynx http://www.raycomm.com/ & calvin.raycomm.com
[2]  Stopped   (tty input)    ssh
[3]  Stopped   (signal)       links http://www.raycomm.com/
[4]+ Stopped    man ssh
[ejr@hobbes ejr]$ bg %3
[3]- lynx http://www.raycomm.com/ &
[ejr@hobbes ejr]$
```

**Code Listing 9.8** Typing **fg** plus the job number brings that job into the foreground. When you bring suspended jobs into the foreground, you'll sometimes see the job activities onscreen. At other times, you'll see only a prompt and you'll need to summon help to see anything of the program.

```
[ejr@hobbes ejr]$ jobs
[1]+ Stopped    ftp ftp.example.com
[ejr@hobbes ejr]$ fg %1
ftp ftp.cdrom.com
```

# Running Jobs in the Foreground with fg

When you're ready to resume a suspended or backgrounded job, you can do so using **fg**. Remember, when you suspend a job, what you're doing is moving the job into limbo. **fg** just moves the job into the foreground again (**Code Listing 9.8**), so you can see, for example, what it's doing or provide input.

## To run jobs in the foreground with fg:

1. **jobs**

    At the shell prompt, type **jobs** to list all stopped or running jobs. Note the job numbers at the left.

2. **fg %1**

    Enter **fg** followed by the number of the job that you want to bring back into the foreground (Code Listing 9.8).

    Depending on the job you're bringing back into the foreground, you may or may not get to see the job running onscreen. Sometimes you'll be plunked back into the job and be able to enter information as prompted. Other times, you'll just see the prompt for the program you returned to the foreground. If this is the case, try typing **?** (for help), which often forces the program to display something onscreen and refresh the display.

**TIP** You can bring the last suspended job into the foreground by typing **fg** (with no job number) at the shell prompt.

# Controlling Job Priority with nice

Suppose you need to process an enormous file from the Internet that would take practically all afternoon. By processing it, you would hog system resources and make the system response time much slower for other users. OK, bad example. Suppose your co-worker needs to process an enormous file and would hog system resources all afternoon. You'd hope that she'd have the courtesy to not tie up system resources that you need to use.

Fortunately, she can, using **nice**, which lets her control job priority. As **Code Listing 9.9** shows, you rank your job's priority using numbers from 1 to 19, with 1 being somewhat nice (higher priority) and 19 being fabulously nice (lower priority). The Unix system uses the number you provide to determine how much attention to devote to the job.

## To control job order with nice:

### nice -n 19 slowscript

At the shell prompt, type **nice**, the **-n** flag followed by the appropriate adjustment (**19**, here), and the name of the program or script to run (Code Listing 9.9). In this example, **slowscript** is run with the lowest priority possible.

Code Listing 9.9 By using **nice** plus an adjustment, you can let Unix determine how hard to work on your job.

```
[ejr@hobbes ejr]$ nice -n 19 slowscript
```

**TIP** To find out how nice you need to be, you might check out how many processes (and which kinds) are currently running on the Unix system. You can do this using ps, as described later in this chapter.

**TIP** You could use nice and run a job in the background—for example, use nice -n 12 funscript & to run funscript in the background with a niceness level of 12.

**TIP** You can just type nice plus the job name (as in nice sortaslow). Doing so will automatically specify 10 as the niceness level (the default setting).

**TIP** If you are the system administrator and logged in as root, you can use negative numbers (down to –20) with nice to increase the priority (nice -n -16 priorityjob).

**TIP** Use renice to change the niceness of a running job. For example, use renice -n 18 2958 (the job number). If you're the system administrator, you can increase or decrease the niceness of any job; if you're a peon—whoops, we mean a regular computer user at your company—you can only decrease the priority of your own jobs, not increase it. In a pinch, you could ask your system administrator to increase the priority of your job.

```
[ejr@hobbes running]$ time slowscript
real    0m0.003s
user    0m0.000s
sys     0m0.003s
 [ejr@hobbes running]$ time ls
bigdog.tar.gz   slowscript   testing.gif
real    0m0.004s
user    0m0.001s
sys     0m0.002s
 [ejr@hobbes running]$ time nice -19 ls
bigdog.tar.gz   slowscript   testing.gif
real    0m0.003s
user    0m0.003s
sys     0m0.006s
 [ejr@hobbes running]$ time -p nice -n 19 ls
foo
real    0m0.003s
user    0m0.004s
sys     0m0.003s
 [ejr@hobbes running]$
```

# Timing Jobs with time

Sometimes, you might want to know how long a job takes to complete. You can do so using the **time** command, which times jobs according to the built-in Unix timer. As **Code Listing 9.10** shows, all you have to do is enter **time** followed by the command you want to time.

## To time a job using time:

**time slowscript**

At the shell prompt, type **time** followed by the complete command. After the command finishes, the system will tell you how long it took, as shown in Code Listing 9.10.

## To compare job times with time:

1. **time ls /usr**

   At the shell prompt, type **time** followed by a job (here, **ls**).

2. **time nice -n 19 ls /usr**

   Then, type **time** followed by another job. In this example, we're comparing a regular **ls** command to a **nice ls** command. As Code Listing 9.10 shows, the elapsed time for the **nice ls** command was considerably longer than for the regular **ls** command.

**TIP** Keep in mind that the time a job takes to run may vary according to the system's current load or capacity. For example, a job might take less time to run at 2 a.m., when few people are using the Unix system, compared with 2 p.m., when many more people are using the system.

**TIP** Different systems produce slightly different `time` outputs. On some systems, you'll get real (clock) time, user time, and system time. *Real time* is how many seconds on the clock elapsed while the program was running, while *user* and *system time* both refer to different measures of how long it took the system to run the job. On other systems, you might get a ton of supplemental information that looks like garbage, as shown in Code Listing 9.11, but the gist of the information is the same.

**TIP** In the case of the `ls` example, you're really not concerned with either the output or the errors—just the time—so you can creatively dispense with all of it. Try `time ls /usr > /dev/null 2>&1` to send standard output to `/dev/null` (the bitbucket) and send error messages to standard output (and thence to the bitbucket). See Chapter 16 for details.

**TIP** Try `time -p` to get a more human-readable output.

Code Listing 9.11 `time` output varies from system to system. Here, we get a bunch of garbage to decipher in addition to the time information.

```
$ time slowscript
0.07user 0.05system 0:50.13elapsed 0%CPU (0avgtext+0avgdata 0maxresident)k
0inputs+0outputs (219major+59minor)pagefaults 0swaps
$
```

Code Listing 9.12 **Code Listing 9.12** Using **ps**, you can find out what processes are currently running.

```
[jdoe@frazz jdoe]$ ps
  PID TTY        TIME CMD
21016 pts/22   00:00:00 bash
21707 pts/22   00:00:00 ps
[jdoe@frazz jdoe]$ ps -a
  PID TTY        TIME CMD
21407 pts/3    00:00:00 su
21411 pts/3    00:00:00 bash
21441 pts/3    00:00:00 su
21444 pts/3    00:00:00 bash
19274 pts/11   00:00:05 xterm
23357 pts/12   00:00:04 xterm
13369 pts/5    00:00:00 zsh
23815 pts/9    00:00:00 su
23818 pts/9    00:00:00 bash
23878 pts/9    00:00:00 csh
23942 pts/9    00:00:01 ssh
23972 pts/18   00:00:00 su
23975 pts/18   00:00:00 bash
24103 pts/5    00:00:00 ssh
 4658 pts/15   00:00:11 ssh
24318 pts/8    00:00:01 xterm
29188 pts/4    00:00:00 rxvt-2.7.9
29368 pts/4    00:00:00 rxvt
29440 pts/8    00:00:00 vi
23883 pts/20   00:00:02 xterm
27257 pts/16   00:00:01 ssh
 6004 pts/20   00:00:00 xterm
20531 pts/20   00:00:02 xterm
21013 pts/22   00:00:00 su
21016 pts/22   00:00:00 bash
21708 pts/22   00:00:00 ps
[jdoe@frazz jdoe]$
```

# Finding Out What Processes Are Running with ps

The jobs that we've been talking about so far are actually types of processes. *Processes* are programs, scripts, or commands—including anything you do in the Unix or Linux system. All jobs are processes, but not all processes are jobs.

Occasionally, you may want to find out what processes are running on the system. You can do this using **ps**, as shown in **Code Listing 9.12**.

## To find out what processes are running with ps:

**ps**

At the shell prompt, type **ps** to see the list of the current processes that you're running in your current shell, including processes for your current shell, as well as any other jobs (Code Listing 9.12).

The exact information you see will vary from system to system. In general, though, you'll find the *PID* (process identification) number at the far left and the process name at the right.

**TIP** You can find out what processes other people are running by typing ps -a at the shell prompt, and you can find out what processes the system is running (also called *daemons*) with ps -ax. The ps -ef variant is usually pretty useful for us.

**TIP** You can often, depending on the system, get a broader look at currently running processes by typing ps -a f (that's a -a, a space, and f). The f flag indicates "forest" view, which lets you see not only the processes, but also how they relate to each other, as shown in Code Listing 9.13.

**TIP** The results ps offers vary greatly depending on the Unix flavor you're using. Type man ps at the shell prompt to find out more about your specific ps capabilities.

Code Listing 9.13 The forest view gives you a broader look at running processes.

```
$ ps -a f
 PID TTY STAT  TIME COMMAND
15043 p0 S     0:00 /bin/login -h calvin raycomm.com -p
15044 p0 S     0:01   \_ -bash
16344 p0 T N   0:00         \_ sh ./slowscript
16345 p0 T N   0:00         | \_ sleep 50
16449 p0 R     0:00         \_ ps f
15911 p1 S     0:00 /bin/login -h calvin raycomm.com -p
15914 p1 S     0:01   \_ -bash
16216 p1 T     0:00.        \_ ssh
16217 p1 T     0:00         \_ links http://www.raycomm.com/
16267 p1 T     0:00         \_ man ssh
16268 p1 T     0:00             \_ sh -c (cd /usr/man ; (echo -e ".pl 1100i"; cat /
16269 p1 T     0:00                 \_ sh -c (cd /usr/man ; (echo -e ".pl 1100i"; c
16270 p1 T     0:00                     \_ sh -c (cd /usr/man ; (echo -e ".pl 1100i
16272 p1 T     0:00                     | \_ cat /usr/man/man1/ssh.1
16271 p1 T     0:00                     \_ /usr/bin/gtbl
16273 p1 T     0:00                     \_ sh -c (cd /usr/man ; (echo -e ".pl 1100i
$
```

# Deleting Processes with `kill`

In addition to suspending jobs and running them in the foreground and background, you can also choose to just delete them completely. For example, you might realize midway through a job that you goofed and need to redo it. Or perhaps you have accessed and suspended a `man` page and no longer need to reference it.

Using `kill`, you can delete essentially any process running or suspended on the Unix system. As **Code Listing 9.14** shows, you delete a process by first listing the processes, then using the `kill` command.

**Code Listing 9.14** Using `kill` plus the PID number, you can delete practically any process running or suspended on the system, given the right permissions.

```
$ ps -a f
 PID TTY STAT TIME  COMMAND
15911 p1 S    0:00 /bin/login -h calvin raycomm.com -p
15914 p1 S    0:01 \_ -bash
16216 p1 T    0:00 \_ ssh
16217 p1 T    0:00 \_ links
http://www.raycomm.com/
$ kill 16217
$ ps -a f
 PID TTY STAT TIME COMMAND
15911 p1 S    0:00 /bin/login -h calvin raycomm.com -p
15914 p1 S    0:01 \_ -bash
16216 p1 T    0:00 \_ ssh
```

## To kill a job with `kill`:

**1.** `jobs`

At the shell prompt, type **jobs**, then note the number or name of the job you want to kill.

**2.** `kill %ftp`

In most shells, you can kill jobs with `kill` followed by **%** and the job number or command name—for example, you could kill an **ftp** job with a job number of 1 using **`kill %ftp`** or **`kill %1`**. If your shell doesn't cooperate, read on.

## To delete a process with `kill`:

**1.** `ps`

At the shell prompt, type **ps** to see the list of all your current jobs (Code Listing 9.14). Note the PID number of the process you want to delete.

**2.** `kill 16217`

Type **kill** followed by the PID number of the job you're deleting.

**TIP** Occasionally, you'll use `kill` and find that the process just keeps going. Try `kill -9` followed by the PID number to delete the process. This is a last resort option, since it doesn't give the program any opportunity to close files or clean up before exiting.

**TIP** Be careful not to kill your current shell process, or you'll abruptly find your connection broken. Doing so would be like sawing off the branch you're sitting on.

**TIP** Many newer Unix systems allow you to use `pkill` to kill processes by name, not number. For example, you might use `pkill ftp` to kill a suspended FTP session.

**TIP** Now that you know about `kill -9`, you can search the Internet for "kill dash nine song monzy" and be privy to the inside jokes. Do note that the song is certainly not kid- or workplace-friendly, but it's the only song about obscure Unix commands that we know. Watch at your own risk.

# Writing Basic Scripts

So far in this book, you've been typing commands (or perhaps combining commands), pressing (Enter), then waiting for Unix to execute the command(s) you specified...and typing in commands, pressing (Enter). You get the idea, and you probably have tired fingers by now.

Using shell scripts, you can create a series of commands, save them as a single file, and then execute them any time you want—without having to re-create the commands or do all that tedious typing over and over again. For example, suppose you want to do a complex search-and-replace on all the **.html** files in your home directory. With a shell script, you can take the time to structure the commands just one time, save the commands as a single file, and then apply it to any directory at any time. You do the hard work one time, and then reuse the script any time you need to.

In this book we'll discuss creating scripts using the **bash** shell. Scripts can be written with any shell—and **zsh** and **bash** in particular are quite good for scripting. If you're writing scripts to use on any type of Unix or Linux, including old ones, you might want to consider using the Bourne shell (**/bin/sh**), but for the purposes of this book, that step for portability is probably not relevant.

Revisit Chapter 3, if needed, to learn more about **zsh** and **bash** shells.

In this chapter, we'll show you how to get started creating and using shell scripts, and will give you enough information to create your own scripts and apply them to your particular uses.

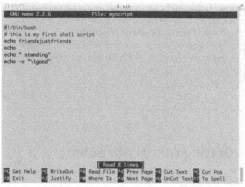

**A** You create shell scripts in an editor one line at a time.

# Creating a Shell Script

A *shell script* is nothing more than a list of commands for Unix to execute. To write a shell script, follow these steps:

1. Open your favorite editor and start a script file.

2. Start the shell script with **#!/bin/bash**.

3. Add the shell script code one line at a time. This code will look strangely famil-iar—it's similar to code you've already used in this book.

4. Save and close the file.

In the following steps, we'll show you how to try out this process by writing a script that prints three lines onscreen **A**. Yeah, we know—whoopee!—but you have to start somewhere, and you can apply the same principles to other shell scripts you create.

### To create a shell script:

1. **nano myscript**

   For starters, access the editor of your choice and start a new file. In this case, we name It **myscript**.

2. **#!/bin/bash**

   On the first line of the script, enter **#!/bin/bash**, which specifies the complete path to the shell that should run the script (**bash**, in this case).

3. **# this is my first shell script**

   On the next line, type a **#** (to indicate a comment), and then add any other notes you want to make. It's always a good idea to use extensive comments in your scripts to help you see what's going on. Remember, comments are for your reference only and won't show up onscreen or do anything.

   *continues on next page*

**4. echo friendsjustfriends**

On the next line of the script, type **echo** followed by the text you want to see onscreen. Here, **echo** tells Unix to display **friendsjustfriends** onscreen—a message just between friends.

**5. echo**

Add another line with **echo** and nothing else to display a blank line.

**6. echo " standing"**

Add another **echo** command. Note that if you use leading spaces or tabs, as we've done here, you must use quotes, as Ⓐ shows.

**7. echo -e "\tgood"**

Using the **-e** flag plus **\t**, you can insert a tab character. See "Getting Fancy with echo" for more **echo** options.

**8. Save and close your script.**

Check Chapter 4 if you need help saving a file and closing your editor.

**9. bash myscript**

Use **bash myscript** to run your new script. In doing so, you get good understanding (literally), as shown in **Code Listing 10.1**.

Ta-daaaaa! You just wrote your first shell script! (See the following section for more information and details on running scripts.)

**TIP** Unless you have some compelling need to use a different shell (for example, if you're using a zsh script because you are taking advantage of functions that exist only in zsh, or striving for a script that will run on antique Unix systems), just stick with bash for your scripts for now.

**Code Listing 10.1** Using **echo** options, you can get a good understanding—or, perhaps, a good understanding just between friends.

```
[unixvqs@LinuxMint scripting]$ sh myscript
friendsjustfriends
    standing
        good
```

## Getting Fancy with echo

In addition to the basic print-to-screen function that **echo** offers, you can also use these formatting flags with **echo -e** (the **-e** enables these special formatting characteristics):

- **\b** moves the cursor back one space.

- **\c** instructs echo not to print a new line after printing the text.

- **\f** forces the following text to appear on the next line at a specified horizontal location.

- **\n** forces the following text to appear on a new line.

- **\t** indents the following text output by one tab.

For example, **echo -e "\tGreetings! \c"** would move "Greetings!" one tab space to the right (as specified by the **\t**) and not insert a new line for any text following it (as specified by the **\c**).

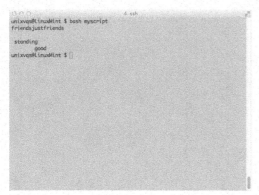

**A** Running a script is as easy as typing **bash** plus the filename of the script.

# Running a Shell Script

After you've created a script in your editor and saved the script file, your next step is to run it, which means to execute every command in the script in the order provided. (Yes, you did this in the previous section, but we'll expand on it here.) As **A** shows, you do this using the **bash** command (or the name of the shell you're using) followed by the name of the shell script you want to run.

## To run a script:

**bash myscript**

At the shell prompt, type **bash** (or the name of the shell, like **ksh** or **csh**, you want to run the script) followed by the name (or full path and name) of the script. In this case, you're really just telling **bash** to run and to use the list of commands in the **myscript** file. You'll see the results of the script—in this case, words appear onscreen, as shown in **A**.

**TIP** Note that in this example, you're explicitly telling Unix the name of the script to run (**myscript**). When you do so, the **#!/bin/bash** line at the top of the script in the previous section is technically superfluous. It's essential only when the script is executable, as in the following section.

# Making a Script Executable

In the previous section, we showed you that you can run a shell script by typing **bash** followed by the name of the shell script file. You can also make a script *executable*, which means that you can run it simply by typing the script name at the shell prompt (omitting the name of the shell). Doing so is handy because it allows you to use the script as conveniently as you'd use any other command. As **Code Listing 10.2** shows, you must set up a little before you can just execute the script.

1. **head -2 myscript**

   At the shell prompt, check to verify that your script does have the **#!/bin/bash** line at the top to specify the shell that runs it. Remember from Chapter 6 that **head -2** will list the top two lines of the file specified.

**Code Listing 10.2** After a little one-time preparation, you can run executable scripts by typing the script name at the shell prompt.

```
[unixvqs@LinuxMint scripting]$ head -2 myscript
#!/bin/bash
# This is my first shell script
[unixvqs@LinuxMint scripting]$ chmod u+x myscript
[unixvqs@LinuxMint scripting]$ pwd ; echo $PATH
/home /scripting
/usr/local/bin:/bin:/usr/bin:/usr/X11R6/ bin:/usr/local/games:home/ scripting
[unixvqs@LinuxMint scripting]$ myscript
friendsjustfriends
    standing
        good
[unixvqs@LinuxMint scripting]$
```

2. **chmod u+x myscript**

   Here, use the **chmod** command to give the user (that's you) execute permission. See the section in Chapter 5 called "Changing Permissions with **chmod**" for details on setting permissions.

3. **pwd ; echo $PATH**

   Display the name of your current directory and the full path, and verify that the current directory is in the path. The current directory (the one in which you just granted yourself execute permission) must be contained in the path; otherwise, the script will not be as easily executable from the shell prompt.

4. **myscript**

   At the shell prompt, type the name of the script. Assuming that your current directory is in the path, the script will run.

**TIP** Every time you open up a new script, check to verify that the first line is #!/bin/bash so the file will run correctly. Also, check the permissions and your path to make sure you can run the script from the shell prompt. (You'll almost always find it more convenient to use executable scripts than to specify the shell or path each time you want to run a script.)

**TIP** If the current directory isn't in the path (either explicitly or through a . notation, as in PATH=/usr/bin:.:), you'll have to take an additional step to execute the script. You could

- Add the current directory to the path with something like PATH=$PATH:/home/yourid/tempdir. Read more about this option in Chapter 8.

- Execute the script with ./myscript instead of just myscript.

- Move the script to a directory in the path.

# Getting a Head Start on Scripts with history

If you find yourself performing a particular process over and over again, consider making that process into a script. An easy way to create a script is to work from the session history, as shown in . Basically, all you have to do is complete the procedure one time, and then use the session history to help build the script for you.

## To get a head start on your script with history:

1. Go through the process that you want to include in the script.

   We'll wait.

2. Keep a rough count of the commands you issue.

   Don't worry about the exact number of commands you use, but have an idea as to whether it's 3, 30, or 300 commands.

3. **history 20 > standyou**

   When you've finished the process, type **history** followed by the approximate number of commands for your script. When estimating the number of commands, err on the high side, because it's easy to delete extra commands. Then, redirect the output to the desired filename, and you'll see your in-the-making script.

4. **vi standyou**

   Use the editor of your choice to edit your script file, deleting the initial line numbers and spaces and generally whipping that script into shape. See the section "Creating a Shell Script" earlier in this chapter for more details.

```
159  history
160  alpine
161  ./myscript
162  nano myscript
163  echo "Testing"
164  cd
165  cd /media/sf_Dropbox/UnixVQS_Revision/Examples/
166  cd scripting
167  history
168  man test
169  at 12:01 1 jan 2014
170  at 12:01 1 jan 2015
171  pwd
172  ls
173  cd ..
174  cd scripting
175  ls
176  which nano
177  history
178  history 20 > standyou

"standyou" 20 lines, 387 characters
```

**A** You can enter a series of commands and then use the code provided with **history** to help create a shell script.

**TIP** If you use **vi**, do a global search-and-replace to get rid of the line numbering (that **history** introduced) at the left—just use **:%s/^ *[0-9]* *//** (one space after the ^), and you're in business. See Chapter 4 for more about clever **vi** tricks.

```
#!/bin/bash
# this is my first shell script
echo -e "Greetings! \c"
echo -e "Say, you're looking mighty sharp today!\n"
echo -e "You were most recently working on `ls -1Fc ~/ | head -1`."




"myscript" 7 lines, 190 characters
```

 Embedding commands just requires an additional couple of lines in the script.

# Embedding Commands

Suppose you create a script that will automatically run when you log in each day. The script might, for example, print "Greetings!" onscreen and possibly deliver a cle(a)ver message: "Say, you're looking sharp today!" You could easily do this with the information you've learned so far in this chapter.

What would be handy here would be to add a line to the script that tells Unix to do all those things plus name the most recently used file—for those of you who need a reminder about what you were last working on. You could just use an **ls** command, but that would only list the filenames and not integrate the information with the rest of your morning greeting. Instead, a better (and more attractive) idea would be to bundle a couple of commands and use them with **echo**  to embed the information right into the greeting.

## To embed a command:

**1.** `vi myscript`

To begin, open **myscript** or another script in your favorite editor. Your script might look like Ⓐ, with the greeting onscreen.

**2.** `echo "You were most recently working`
   `→ on ‵ls -1Ft ~ | head -1‵."`

Type **echo** followed by the descriptive text you want to see. Then embed the **ls** command (`‵ls -1Fc ~/ | head -1‵`) within the descriptive text. Note that the embedded code begins and ends with ‵ (back ticks) before the **.** (dot).

The embedded command here lists just the most recently changed file or directory in the home directory. **1** provides for one entry per line, **F** formats the directory names with a **/** so we can tell whether we're working in a subdirectory or on a file, and **c** (or **t**) sorts by the modification date. We then pipe the output to **head -1**, which displays the top line of the file listings.

**3.** Save your script and exit the editor, and then try it out, as in **Code Listing 10.3**.

**TIP** You can embed dates into scripts, too. Try echo -e "Today is ‵date +%A‵" if you work so much that you forget what the day of the week is. See the sidebar "Using Clever Dates" for more date details.

**TIP** When you embed commands that are directory dependent—such as ls or find—be sure to specify the complete path. If you don't, you'll get paths relative to where the script is rather than relative to where you're running the script from.

**TIP** Embedded commands are useful in many ways. You can use them any time that you want to have one program act based on the output of another program, just as echo displays something based on the output of a program.

**Code Listing 10.3** The results of embedded commands can be impressive.

```
[unixvqs@LinuxMint scripting]$ myscript
Greetings! Say, you're looking mighty
→ sharp today!
You were most recently working on figlet.
[unixvqs@LinuxMint scripting]$
```

## Using Clever Dates

You can use the **date** command to deliver any date with any format. In general, use **date +"Today is %A"**, but you can use any or all of the following bits:

- **%d** includes the two-digit day of month.
- **%y** includes the two-digit year.
- **%Y** includes the four-digit year.
- **%m** includes the numeric month.
- **%b** includes an abbreviated month.
- **%B** includes the full month name.
- **%a** includes the abbreviated day of the week.
- **%A** includes the full day of the week.
- **%R** includes the time in hours and minutes.
- **%D** includes the date in month/date/year format.

Check the **man** pages for the remaining several dozen options.

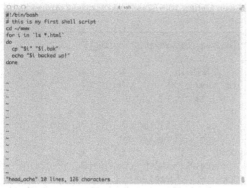

```
#!/bin/bash
# this is my first shell script
cd ~/www
for i in `ls *.html`
do
    cp "$i" "$i.bak"
    echo "$i backed up!"
done
```

"head_ache" 10 lines, 126 characters

**A** Using a loop with an embedded command, you can automatically apply a script to several files.

# Looping Your Scripts

Suppose you've created a script that you'd like to apply to several files. For example, say that at the end of each day you need to make backup copies of all **.html** files in your **www** directory. You could make a backup of each individual **.html** file, but that's a lot of work. An easier way would be to create a short script to copy a single **.html** file, and then *loop* (repeat) the script to apply to all **.html** files in your **www** directory **A**. You create one short script; Unix does the tedious work for you.

## To make a loop:

1. **vi head_ache**

   At the shell prompt, start your editor and open the script you want to loop. In this case, we're using **vi** and the **head_ache** file. (Of course, you could name the script **html_backup** or something mundane like that.)

2. **#!/bin/bash**

   Tell your Unix system which shell to use to run the shell script. In this example, we're telling it (with **#!**) to run the shell script with **/bin/bash**.

3. **cd ~/www**

   Make sure that you're in the directory in which the loop will take place. In this example, our shell script resides in our home directory, but the files to which the loop will apply reside in the **www** directory.

*continues on next page*

**4. `for i in `ls *.html``**

OK, don't panic. Read this as: "Look **for** items **in** the list of **.html** files." In this code, we're providing the output of the embedded command (```ls *.html```) to the **for** loop (the **.html** files), as shown in Ⓐ. The **-1** flag on the **ls** command, as mentioned in the previous section, forces a single list of output (which is ideal for script use) rather than several columns (which is easy to read onscreen but doesn't work well for scripts).

**5. do**

On the line immediately after the **for** statement, type **do**. This tells the Unix system that the following information will be the loop to apply.

**6. `cp "$i" "$i.bak"`**

Here, we copy (**cp**) the specified items (**$i**) to a backup file (**$i.bak**)—that is, one backup file per file copied. So, if you have 72 **.html** files to begin with, you'll end up with those original 72, plus 72 new backup files.

**7. `echo "$i backed up!"`**

Add **echo "$i backed up!"** so that the system displays onscreen what it has done.

**8. done**

On the next line, announce that you're done with the loop.

**9. Save it, make it executable, and try it out.**

This example script will make backup copies of all **.html** files in the **www** directory, as in **Code Listing 10.4**.

**Code Listing 10.4** This loop reports progress as it backs up each file.

```
[unixvqs@LinuxMint scripting]$
→ more head_ache
#! /bin/bash
cd ~/www
for i in `ls -1 *.html`
do
    cp "$i" "$i.bak"
    echo "$i backed up!"
done
[unixvqs@LinuxMint scripting]$ ./head_ache
above.html backed up!
file1.html backed up!
html.html backed up!
reference.html backed up!
temp.html backed up!
[unixvqs@LinuxMint scripting]$
```

**TIP** Loop instructions can be much more complex. For example, you could make a loop to spell-check each of the chapter files in the directory and report how many misspelled words there are in each file. To do that, use this line in the loop: echo -e "$i has \t `cat $i | spell | wc -l` misspelled words". Here again, just build the loop one step at a time.

**TIP** Loops are particularly handy for searching and replacing throughout multiple documents. For example, if you're the new webmaster and you want to replace the old webmaster's name at the bottom of all .html files with your name, you can do so using a loop with sed. Check out Chapter 6 for more information about sed.

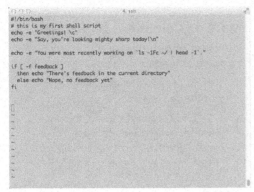

```
#!/bin/bash
# this is my first shell script
echo -e "Greetings! \c"
echo -e "Say, you're looking mighty sharp today!\n"

echo -e "You were most recently working on `ls -1Fc ~/ | head -1`."

if [ -f feedback ]
    then echo "There's feedback in the current directory"
    else echo "Nope, no feedback yet"
fi
```

**A** Using if-then conditional statements, you can let the computer determine whether something is true or not, and then act accordingly.

# Creating If-Then Statements

The basic principle of *if-then statements* is that if a certain condition is met, then one thing happens; if the condition is not met, then another thing happens. That is, if you walk into your office in the morning and you see your daily to-do list, then you sit down and work. If you walk into your office in the morning and you don't see your to-do list, then you get to lounge all day. Or something like that.

As **A** shows, you can create if-then statements using **if**, **then**, and **else** commands. When you set up these conditional statements, the computer then has to test the condition to determine whether it's true or false, and act accordingly. In the next example, we set up a fairly simple if-then conditional statement requiring the computer to test whether or not a file exists and tell us what it finds. Use the following steps to get started with if-then statements, and see the "More on Conditions for If-Then" sidebar in this section to learn how to expand your if-then statements.

## To write an if-then conditional statement:

1. `vi deef`

   To begin, access your editor and the script file. Here we're adapting an existing script (for feedback) in **vi**.

2. `if [ -f feedback ]`

   Start the loop with **if**, and then follow it with a conditional statement, in this case `[ -f feedback ]`, which checks for the existence of a file named **feedback** in the current directory. If that file exists, then the expression is true.

3. `then echo "There's feedback in the`
   `→ current directory"`

   On the line immediately after the **if** statement, enter the command to be carried out or message to be displayed if the **if** statement is true. In this example, a true **if** statement would result in "There's feedback in the current directory" being printed onscreen.

## More on Conditions for If-Then

Using the steps provided in this section, try some of these if-then possibilities:

- `[ -f filename ]` checks to see whether a file exists.

- `[ ! -f filename ]` checks to see whether a file does not exist. The **!** symbol (not) makes this test report "true" when the previous example would be "false."

- `[ -d name ]` checks to see whether **name** exists and is a directory.

- `[ first -nt second ]` checks to see whether the modification date of the first file or directory is newer than the second.

- `[ first -ot second ]` checks to see whether the modification date of the first file or directory is older than the second.

- `[ -n string ]` checks to see whether the string has a length greater than 0.

- `[ -z string ]` checks to see whether the string is 0 length.

- `[ string1 = string2 ]` checks to see whether the first string is equal to the second.

- `[ string1 != string2 ]` checks to see whether the first string is not equal to the second.

- `[ \( condition1 \) -a \`
  `( condition2 \) ]` checks to see whether both conditions are true (conditions can include other conditions).

- `[ \( condition1 \) -o \`
  `( condition2 \) ]` checks to see if either **condition1** or **condition2** is true.

Type **man test** for more information about creating conditional statements.

**4.** `else echo "Nope, no feedback yet"`

On the next line, use **else** followed by a statement specifying what should happen if the **if** statement is false. Here, we specify that "Nope, no feedback yet" will be printed onscreen if the **feedback** file is not found.

**5.** `fi`

Immediately after the **else** statement, announce that you're finished with **fi**.

**6.** Save the script and try it out.

In this example, the script will check to see if **feedback** exists and print a different message depending on what it finds (**Code Listing 10.5**).

You can specify any path to the file **feedback** from this example. Perhaps you want to specify **~/feedback** to check for feedback in your home directory, or **/export/shared/critical/projects/feedback**.

**Code Listing 10.5** The last line produced by the **feedback** script differs, depending on the files found.

```
[unixvqs@LinuxMint scripting]$ ./deef
Greetings! Say, you're looking mighty sharp today!
You were most recently working on scripting/.
Nope, no feedback yet
[unixvqs@LinuxMint scripting]$ touch feedback
[unixvqs@LinuxMint scripting]$ ./deef
Greetings! Say, you're looking mighty sharp today!
You were most recently working on scripting/.
There's feedback in the current directory
[unixvqs@LinuxMint scripting]$
```

# Accepting Command-Line Arguments in Your Scripts

Suppose that at the end of every month you need to send a progress report to your boss. You might set up a script to address an email message to your boss, provide an appropriate subject line, and send the file containing the progress report. You'd likely have this script automatically address a message to your boss and put in the subject line, but you'd want to use command-line input to tell the script which file you want to send. By using command-line input, you can give your scripts a bit more flexibility and still have much of a process automated for you. You run the script and specify the input at the shell prompt, as shown in **A**.

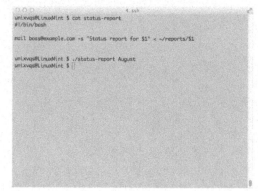

**A** Using command-line input, you can add flexibility to a script and still have the script do the grunt work for you.

## To accept command-line arguments in a script:

1. `vi status-report`

   Use your favorite editor to edit your script.

2. `mail -s "Status report for $1"`
   `↪ boss@example.com < ~/reports/$1`

   Enter a command, with **$1** appearing in each place you want to use the first item of input from the command line. In this example, the script starts a message to the boss, fills in the subject line (adding the month automatically), and sends the appropriate monthly report (the one specified on the command line) from the **reports** directory under your home directory.

   See Chapter 11 for more information about sending email.

3. Save and exit, and then run the script (**Code Listing 10.6**), though you might first have to provide the content for the status report and find a boss to take your status report.

**TIP** To see the information provided at the command line, echo it back out with `echo $*`. The $* variable provides all the command-line input, with $1, $2, $3, and so on (up to $9) containing the individual arguments.

**TIP** You can also accept input at specified points while a script is running. See the next section for more details.

**Code Listing 10.6** By providing command-line input (in this case **August**), you can control what the script does.

```
[unixvqs@LinuxMint scripting]$ more status-report
#! /bin/bash
mail -s "Status report for $1" boss@example.com < ~/reports/$1
[unixvqs@LinuxMint scripting]$ ./status-report August
[unixvqs@LinuxMint scripting]$
```

# Accepting Input While a Script Is Running

In the previous section, we showed you that you can require that information be provided along with the script in order for the script to run, but it's easy to forget to input the information and thus not get the results you expected. You can also require input while a script is running. The script runs, you input some information, and then the script continues (probably) using the information that you input . In this case, the script counts misspelled words, but you can apply it to anything you want.

Ⓐ You can also input information while a script is running.

## To accept input while a script is running:

1. **`nano retentive`**

   Use your favorite editor to edit your script.

2. **`echo -e "Which file do you want to`**
   **`→ analyze?"`**

   Specify the text for the prompt that you'll see onscreen. Here, the onscreen text will read, "Which file do you want to analyze?"

3. **`read choice`**

   At whatever point in the script you want the script to accept information, type **read** followed by the name of the variable to accept the input. Here, we name the variable **choice**.

**Code Listing 10.7** Accepting input while a script runs helps ensure that you don't forget to type it in, and still gives customized results.

```
[unixvqs@LinuxMint scripting]$ ./retentive
Which file do you want to analyze?
testfile
testfile has 11 misspelled words
and was last changed at 08:44 on Mar 30
→ [unixvqs@LinuxMint scripting]$
```

4. `echo "$choice has `cat $choice |`
   → `spell | wc -l` misspelled words"`

   Echo a phrase (and embedded command) to check the spelling, count the misspelled words, and report the number for the file specified. At each place where the filename should appear, substitute **$choice**.

5. `echo -e "and was last changed \c"`

   Echo another line with text and (because of the **\c**) no line break at the end of the line.

6. `ls -l $choice | awk '{ print " at`
   → `" $8 " on " $6 " " $7 }'`

   This very long and complex line uses **awk** to pluck the time, month, and day of the month fields out of the **ls -l** listing for the file given as **$choice** Ⓐ. See Chapter 6 for details about **awk**.

7. Save and exit.

   You have the hang of this by now.

8. `./retentive`

   Run the script (after making it executable and specifying the current directory, if necessary) and provide a filename when prompted, as shown in **Code Listing 10.7**.

> **TIP** A great example of a use of prompted input is configuration files. See "Using Input to Customize Your Environment" in Chapter 16 for details and a specific example.

> **TIP** See Chapter 8 for more information about setting up configuration files and starting scripts upon login.

> **TIP** You can use a set of lines like echo -e "Please enter the name: \c" and read name to have both the input line and the introduction to it appear on the same line.

# Debugging Scripts

As you're developing scripts, you'll no doubt encounter a few problems in getting them to run properly. As **A** shows, you can help debug your scripts by printing the script onscreen as it runs. That way, you can follow the script as it runs and see where the problems might be.

## To print the script onscreen as it runs:

`sh -x retentive`

At the shell prompt, type **sh -x** followed by the script name (and any additional information you need to provide). The **-x** tells the shell to execute the script (as usual) and print out the individual command lines, as shown in **A**.

**TIP** Use the name of an appropriate shell, followed by -x, followed by the script name for this kind of debugging output. For example, try **bash -x** `retentive`.

```
unixvqs@LinuxMint $ bash -x retentive
+ echo -e 'Which file do you want to analyze?'
Which file do you want to analyze?
+ read choice
testfile
++ wc -l
++ spell
++ cat testfile
+ echo 'testfile has 11 misspelled words'
testfile has 11 misspelled words
+ echo -e 'and was last changed \c'
and was last changed + awk '{ print "at "$8 " on " $6 " " $7 }'
+ ls -l testfile
at 08:44 on Mar 30
unixvqs@LinuxMint $
```

**A** Printing the script onscreen as it runs is a great way to debug it.

# Sending and Reading Email

If you're anything like us, your whole day revolves around getting goodies in your email inbox and sending "highly important" messages (of course they're important, right?). In any case, sending and receiving email will probably be rather common tasks in your Unix or Linux experience.

In this chapter, we'll introduce you to a few Unix and Linux email programs and show you how to get started with them. (Of course, just use the instructions that apply to the program you're using!) Then, we'll show you some clever things you can do with email in Unix, such as creating signature files and sending automatic vacation email replies.

Throughout this chapter, we'll be referring to a program called **alpine**. The program called **alpine** is simply a newer version of **pine** (well, there are some licensing changes similar to those with **pico** and **nano** back in Chapter 4, but those won't affect your daily life with email). If **alpine** is not available and you are on an older system, say, at your office, you might possibly have **pine**. If so, you can pretty much use the **alpine** instructions for **pine**.

# Choosing an Email Program and Getting Started

In general, you'll have a choice of three kinds of programs for sending and receiving email on a Unix or Linux system:

- An email program installed on your local computer or network that interacts with the mail system for you. You might know these programs as mail clients and might have used ones like Mail.app, Evolution, Thunderbird, or Outlook Express. These are handy because they usually have a spiffy interface and can handle attachments without a lot of hassle on your part, but they're not really Unix email programs. These programs also let you store your mail on your desktop system (Windows or Macintosh or even Unix desktops, but those are beyond the scope of this book).

- A web-based email program that you access through your web browser on your local computer. These include Gmail, Yahoo Mail, Outlook.com, and many more. These are also outside the scope of the book (although most of the servers that host webmail programs actually run Unix or Linux).

- An email program that you access and use directly on the Unix or Linux system. These programs, such as **alpine**, **mutt**, and **mail**, let you send and receive with varying degrees of ease. Additionally, **alpine** and **mutt** let you send attachments with not a lot of hubbub. Because the mail remains on the Unix system, you can access your mail from anyplace you can access your Unix or Linux system.

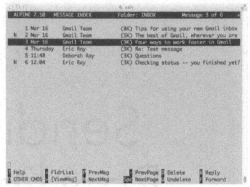

**A** **alpine**'s interface and features are intuitive and easy to use.

**B** **mutt**'s interface and features are fairly easy to use but not as easy as **alpine**'s.

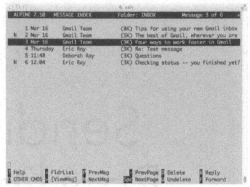

**C** **mail**'s interface and features are, well, kind of a pain to use.

**Code Listing 11.1** Read with great interest the line that says "You have mail" when you log in.

```
login: unixvqs
Password:
Last login: Sun Aug 2 07:41:00 on tty4
You have mail.
unixvqs@FreeBSD $
```

**TIP** How do you know whether someone has sent you something? The shell will often announce (but not usually audibly) "You have mail" or "You have new mail" when you log in, as shown in Code Listing 11.1—that is, if you do in fact have email waiting for you.

**TIP** You're not limited to using just a regular Unix or Linux email program or a webmail program; you can use either or both, depending on your specific preferences and needs. You're also not limited to using just one email program if you have more than one available, although reading mail from two different Unix programs can sometimes make it a little hard to keep track of what's where. Try them out and see which program or combination of programs meets your needs.

**TIP** Yes, you can read Gmail (or nearly any other IMAP mail service) with alpine or mutt. Just do an Internet search for "configure alpine for gmail" or "muttrc for gmail," follow the (straightforward) instructions, and you'll be in business.

**TIP** We often recommend using character-based email programs like these to read mail. After you get used to the interface, you can whiz through your email much faster than you can with a GUI (graphical user interface) mailer (like Outlook or Thunderbird mail) or with a webmail application, and you don't have spam graphics opened in your face either.

In this chapter, we'll focus on the email programs that you access directly from the system, because these are the true email programs. Although there are a bazillion different ones available, you'll likely have access to one (or more) of these:

- **alpine**: This program is intuitive to use and lets you send and receive email and attachments very easily. **alpine** is our recommendation if you have it available. Ⓐ shows **alpine**'s relatively simple interface. Just use the menu commands listed at the bottom of the screen.

  Another mail program—**cone**—is fairly similar to **alpine**. We could not see a compelling reason to choose **cone** over **alpine**, so we opted to cover only **alpine** in this book. However, if you see **cone** available and you like **alpine**, give it a shot.

- **mutt**: This program is a bit less user-friendly, but it lets you send and receive email and can deal with attachments nicely. **mutt** is our second choice if **alpine** is not available, but **mutt** is very powerful and quite friendly if you put a bit of time into customizing it for your needs. Ⓑ shows its interface, which provides ample features for most purposes.

- **mail**: This program is available on practically every Unix system; however, it's fairly difficult to use and does not provide intuitive options or commands, as Ⓒ shows. We recommend choosing another email program if at all possible. Use this program for emergencies only.

# Reading Email with alpine

It's likely that your first step in using **alpine** will be to read email. As Ⓐ through Ⓓ show, you start by entering the **alpine** command, and then work screen by screen, depending on what you want to do.

## To read email with **alpine**:

1. **alpine**

   At the shell prompt, type **alpine** to start the program. The first time you use **alpine**, it will greet you (see Ⓐ) before you get started. Thereafter, you'll see the normal main screen, as shown in Ⓑ.

   If you get an error message about the **alpine** command not being found, look around on the system to find the program. See Chapter 1 for details on where to look.

2. Ⓛ

   Press Ⓛ to view the folder list, which includes an inbox folder as well as (eventually) other folders that you set up.

3. Use the arrow keys to navigate the folder list (if you have other folders).

4. Ⓥ

   Press Ⓥ to view the selected folder. Note that the default selection in the bottom menu is shown with brackets, [ ] (see Ⓒ). Rather than use arrow keys to select the default, you can press Enter.

5. Use the ↑ and ↓ keys to move up and down in the message list.

   Your unread messages will appear at the bottom of the list by default.

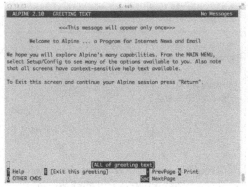

Ⓐ When you start **alpine** for the first time, it will greet you.

Ⓑ You'll become well acquainted with **alpine**'s main screen.

Ⓒ All you have to do is press Enter to select the default selection, which is shown at the bottom in brackets.

**D** Do you really want to quit **alpine**? Just checking.

## Printing with alpine

Although many Unix email programs don't let you print to your local printer, **alpine** does. All you have to do is choose %, take the default printout on "attached to ansl," as **alpine** suggests, and your printout will appear, most likely on your regular printer. Printing to a local printer this way doesn't work with some communications programs (notably Windows **telnet**), but it does work with many. If you're sitting in front of a Linux or OS X system, you could also use other printing utilities on your system—the "attached to ansi" option is intended for people who are connected to the Unix system with **ssh** or **telnet**.

6. Enter

   Press Enter to read the selected message.

7. Hmmm. Uh-huh. Wow. Marvy.

   Read your messages. Press < to get out of the current message and back to the message index for the current folder.

8. Q

   Press Q when you're ready to quit **alpine**. You'll be prompted to verify that you want to quit, as shown in **D**. Just press Y to quit, or N if you didn't really want to quit.

**TIP** Notice the menu commands listed at the bottom of the **alpine** screen. You can choose any of these options by pressing the appropriate key. **alpine** is conveniently case-insensitive, so either lowercase or uppercase commands will work.

**TIP** Start with **alpine -i** to start in your inbox, rather than at the main menu.

**TIP** As you're perusing your email, you can use Tab to jump to the next unread message in the folder.

**TIP** Delete messages by pressing Delete, either when the message is highlighted in the message list or when the message is open onscreen. When you quit the program, **alpine** will verify that you want to discard the deleted messages. Just press Y to confirm the deletion, or N if you really didn't want to get rid of the messages. (Note that deleting in **alpine** does not send them to the Recycle Bin, as the Delete key does when using a Windows email program. In Unix, pressing Delete really deletes messages... they're gone!)

**TIP** You can reply to messages by pressing R with a message selected or while reading a message.

**TIP** When using **alpine**, keep your eyes open for an O in the menu at the bottom of the screen, indicating that there are other options.

Sending and Reading Email   **213**

# Sending Email with alpine

Our next favorite thing to do with **alpine** is to send new messages. Commonly, you'll send messages after you've already started **alpine** , but you can also start a new message directly from the shell prompt (see the accompanying tips).

**A** Preparing a message in **alpine** is as easy as filling in the blanks.

## To compose and send a message using alpine:

1. **alpine**

   Type **alpine** at the shell prompt to start **alpine**, if it isn't already running.

2. C

   Press C to compose a new message.

## Our Two Cents on the Subject of Subjects

- Always include a descriptive subject line that succinctly summarizes the message's contents. For example, rather than say "Here you go," say "Comments on the Baskins proposal."

- Never leave the subject line blank. Many people toss subjectless messages, thinking that they might be spam or otherwise not important enough to read.

- Never use ALL CAPS in the subject line, or anywhere else, for that matter), as recipients may perceive this as being YELLED AT VERY LOUDLY.

- Be aware of how spam filters work. Many ISPs use them to reduce the amount of spam (bulk messages, like junk mail, that are sent out to hundreds or thousands or even millions of people at the same time) that goes through.

  - Some filters are set to discard messages with subject lines in ALL CAPS.

  - Other filters discard messages with a lot of exclamation points in the subject.

  - Many filters eliminate messages with subject lines that sound "spammy," like "Make money now," "Eliminate bad credit," "This isn't spam," "Lose weight now," and the like. Obviously, many phrases and subjects that are not appropriate to print here in this book would also be discarded.

**3.** `Tab`

Press `Tab` to move through the message header fields. Fill in carbon copy recipients (**cc:**) and the **Subject:** line. See the sidebar called "Our Two Cents on the Subject of Subjects" for details about including subject lines.

If you're sending an attachment, type in the Unix filename (and path, if appropriate) on the **Attchmnt:** line. For example, type **~/myfile**, which includes the full path name and the filename.

**4. Hi, Kelly, when should we schedule**
→ **that golf game -- er, um --**
→ **business meeting?**

In the message window, type in your message. **A** shows our message, complete with the header information and the message body.

**5.** `Ctrl`+`X`

When you're ready to send, press `Ctrl`+`X`. **alpine** will ask you to confirm that you really want to send the message. Press `Y` (or press `Enter`) to send it, or `N` if you don't want to send it.

**TIP** Rather than type in someone's lengthy email address (such as joeblow @acmefancompany.com), set up an alias— a shortened name that replaces the long-winded address. Yeah, you'd be able to just type in Joe or whatever, and Unix will know which long-winded address goes with that name. To set up aliases, use the address book (press `A` from the main menu) and follow the instructions given.

**TIP** If you're at the shell prompt and want to send email without bothering with the main alpine interface, type alpine followed by the email address you want to send mail to (for example, alpine bigputz@raycomm.com). If you want to send email to multiple addresses, just separate them with commas or spaces, as in alpine unixvqs@raycomm.com, bigputz@raycomm.com.

# Customizing alpine

Although **alpine** is rather intuitive to use, it is also quite powerful, giving you ample options for customizing it.  shows **alpine**'s customization screen, as well as a few of the options you can choose.

## To customize alpine:

1. **alpine**

   At the shell prompt, type **alpine** to start the program.

2. M

   Press M to visit the main menu.

3. S

   Press S to summon the setup menu.

4. C

   Press C to access the configuration setup menu, which is shown in A.

5. Scroll through the configuration list using the ↑ and ↓ keys.

   **alpine** offers you gobs of options to configure. **Table 11.1** describes the ones you might find most useful.

A By using the configuration setup menu, you can tailor **alpine** to your needs.

**6.** `[Enter]`

Press `[Enter]` to select the option you want to change.

**7.** Make your selection or fill in the necessary information.

**8.** `[Enter]`

Press `[Enter]` to exit the configuration menu and return to the setup menu. You'll be prompted to save your changes. If you want to do so, press `[Y]`; if not, press `[N]`. You'll then whiz back to the main menu.

> **TIP** You can customize `alpine` so that it automatically opens your inbox whenever you start it. In the `initial-keystroke-list`, just type `l,v`, and then press `[Enter]` to specify the initial characters.

### TABLE 11.1 Commonly Used Configuration Options

| Option | Description |
|---|---|
| `initial-keystroke-list` | Specifies key commands for `alpine` to use when starting, just as if you'd typed them in directly. |
| `quit-without-confirm` | Allows you to exit `alpine` without the "are you sure?" message. |
| `signature-at-bottom` | Puts your automatic signature at the end of the message you're replying to, rather than above it. |
| `saved-msg-name-rule` | Sets `alpine` to automatically file your saved messages in a specific folder, based on the characteristics (sender, etc.) of the message. |
| `fcc-name-rule` | Sets your file copy of outgoing messages to be saved in a particular folder. We like the **by-recipient** option, which files messages according to whom we sent them to. |
| `use-only-domain-name` | Sets `alpine` to send all outgoing messages with just the domain name and not the machine name on the **From:** line. For example, our messages come from **@raycomm.com**, not from **@frazz.raycomm.com**. |

# Reading Email with mutt

If you're using **mutt**, you'll probably find that reading email messages is rather straightforward. As **Ⓐ** shows, you just scroll through your list of messages with the ⬆ and ⬇ keys and press Enter to open the message you want to read.

## To read email with mutt:

1. **mutt**

   Type **mutt** at the shell prompt to start the program. The system might ask you if you want it to create folders for you, as shown in **Code Listing 11.2**. We say let it do the work for you and enter **[yes]**. Enter **[no]** if you don't want folders created. **Ⓐ** shows the main **mutt** screen.

2. Use the ⬆ and ⬇ keys to move up and down in your list of email messages.

   Your unread messages will be at the bottom of the list.

**Ⓐ** **mutt**'s main index screen shows many of your options.

Code Listing 11.2 **mutt** will create a mail directory for you.

```
[awr@hobbes awr]$ mutt
/home/jdoe/Mail does not exist. Create it? ([yes]/no):
```

**3.** `Enter`

Press `Enter` to open a message to read.

**4.** `I`

Press `I` to return to the list of messages (index) or press `Spacebar` to scroll down through the current message. **A** shows the menu of commands, which should help you remember some of the basics of **mutt**.

**5.** `Q`

Press `Q` (for quit), then wave goodbye to **mutt**. You might be prompted with questions to answer (for example, about discarding deleted messages or moving read messages to your read-mail folder). Answer yes only if you'll be using **mutt** as your primary mailer in the future.

**TIP** You can customize virtually every aspect of **mutt** but only by editing the ~/.muttrc configuration file. If you think you might like the flexibility of **mutt**, search the Internet for sample .muttrc files to get an idea of what you can do with it.

**TIP** You can delete a message by pressing `D` when you're viewing it or when it's selected in the message index screen. When you quit **mutt**, you'll be asked whether **mutt** should "Move unread messages to /home/yourid/ mbox." At that time, press `N` to keep them in your inbox or `Y` to move them.

**TIP** You can reply to messages by pressing `R` with the message selected in the message list or while reading the message.

**TIP** You can access **mutt** help, such as it is, from almost any screen by pressing `?`.

**TIP** You can move to a specific message in the message index by typing the message number.

# Sending Email with mutt

Sending messages with **mutt** is similar to sending messages with alpine. Most commonly, you'll compose a message while you're already messing around in **mutt** .

## To compose and send a message using mutt:

1. **mutt**

   To begin, type **mutt** at the shell prompt to start **mutt**.

2. M

   Press M to start a new message.

3. Enter

   Press Enter after entering each bit of information that **mutt** asks for **A**. Fill in the **To:** and **Subject:** lines. (See the sidebar "Our Two Cents on the Subject of Subjects" earlier in this chapter.)

4. Say hello to **vi**.

   Huh? After you enter the message header contents (filling in what you want), you'll be plunked right into **vi**, facing the top of a very blank message. See Chapter 4 for a quick reminder about using **vi**.

**A** You fill in the message header by answering questions or filling in blanks (**Subject:**, in this case), and then move on using the (Enter) key.

**5.** Kelly, I was having this dream that
→ I had my alarm clock installed
→ in my stomach. I remembered this
→ because, when my alarm went off,
→ I found myself pushing my belly
→ button trying to turn off the
→ noise. Good grief...I need a
→ vacation!

Type your message, whatever it may be.

**6.** Esc

When you're finished, press Esc (to get into command mode).

**7.** **:wq**

Then type **:wq** to save your work and exit the editor.

**8.** Y

Press Y to send the message. If you decide you don't want to share details about your belly button after all, you can press E to edit your message or press Q to quit and forget the whole thing.

**TIP** You can change the default editor from **vi** to something else available on your Unix system. All you have to do is edit your ~/.muttrc file (or create one if it doesn't exist) and add **set editor="nano"** (or whatever editor) to the file.

**TIP** To send a quick message from the shell prompt, type **mutt** followed by the recipient's email address, as in **mutt winchester@raycomm.com**. If you want to send email to multiple addresses, just separate them with commas or spaces, as in **mutt unixvqs@raycomm.com, info@raycomm.com**.

# Reading Email with `mail`

In general, using `mail` is a bit less intuitive than using either **alpine** or **mutt**; however, reading email with `mail` is particularly—um—challenging. Although we'd recommend using another program to read email if at all possible, here are the steps for reading email with `mail` if you're daring enough or if you have no other options.  illustrates this fairly quick task.

 The **mail** screen is anything but intuitive, but you can see the messages you have.

## To read email with `mail`:

1. `mail`

   Type `mail` at the shell prompt. You'll get a list of messages and a prompt .

2. `3`

   Type the number of the message you want to read and press Enter.

3. `Marvelous...he's such a jerk...`
   `→ oh, that's neat....`

   Read your messages. Press the number of the next message to move on to the next message, or Spacebar to page through the message a screen at a time.

4. `q`

   Press q to quit `mail` when you're ready.

---

**TIP** If somebody really long-winded sends you a long message, your Unix system might just zip the message on by, leaving you reading only the bottom few lines. To read the message in its entirety, either type more to page through the message, or type s followed by the message number, followed by a filename (s 18 message-in-a-file) to save it to a file, then use the editor of your choice to read it.

**TIP** Type h followed by a message number to see different message headers. For example, type h 117 to see the messages leading up to number 117.

**TIP** Find a different mail program if at all possible—it's useful to be able to cope with `mail` for times of need, but it's not a good long-term solution.

# Sending Email with `mail`

Despite **mail**'s unintuitive interface and features, it is a great program to use if you just want to dash off a quick message without fussing with niceties. As **Code Listing 11.3** shows, you can send messages while in **mail** or from the shell prompt. You can also use **mail** to send files fairly easily.

## To compose and send a message using `mail`:

1.  **mail unixvqs@raycomm.com**

    At the shell prompt, type **mail** followed by the recipient's address. If you want to send email to multiple addresses, just separate them with commas but no spaces, as in **mail putz@raycomm.com, putz2@raycomm.com**.

    If you're already in **mail**, just type **m** followed by the address or addresses, as in **m putz@raycomm.com,deb@raycomm.com**.

    *continues on next page*

Code Listing 11.3 Using **mail**, you can dash off a quick note by including the recipient's address and the message text.

```
[ejr@hobbes ejr]$ mail unixvqs@raycomm.com
Subject: You're in big trouble now!
So, anyway, Winchester had perched
himself on my stereo turntable (those were sooooo low-tech, weren't they?!). He was
waiting for me to turn on the stereo so he could go back to sleep while spinning in
circles. I used to let him sleep that way
at night. Well, that was until one night
when the lid closed on him...
EOT
[ejr@hobbes ejr]$
Code Listing 11.4 To send a text file through the mail, you just redirect the file to mail.
[ejr@hobbes ejr]$ mail unixvqs@raycomm.com < sendit.txt
[ejr@hobbes ejr]$
```

2. So, anyway, Winchester had perched
    → himself on my stereo turntable
    → (those were sooooo low-tech,
    → weren't they?!). He was waiting
    → for me to turn on the stereo so
    → he could go back to sleep while
    → spinning in circles. I used to
    → let him sleep that way at night.
    → Well, that was until one night the
    → lid closed on him...

    Type in your message text (see Code
    Listing 11.3).

3. Ctrl+D

    Announce that you're finished with
    either a . (dot) by itself on the last line
    or with Ctrl+D, and the message will
    zip off to the recipient(s).

## To send text files with mail:

mail unixvqs@raycomm.com < sendit.txt

At the shell prompt, type **mail** followed
by the recipient's address. Then use **<**
and the filename to redirect the file
(**< sendit.txt**), which tells Unix to send
the file to the address provided (**Code
Listing 11.4**).

**TIP** See "Scheduling Regularly Occurring
Jobs with cron" in Chapter 9 for a spiffier way
of using mail to send messages directly.

**TIP** See the section in Chapter 1 called "Redirecting Output" for a refresher on redirection.

**TIP** You'll notice that the mail interface on
some systems does not provide for a subject
line. On some systems, you can add one by
including -s plus the subject text, like this:
mail -s "An old Winchester story...dumb
cat!" unixvqs@raycomm.com.

**TIP** You can accomplish all of these command-line mail sending options with mutt
as well as mail, but you get added benefits
with mutt, including being able to send
attachments. For example, mutt -s "Sending
that file" -a bigolefile.tgz suggest@
example.com < /dev/null will do the whole
nine yards at once, including attaching the big
ol' file. Don't try that with mail!

**A** Your signature file can contain any information you want. Be creative, but keep it concise!

# Creating a Signature File

If you've been using email for any length of time, you've undoubtedly noticed *signature files*, which appear at the bottom of messages and include contact information, company name, and perhaps a short funny quote or saying. You can add a signature to your outgoing messages by creating a **.signature** file **A**.

## To create a signature file:

1. **nano ~/.signature**

   At the shell prompt, type an editor's name (here we use **nano**, but you can use the editor of your choice), specify the home directory (with **~/**), and then specify the **.signature** filename. Note the leading dot in the filename, which makes the file hidden.

2. **Kelly Jones      kelly@example.com**
   **My thoughts are my own ... is that OK,**
   **→ honey?**

   Go ahead, type your signature information **A**. We recommend that your **.signature** file include, at minimum, your name and email address. You can also add funny sayings ("You know you're a geek when you refer to going to the bathroom as 'downloading.'") or disclaimers ("My opinions are mine and not my company's."). Whatever you want, really. Keep your signature as short as possible; long signatures are hard to wade through.

3. Save and exit the file.

   If you're using **nano** or **vi**, you can get a quick reminder about this in Chapter 4.

**TIP** If you want to get really fancy with your signature, use a *figlet*, which is a text representation of letters, as shown in Code Listing 11.5. Check out your favorite Internet search engine and search for "figlet" or "figlet generator" for more information about creating your own.

**TIP** Many email purists think that four lines is the longest signature anyone should have. If you create one that's longer, expect some people to chew you out for it.

**TIP** Both `mutt` and `alpine` automatically include a `.signature` file in outgoing mail.

Code Listing 11.5 Figlets are fun and fancy.

```
[ejr@hobbes ejr]$ more figlet
  ___ ___ ___
 |   \ \ /  _| | _ |
 | |_) |  __| | |_ __ __  _  ___  | |__ __
 |  _// .'| | | | | | / _\| '.' _ \| | |'. \ / _|
 | | \ \( | |_| |  _( )| | | | | | | |_ || | | |(_
 |_| \\_, |_\,|_____/|_| |_|_|_| |_| |_( ) |___|_| |_|\__()
   _/ | |/
  |__/
```

**A** All you have to do is tell Unix where you want your messages forwarded to.

**TIP** Check with your system administrator to see if a `.forward` file will really do what you want. Many newer Linux and Unix systems automatically send mail to `procmail` (and ignore the `.forward` file), so you might need to use a `procmail` recipe to forward your mail. It's equally effective, but just different. See "Managing email with `procmail`" later in this chapter for details.

**TIP** If you want, you can keep a copy of all incoming messages (in your incoming email box, just where they'd usually be) and forward them to unsuspecting recipients. Just type `\yourid, other@address.com` (substituting your userid on the current system for `yourid` and the address to which to forward the mail for `other@address.com`).

**TIP** Forwarding messages is also handy when you change ISPs. You can forward all messages sent to your old address to your new one, which helps tremendously in ensuring that you receive all your important messages while your friends and coworkers update their address books.

# Automatically Forwarding Incoming Messages

Suppose you're the boss of a big project, and everyone sends you all the important related email messages. You can tell Unix to *automagically* forward these incoming messages to the people who will actually do something about them. Hey, you're the boss, right? Or maybe you just got a different email account, and you want incoming mail sent to your old address forwarded to your new address. As **A** shows, all you have to do is create a **.forward** file.

## To forward incoming email messages:

1. `vi ~/.forward`

   To begin, type **vi** at the shell prompt (or the appropriate command for whichever editor you are using), indicate your home directory (with **~/**), and then type **.forward** as the filename.

2. `mynewid@raycomm.com`

   Add, as the first line of the file, the address to which you want your email forwarded **A**. In addition to forwarding to a single address, you can also use a **.forward** file with multiple addresses on multiple lines to send incoming email to several addresses at once.

3. Save and close the file.

   Check out Chapter 4 for details about saving and closing files using **nano** or **vi**.

# Announcing an Absence with vacation

If you're planning a vacation and will be away from your email for a while, let Unix or Linux announce your absence for you . Using the **vacation** program, you can have the system send a reply saying that you're out of the office to everyone who sends you email.

Keep in mind that **vacation** is quite variable among different Unix systems and ISPs. What you have might be different from the "standard" form used here. Be sure to check with your system administrator for specific instructions if you have any problems, and also look at "Configuring **procmail**," later in this chapter, as many newer Linux and Unix systems use **procmail** instead of a **.forward** file to tell **vacation** to respond to your messages.

Ⓐ Using a template, you can customize the vacation message—even extensively, as we've done.

## To send "I'm on vacation" messages using vacation:

1. **vi ~/.vacation.msg**

   At the shell prompt, type **vi ~/ vacation.msg**. You'll need to edit a message (a template, actually) for the response that people should receive when they email you, as shown in Ⓐ.

2. **Subject: away from my mail Thanks**
   → **for emailing me about $SUBJECT.**
   → **Fortunately for me, I'm taking a**
   → **fabulous vacation mowing my lawn,**
   → **doing laundry, and catching up on**
   → **other things I can't do because I**
   → **usually work so much. If you would**
   → **like me to stay on vacation, please**
   → **email my boss (boss@example.com)**
   → **and let her know. Thanks!**

**Code Listing 11.6** Your **.forward** file should reference the **vacation** file.

```
[ejr@hobbes ejr]$ cat ~/.forward
\ejr, "|vacation ejr"
[ejr@hobbes ejr]$
```

Create and edit the text to say what you want.

The **$SUBJECT** term in the text will be replaced with the actual subject of the email sent to you.

3. Save your text and exit the editor.

    Chapter 4 has the gory details about saving and exiting in **nano** and **vi**.

4. **vacation -I**

    Type **vacation -I** at the shell prompt to start **vacation** and tell it to respond to all incoming messages. You'll still get the incoming messages in your inbox. In fact, they'll pile up in your inbox and wait for you to return.

5. **cat ~/.forward**

    Look at the **.forward** file in your home directory to verify that it contains a reference to the **vacation** program. Your **.forward** file specifies what should happen to your mail upon receipt. In this example, it should be processed by **vacation**. The reference to **vacation** is usually inserted automatically by the **vacation** program, but if it's not there, you'll need to edit the **.forward** file and add text like **\yourid, "|vacation yourid"**. Of course, substitute your real userid for the placeholder, and possibly include the full path to **vacation** (**/usr/bin/vacation** on our system). (See Code Listing 11.6.)

## To stop vacation emails:

**mv .forward vacation-forward**

At the shell prompt, move the **.forward** file that references the **vacation** program to a different name (in this case, **vacation-forward**). You could just delete it or remove the reference to **vacation**, but it's easier to save it so you can reuse it for your next vacation.

**TIP** Remember to unsubscribe to all mailing lists before you start **vacation**. If you don't, you may send a vacation announcement to a whole list of people who likely don't care (not to mention that you'll irritate the list administrator!). Or, worse, you might cause a *mail loop* (in which your messages to the list are acknowledged by the server, and the acknowledgments are in turn sent vacation announcements), causing hundreds or thousands of messages to accumulate in your account. It shouldn't happen, but it sometimes does.

# Configuring procmail

Let's see...two messages from the boss...17 messages from the string collectors' discussion group...oh, hey, a message from Mom...and....

One of the handiest things you can do to make your Unix life easier is to use **procmail** (a mail-filtering program) to handle some of your incoming email automatically.

In this section, we'll show you how to configure **procmail** so you can manage incoming messages. As  and **B** show, you need to do two things to set up your system to manage mail with **procmail**:

- Specify settings for **procmail** **A**. For example, incoming mail normally gets plunked directly into your inbox; however, **procmail** filters mail before it even gets to your inbox, so you need to tell **procmail** where your mail folders are, among other things.

- Tell **procmail** to do its thing **B**. Essentially, you create a **.forward** file that sends your incoming mail to **procmail** for processing before you ever see it. This step is not necessary for many systems, particularly newer Linux and Unix systems.

## To specify settings for procmail:

**1. nano ~/.procmailrc**

To begin, access your editor and create a **.procmailrc** file in your home directory.

**2. LOGFILE=$HOME/.maillog**

Give **procmail** a place to log all its activities, so it can tell you what it's done: "I threw away 7 messages from your boss... filed 3 messages from Joe in the GolfBuddies folder...." In this example, we tell **procmail** to keep a log file called **.maillog** in our home directory **A**. Keep an eye on this file, because it can grow large over time.

**A** You specify the **procmail** settings you need, and then you're off and running.

**B** Tell the Unix system to send incoming messages to **procmail** for processing to ease your mail management.

3. **PATH=/usr/bin:/usr/local/bin:/bin**

   Specify the path for your executable programs. It's a good idea to do this now, just in case you eventually use **procmail** to more extensively filter or autorespond to messages.

4. **DEFAULT=/var/spool/mail/yourid**

   Specify the location for your incoming mail. Remember, the filter gets the mail before it ever reaches the inbox, so you need to tell **procmail** where your inbox is. Check with your system administrator to confirm the **DEFAULT**. (**/var/spool/mail/yourid** is typically, but not always, the location, but obviously with your real userid, not **yourid**.)

5. **MAILDIR=$HOME/mail**

   Specify where **procmail** should find your mail program and all the folders and information it creates. If you're using **alpine**, you will probably type this line exactly as shown. If you're using **mutt**, you might need to use **Mail** instead of **mail**.

## To turn on procmail filtering:

1. **nano ~/.forward**

   Use your favorite editor to create a **.forward** file in your home directory.

2. **"| /usr/bin/procmail"**

   If **procmail** is not located at **/usr/bin**, type in the actual location. **/usr/local/bin** would be another likely directory.

3. Save and close the file.

   That's it! Now all you have to do is wait for incoming messages and see if they get filtered as you intended (as you'll set up in the next section). It's a good idea to use a different email account to send yourself email and confirm that your changes work as you expect.

**TIP** Don't forget that many newer Unix and Linux systems are configured to send your email automatically through **procmail**, even without you having to turn it on. We recommend trying the steps in the task "To specify settings for **procmail**" first and see if that works, and only try the steps in the "To turn on **procmail** filtering" task if just specifying settings isn't sufficient.

# Managing Email with procmail

procmail can help you automatically—or selectively—respond to email. As you'll see, procmail is similar to forwarding email and using the **vacation** program, but you'll probably find procmail much more flexible.

## To specify how messages should be filtered (to "write a recipe"):

1. **vi ~/.procmailrc**

   In **vi**, access your **.procmailrc** file.

2. Move to the end of the file, below the setup information.

3. **:0:**

   Start a new recipe with **:0:**, as shown in . (Don't ask why you use **:0:**. That's just the way it is.)

4. **\* ^TOGolfBuddies**

   Set the criteria for **procmail** to filter with. Here,

   ▸ **\* ^TO** tells procmail to examine the **TO** line (and, actually, the **CC** line, too) of all incoming messages.

   ▸ **GolfBuddies** is the text to match in the **TO** line (as in **To: GolfBuddies@ nowhere.nowhen.com**). Of course, you'd put in the actual name of the list to look for (or the alias for your mailing list, or whatever) rather than **GolfBuddies**.

5. **$MAILDIR/FriGolfBuddies**

   Specify where the filtered mail should go. In this case, filtered mail would go in the **FriGolfBuddies** folder, but you might filter messages from mailing lists into a **listmail** folder.

6. Save and close the file.

Ⓐ Add the recipes of your choice to your .procmailrc file.

## Use procmail to Toss Spam Messages

The following recipe,

```
:0:
* !^TO.*awr@.*raycomm.com
$MAILDIR/spam
```

uses a regular expression to filter messages that aren't explicitly addressed to a userid with **awr** before the **@** and **raycomm.com** at the end and places them into a special folder called **spam**. Put the spam filter at the end of your list of rules so all the messages originating from your mailing lists and other important messages are filed first. After testing this and making sure that you like it and it doesn't pitch valuable messages, you could change the last line to **/dev/null** to just throw away the garbage.

For more complex and sophisticated spam solutions, check the options with an online search for "procmail spam filter."

## To forward mail with procmail:

1. `nano ~/.procmailrc`

   To begin, access your editor and edit the `.procmailrc` file that you previously created in your home directory.

2. `:0:`

   On a new line at the bottom of the file, add `:0:`, which starts a **procmail** recipe. This basically tells **procmail** to "lock" your mail directory while it's processing mail.

3. `! myotheremail@example.com`

   Provide an exclamation point (**!**) and the address to which to send the mail.

4. Save and close the file.

   Now all email that you receive will be forwarded automatically to `myotheremail@example.com`.

## To invoke vacation with procmail:

1. `pico ~/.procmailrc`

   To begin, access your editor and edit the `.procmailrc` file that you previously created in your home directory.

2. `:0 c`
   `| /usr/bin/vacation jdoe`

   On a new line at the bottom of the file, add the recipe shown to send a copy (the **c** at the end of the first line) of your email to the **vacation** program. See "Announcing an Absence with **vacation**" earlier in this chapter for more information about the **vacation** program.

3. Save and close the file.

   Now all email that you receive will be stored and passed along for the **vacation** program to respond to.

**TIP** Your `.procmailrc` file gets processed in order. As soon as a recipe matches an incoming email message, it's applied. So if your first recipe is the forwarding recipe, `procmail` will never even get to any later recipes. If no recipes are matched, mail will be delivered to the DEFAULT location you specified (see "Configuring `procmail`," earlier).

**TIP** After you set up your `procmail` processing, be patient. Sometimes `procmail` processes email on a specific schedule (hourly, for example), so testing it may be a little time-consuming.

## Sample procmail Recipes

The following recipes, with annotations, should help you get started filtering with **procmail**:

```
# Filter based on the To:, Cc: and similar headers

:0:
* ^TO.*awr@.*raycomm.com
$MAILDIR/interesting
# Filter based on the subject

:0:
* ^Subject:.*Status Report.*
$MAILDIR/status-reports
# Filter based on sender

:0:
*^From:.*spammer@example.com
$MAILDIR/IN.TO-DELETE
# Filter directly to garbage, irrevocably, based on sender

:0:
*^From:.*spammer@example.com
/dev/null
# Filter based on size (greater than 1000 bytes)

:0:
* > 1000
$MAILDIR/longish
```

# Accessing the Internet

So far in this book, you've been working with files and scripts located directly on the Unix or Linux system. In this chapter, we'll show you how to venture beyond your Unix or Linux system and take advantage of the information on the Internet.

# Getting Familiar with Internet Lingo

Before you venture out onto the Internet using the information in this chapter, you should become familiar with some concepts and terminology.

A *server* is a computer that stores data and "serves" it whenever requested. For example, you might think of a web server as a big storehouse for `.html` files. Its job is to store `.html` files, wait for another computer to request files, and then find the requested files and "serve" them to the requesting computer. And, yes, your Unix or Linux system might be a web server, but it doesn't have to be.

A *client* is a program that runs on your Unix system and is used to access data on a server. For example, your **links** web browser is a client—that is, it runs on your Unix or Linux system and is used to access files on a web server.

An *IP* (Internet Protocol) *address* is the address of a specific computer. This address identifies a computer, much the way your street address identifies your home. You use IP addresses, for example, every time you access a webpage. You may type **www.raycomm.com** (which is called the *host name*), but behind the scenes, that's translated into a specific IP address, such as **192.168.141.12**. You will use host names (such as **www.oracle.com** or **www.sun.com**) more often, because they're easier to remember than a string of numbers. Whether you type in a character address or a numeric address, all you're doing is accessing a specific address for a specific computer.

**TABLE 12.1  Internet Ports and Protocols**

| Port | Protocol |
|------|----------|
| 21 | ftp |
| 22 | ssh |
| 23 | telnet |
| 70 | gopher |
| 80 | http |
| 119 | nntp |
| 8080 | http (usually for test servers) |

*Protocols* are the languages that computers use to communicate with one another. For example, *FTP* (File Transfer Protocol) is used to transfer files from one computer to another. *HTTP* (Hypertext Transfer Protocol) is used to transfer data on the web, usually by web browsers.

*Ports* are like a computer's ears—they're "places" that computers listen for connections. Most web servers run at port 80, and if you connect to **http://www.raycomm.com:80/**, you're explicitly saying that you want to talk to the **www.raycomm.com** computer, at port **80**, using HTTP. You could specify a different protocol (FTP, for example) or a different port (**8080**, for example) to communicate with the same computer in a different way, as **Table 12.1** shows.

# Logging In to Remote Systems with ssh

You might already be using **ssh** to connect to your Unix or Linux system. You can, though, use it to connect to and use practically any other computer system on the Internet (assuming you have rights to log in to it), as **Code Listing 12.1** shows.

## To connect to another computer using ssh:

1. **ssh server.example.com**

   At the shell prompt, type **ssh** followed by the name of the system to which you want to connect.

2. Log in using the instructions you have for accessing the system.

   Presumably, if you're accessing a system over the Internet, you have some reason and permission to do so. In some cases, you'll type the name of the application, or you might be using the remote system just as you use the system from which you are connecting.

3. After you've finished using the remote system, log out according to the instructions and policies of the remote system. In other words, do what the system administrator tells you to do.

**TIP** For help with **ssh**, type **ssh** at the shell prompt and look at the list of options, or type man **ssh** for more help. When you have an active session, use ⌤ ? (press keys sequentially, not simultaneously) to get help with the current session.

**TIP** If you have a different login name on the remote system, you can specify that to ssh with **ssh server.example.com -l otherusername** to log in more easily. Or, if it's easier to remember, try **ssh otherusername@ server.example.com**.

Code Listing 12.1 Use **ssh** to connect securely to other systems on the Internet.

```
[jdoe@frazz jdoe]$ ssh server.example.com
jdoe@server's password:
jdoe /home/jdoe $ whoami
jdoe
jdoe /home/jdoe $ uname -a
Linux server.example.com 2.4.19-ac4 #13 SMP
→ Sat Nov 16 05:30:56 MST 2002 i686 unknown
→ unknown GNU/Linux
jdoe /home/jdoe $ logout
[jdoe@frazz jdoe]$
```

**TIP** You can use the **wall** (Write ALL) command to send **write**-type messages to everyone logged in to the system. System administrators commonly use **wall** when they need to warn people that the system is being brought down.

**TIP** Use w or who to find out who else is logged in to the system. See the sections "Learning Who Else Is Logged In with who" and "Learning Who Else Is Logged In with w" in Chapter 7 for more information.

**TIP** If you want to practice logging in to remote systems, use your favorite search engine to search for "free shell account" and you'll find a trove of valuable resources.

```
000                          4.ssh
unixvqs@LinuxMint $ telnet telehack.com
Trying 64.13.147.30...
Connected to telehack.com.
Escape character is '^]'.

Connected to TELEHACK port 32

It is 8:24 am on Sunday, March 30, 2014 in Mountain View, California, USA.
There are 32 local users. There are 24415 hosts on the network.

May the command line live forever.

Command, one of the following:
  ?          ac          advent      cal         calc        ching
  clear      cowsay      date        eliza       factor      figlet
  finger     fnord       geoip       help        hosts       ipaddr
  joke       login       morse       newuser     octopus     phoon
  ping       primes      rain        rand        rig         rot13
  starwars   traceroute  units       uptime      users       zc

.
```

**A** Note the Escape character as it flashes by.

# Logging In to Remote Systems with `telnet`

You might already be using **telnet** to connect to your Unix or Linux system, but you probably aren't because **telnet** is a huge, gaping security hole. You can, though, use it to connect to and use some other computer systems on the Internet (assuming you have rights to log in to it and that the system administrator allows **telnet** access rather than requiring SSH), as **A** shows.

## To connect to another computer using `telnet`:

1. `telnet telehack.com`

   At the shell prompt, type **telnet** followed by the name of the system to which you want to connect. In this example, we're connecting to a system in Mountain View, California.

2. Make note of the Escape character announced when you log in—look quickly, because it'll whiz by onscreen. The *Escape character* is what you'll press should your **telnet** connection stall or the system lock up. In our example, the Escape character is Ctrl+], which will return us to the **telnet** prompt so we can **quit** the connection **A**.

   *continues on next page*

3. Log in using the instructions you have for accessing the system.

   Presumably, if you're accessing a system over the Internet, you have some reason (and permission) to do so. In some cases, you'll type the name of the application. In most other systems, you'll log in with a userid and password, just as you log in to your Unix system 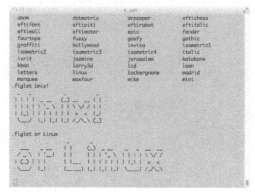.

4. After you've finished using the remote system, log out according to the instructions and policies of the remote system.

**B** After you're connected, you can use the remote system just like your own.

**TIP** For help with `telnet`, type `telnet` at the shell prompt, and then enter a **?** at the `telnet>` prompt. `open`, `close`, and `exit` will be the most useful tools for you.

**TIP** You'll find that `telnet` connections to libraries and other mainframe computers are often difficult to use because of oddities in keyboard emulations. Your best bet is to contact the site owner and ask for an **FAQ** list (with answers!). You won't be the first to have questions.

**TIP** A program closely related to `telnet`, `tn3270` is designed specifically for communicating with IBM mainframes, which are commonly used for college library catalogs as well as other professional and academic systems. If you know that you're communicating with an IBM mainframe, `tn3270` will probably be better to use.

**TIP** As you probably gathered, telnet is very much a throwback to the earlier days of the Internet. You can find some good (fun, interesting, entertaining) information about telnet at `www.telnet.org`, including places to `telnet` to.

**TIP** If you want to hear the gory details on why `telnet` is well and truly dead on the Internet, search online for "telnet worm."

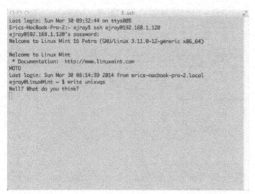

A You can send quick messages to another user on your system with **write**.

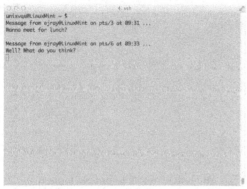

B The message suddenly appears on the user's screen.

# Communicating with Others Using write

Most of the time when you connect to a Unix or Linux system, you'll be communicating with the computer. You can, though, communicate with other people logged in to the same system. **write** is ideal for getting a quick message to other users—kind of like putting a yellow sticky note on their computer, as A shows.

## To communicate with others using write:

1. **write userid**

   At the shell prompt, type **write** followed by the userid of the person to whom you want to send a message. You'll get a blank line with a blinking cursor on it, just waiting for you to type something.

2. **Wanna meet for lunch?**

   Go ahead and type your message A.

3. Ctrl+D

   When you're finished typing, press Ctrl+D to send the message. What you typed will appear on the other user's screen B.

> **TIP** Keep in mind that a **write** message will suddenly appear on the recipient's screen and can be an intrusive surprise!

> **TIP** If you don't want to receive **write** messages, type **mesg n** at the shell prompt. This command will keep other people from sending you **write** messages for the current session. Type **mesg y** to enable **write** again.

# Communicating with Others Using talk

You can also have a real-time, two-way conversation (very much like an instant-messaging chat) with another user logged in to the system by using **talk**. As  shows, you type your messages, the other person types his, and you can both see the exchanges onscreen.

**A** **talk** lets you have a real-time, two-way online conversation.

## To communicate with others using **talk**:

1. **talk deb**

   At the shell prompt, type **talk** and the userid of the person to whom you want to talk. The other user will be prompted to enter **talk** and your userid. Then, you'll see the **talk** screen, as shown in **A**.

2. **You just wouldn't have believed it!**
   → **I had just chased the dog for six**
   → **blocks...Yeah, the stinkin' pooch**
   → **always thinks the garbage truck**
   → **is stealing our stuff... Right.**
   → **Hilarious. Anyway, there I was**
   → **huffing and puffing on the front**
   → **porch, when a neighbor informed**
   → **me that some kids were rooting**
   → **through my trash. Like, what did**
   → **they expect to find? Old panty**
   → **hose and coffee filters? Nawww.**
   → **I stopped using panty hose for**
   → **coffee filters a long time ago.**
   → **It made me look too tan.**

   Type anything you want. Each keystroke will show up on the other person's screen, so they'll see exactly how quickly (and how well) you type.

3. Ctrl+C

   When you're finished, break the connection.

**TIP** You can also talk to people logged in to other Unix systems. Just use talk userid@wherever.com. Of course, fill in the other person's actual userid and address, which will often be the same as that person's email address. Firewalls often—but not always—block these chats, though.

**TIP** If someone requests a talk with you, just type talk and the person's userid (or userid@wherever.com, if the person's host name isn't the same as yours).

**TIP** As with write, you can type mesg n and mesg y at the shell prompt to turn talk off and on for the current session.

**TIP** Though talk is not as groovy as some of the GUI-based instant messaging programs, it's still pretty cool, huh? It's also a good way to ask for help from more experienced users on your system, particularly if you checked first to see if it's OK to do so.

# Getting Files from the Internet with ftp

Some of the Internet's great information resources are FTP sites, which contain hundreds of thousands of files from all over the Internet. FTP sites are similar to websites but are directory oriented and speak a different protocol. They're less fun than the web usually is but often more practical.

One of the easiest ways to access information on FTP sites is to use **anonymous ftp**, which lets you access the sites and download files to your computer (**Code Listing 12.2**).

## Getting a single file through anonymous ftp:

1. `ftp calvin.raycomm.com`

   At the shell prompt, type **ftp** followed by the name of the FTP site to which you're connecting. Of course, if the computer has an IP address but no name, type the IP address instead. You'll be prompted to log in, as shown in Code Listing 12.2.

2. **anonymous**

   For the user name, type **anonymous**. (Type **ftp** if you get tired of typing **anonymous**—it nearly always works.)

3. `you@wherever.com`

   Use your email address for the password. It's polite to identify yourself to the people who provide the FTP service. Just **you@** is usually sufficient.

4. `cd /pub/files`

   Use standard Unix **cd** commands to move through the directory tree to the file you want.

*continues on page 245*

**Code Listing 12.2** Use **anonymous ftp** to get files from archives across the Internet.

```
[ejr@hobbes ejr]$ ftp calvin.raycomm.com
Connected to calvin.raycomm.com.
220 calvin Microsoft FTP Service (Version 2.0).
Name (calvin.raycomm.com:ejr): anonymous
331 Anonymous access allowed, send identity (email name) as password.
Password:
230 Anonymous user logged in.
Remote system type is Windows_NT.
ftp> cd /pub/files
250 CWD command successful.
ftp> binary
200 Type set to I.
ftp> hash
Hash mark printing on (1024 bytes/hash mark).
ftp> get jokearchive.gz
local: jokearchive.gz remote: jokearchive.gz
200 PORT command successful.
150 Opening BINARY mode data connection for jokearchive.gz(1481035 bytes).
################################################################################
################################################################################
################################################################################
################################################################################
################################################################################
################################################################################
################################################################################
################################################################################
################################################################################
################################################################################
################################################################################
################################################################################
################################################################################
################################################################################
################################################################################
################################################################################
################################################################################
######
226 Transfer complete.
1481035 bytes received in 4.07 secs (3.6e+02 Kbytes/sec)
ftp> quit
221
```

5. **binary**

   Specify the file type—in this case, **binary**, because we're downloading a gzipped archive file. Specify **ascii** for README files, text, and HTML files.

6. **hash**

   Next, you have the option of typing **hash** to tell the FTP client to display a hash mark (**#**) for every 1024 bytes transferred. If you're transferring a small file or using a fast connection, this might not be necessary; however, for large files and slow connections, the hash marks will let you know that you're making progress.

   If you'll be downloading multiple files, check out the sidebar "Getting Multiple Files" in this section before proceeding. The instructions for getting single and multiple files differ at this point in the process.

7. **get jokearchive.gz**

   At the **ftp>** prompt, type **get** and the filename to get the file from the remote system and plunk it into your own account.

8. **quit**

   When it's finished, just type **quit**.

**TIP** If the FTP connection seems to get stuck as soon as you log in, try -yourid@ wherever.com as the password. The - character disables system announcements and helps keep your FTP client happy.

**TIP** Some firewalls—particularly the ones on home networks—do not deal gracefully with some of the intricacies of the FTP protocol. If you can connect and log in but not list files or get anything, the firewall might be the problem. As soon as you log in, type pass (for passive) and the problem should go away.

**TIP** Another handy use for - is to view text files onscreen. For example, type get filename - to have the text just scroll by on the screen.

**TIP** Instead of using get, use newer (as in newer goodjokes.gz) to get a more recent file with the same name as the one you have.

**TIP** If you start downloading a file and the FTP connection breaks, type reget and the filename to continue the transfer from wherever it left off. (You'll have to reestablish the connection first, of course.)

**TIP** You can tell the FTP client to make sure that all the transferred files have unique names by using runique instead of get. That way, you can ensure that files don't overwrite existing files on your local system.

**TIP** Use regular Unix commands like ls and cd to move around in the remote system, and preface them with an l to apply to your system. For example, cd .. would change to the next higher directory on the remote system, and lcd .. (from within the FTP client) would change to the next higher directory on the local system. The current local directory is where your files will be saved.

## Getting Multiple Files

If you'll be getting multiple files with **ftp**, follow steps 1 through 6 in this section, then

- **prompt**

  Optionally, type **prompt** to tell the FTP client not to prompt you for each individual file that you want to get. You'll be informed that **prompt** is set to no. If you want to turn it back on, issue **prompt** again.

- **mget start\***

  At the **ftp>** prompt, type **mget** (for "multiple get") followed by the string or filenames to match. In this example, we use **start\*** to get all files with names that begin with "start." You could also use **mget \*.gz**, for example, to get files with the **.gz** file extension. See Chapter 1 for more about using wildcards.

- **quit**

  When you're finished getting files, just type **quit**.

# Sharing Files on the Internet with ftp

Sharing files on the Internet with **ftp** is similar to getting files; instead of retrieving files, however, you give files to other people (**Code Listing 12.3**). Do note that **ftp** is not secure, so don't use it to share passwords, bank statements, loan applications, or anything else that you do not want to have on the nightly news.

Code Listing 12.3 Using **put**, you can share your files with other people on the Internet.

```
[ejr@hobbes ejr]$ ftp ftp.raycomm.com
Connected to www.raycomm.com.
220 ftp.raycomm.com FTP server (NcFTPd 2.1.2, registered copy) ready.
Name (ftp.raycomm.com:ejr): ejray
331 User ejray okay, need password.
Password:
230-You are user #8 of 100 simultaneous users allowed.
230-
230 Logged in.
Remote system type is UNIX.
Using binary mode to transfer files.
ftp> cd incoming
250 "/home/ftp/pub/users/e/ejray/incoming" is new cwd.
ftp> binary
200 Type okay.
ftp> put myjokes.gz
local: myjokes.gz remote: myjokes.gz
200 PORT command successful.
150 Opening BINARY mode data connection.
226 Transfer completed.
128889 bytes sent in 15.5 secs (8.1 Kbytes/sec)
ftp> quit
221 C-ya!
[ejr@hobbes ejr]$
```

## To share files on the Internet with `ftp`:

1. `ftp ftp.raycomm.com`

   Open the FTP connection as shown in the previous section.

2. `youruserid`

   Log in with your userid.

3. `password`

   Enter your password.

4. `cd incoming`

   Use standard Unix directory commands (`ls`, `cd`, and so on) to move into the directory into which you want to put the files (Code Listing 12.3). `incoming` is often the right directory name to use, particularly on public FTP servers.

5. `binary`

   Set the file type. You'll want to use the **binary** file type for any files other than text or HTML files; use **ascii** for text or HTML.

6. `put myjokes.gz`

   Type **put** followed by the name of the file you're making available.

7. `quit`

   Type **quit** when you're done.

**TIP** On public FTP servers that accept incoming files, you might not be able to list the files in the `incoming` directory or see anything in there. In that case, you essentially just cast your file into a big open room and close the door. This allows FTP administrators to screen the incoming files before making them available for downloading. In case you're wondering, this is called a *dropbox*, and that's precisely where the name of the common Internet service came from.

**TIP** You can use the `mput` command to make multiple files available.

**TIP** If you're transferring a lot of files at once—say, for example, you're moving all of your files from your old ISP to your new one—consider using `tar` and `gz` to collect and zip up all of your files, and then transferring just a single file. See Chapter 13 for more information about these commands.

**TIP** Navigate in your local system (for example, to change to a directory containing files to put) with regular Unix commands like `ls` and `cd`, prefaced with an `l`.

**TIP** Use `!` to execute a command on your local system from within the `ftp` application. For example, `pwd` would display the path and name of the current directory on the other system, and `!pwd` would display the path and name of the current directory on the local system.

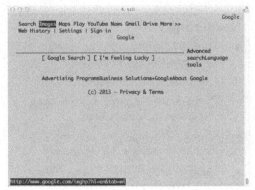

**(A)** The `links` browser provides great surfing capabilities, even without images.

# Surfing the Web with `links`

Using `links`, a really fancy text-based web browser, you can surf the web just as you might with Firefox or Internet Explorer, except with no graphics. That's really not a bad thing; consider that you don't have to deal with pop-up ads, banner ads, or similar junk. Just content, all the time. `links` even supports tables and complex webpage designs, which is unusual for a text-based browser **(A)**. Related advantages of using `links` are that you won't have to deal with slow download times for graphics, annoying sound files, plug-ins, or other showy webpage features.

## Useful `links` Keystrokes

- **/findme** finds text within the file. (Replace **findme** with the text you're looking for.) This is also handy to quickly navigate through a page.

- (?) finds text backward (moving up from the cursor) through the file.

- (D) downloads the current link.

- (G) goes to an address or file. You enter the address at the prompt.

- (Shift)+(G) lets you edit the current address.

- (Esc) usually lets you back out (escape from) the current menu.

- (S) brings up a menu to manage your bookmarks, including bookmarking the current page.

- (\) lets you toggle back and forth between viewing the formatted page and viewing the HTML source.

- (Ctrl)+(R) reloads the current page and refreshes the screen.

## To surf the web with `links`:

1. `links http://www.google.com/`

   At the shell prompt, type **links** followed by the name of an **.html** file or a website address. Here, we're accessing the Google website **A**.

2. Surf the web or search online for your favorite subject.

   See the sidebars "Navigating with **links**" and "Useful **links** Keystrokes" in this section for details.

3. Q

   Press Q to quit and return to the shell prompt. That's it!

> **TIP** Press Esc to bring up a handy—and very familiar—menu at the top of the screen. Use the arrow keys to navigate through the menu and Esc to get out of it.

### Navigating with `links`

- → (or Enter) follows the currently highlighted link to a new page.

- ← returns to the previous page.

- ↓ moves the highlight down to the next link in the document.

- ↑ moves the highlight up to the previous link in the document.

- Spacebar or Page Down scrolls down to the next page.

- Page Up or B scrolls up to the previous page.

- Q quits **links**.

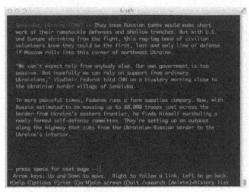

**A** You can use **lynx** to navigate to any site on the web.

# Surfing the Web with lynx

You can also surf the web using **lynx**, a text-based web browser. It's not as spiffy as **links** and doesn't handle many webpages as gracefully, but it has its place in your toolbox too. Generally, you can access the wealth of information available on the web **A**, and you can use **lynx** to download and reformat pages easily.

## Useful lynx Keystrokes

- **/findme** finds text within the file. (Replace **findme** with the text you're looking for.)
- ? lets you access help.
- D downloads the current link.
- G goes to an address or file. You enter the address at the prompt.
- Shift+G lets you edit the current address.
- A+L adds the current link to your bookmark list.
- V lets you view the bookmark list.
- Backspace lets you see a list of pages you've visited (your history).
- \ lets you toggle back and forth between viewing the formatted page and viewing the HTML source.
- Ctrl+R reloads the current page and refreshes the screen.

## To surf the web with `lynx`:

**1.** `lynx http://www.cnn.com/`

At the shell prompt, type **`lynx`** followed by the name of an **`.html`** file or a website address. Here, we're accessing the CNN website 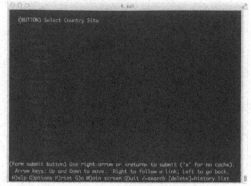.

If you only type in **`lynx`**, you'll get the default page for your system, which is likely the **`lynx`** home page or the main page for your ISP.

**2.** Surf, surf, surf!

See the sidebars "Navigating with **`lynx`**" and "Useful **`lynx`** Keystrokes" in this section for details.

**3.** Ⓠ

Press Ⓠ to quit and return to the shell prompt. That's it!

> **TIP** If you access a `lynx`-unfriendly page, like the one shown in Ⓑ, press ↓ to scroll down a few times. Usually you'll be able to find the content.

> **TIP** `lynx` is a great way to get a spiffy plain-text file out of an `.html` document. Try `lynx -dump http://example.com/goodpage.html > newname.txt` to start `lynx` and direct it to send the display to standard output and then redirect the output to the file called `newname.txt`. This will give you the text from the page, without HTML code, in a file in your Unix account.

> **TIP** `lynx` makes it really easy to get a quick view of a local `.html` document, but it isn't as flexible as `links` for web browsing in general.

Ⓑ Some sites are considerably less friendly than others if you're not using graphics.

## Navigating with `lynx`

- → (or Enter) follows the currently highlighted link to a new page.

- ← returns to the previous page.

- Tab moves the highlight down to the next link in the document.

- Shift+Tab moves the highlight up to the previous link in the document.

- M returns you to the first screen you accessed in the session—the one you saw in step 1 in "To surf the web with `lynx`."

- Spacebar scrolls down to the next page.

- B scrolls up to the previous page.

**Code Listing 12.4** You can use **wget** to download as much of the web as you can handle.

```
jdoe /home/jdoe $ wget http://www.cnn.com/
 18:07:51 http://www.cnn.com/
    => 'index.html'
Resolving www.cnn.com... done.
Connecting to www.cnn.com[64.236.24.4]:
 → 80... connected.
HTTP request sent, awaiting response...
 → 200 OK
Length: unspecified [text/html]
  [ <=>            ] 51,290  53.28K/s
18:07:53 (53.28 KB/s) - 'index.html' saved
 → [51290]
jdoe /home/jdoe $
```

# Downloading Websites with wget

The **wget** utility allows you to download webpages—and whole websites—to use offline. You just specify a URL and how many levels (links away from the starting page) you want to download, and let **wget** do its thing (as in **Code Listing 12.4**). Then you can use the webpages when you're not connected to the Internet, as when you're on an airplane, in a hotel, or in a waiting room, for example.

## To download websites with wget:

1. **wget http://www.cnn.com/**

   At the shell prompt, type **wget** followed by the URL of a website or FTP site. Here, we're accessing the CNN website (Code Listing 12.4) and downloading the home page.

2. Slurp!

3. **links index.html**

   Then use your favorite web browser to check out your handiwork.

**TIP** wget --recursive --level=2 http://www.example.com/ lets you get several (two, in this case) levels of a website. Be careful, because it's easy to bite off more than you can chew. If you use wget -r http://www.example.com/, wget will try to recursively download the whole thing. We ended up with more than 20 MB from the first command on www.cnn.com.

**TIP** wget also works for FTP sites. Just use wget ftp://ftp.example.com or wget jdoe:imAsecret@ftp.example.com if you need to specify a password.

**TIP** Check out the man page for wget (man wget) for more on the extensive options available.

**TIP** We recommend using a separate directory to contain the contents of different websites. Otherwise, wget will either rename files to avoid clobbering (or overwriting) existing files (thus breaking links) or clobber existing files (thus making it highly likely that only the last website you downloaded will be complete). If you use wget with the -x option (as in, wget -x http://www.example.com/), it'll do this automatically. See Chapter 2 for more on using directories.

# Checking Connections with ping

Think of using **ping** as saying "Are you there?" to a remote computer. For example, suppose you're trying to connect to a webpage but getting no response from the computer. Rather than wait and wonder what's going on, type **ping** to find out if the computer is up and functional (**Code Listing 12.5**).

## To check a computer with ping:

ping www.raycomm.com

At the shell prompt, type **ping** and the host name to test the connection to a specific host, as shown in Code Listing 12.5.

Depending on your Unix system, it may check the connection one time and report the results. Or, it may continue to pester the other computer every second or so until you tell it to stop. If that's the case, just press Ctrl+C to stop it.

**TIP** If you're having problems connecting to a particular computer, you might consider using traceroute, which pings all the computers on the path between point A and point B. While ping tells you if a host responds or not, traceroute will give you an idea of where the problem might lie. See the next section for more details about traceroute.

**TIP** The ping command doesn't provide a definitive answer to the status of the remote computer. Some systems are configured not to respond to pings for security reasons. If you get a response from ping, the system is definitely up and you can communicate with it; however, a lack of response from ping may not mean anything about that system's status.

**Code Listing 12.5** Using **ping**, you can find out whether you can connect to a specific computer.

```
[ejr@hobbes ejr]$ ping www.raycomm.com
PING www.raycomm.com (204.228.141.12): 56 data bytes
64 bytes from 204.228.141.12: icmp_seq=0 ttl=251 time=190.3 ms
64 bytes from 204.228.141.12: icmp_seq=1 ttl=251 time=197.7 ms
64 bytes from 204.228.141.12: icmp_seq=2 ttl=251 time=166.5 ms
64 bytes from 204.228.141.12: icmp_seq=3 ttl=251 time=157.5 ms
 - www.raycomm.com ping statistics -
4 packets transmitted, 4 packets received, 0% packet loss
round-trip min/avg/max = 157.5/178.0/ 197.7 ms
[ejr@hobbes ejr]$
```

# Tracing Connections with traceroute

When you're connecting to a remote computer, you're actually connecting through a series of computers (and routers and other expensive Internet stuff). That is, your computer connects to another computer, which connects to another, which connects to yet another, and so on until your computer connects to the one you're trying to reach.

The data that you're sending or receiving actually meanders through the path in *packets* (little chunks of data) that are reassembled into the correct sequence at the other end. But not all packets take precisely the same route from the sending computer to the destination computer. Communication on the Internet is much more like sending a lot of letters than making a telephone call. It's a bunch of little messages being passed along, not a continuous connection.

Using **traceroute**, you can satisfy your curiosity or possibly identify bottlenecks. How? You find out what route the packets take to arrive at the destination computer, as shown in **Code Listing 12.6**. If, for

**Code Listing 12.6** Using **traceroute**, you can see how data meanders between your computer and a remote computer.

```
ejray> traceroute www.yahoo.com
traceroute to www10.yahoo.com (204.71.200.75), 30 hops max, 40 byte packets
 1 198.60.22.1 (198.60.22.1) 8 ms 2 ms 3 ms
 2 903.Hssi5-0-0.GW1.SLT1.ALTER.NET (157.130.160.141) 18 ms 13 ms 14 ms
 3 124.ATM4-0-0.CR1.SFO1.Alter.Net (137.39.68.9) 68 ms 65 ms 52 ms
 4 311.atm3-0.gw1.sfo1.alter.net (137.39.13.49) 60 ms 50 ms 39 ms
 5 Hssi1-0.br1.NUQ.globalcenter.net (157.130.193.150) 40 ms 39 ms 28 ms
 6 pos0-1-155M.wr1.NUQ.globalcenter.net (206.132.160.25) 30 ms 48 ms 42 ms
 7 pos1-0-622M.wr1.SNV.globalcenter.net (206.251.0.74) 50 ms 67 ms 61 ms
 8 pos5-0-0-155M.cr1.SNV.globalcenter.net (206.251.0.105) 48 ms 40 ms 41 ms
 9 www10.yahoo.com (204.71.200.75) 43 ms 50 ms 53 ms
ejray>
```

example, you see that the routes to your three favorite (but currently inaccessible) websites all end at a specific computer, that's where the network outage is and that's who you're waiting for to get things up and running.

## To trace a connection with traceroute:

**traceroute www.yahoo.com**

At the shell prompt, type **traceroute** plus the address of the other computer in the connection. You'll see results similar to those shown in Code Listing 12.6. Each line in the **traceroute** output represents a computer (or other device) on the Internet that receives your packets and passes them on to the next computer.

**TIP** If you're experiencing connectivity problems, try using **traceroute** to several different, geographically dispersed hosts to isolate the problem. For example, if you're in the Midwest and you can **traceroute** all the way to www.stanford.edu (physically located in Palo Alto, California) but not to www.mit.edu (in Boston, Massachusetts), there's likely trouble on the Internet between you and the East Coast.

**TIP** You can speed the **traceroute** process by using the -n flag; for example, **traceroute** -n hostname. This checks the path using only IP addresses and does not translate the IP addresses into the DNS (Domain Name Server) host names with which you're familiar.

**TIP** Many firewalls do not pass through the ICMP (Internet Control Message Protocol, or ping) packets (there's a techie term for you) that **traceroute** uses. If you get a lot of lines with * * * in them, as shown in Code Listing 12.7, that might be the problem.

**Code Listing 12.7** Sometimes, **traceroute** has problems with firewalls between you and the target system.

```
jdoe /home/jdoe $ /usr/sbin/traceroute
→ www.google.com
traceroute to www.google.com
→ (216.239.51.101), 30 hops max, 38 byte
packets
 1 192.168.1.1 (192.168.1.1) 0.907 ms
→ 0.683 ms 0.632 ms
 2 * * *
 3 * * *
 4 * * *
 5 * * *
 6 * * *
 7 * * *
 8 * * *
 9 * * *
10 * * *
11 * * *
12 * * *
13 * * *
14 * * *
15 * * *
16 * * *
17 * * *
18 * * *
19 * * *
20 * * *
21 * * *
22 * * *
23 * * *
24 * * *
25 * * *
26 * * *
27 * * *
28 * * *
29 * * *
jdoe /home/jdoe $
```

**Code Listing 12.8** You can manually translate a domain name into an IP address using **nslookup**.

```
jdoe /home/jdoe $ nslookup www.raycomm.com
Note: nslookup is deprecated and may be
→ removed from future releases.
Consider using the 'dig' or 'host' programs
→ instead. Run nslookup with
the '-sil[ent]' option to prevent this
→ message from appearing.
Server: ns1.netrack.net
Address: 206.168.112.16#53
Non-authoritative answer:
Name: www.raycomm.com
Address: 206.168.112.83
```

# Matching Domain Names with IP Addresses

When accessing a computer on the Internet, you generally type in a domain name (such as **www.raycomm.com**) and your system translates it into an IP address (such as **204.228.141.12**). As a rule, the translation from domain name to IP address proceeds without a problem. Heck, most of the time, you won't even notice that it happened. Occasionally, though, you'll come across an error message that says something like "failed DNS lookups." All that this message means is that the domain name server (probably on your Unix system) cannot match the domain name you provided to an IP address.

So, what do you do?

- Just be patient for a day or two until the problem is resolved. (In the meantime, make sure the problem isn't a typo on your part.)

- Use **nslookup** or **dig**. These commands manually convert a domain name to the matching IP address (**Code Listing 12.8**). Then you can connect directly to the IP address rather than use the domain name.

## To match a domain name with an IP address using `nslookup`:

`nslookup www.raycomm.com`

At the shell prompt, type **nslookup** followed by the domain name you want to look up and the server you want to do the looking for you (Code Listing 12.8). Remember, if you get one of those pesky "failed DNS lookup" messages, the problem likely resides with your name server; therefore, you'll need to specify a different name server to match the domain name and IP address for you.

## To match a domain name with an IP address using `dig`:

`dig @ns1.example.com www.raycomm.com`

At the shell prompt, type **dig** followed by **@server-you-want-to-query** and the domain name you want to look up (**Code Listing 12.9**). Specifying the name server isn't essential but can often be useful.

**TIP** You can also do reverse lookups (matching address to name). This can be handy for identifying the origins of unknown email (from the IP addresses in the email headers), among many other tasks. Use `nslookup 192.168.1.23` (substituting the appropriate IP address) or `dig -x 192.168.1.82` to match an address to a name. Note that many servers have a single IP address that supports many domain names, so the answer from this may not be as definitive as it looks.

**TIP** For most purposes, `nslookup` provides more quickly comprehensible output (Code Listing 12.8) than `dig` does. However, `dig` (with appropriate options) can help provide extra information that can be useful in some cases. See `man dig` for information about available options.

**TIP** You can find alternate domain name servers by using the `whois` query server at `www.internic.net/whois.html` and looking up the domain name you want. All domain names have to be listed with two different domain name servers that are responsible for the domain names. Either of those listed servers should be able to provide the IP address for the domain name you enter.

**Code Listing 12.9** You can use **dig** to look up domain names and IP addresses.

```
jdoe /home/jdoe $ dig @ns1.netrack.net www.raycomm.com
; <<>> DiG 9.2.1 <<>> @ns1.netrack.net www.raycomm.com
;; global options: printcmd
;; Got answer:
;; ->>HEADER<<- opcode: QUERY, status: NOERROR, id: 32957
;; flags: qr rd ra; QUERY: 1, ANSWER: 1, AUTHORITY: 2, ADDITIONAL: 0
;; QUESTION SECTION:
;www.raycomm.com.             IN   A
;; ANSWER SECTION:
www.raycomm.com.     3585    IN   A 206.168.112.83
;; AUTHORITY SECTION:
raycomm.com.         3585    IN   NS ns2.raycomm.com.
raycomm.com.         3585    IN   NS ns1.raycomm.com.
;; Query time: 60 msec
;; SERVER: 206.168.112.16#53(ns1.netrack.net)
;; WHEN: Sun Jan 26 18:20:47 2003
;; MSG SIZE rcvd: 85
jdoe /home/jdoe
```

# Working with Encoded and Compressed Files

As you use Unix, you will quite possibly encounter encoded or compressed files and have to extract, unencode, encode, or otherwise manipulate the files to be able to view or use them. This chapter discusses ways of encoding and compressing files.

# Encoding Files with uuencode

You'll use *encoding* whenever you're sending a *binary* file (a nontext file) through email. Although many email programs will take care of encoding for you (and, therefore, you won't need to concern yourself with the information here), you may occasionally have to do it yourself.

Files must be encoded so that they can pass through Internet email gateways unscathed. If you don't encode a file and your email program doesn't do it for you (although most do), the file will arrive as a bunch of unusable gibberish. This is because the gateways assume that all text passing through uses 7-bit words, whereas binary files use 8-bit (1 byte) words; therefore, binary files are garbled.

Realistically, most email programs take care of this for you, but it's useful to understand, and to be able to do on your own, in a pinch.

To prevent gibberish, just **uuencode** your files before you send them along, as shown in **Code Listing 13.1**.

## To encode a file using uuencode:

**uuencode ournewhouse.jpg**
**→ ourhouse.jpg > house.uue**

At the shell prompt, type **uuencode** followed by

- The name of the unencoded file (ournewhouse.jpg, in this case).

- The name you want the (eventually) unencoded file to have (**ourhouse.jpg**).

- A command to redirect the output to a new filename (**> house.uue**). You add this bit so the file will be saved on disk and not displayed on the screen instead. We've used the **.uue** extension so we'll more easily remember that the file is uuencoded.

Code Listing 13.1 lists the files in a directory (to verify the name) and then **uuencodes** the file. Also, notice that it shows what the top of a **uuencoded** file looks like.

**Code Listing 13.1** Use **uuencode** to encode files and, optionally, to redirect the output to disk.

```
[unixvqs@LinuxMint compression]$ ls
Folder              bigfile.uue    folderzip.zip    home.gz.uue
Zipadeedoodah       file1.htm      fortunes1.txt    newzip.zip
bigfile.gz          file2.html     fortunes1.zip    ournewhouse.jpg
bigfile.new.gz      folder.tar     gzip             temp
[unixvqs@LinuxMint compression]$ uuencode ournewhouse.jpg ourhouse.jpg > house.uue
[unixvqs@LinuxMint compression]$ head house.uue
begin 664 ourhouse.jpg
M"<@>H@("'("'@("'@("'@("'@("'@("'@("'@("'@("'@("'@
M("'@4F%N9&]M(%5.25@@1F]R='5N97,,A"@H*"@I)9B!Y;W4G<F4@;;@;F]T(';A
M<G0@;V\@@=&AE;'-O;2;'Y;:#V;W=G<E4@@@N%R=(<&QT'U09B!T<&;0<'(I E8VEP
M:71A=&4@N"@o@<I4:@;VYL>2!R96R%L;'D@9VVV]09b"1P;;%C92!T;R18=70
M;'5M8F5R('I&,@:%T'($$$<%7@=c<F4@=@7IE%E@A&QU;06)E:IH;@@@@6IR
M96%D>2!B965N('&-U>"!;A;FD;F960@@=]G971H97($:&:@X@@d&B@@90
M<&;@@@V8@9G5R('I:6-6YED@9@'!U=;"!;'I@@-I9;1:%$8@F]8@8@8F
M9C,N\\N"'@@("'@("'@("'@(''M+!@879E$($)A)A<G)++@89B5(@6EN
M9R!!09B!T:&4@4V52B8V\@@@@H;81:&1#L:@&@@;;2,,@@;&=@D=;@@;=@8(@@
[unixvqs@LinuxMint compression]$
```

## To encode with uuencode and email at once:

uuencode ournewhouse.jpg house.jpg |
→ mail -s "Here's the new picture"
→ debray@raycomm.com

At the shell prompt, use **uuencode** followed by

- The name of the **unencoded** file (**ournewhouse.jpg** in this case).

- The name you want the (eventually) unencoded file to have (**house.jpg**).

- A command to pipe the output (| **mail -s "Here's the new picture" debray@raycomm.com**). This mails the file to a specific email address with specific text in the subject line, which the **-s** flag sets. See Chapter 11 for more about mailing files and mailing from the shell prompt.

**Code Listing 13.2** shows this command, and Code Listing 13.1 gives a glimpse into a **uuencoded** file.

---

**TIP** Also check out Chapter 11 for information about email programs that will automatically handle attachments, such as encoding attached files for you.

**TIP** You must (either manually or automatically) encode all binary files (graphics, programs, compressed files, and so on) before emailing them. Plain text files (text files, scripts, or HTML documents) don't need to be encoded.

**Code Listing 13.2** You can **uuencode** and mail all in one step to work more efficiently.

```
[unixvqs@LinuxMint compression]$
→ uuencode ournewhouse.jpg house.jpg |
→ mail -s "Here's the new picture"
→ debray@raycomm.com
```

# Decoding Files with uudecode

You'll decode files whenever you receive binary files through email—it's the only way you can use encoded files. Although most email programs will take care of decoding files for you (and, therefore, you won't need the information here), you may need to do it manually on occasion. If you open a file or an email message and see something like **Code Listing 13.4**, you've got a little decoding to do. To avoid the gibberish, decode your files, as shown in **Code Listing 13.3**.

## To decode files with uudecode:

**uudecode rowboat.uue**

At the shell prompt, type **uudecode** followed by the name of the file to decode (Code Listing 13.3).

**TIP** When you receive an encoded file, you might have to uncompress or unzip it in addition to decoding it. See the appropriate sections later in this chapter for details.

**TIP** If you have a file that you suspect is uuencoded, use head plus the filename to view the top ten lines of the file. If it's really uuencoded, you'll see a line saying so at the top, as shown in Code Listing 13.4. The 664 in the line is the file's permissions, and rowboat.jpg is the filename that the extracted file will have. See Chapter 5 for highly interesting details about file permissions.

Code Listing 13.3 **uudecoding** files is straightforward.

```
[unixvqs@LinuxMint compression]$ uudecode  rowboat.uue
[unixvqs@LinuxMint compression]$ ls -l row*
-rw-rw-r-  1 ejr    users   128886 Jul 27  09:52 rowboat.jpg
-rw-r-r-   1 ejr    users   177606 Jul 27  09:51 rowboat.uue
[unixvqs@LinuxMint compression]$
```

Code Listing 13.4 Use the **head** command to view the top of a file. The **begin** line is the tipoff that it's a **uuencoded** file, with 664 permissions and the name **rowboat.jpg**.

```
[unixvqs@LinuxMint compression]$ head rowboat.uue
begin 664 rowboat.jpg
M"<@>H@("'@("'@("'@("'@("'@("'@("'@("'@("'@("M("'@4F%N9&]M(%5.25@@1F]
R='5N97,A"@H@@H*"'@I)9B!Y;W4G<F4@;;F]T('!A
M<G0@;;;V8=&AE(''-0;;;5T;6]N"@H@@H*"'@I)9B!Y;W4G<F4@;;F]T(''&@@&']E8VEP
M:71A=&4@;;;''@H@@H*"''&''4C..!2$R.!T;R!B!=7D@
M;'5M8F5F5R(&ES(&$$<&%<W10<F=4@=$&=$AE(&$$<&&<V\X87('@86)QR
M96%D>2!C965E:&E=''(&';F=''(F96]@=@.'6X@=&AE(&$90R
M<F%T@;V8Q!965N(&!-=.:#H-9640@@G971H97((@6X@=&AE(&$90
M<FT@;V8@@9G5R;FET=7?7)E.E'$'+''@''''I;?9$&$8E]X
M97,N"B!B@("''@("''@("''M+2$$'879E($$<G%Y+"''B'$$8E(%1A;$%6$N
M9R!09B!T;:&4V4-R-97<B''@@HB:1&S8V5V\X.07,\&$X=@@.;'55A="''!!%
[unixvqs@LinuxMint compression]$
```

# Archiving with tar

Occasionally, you'll want to take a bunch of files and make them into one file, such as when you're archiving information, for example. You might think of it as tossing a bunch of toys into a toy box—that is, taking a bunch of related things and storing them all in one place.

Using **tar** (which came from "tape archive"), you can take a bunch of files and store them as a single, uncompressed file (see **Code Listing 13.5**). You'll use **tar** files not only to store information, but also to create a single source for compressing and **gzip**ping files, which is discussed later in this chapter.

**Code Listing 13.5** Tarring files binds them all together into a single file.

```
[unixvqs@LinuxMint compression]$ ls -l
total 2290
drwxrwxr-x   2 ejr     users     1024 Jul 23 10:56  Feather
drwxrwxr-x   2 ejr     users     1024 Jul 23 10:49  Zipadeedoodah
-rw-rw-r-    1 ejr     users    53678 Jul 23 06:42  bigfile.gz
-rw-rw-r-    1 ejr     users    53678 Jul 23 10:16  bigfile.new.gz
-rw-rw-r-    1 ejr     users    73989 Jul 23 10:16  bigfile.uue
-rw-rw-r-    1 ejr     users   128886 Jul 23 11:45  file1.htm
-rw-rw-r-    1 ejr     users   128886 Jul 23 11:45  file2.html
-rw-rw-r-    1 ejr     users   686080 Jul 23 10:41  folder.tar
-rw-rw-r-    1 ejr     users   268156 Jul 23 06:53  folderzip.zip
-rw-rw-r-    1 ejr     users   128886 Jul 23 06:37  fortunes1.txt
-rw-rw-r-    1 ejr     users    55124 Jul 23 06:38  fortunes1.zip
-rw-rw-r-    1 ejr     users        0 Jul 23 11:2   gzip
-rw-rw-r-    1 ejr     users    73978 Jul 23 11:15  home.gz.uue
-rw-r-r-     1 ejr     users   177607 Jul 27 09:34  house.uue
-rw-rw-r-    1 ejr     users    53792 Jul 23 06:52  newzip.zip
-rw-rw-r-    1 ejr     users   128886 Jul 23 08:19  ournewhouse.jpg
-rw-rw-r-    1 ejr     users   128886 Jul 27 09:52  rowboat.jpg
-rw-r-r-     1 ejr     users   177606 Jul 27 09:51  rowboat.uue
drwxrwxr-x   3 ejr     users     1024 Jul 23 12:56  temp
[unixvqs@LinuxMint compression]$ tar -cf tarredfilename.tar Feather
[unixvqs@LinuxMint compression]$
```

## To archive a directory with `tar`:

**1.** `ls -l`

For starters, type `ls -l` at the shell prompt to verify the name of the directory you're going to `tar`.

**2.** `tar -cf tarredfilename.tar Feather`

Type `tar` followed by

- ▶ The `-cf` flags (to create a file and specify the desired filename for it)

- ▶ The name you want the tarred (archived) file to have (**tarredfilename.tar** in this example)

- ▶ The name (or names) of the directory or files to tar (**Feather**, here)

**TIP** See the "Combining Commands" section later in this chapter for timesaving ideas for combining and compressing files all in one fell swoop.

**TIP** Some versions of `tar` also support `gzip`, so you can use `tar -czf tarredfilename.tgz Feather` to `tar` and `gzip` all at once.

**TIP** You can add the `v` flag to the `tar` command flags (`-vcf`) to get a verbose description of what's being tarred.

**TIP** If you want to sound like a real Unix geek, refer to tarred files as "tarballs."

# Unarchiving Files with tar

You'll also use **tar** to unarchive files, where you take all the individual files out of the single tarred file, as shown in **Code Listing 13.6**.

## To unarchive files with **tar**:

`tar -xf labrea.tar`

At the shell prompt, type **tar -xf** (here, **x** means extract) followed by the name of the tarred file you want to unarchive. The bunch of once-tarred files will be separated into the original files or directories, as shown in Code Listing 13.6.

## To unarchive selected files with **tar**:

`tar -xf labrea.tar mammoth`

You can also extract only specified files from a **tar** file. You might do this to restore just a couple of files from a backup archive, for example. This command extracts the file named **mammoth** from the **labrea.tar** file and places it back where it belongs (**Code Listing 13.7**).

**TIP** Consider moving tarred files into a temporary directory before you unarchive them. When you unarchive, **tar** overwrites any files with the same names as files that are extracted. Using a temporary directory—ideally a new and empty temporary directory—will prevent this.

**TIP** Use **tar -tf filename** to list the files (to check your work, perhaps, or find a backup file) without actually unarchiving the files.

**TIP** Use **tar -xvf filename** to see the names of the files as they're extracted from the archive.

**Code Listing 13.6** Untarring files reconstructs the original directory structure.

```
[unixvqs@LinuxMint compression]$ tar -xf labrea.tar
[unixvqs@LinuxMint compression]$ ls -l Labrea/
total 483
-rw-r-r-  1 ejr  users   53678 Jul 27 10:05 bigfile.gz
-rw-r-r-  1 ejr  users  128886 Jul 27 10:06 mammoth.jpg
-rw-r-r-  1 ejr  users  177607 Jul 27 10:05 house.uue
-rw-r-r-  1 ejr  users  128886 Jul 27 10:06 rowboat.jpg
[unixvqs@LinuxMint compression]$
```

**Code Listing 13.7** Unarchive just a single file to replace a missing or corrupted file.

```
[unixvqs@LinuxMint compression]$ tar -xf labrea.tar mammoth
[unixvqs@LinuxMint compression]$ ls -l Labrea/m*
-rw-r-r-  1 ejr  users  128886 Jul 27 10:06 Labrea/mammoth
[unixvqs@LinuxMint compression]$
```

# Compressing Files with compress

*Compressing* a file just means making it smaller so that it takes up less hard disk space. It's like overfilling a toy box, closing the lid, then sitting on it to smoosh the contents so that they fit into a smaller space. Many times when you create a file that you'll be sending via FTP or that people will access through the web, you'll want to compress the file so that it takes less time to send and download. As **Code Listing 13.8** shows, you compress files using the **compress** command (or also using **gzip**, later in this chapter).

## To compress a file with compress:

### compress labrea.tar

At the shell prompt, type **compress** followed by the filename. Here, we're compressing a tarred file, which contains multiple files. As you can see in Code Listing 13.8, the compressed file has a new extension (**.Z**) that shows that it's compressed, and it replaces the original, uncompressed file.

**TIP** You can compress only one file at a time. If you have multiple files you want to compress, consider archiving them first using `tar`, and then compressing the single archived file. See the section called "Archiving with `tar`" earlier in this chapter.

**TIP** You can add the -c flag to `compress` to leave the original file untouched and send the compressed version to standard output (where you'll probably specify a name and save it to a file). For example, you might use `compress -c labrea.tar > labrea.tar.compressed.Z`. See Chapter 1 for some mighty interesting information on redirecting output.

**Code Listing 13.8** Listing files before and after compressing them lets you see how much smaller the new file is.

```
[unixvqs@LinuxMint compression]$ ls -l l*
-rw-r-r-  1 ejr  users  501760 Jul 27 10:06 labrea.tar
[unixvqs@LinuxMint compression]$ compress labrea.tar
[unixvqs@LinuxMint compression]$ ls -l l*
-rw-r-r-  1 ejr  users  297027 Jul 27 10:06 labrea.tar.Z
[unixvqs@LinuxMint compression]$
```

# Uncompressing Files with uncompress

Compressing a file is handy for reducing the amount of disk space it uses, but you can't do much with a compressed file—directly, at least. You'll need to uncompress it first. As **Code Listing 13.9** shows, you do so using the **uncompress** command.

## To uncompress a file with uncompress:

**uncompress labrea.tar.Z**

At the shell prompt, type **uncompress** followed by the full filename of the file to uncompress. The compressed file is replaced by the uncompressed file, which is named like the original, but without the **.Z** (see Code Listing 13.9).

**TIP** Remember that uncompressed files take up more space—sometimes a lot more space—than compressed files. You might want to check your storage quota with your ISP before you uncompress a file to make sure that you don't exceed your limit. As Chapter 7 explains, you can often check your quota by typing **quota -v** at the shell prompt.

**TIP** You can add the **-c** flag to **uncompress** to leave the original file untouched and send the uncompressed version to standard output. For example, you might use **uncompress -c tarred.tar.Z > tarred.tar**. See Chapter 1 for more information on redirecting output, as is shown here.

**TIP** You can also use **gunzip** to uncompress compressed files. Check out "Unzipping a **gzip** File with **gunzip**" later in this chapter.

**Code Listing 13.9** You can uncompress files with a single swift command and possibly double your disk usage at the same time, as shown here.

```
[unixvqs@LinuxMint compression]$ ls -l l*
-rw-r-r-  1 ejr  users  297027 Jul 27 10:06 labrea.tar.Z
[unixvqs@LinuxMint compression]$ uncompress labrea.tar.Z
[unixvqs@LinuxMint compression]$ ls -l l*
-rw-r-r-  1 ejr  users  501760 Jul 27 10:06 labrea.tar
[unixvqs@LinuxMint compression]$
[unixvqs@LinuxMint compression]$ ls -l z*
-rw-r-r-  1 ejr  users  501760 Jul 27 10:22 zipadeedoodah.tar
[unixvqs@LinuxMint compression]$ gzip zipadeedoodah.tar
[unixvqs@LinuxMint compression]$ ls -l z*
-rw-r-r-  1 ejr  users  239815 Jul 27 10:22 zipadeedoodah.tar.gz
[unixvqs@LinuxMint compression]$
```

# Zipping a File or Directory with gzip

If you want to compress only a single file or directory, you might choose **gzip** rather than **compress**. The **gzip** command is more efficient, so you wind up with smaller files than you do with **compress**. As **Code Listing 13.10** shows, you use **gzip** in much the same way that you use **compress**.

## To zip a file or directory with gzip:

1. **ls -lh z***

   At the shell prompt, use **ls -l** to confirm the name of the file or directory you want to zip. In this example, we're looking for **z** (as in zipadeedoodah) files.

2. **gzip zipadeedoodah.tar**

   Type **gzip** followed by the name of the file or directory to **gzip**. The zipped file will replace the unzipped version and will have a new **.gz** extension.

**TIP** If you want to keep a copy of the original, unzipped file, try gzip -c filetogzip > compressed.gz.

**TIP** If the compressed files will be accessed by someone using Windows, you should consider using zip, which is discussed later in this chapter. Although gzip is more convenient in the Unix world, gzip is not the same as traditional .zip files used in Windows.

**TIP** Another utility used for compressing files is bzip (bzip2, actually). You can find more information about it at www.bzip.org. It's quite powerful, slightly more efficient than gzip, and quickly gaining popularity.

**TIP** You can tar a group of files and then compress the single file using gzip.

Code Listing 13.10 Using **gzip**, you can compress a single file.

```
unixvqs@LinuxMint $ ls -lh z*
-rwxrwx--- 1 unixvqs unixvqs 12M Mar 30 10:20 zipadeedoodah.tar
unixvqs@LinuxMint $ gzip zipadeedoodah.tar
unixvqs@LinuxMint $ ls -lh z*
-rwxrwx--- 1 unixvqs unixvqs 6.2M Mar 30 10:20 zipadeedoodah.tar.gz
unixvqs@LinuxMint $
```

# Unzipping a gzip File with gunzip

To access gzipped files, you'll need to unzip them. You do so using **gunzip**, as Code Listing 13.11 shows.

## To unzip a gzip file with gunzip:

1. **ls -l *.gz**

   At the shell prompt, verify the name of the gzipped file with **ls -l** (Code Listing 13.11).

2. **gunzip zipadeedoodah.tar**

   Enter **gunzip** and the name of the file to unzip. **gunzip** will uncompress the file(s) and return you to the shell prompt.

**TIP** When you're unzipping files with **gunzip**, you're not required to enter the file extension. **gunzip zipadeedoodah** would work just as well as **gunzip zipadeedoodah.gz**.

**TIP** You might encounter gzipped files with a .tgz (tarred, gzipped), **tar.gz**, or just .gz extension. It'll handle any of those gracefully.

**TIP** Some systems don't recognize the **gunzip** command, so you might need to use **gzip -d** to uncompress the files.

**TIP** If you have a compressed file that you know is text—**oldfunnysayingsfromthenet.gz**, for example—you can uncompress it (without deleting the original file) and view it with a single command: **gzcat oldfunnysayingsfromthenet | more**. Yes, that's gz (as in **gzip**) and **cat** (Chapter 1) concatenated together. Unix people are funny, eh?

**TIP** **gunzip** understands how to uncompress most (compressed) files, including those co pressed with **compress** or **.zip** files from Windows systems.

Code Listing 13.11 Use **gunzip** to uncompress zipped files.

```
[unixvqs@LinuxMint compression]$ ls -l *.gz
-rw-rw-r-    1 ejr  users    53678 Jul 23 06:42 bigfile.gz
-rw-rw-r-    1 ejr  users    53678 Jul 23 10:16 bigfile.new.gz
-rw-r-r-     1 ejr  users   239819 Jul 27 10:22 zipadeedoodah.tar.gz
[unixvqs@LinuxMint compression]$ gunzip zipadeedoodah.tar
[unixvqs@LinuxMint compression]$ ls -l z*
-rw-r-r-   1 ejr  users   501760 Jul 27 10:22 zipadeedoodah.tar
[unixvqs@LinuxMint compression]$ ls -l *.gz
-rw-rw-r-  1 ejr  users   53678 Jul 23 06:42 bigfile.gz
-rw-rw-r-  1 ejr  users   53678 Jul 23 10:16 bigfile.new.gz
[unixvqs@LinuxMint compression]$
```

# Zipping Files and Directories with zip

If you're working with files and directories that will be accessed on the Windows platform, you might need to use **zip** (rather than **gzip**). This **zip** is like Windows **zip**, so it's a safer option than **gzip**, which can work, but it depends on the software available on the Windows system. **zip** files are compressed to save disk space and sometimes contain multiple files (see **Code Listing 13.12**).

## To zip files or directories with zip:

1. **ls -l z***

   At the shell prompt, use **ls -l** to confirm the names of the files or directories you want to zip.

2. **zip -r zipped zipadeedoodah**

   Type **zip -r** followed by the name of the **zip** file you're creating (without an extension), followed by the name of the file or directory to zip, where **-r** means recursive. Then just twiddle your thumbs while waiting for Unix to zip your files (Code Listing 13.12).

**TIP** Some Unix systems don't offer the **zip** command. In that case, if you need to share files with Windows users, use either **gzip** or **compress**, send the file, and tell your colleagues that they can use WinZip, among other programs, to extract the files.

**TIP** If you zip a directory (remember to include the **-r** for recursive argument), you zip all the files within it.

**TIP** If you can't get the tune "Zip-A-Dee-Doo-Dah" out of your head after these examples, try humming "The Candy Man" or "I'd Like to Teach the World to Sing" or whistling the "Colonel Bogey March" (theme from *The Bridge on the River Kwai*).

Code Listing 13.12 Use **zip** to compress files, particularly those you'll share with Windows users.

```
[unixvqs@LinuxMint compression]$ ls -l z*
-rw-r-r-  1 ejr  users  501760 Jul 27 10:22 zipadeedoodah
[unixvqs@LinuxMint compression]$ zip -r zipped zipadeedoodah
  adding: zipadeedoodah (deflated 52%)
[unixvqs@LinuxMint compression]$ ls -l z*
-rw-r-r-  1 ejr  users  501760 Jul 27 10:22 zipadeedoodah
-rw-r-r-  1 ejr  users  239943 Jul 27 10:41 zipped.zip
[unixvqs@LinuxMint compression]$
```

# Unzipping Zipped Files with unzip

You can unzip zipped files using **unzip**, which is logical because you certainly wouldn't unzip zipped files with un-Velcro or unsnap (**Code Listing 13.13**).

## To unzip a zip file using unzip:

1. `ls -l *.zip`

   At the shell prompt, verify the name of the zip file with `ls *.zip`.

2. `unzip zipped.zip`

   Enter **unzip** and the name of the file to unzip (with or without the **.zip** extension). **unzip** will uncompress the file(s) and return you to the shell prompt.

**TIP** If you attempt to unzip a file and the file or files to be unzipped already exist, unzip will prompt you for each one to determine if you want to overwrite (destroy) the existing file, cancel the unzipping process, or rename the file you're unzipping to a safe name. Alternatively, use the -n (never overwrite) or -o (always overwrite) flag to avoid this prompt entirely.

**TIP** gunzip also understands how to uncompress some .zip files, so you can use gunzip instead of unzip, if you'd like. On the Unix side of things, use whatever seems easiest to you, or gunzip if you really don't care.

**TIP** To see the contents of a zip file, use unzip -l zipped.zip.

Code Listing 13.13 **unzip** lets you uncompress files without accidentally obliterating them.

```
[unixvqs@LinuxMint compression]$ ls -l *.zip
-rw-rw-r-  1 ejr  users  268156 Jul 23 06:53 folderzip.zip
-rw-rw-r-  1 ejr  users   55124 Jul 23 06:38 fortunes1.zip
-rw-rw-r-  1 ejr  users   53792 Jul 23 06:52 newzip.zip
-rw-r-r-   1 ejr  users  239943 Jul 27 10:41 zipped.zip
[unixvqs@LinuxMint compression]$ unzip zipped.zip
Archive: zipped.zip
replace zipadeedoodah.tar? [y]es, [n]o, [A]ll, [N]one, [r]ename: y
  inflating: zipadeedoodah.tar
[unixvqs@LinuxMint compression]$
```

# Combining Commands

As we've shown you in this chapter, you use separate commands to **uuencode/uudecode**, **tar/untar**, **compress/uncompress**, and **zip/unzip** files and directories. A lot of times, however, you can pipe commands together and run them in sequence, saving you time and hassle. For example, as **Code Listing 13.14** shows, you can **uudecode** and **gunzip** files at the same time by piping the commands together. You can also **uncompress** and **untar** at one time, and you can **tar** and **gzip** at one time.

### To uudecode and gunzip at one time:

1. **ls -l h***

   Use **ls -l** to verify the existence of your uuencoded and zipped file.

2. **uudecode -o /dev/stdout home.gz.uue**
   **→ | gunzip > home**

   Here, we use **-o /dev/stdout** to send the **uudecode** output to the standard output, then pipe the output of the **uudecode** command to **gunzip**, then redirect the output of **gunzip** to the **home** file. Whew! See Code Listing 13.14 for the details.

**Code Listing 13.14** Decoding and unzipping at once is a little cryptic but saves your typity typity fingers.

```
[unixvqs@LinuxMint compression]$ ls -l h*
-rw-rw-r-  1 ejr   users   73978 Jul 23 11:15 home.gz.uue
-rw-r-r-   1 ejr   users  177607 Jul 27 09:34 house.uue
[unixvqs@LinuxMint compression]$ uudecode -o /dev/stdout home.gz.uue | gunzip > home
[unixvqs@LinuxMint compression]$ ls -l h*
-rw-r-r-   1 ejr   users  128886 Jul 27 10:48 home
-rw-rw-r-  1 ejr   users   73978 Jul 23 11:15 home.gz.uue
-rw-r-r-   1 ejr   users  177607 Jul 27 09:34 house.uue
[unixvqs@LinuxMint compression]$
```

## To uncompress and untar
## at one time:

**zcat filename.tar.Z | tar -xf -**

At the shell prompt, type **zcat** followed by
the filename (as usual) and pipe that output
to **tar**. Follow the **tar** command and flags
with a - so that **tar** will be able to save the
file to the intended name (**Code Listing 13.15**).

## To tar and gzip at one time:

**tar -cf - Feather | gzip > feather.tar.gz**

At the shell prompt, enter your **tar** command as usual but add a - (and a space)
before the filename so the output can be
piped. Then, pipe the output to **gzip** and
redirect the output of that to a filename
with the **.tar** and **.gz** extensions to show
that the file has been tarred and gzipped
(**Code Listing 13.16**).

**Code Listing 13.15** After you find the compressed files, you can **uncompress** and **untar** them at once,
and then use **ls -ld** (long and directory flags) to check your work.

```
[unixvqs@LinuxMint compression]$ ls -l *.Z
-rw-r-r-   1 ejr  users  297027 Jul 27 10:06 labrea.tar.Z
[unixvqs@LinuxMint compression]$ zcat labrea.tar.Z | tar -xf -
[unixvqs@LinuxMint compression]$ ls -ld L*
drwxr-xr-x 2 ejr  users  1024 Jul 27 10:16 Labrea
[unixvqs@LinuxMint compression]$
```

**Code Listing 13.16** You can efficiently **tar** and **gzip** all at once as well.

```
[unixvqs@LinuxMint compression]$ ls -ld F*
drwxrwxr-x 2 ejr  users  1024 Jul 23 10:56 Feather
[unixvqs@LinuxMint compression]$ tar -cf - Feather | gzip > feather.tar.gz
[unixvqs@LinuxMint compression]$ ls -l f*
-rw-r-r-   1 ejr  users  106752 Jul 27 10:54 feather.tar.gz
-rw-rw-r-  1 ejr  users  128886 Jul 23 11:45 file1.htm
-rw-rw-r-  1 ejr  users  128886 Jul 23 11:45 file2.html
-rw-rw-r-  1 ejr  users  686080 Jul 23 10:41 folder.tar
-rw-rw-r-  1 ejr  users  268156 Jul 23 06:53 folderzip.zip
-rw-rw-r-  1 ejr  users  128886 Jul 23 06:37 fortunes1.txt
-rw-rw-r-  1 ejr  users   55124 Jul 23 06:38 fortunes1.zip
[unixvqs@LinuxMint compression]
```

# Using Handy Utilities

Just when you thought Unix was great... it gets better! Unix gives you a plethora of handy-dandy utilities—small programs— that can make your life a bit easier. For example, you might want to use the calendar, calculator, or interactive spell-checker. None of these utilities is likely to be essential to your day-to-day Unix doings; however, they are handy to have and use. Ask your system administrator about which utilities you have available, or return to Chapter 1 to explore your system and find out what's there. In this chapter, we'll look at a few of the most useful ones.

# Calendaring with cal

One of the handiest Unix utilities is **cal**, which—logically—is a calendar. Find out what today's date is, what day of the week December 31 is, or what the calendar year looks like. As **Code Listing 14.1** shows, all you have to do is type **cal** and any specific options you want.

## To use the cal utility:

**1. cal**

Type **cal** at the shell prompt to see the current month's calendar, as shown in Code Listing 14.1. Then, start playing with options, as shown in the next few steps.

**2. cal -j**

Use **cal -j** to see the Julian calendar, which shows each day numbered from the beginning of the year. (This argument doesn't work on all systems.)

**3. cal 2015 | more**

Pipe **cal 2015** to **more** to see the whole year's calendar.

**4. cal 12 1941**

Type **cal** plus specific dates to view dates for a particular year.

---

**TIP** Note that **cal** is very flexible, and takes whatever date you provide without complaint. If you ask for **cal 98**, you'll get the calendar for the year 98—that is, 1900 and three quarters of a score years ago, if you want to keep track like that.

**TIP** Put **cal** into your startup configuration files to get a reminder of the date whenever you log in. Check out Chapter 8 for details.

**Code Listing 14.1** Just type **cal** to see the current month's calendar, or check out other calendar options with flags.

```
unixvqs@LinuxMint $ cal
      April 2014
Su Mo Tu We Th Fr Sa
       1  2  3  4  5
 6  7  8  9 10 11 12
13 14 15 16 17 18 19
20 21 22 23 24 25 26
27 28 29 30

unixvqs@LinuxMint $ cal -j 3 2015
       March 2015
Su  Mo  Tu  We  Th  Fr  Sa
60  61  62  63  64  65  66
67  68  69  70  71  72  73
74  75  76  77  78  79  80
81  82  83  84  85  86  87
88  89  90

unixvqs@LinuxMint $ cal 2015
```

*code listing continues on next page*

```
                          2015
        January               February                March
   Su Mo Tu We Th Fr Sa   Su Mo Tu We Th Fr Sa   Su Mo Tu We Th Fr Sa
              1  2  3       1  2  3  4  5  6  7       1  2  3  4  5  6  7
    4  5  6  7  8  9 10     8  9 10 11 12 13 14     8  9 10 11 12 13 14
   11 12 13 14 15 16 17    15 16 17 18 19 20 21    15 16 17 18 19 20 21
   18 19 20 21 22 23 24    22 23 24 25 26 27 28    22 23 24 25 26 27 28
   25 26 27 28 29 30 31                            29 30 31

         April                  May                    June
   Su Mo Tu We Th Fr Sa   Su Mo Tu We Th Fr Sa   Su Mo Tu We Th Fr Sa
           1  2  3  4                   1  2       1  2  3  4  5  6
    5  6  7  8  9 10 11     3  4  5  6  7  8  9     7  8  9 10 11 12 13
   12 13 14 15 16 17 18    10 11 12 13 14 15 16    14 15 16 17 18 19 20
   19 20 21 22 23 24 25    17 18 19 20 21 22 23    21 22 23 24 25 26 27
   26 27 28 29 30          24 25 26 27 28 29 30    28 29 30
                           31

          July                 August                September
   Su Mo Tu We Th Fr Sa   Su Mo Tu We Th Fr Sa   Su Mo Tu We Th Fr Sa
           1  2  3  4                      1       1  2  3  4  5
    5  6  7  8  9 10 11     2  3  4  5  6  7  8     6  7  8  9 10 11 12
   12 13 14 15 16 17 18     9 10 11 12 13 14 15    13 14 15 16 17 18 19
   19 20 21 22 23 24 25    16 17 18 19 20 21 22    20 21 22 23 24 25 26
   26 27 28 29 30 31       23 24 25 26 27 28 29    27 28 29 30
                           30 31

        October               November                December
   Su Mo Tu We Th Fr Sa   Su Mo Tu We Th Fr Sa   Su Mo Tu We Th Fr Sa
              1  2  3       1  2  3  4  5  6  7             1  2  3  4  5
    4  5  6  7  8  9 10     8  9 10 11 12 13 14     6  7  8  9 10 11 12
   11 12 13 14 15 16 17    15 16 17 18 19 20 21    13 14 15 16 17 18 19
   18 19 20 21 22 23 24    22 23 24 25 26 27 28    20 21 22 23 24 25 26
   25 26 27 28 29 30 31    29 30                   27 28 29 30 31

unixvqs@LinuxMint $ cal 12 1941
    December 1941
Su Mo Tu We Th Fr Sa
    1  2  3  4  5  6
 7  8  9 10 11 12 13
14 15 16 17 18 19 20
21 22 23 24 25 26 27
28 29 30 31

unixvqs@LinuxMint $
```

# Calculating with bc

Unix even offers a handy calculator utility that lets you...er...calculate things. Just use **bc**, as shown in **Code Listing 14.2**.

## To calculate with bc:

**1. bc**

At the shell prompt, type **bc**. You'll find yourself at a blank line, waiting for math to do.

**2. 6*5** [Enter]

Enter the numbers, operators, expressions, or whatever you want to calculate. Use **+** to add, **-** to subtract, ***** to multiply, and **/** to divide. The answer appears on the next line (Code Listing 14.2).

**3.** [Ctrl]+[D]

Quit **bc** when you're done.

> **TIP** You can tell **bc** to calculate expressions within a file by using bc `filename`. (Of course, replace `filename` with the real filename.) Then, **bc** waits for more to do from the command line.

> **TIP** Type man **bc** for more details about **bc**'s capabilities.

**Code Listing 14.2** Using the **bc** utility, you can calculate and calculate and calculate...

```
unixvqs@OSX $ bc
6*5
30
unixvqs@OSX $
```

**Code Listing 14.3** Using the **expr** utility, evaluating the value or the truth (or lack thereof) of expressions is straightforward.

```
unixvqs@OSX $ expr 3 \* 4
12
unixvqs@OSX $ expr 5 % 3
2
unixvqs@OSX $ a=$PWD; b=$HOME; expr $a = $b
1
unixvqs@OSX $ cd bin
unixvqs@OSX $ a=$PWD; b=$HOME; expr $a = $b
0
unixvqs@OSX $
```

# Evaluating Expressions with expr

Unix also provides **expr**, which you can use for evaluating expressions. (In this use, the term *expressions* refers to the mathematical, logical, scientific meaning of the word.) In addition to evaluating mathematical expressions, you can evaluate darn near anything else. The **expr** utility is often used in shell scripts—and you'll probably find the most value in **expr** in that context—but it works just fine at the command line, too, as shown in **Code Listing 14.3**.

## To evaluate with expr:

- **expr 3 \* 4**

  At the shell prompt, enter **expr** followed by the expression it should evaluate. In this example, we're multiplying 3 times 4. (We have to use a \ to escape [protect] the * from being interpreted as a wildcard by the shell.)

- **expr 5 % 3**

  Determine the modulo (remainder) of 5 divided by 3. The answer appears on the next line (Code Listing 14.3).

- **a=$PWD; b=$HOME; expr $a = $b**

  This cryptic expression sets **a** equal to the current directory and **b** equal to the home directory, and then compares the two. If it returns **1** (true), you're in your home directory. If it returns **0** (false), you're not.

**TIP** Comparisons within shell scripts allow you to check to see whether or not something is true, and then act accordingly. See Chapter 10 for more information.

**TIP** The **expr** man page isn't particularly helpful; search the Internet to get help with **expr**.

# Converting with units

Do you always forget how many drams there are in an ounce? Never fear. The **units** utility makes converting measurements a snap. See **Code Listing 14.4** to learn how to convert with units.

## To convert with units:

**1. units**

At the shell prompt, type **units**. The Unix system will prompt you with "You have:" as shown in Code Listing 14.4.

**2. inch**

Enter the units you're starting with. You'll then be prompted with "You want:"

**3. feet**

Enter the kind of units you want, and watch with amazement as Unix counts on its fingers and toes to figure out the answer.

**4.** Ctrl +D

Quit **units** when you're finished.

---

**TIP** You can create your own **units** file, if you want, defining relationships between units and values of constants. That way, if the value of pi changes, you can create your own file with the new value. Type `man units` for more information.

**TIP** Mess around with **units** more, and you'll be astounded at the many units it can convert.

**Code Listing 14.4** Use the **units** utility to find out how to convert from anything to anything else—really!

```
unixvqs@OSX $ units
1948 units, 71 prefixes, 28 functions
You have: inch
You want: feet
 * 0.083333333
 / 12
You have:
unixvqs@OSX $
```

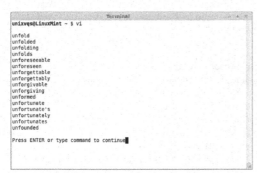

**A** Use **look** to find words, even within **vi**.

Code Listing 14.5 Look up words with **look**.

```
unixvqs@OSX $ look unfo
unfold
unfolded
unfolding
unfolds
unforeseen
unforgeable
unforgiving
unformatted
unfortunate
unfortunately
unfortunates
unfounded
unixvqs@OSX $
```

# Looking It Up with look

Speaking of spelling, you can also have Unix just look up a word for you in the system dictionary. It's just like saying, "Hey, honey, how do I spell 'unforgivably,' as in 'unforgivably lazy?'" Just type **look** and the beginning of the word you want to look up (Code Listing 14.5).

## To look up a word with look:

**look unfo**

At the shell prompt, type **look** followed by the first letters—all you know—of the word you want to look up. You'll see a listing of all the words that start with those letters, as shown in Code Listing 14.5.

**TIP** You can use **look** from within **vi**, with Esc **:!look unfo**, as shown in **A**.

# Keeping a Record of Your Session with script

Occasionally, you may need to keep a record of a Unix or Linux session—for example, if you're using Unix or Linux as part of a class assignment or you need a session record to submit to your untrusting boss. You can do this using **script**, which keeps a record of every command you type from the shell prompt (**Code Listing 14.6**). You might think of typing **script** as pressing the Record button on a tape recorder.

## To record your session with script:

1. **script covermybutt**

   At the shell prompt, type **script** to start recording your actions. You can save the transcript to a specified filename, as in **script covermybutt**. If you don't specify a file, Unix will save the transcript in the current directory as **typescript**.

2. Do your thing. See you in a couple of hours.

3. ⌨Ctrl⌨+⌨D⌨

   When you're finished, press ⌨Ctrl⌨+⌨D⌨ to stop recording the session.

4. **more covermybutt**

   Use **more** or the editor of your choice to view the script. Code Listing 14.6 shows a sample transcript.

**Code Listing 14.6** Using **script** is a great way to keep records.

```
[
ejr@hobbes ch14]$ more covermybutt
Script started on Sun 30 Mar 2014
→ 04:14:23 PM MDT
unixvqs@OpenIndiana $ pwd
/home/ejr/ch14
unixvqs@OpenIndiana $ who
root    tty1    May 15 14:18
ejr     ttyp0   May 15 14:20 (calvin.raycomm.com)
ejr     ttyp1   May 15 14:28 (calvin.raycomm.com)
unixvqs@OpenIndiana $ ps ax
 PID TTY STAT TIME COMMAND
   1 ? S 0:02 init [3]
   2 ? SW 0:00 (kflushd)
   3 ? SW< 0:00 (kswapd)
  48 ? S 0:00 /sbin/kerneld
 229 ? S 0:00 syslogd
 238 ? S 0:00 klogd
 260 ? S 0:00 crond
 272 ? S 0:00 inetd
 283 ? S 0:00 lpd
 298 ? S 0:00 sendmail: accepting
→ connections on port 25
 310 ? S 0:00 gpm -t ms
 321 ? S 0:00 httpd
 355 ? S 0:00 nmbd -D
 368 1 S 0:00 /bin/login - root
 369 2 S 0:00 /sbin/mingetty tty2
 370 3 S 0:00 /sbin/mingetty tty3
 371 4 S 0:00 /sbin/mingetty tty4
 372 5 S 0:00 /sbin/mingetty tty5
 373 6 S 0:00 /sbin/mingetty tty6
 375 ? S 0:00 update (bdflush)
 381 1 S 0:00 -bash
 402 ? S 0:00 in.telnetd
 436 ? S 0:00 in.telnetd
 249 ? S 0:00 /usr/sbin/atd
 327 ? S 0:00 httpd
 328 ? S 0:00 httpd
 329 ? S 0:00 httpd
 330 ? S 0:00 httpd
 331 ? S 0:00 httpd
 332 ? S 0:00 httpd
 333 ? S 0:00 httpd
 334 ? S 0:00 httpd
 335 ? S 0:00 httpd
```

*code listing continues on next page*

**Code Listing 14.6** *continued*

```
403 p0 S 0:00 /bin/login -h calvin
→ raycomm.com -p
404 p0 S 0:00 -bash
437 p1 S 0:00 /bin/login -h calvin
→ raycomm.com -p
438 p1 S 0:00 -bash
449 p1 S 0:00 ispell gudspeler
450 p0 S 0:00 script covermybutt
451 p0 S 0:00 script covermybutt
452 p3 S 0:00 bash -i
455 p3 R 0:00 ps ax
unixvqs@OpenIndiana $ exit
Script done on Sun 30 Mar 2014
→ 04:24:53 PM MDT
unixvqs@OpenIndiana $
```

**TIP** Screen-based programs, such as `vi`, `nano`, `alpine`, `mutt`, and `links`, tend to wreak havoc with the output of `script`. You can still read the content, but the formatting is often badly out of whack, as shown in **A**.

**TIP** You would use `script` if you want to record both what you did and what happened ("Geez, I typed `rm unbackedupdata`, then `ls`, and sure enough, the `ls` listing showed that I was in big trouble"). On the other hand, if you just want the list of commands you typed with no indication of what happened, check out `history` from Chapter 3 ("Geez, I typed `rm unbackedupdata`, then I typed `ls`, then I logged out and cried").

**A** Some programs give you oddly formatted script output and strange beeps when you view the script.

# Getting Back to Your Place with screen

One of the challenges of working in a remote terminal session is that if the connection breaks (because the Wi-Fi connection at the coffee shop failed, for example), you've completely lost the context of what you were doing. Unsurprisingly, there's a tool to fix that.

The **screen** utility lets you easily start a session that you can reconnect to whenever you want, and it's easy to use. Using **screen** and various flags, you can start a screen session

## To start a screen session with **screen**:

**screen**

To start a screen session, just type **screen**. Every command you type next will be part of the screen session, and you can get back to it as needed.

## To detach from a screen session

Ctrl+A D

Use Ctrl+A (to enter command mode, much like Esc for vi), then D to detach from the screen session.

```
unixvqs@LinuxMint $ screen -list
There are screens on:
        8996.pts-7.LinuxMint    (03/30/2014 04:11:35 PM)     (Detached)
        8892.pts-11.LinuxMint   (03/30/2014 04:10:46 PM)     (Detached)
        8281.pts-7.LinuxMint    (03/30/2014 04:09:06 PM)     (Detached)
3 Sockets in /var/run/screen/S-unixvqs.

unixvqs@LinuxMint $ screen -r
There are several suitable screens on:
        8996.pts-7.LinuxMint    (03/30/2014 04:11:35 PM)     (Detached)
        8892.pts-11.LinuxMint   (03/30/2014 04:10:46 PM)     (Detached)
        8281.pts-7.LinuxMint    (03/30/2014 04:09:06 PM)     (Detached)
Type "screen [-d] -r [pid.]tty.host" to resume one of them.
unixvqs@LinuxMint $ screen -r
There are several suitable screens on:
        8996.pts-7.LinuxMint    (03/30/2014 04:11:35 PM)     (Attached)
        8892.pts-11.LinuxMint   (03/30/2014 04:10:46 PM)     (Detached)
        8281.pts-7.LinuxMint    (03/30/2014 04:09:06 PM)     (Detached)
Type "screen [-d] -r [pid.]tty.host" to resume one of them.
unixvqs@LinuxMint $
```

**A** Use **screen** to reconnect to an existing Unix or Linux session and get back to the same place you were.

## To list screen sessions:

**screen -list**

Enter **screen -list** to see all the screens currently running.

## To reconnect to a screen session:

**screen -r**

Just type **screen -r** to reconnect to an existing screen session. If you have multiple screen sessions running, you will be prompted to choose which one you want to connect to **A**.

## To close a screen session:

Ctrl+A : **quit**

To close a screen session, enter Ctrl+A to enter command mode (again, like **vi**). Type : next, to get to the screen command prompt. Then type **quit** to exit **screen**.

**TIP** If **screen** isn't quite to your liking, but you think the concept is a good one, **tmux** is an increasingly popular alternative. It provides fundamentally similar capabilities and adds some interesting features, but it isn't as universally available as **screen**.

**TIP** Many people use **screen** for things like developing software, because **screen** makes it easier to resume where you left off.

# Acting On Found Files with xargs

Sometimes, much like the use of pipes from Chapter 1, you need to both find files and take action on their contents. Using plain pipes just acts on the filenames. For example, **ls -1| sort** will list the files in a directory, then sort them by name. If you wanted to list and sort the contents of the files, then you would use **xargs (Code Listing 14.7)**.

## To find files, then view them

1. **find . -name "*jungle*"**

   At the shell prompt, enter **find . -name "*jungle*"** to find all the files with "jungle" in the name in the current directory and directories below.

2. **find . -name "*jungle*" | wc -l**

   If you just pipe the output of the **find** command to **wc**, you'll get the count of the files that were found—two files, in this case.

3. **find . -name "*jungle*" | xargs wc -l**

   By adding **xargs** to the command, you ensure that the command is applied to the content of the found files, not just to the individual file names. In Code Listing 14.7, you see that the files with "jungle" in the name contain 20042 total lines.

**TIP** If you have files with spaces in the name—not as uncommon as it used to be, for sure—**xargs** will end up giving you some unexpected results and errors. That too is fixable. Add **-print0** to the **find** command, and **-0** to the **xargs** command. (They do make it simple, eh?). For example, enter **find . -name "*jungle*" -print0 | xargs -0 wc -l** to ensure that you get the right results even if the file name is "bungle in the jungle."

**TIP** You can use **xargs** to issue other commands on found files. If you want to delete files that you find, much as you did in Chapter 2, you can use **xargs** too. Try **find . -name "*.bak" | xargs rm** to delete all the files found.

**TIP** Check out the **man** page for **xargs** for some of the cool stuff it can do. It takes a while to get your head around the power it offers, but with time, the value becomes clear.

**Code Listing 14.7** Use **xargs** to apply a command to everything that **find** can find. Really.

```
unixvqs@LinuxMint $ find . -name "*jungle*"
./the_jungle.txt
./the_jungle_book.txt
unixvqs@LinuxMint $ find . -name "*jungle*" | wc -l
2
unixvqs@LinuxMint $ find . -name "*jungle*" | xargs wc -l
  14239 ./the_jungle.txt
   5803 ./the_jungle_book.txt
  20042 total
unixvqs@LinuxMint $
```

# 15

# Being Root

Up to now, we've been addressing Unix tools and tips that you, as a normal user of the system, can take advantage of. And as a normal user, you can't hurt the system as a whole—you can mess up your own files, certainly, but that's as far as it goes. As we've mentioned, though, there's also a different class of user, called "superuser," or **root**. The **root** user has complete power within the system and can (must) handle configuration issues, software installation for everyone using the system, and troubleshooting. The **root** user can also easily wreck the system with a single tpyo. Thorough coverage of system administration and being **root** is outside the scope of this book, but it's important to have some tools in your arsenal. In this chapter, we'll give you some basic tools to use as **root**.

# Acting Like root with sudo

As you know by now, logging in as **root** gives you the power to make changes across the entire Unix system, not just within the directories and files that you individually have permissions to access, read, or modify. Of course, having all this power also comes with responsibilities— not to screw up the entire system, among other possibilities. Especially as you're learning about system administration, you may want to experiment with these skills by logging in as **sudo** instead. Using the **sudo** utility, you can run some commands as if you were **root**, but it's not as risky as being **root**. The real **root** user has to give permission to use **sudo**, and sometimes the permission is limited to using specific utilities—you'll have to experiment.

If you are on a shared system—any system other than one that you are the sole administrator of—make sure that you have permission before using **sudo**. All **sudo** uses are usually logged, as are attempts to use **sudo**. If your system administrator won't be happy with you experimenting with being **root**, don't use **sudo** on any system other than your own.

In **Code Listing 15.1**, we show the difference between being a normal user and acting with authority with **sudo**.

**Code Listing 15.1** The **sudo** command lets you do things that you can't do as a normal user, but that isn't as risky as being **root**.

```
unixvqs@LinuxMint ~ $ cd /var/log
unixvqs@LinuxMint /var/log $ tail syslog
tail: cannot open 'syslog' for reading: Permission denied
unixvqs@LinuxMint /var/log $ sudo tail syslog

We trust you have received the usual lecture from the local System
Administrator. It usually boils down to these three things:

    #1) Respect the privacy of others.
    #2) Think before you type.
    #3) With great power comes great responsibility.

[sudo] password for unixvqs:
Mar 30 10:34:05 LinuxMint postfix/smtp[4228]: connect to smtp.gmail.com[2607:f8b0:4001:c03::6d]:25:
→ Network is unreachable
Mar 30 10:34:05 LinuxMint postfix/smtp[4230]: connect to smtp.gmail.com[74.125.142.108]:25:
→ Connection timed out
Mar 30 10:34:05 LinuxMint postfix/smtp[4231]: connect to smtp.gmail.com[74.125.142.109]:25:
▸ Connection timed out
Mar 30 10:34:05 LinuxMint postfix/smtp[4231]: connect to smtp.gmail.com[2607:f8b0:4001:c03::6d]:25:
→ Network is unreachable
Mar 30 10:34:05 LinuxMint postfix/smtp[4228]: B22A32A61B8: to=<boss@example.com>, relay=none,
→ delay=6963, delays=6903/0.01/60/0, dsn=4.4.1, status=deferred (connect to smtp.gmail.com
→ [2607:f8b0:4001:c03::6d]:25: Network is unreachable)
Mar 30 10:34:05 LinuxMint postfix/smtp[4230]: 96A0B2A61B9: to=<boss@example.com>, relay=none,
→ delay=6941, delays=6881/0.01/60/0, dsn=4.4.1, status=deferred (connect to smtp.gmail.com
→ [74.125.142.108]:25: Connection timed out)
Mar 30 10:34:05 LinuxMint postfix/smtp[4231]: E24062A61B6: to=<boss@example.com>, relay=none,
→ delay=6983, delays=6922/0.01/60/0, dsn=4.4.1, status=deferred (connect to smtp.gmail.com
→ [2607:f8b0:4001:c03::6d]:25: Network is unreachable)
Mar 30 10:34:10 LinuxMint postfix/smtp[4229]: connect to smtp.gmail.com[74.125.142.108]:25:
→ Connection timed out
Mar 30 10:34:10 LinuxMint postfix/smtp[4229]: connect to smtp.gmail.com[2607:f8b0:4001:c03::6d]:25:
→ Network is unreachable
Mar 30 10:34:10 LinuxMint postfix/smtp[4229]: 1AEAA2A61BA: to=<boss@example.com>, relay=none,
→ delay=6931, delays=6865/0.01/65/0, dsn=4.4.1, status=deferred (connect to smtp.gmail.com
→ [2607:f8b0:4001:c03::6d]:25: Network is unreachable)
unixvqs@LinuxMint /var/log $
```

## To act like root with sudo:

1. **`cd /var/log; tail syslog`**

   As plain-old you, try to look at the system log files in **/var/log**. On a Linux or Mac system, it's usually **/var/log/syslog**; on a Solaris system, it's usually **/var/adm/messages**. Other Unix flavors will have other, but similar, locations.

   Note that some of these files will require **root** access to view them, while others won't. If you can view a file as you, then choose a different file to see how **sudo** helps.

2. **`sudo tail syslog`**

   Permission was denied on the previous attempt; now use **sudo** before the command to issue the same command with **root** authority.

3. **`*******`**

   Enter your password after the interesting warning, and then note that the command succeeded this time (see Code Listing 15.1).

Code Listing 15.2 More surprisingly, **sudo** sometimes has a sense of humor.

```
1 unixvqs@LinuxMint ~ $ sudo ls
Password:
My mind is going. I can feel it.
Password:
Take a stress pill and think things over.
Password:
He has fallen in the water!
sudo: 3 incorrect password attempts
unixvqs@LinuxMint ~ $
```

**TIP** After you've used **sudo** once, you can use it again within a specific amount of time (usually five minutes) without entering your password again.

**TIP** Some versions of **sudo** have pretty entertaining prompts if you mess up your password (Code Listing 15.2). You're likely to irritate your system administrator tremendously if you try to look at these on purpose, though.

**TIP** If you haven't been given permission (not just technical permission, but actual, "you may do this" permission) to use **sudo**, don't. Everything that happens with **sudo** is logged, and you'll probably have to answer for your actions.

**TIP** Whenever possible, it's better to use **sudo** only when you need it than to become **root**. Any typo can be problematic, and it's a good thing to have to consciously add **sudo** when you want to act with **root** authority. The more time you spend as **root**, the more exposed to security issues you are.

**TIP** Some Solaris and OpenIndiana systems support **pfexec**, which is generally comparable to **sudo** and can be used in just the same way. Under the covers, it's different, but the differences aren't likely to be significant for you right now.

**Code Listing 15.3** Becoming **root** is remarkably easy.

```
unixvqs@LinuxMint ~ $ su
Password:
[root@LinuxMint]# exit
unixvqs@LinuxMint ~ $ su -
Password:
[root@LinuxMint root]#
```

**TIP** As with using **su** to become yourself (or another user), you can use **su -** to ensure that all the **root** environment variables are set correctly. If you just use **su** without the hyphen, environment variables and the like will be set for only the **root** identity and not you. Which is more appropriate depends completely on your situation. If you get unexpected error messages (`file not found`, for example) with one approach, try the other.

**TIP** Usually, you'll have to log in to a system as you, and then become **root**. It's a rare system that will allow you to log directly in remotely as **root**. Again, this is a security measure to help minimize the possibility of break-ins. Even if someone gets the **root** password on a system, they can't act as **root** if they can't also log in as a normal user.

**TIP** There are no real secrets on a Unix system. If you have something that must be a secret, you must encrypt it, or the **root** user (as well as other users) could know it.

# Becoming root with su

Becoming **root**, assuming that you know the **root** password, is really quite easy. To do so, you just apply the **su** command (introduced in the "Changing Your Identity with **su**" section in Chapter 3), where you change to the **root** identity (**Code Listing 15.3**).

Once again, we want to stress that being **root** on a Unix system carries with it a lot of responsibility. First, you must be extraordinarily careful about what you type and where you type it. Every system administrator out there has a horror story about wrecking a system (to a greater or lesser degree) through careless use of the **root** shell. We've done it, too. Second, you must be very responsible about what you do. You can read anything, see anything, watch anything, and change anything. You can, therefore, easily infringe upon the privacy of your users. Don't.

### To become root:

1. **su**

   Enter **su** to become **root**.

2. **\*\*\*\*\*\*\***

   Enter the **root** password when prompted. Note that, after you succeed, you'll see a different prompt (**#**). This is your confirmation that you succeeded and are now **root** (Code Listing 15.3).

3. **exit**

   Use **exit** or Ctrl+D to exit the **root** shell and become yourself again.

# Starting, Stopping, and Restarting Daemons

As **root**, you can do anything on the system, but you shouldn't have much to do at all. Generally, Unix and Linux systems are configured so that the programs that should be running all the time (like the web server software, mail server software, or similar programs) are automatically started in the background when the system is booted. Then you, as **root**, need only handle crises and problems. (Ha! Easier said than done.)

That said, sometimes you'll need to start or stop *daemons* (programs running in the background—see Chapter 9 for details). Say, for example, that you get an email from one of your family members complaining that file sharing (or, technically, the **samba** daemon) isn't running. As the system administrator, you'll have to start it. (The daemon is called **smbd**, but the command is **samba**. Intuitive, right...or not!)

## To start a daemon:

1. **ps -ef | grep smbd**

   Verify that the Samba server really isn't running. Sometimes users are wrong. If you see lines that list **smbd** (other than the one that reports the command you're running), **samba** is active and doesn't need to be started. The problem may lie elsewhere.

2. **cd /etc/init.d**

   Change to the directory containing the generic **init** (for initialization) scripts. This directory is likely **/etc/init.d/** or **/etc/rc.d/init.d/**, as **Code Listing 15.4** shows.

---

3. **sudo service smbd start**

   Use **sudo service smbd** and **start**. The **samba** in the **/etc/init.d** directory is a script to start the daemon with the appropriate options.

4. **ps -ef | grep smbd**

   Verify that the Samba server is now running.

**TIP** To stop a daemon, use the same process, but use **stop** (as in, **sudo service smbd stop**) to stop a daemon cleanly.

**TIP** Sometimes you might need to restart a daemon. You could stop it and then start it, but in many cases you could also use **restart** or **reload** (as in, **sudo service httpd restart**).

**TIP** Be careful about stopping or restarting daemons with which you are not familiar. Unix has a lot of interdependencies that are often not clear, and stopping something you think you don't need might have unexpected consequences.

**TIP** You might think you'd need to use **./smbd** or **/etc/init.d/smbd** to specify the exact command to use, but **service** is very smart—and special—and will only start processes from **/etc/init.d**. Cool, eh?

**Code Listing 15.4** Sometimes you have to manually start system daemons.

```
unixvqs@LinuxMint ~ $ ps -ef | grep smbd
unixvqs     2530  2101  0 09:15 pts/1    00:00:00 grep --colour=auto smb
unixvqs@LinuxMint ~ $ sudo service smbd start
smbd start/running, process 2575
unixvqs@LinuxMint ~ $ !ps
ps -ef | grep smb
root        2575     1  0 09:20 ?        00:00:00 smbd -F
root        2577  2575  0 09:20 ?        00:00:00 smbd -F
unixvqs     2580  2101  0 09:20 pts/1    00:00:00 grep --colour=auto smb
unixvqs@LinuxMint ~ $
```

# Changing the System Configuration

Most (nearly all) the system configuration files for Unix systems are contained in the **/etc** directory. If it's a configuration setting that's specific to a user, the setting will be located in the user's home directory; otherwise, configuration settings for the whole system are located in the **/etc** directory.

We're not going to get into changing much here—you really should know what you're doing before you start futzing with the system configuration. However, if you're **root**, you should have some fun with it, so here's something fun to play with. In the following example, you'll see how to change the Message of the Day (aka the **motd**), which greets users when they log in to the system (Ⓐ and Ⓑ).

## To change the motd:

1. `sudo vi /etc/motd`

   Use **sudo** to gain **root** access and edit the **/etc/motd** file.

2. `Hey, you have wrinkles in your`
   `→ stockings! Oh...sorry, you're not`
   `→ wearing stockings!`

   Uhhh, yikes! Add your favorite slogan, saying, or comment to the file. Keep in mind that everyone who logs in to the system will see this message, so keep it clean...and be nice! (See Ⓑ.)

3. `logout`

   Log out, so you can log back in and see your handiwork.

4. `ssh yoursystem.example.com`

   Log back in to see the new message.

Ⓐ Any user will see the **motd** when logging in.

Ⓑ After a user with **root** privilege edits **/etc/motd**, it's...er...different.

**TIP** The /etc/motd file is really handy for providing warnings, notes, and comments to system users. Particularly if you're planning on having system downtime or maintenance, it's nice to warn users with a message in /etc/motd.

**TIP** Virtually every other change you might make in /etc will also affect everyone on the system. Be careful.

**TIP** Depending on what you choose to change or edit in /etc, you might need to restart the appropriate daemon (as described in the previous section) for your changes to take effect. If it looks like your change didn't work, restart the daemon.

**TIP** Unix man pages also usually describe the configuration files found in /etc. Use man filename (as in, man exports) to find out what the configuration does.

## Installing Software

As **root**, you can also install your own software.

The new way, though, is far easier. On most Unix and Linux systems, you can use a special program that will go out on the web and download the program you need (along with any supplemental programs needed for your choice to run) and install it automatically. Whee!

Online repositories, specific to each different Unix or Linux variety, contain large quantities of packages, which are programs and all of the needed configuration settings to allow them to work. When you install—or upgrade—your software, you are downloading from these repositories.

For example, on Ubuntu or similar Linuxes (like LinuxMint, our favorite of the week), if you want to install the **fortune** application so you can see more cute or clever sayings than you otherwise might, you can simply type **sudo apt-get install fortune** and stand back.

The comparable command on OpenSolaris is **pfexec pkg install fortune**.

On CentOS, RedHat, SuSE, and others, you use **sudo rpm --install fortune**.

For any of these, we encourage you to explore the **man** pages for the command of your choice—you can do a lot with these commands, and it's worth a couple of minutes to read up on the options.

In all of these cases, though, you can accomplish the same thing using a spiffy GUI tool from your Unix desktop. Not only does this tool install the software, but it also tells you what's available to choose from. Poke around in the desktop menus (if you have more than just an **ssh** connection to your system) and see what you can find. Look for things like "Package Manager," and you'll be set.

# Monitoring the System

Monitoring the system is one of the key responsibilities of a system administrator. You need to make sure that everything is as it should be on the system, or yell at people, call the cops, order a new hard drive, or whatever else is required. On a single-user system, there's really not much to do, but on a larger system with many users, monitoring is a significant part of a system administrator's job.

Among other things, you can monitor the system logs (located in **/var/log** or **/var/adm**), the users logged in, overall system load, and available memory.

## To monitor logs:

- **sudo tail -1000 /var/log/syslog |**
  → **more**

  Use **sudo** to gain **root** access and look at the end (last 1000 lines) of the **messages** log file. The output of **tail** is piped to **more** so you can actually read it.

  *or*

- **sudo tail -f /var/log/apache2/**
  → **error_log**

  If you're looking for a specific occur-rence of an event as it happens, you can use **tail -f** to keep displaying the log as new errors, in the case of this log, are added to it. In this example, we're looking at the very end of the web server's error log, as shown in 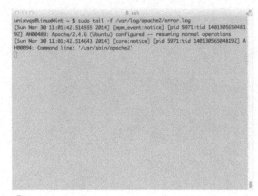.

**A** Monitoring logs is an important responsibility of the **root** user.

**B** The **top** utility helps monitor the system status.

**TIP** There's a lot to monitor and a lot to keep up with. Take time to read man pages, search the web, and ask around for tips and tricks. A wide variety of additional utilities exist to make these processes easier for you.

**TIP** Develop shell scripts that automatically run when you log in and perform the "normal" system checks. By doing so, you don't have to run routine checks manually, and you can come up to speed quickly on what's going on.

**TIP** Use top -d 2 | grep Mem for a running status check on your available memory. Use grep for other characteristics from top output, as appropriate.

**TIP** Anything that's different from usual is worth being concerned about. Check man pages or search the web to find out for sure.

## To monitor users:

- **w; who**

  You don't even need **sudo** for this one, but you do want to keep an eye on the users logged in, and where they're coming from. After a while, you'll be able to recognize patterns and react to them. If **jdoe** usually logs in by 9 a.m. and logs out by 4 p.m., and always logs in from the same system, and then you see **jdoe** suddenly logging in from a different address at 1 a.m., you should wonder if **jdoe**'s secret password isn't quite so secret anymore.

  *or*

- **last**

  The **last** utility tells you who logged in (and out) and when, and from where, as shown in **Code Listing 15.5**. Good stuff to know, particularly if you're not online and actively monitoring **w** and **who** all the time.

## To monitor system load:

**top**

Use **top** to monitor your system loads, as shown in **B**. Different systems will show distinctly different patterns, but if you become accustomed to checking **top** when everything seems normal on your system, you'll be able to better tell if something is abnormal or even what's wrong when the time comes. Press [Q] to quit **top**.

## To monitor memory:

**sudo free**

With the help of **sudo**, use **free** to see how much free memory (RAM in the computer, not storage on the disk) you have. If you get low on RAM, computer processing slows down and you might need to close some applications. If you get very low on RAM, applications might even crash.

**Code Listing 15.5** You can keep an eye on the users logged in and where they're coming from using **w**, **who**, and **last**.

```
[jdoe@frazz init.d]$ w; who
5:05am up 42 days, 18:42, 22 users, load average: 0.44, 0.40, 0.38
USER       TTY        FROM           LOGIN@      IDLE    JCPU   PCPU   WHAT
jdoe       pts/6      192.168.1.104  4:58am      1:12    0.11s  0.02s  tail -f /var/log/httpd/
unixvqs    pts/19     mike.raycomm.c Sat 12pm    12:28m  1.05s  0.94s  ssh sulley
root       vc/1                      Dec 15 10:25
unixvqs    :0                        Dec 16 16:10
unixvqs    pts/0                     Dec 16 16:11
jdoe       pts/6                     Jan 27 04:58 (192.168.1.104)
unixvqs    pts/8                     Dec 23 19:49
unixvqs    pts/17                    Jan 7 18:29
unixvqs    pts/20                    Jan 4 08:31
jdoe       pts/16                    Jan 13 19:39 (192.168.1.104)
unixvqs    pts/19                    Jan 25 12:03 (mike.raycomm.com)
unixvqs    pts/22                    Jan 25 12:03
[jdoe@frazz init.d]$ last
jdoe       pts/6      192.168.1.104  Mon Jan 27 04:58 still logged in
jdoe       pts/6      192.168.1.104  Mon Jan 27 04:57 - 04:58 (00:01)
jdoe       pts/6      192.168.1.104  Mon Jan 27 04:55 - 04:57 (00:01)
jdoe       pts/6      192.168.1.104  Sun Jan 26 18:05 - 20:16 (02:11)
jdoe       pts/6      mike.raycomm.c Sat Jan 25 12:12 - 06:52 (18:40)
unixvqs    pts/19     mike.raycomm.c Sat Jan 25 12:03 still logged in
unixvqs    pts/19     mike.raycomm.c Sat Jan 25 12:02 - 12:02 (00:00)
jdoe       pts/6      mike.raycomm.c Sat Jan 25 10:35 - 12:11 (01:36)
jdoe       pts/19     192.168.1.104  Tue Jan 21 20:59 - 00:11 (03:12)
jdoe       pts/19     192.168.1.104  Mon Jan 13 20:59 - 23:56 (02:57)
jdoe       pts/16     192.168.1.104  Mon Jan 13 19:39 - 23:34 (03:54)
jdoe       pts/23     192.168.1.104  Sun Jan 12 06:02 - 08:14 (02:12)
jdoe       pts/14     192.168.1.104  Mon Jan 6 20:54 - 23:42 (02:47)
unixvqs    pts/17     frazz.raycomm.co Thu Jan 2 20:50 - 06:27 (1+09:36)
unixvqs    pts/4                     Wed Jan 1 04:55 gone - no logout
wtmp begins Wed Jan 1 04:55:40 2010
[jdoe@frazz init.d]$
```

**A** Use **watch** to keep an eye on the system.

# Keeping Up with watch

As a system administrator, you practically have to have eyes in the back of your head and be aware of all kinds of activities that might be going on. The **watch** command is your friend. It keeps an eye on pretty much anything (users, system, or files) you want to monitor.

## To watch:

- **watch last**

  Use **watch** to monitor the output of a specific command. When something changes, you'll see it in the **watch** output **A**. In this case, we're monitoring who logged in and when.

  *or*

- **watch --differences=cumulative ls**
  **→ -l /var/spool/mail**

  You can watch to see if mail's getting delivered by monitoring an **ls -l** output from the **/var/spool/mail** directory. The extra flags show cumulative differences since you started **watch**.

  **TIP** The **watch** utility can be really handy, but sometimes it'd be easier to just type something like **tail -f /var/log/httpd/ access_log** to keep track of the web server access log or to write a shell script to periodically run **last**. Basically, **watch** is useful, but it's not the only way to monitor what's going on.

  **TIP** On the lighter side, you can also use **watch** to periodically run other programs. For example, **watch -n 5 fortune** will display a new fortune every five seconds.

# Checking Boot Messages with dmesg

Sometimes you might need extra information, beyond what is available on the running system, about the configuration or the hardware. The system automatically probes the hardware and generates all kinds of potentially useful information at that time but keeps it socked away in the bowels of the system. Use **dmesg** to get at what you need...in appalling detail.

## To check status with dmesg:

- **dmesg | more**

  Use **dmesg** (with the help of **more**) to gain some insight into the system (**Code Listing 15.6**).

  *or*

- **dmesg | mail -s "Help me understand"**
  **→ goodfriend@example.com**

  Send the output of **dmesg** to a friend for advice, if you're really stuck.

> **TIP** See Chapter 11 for more information about mailing files and data from the command line.

**Code Listing 15.6** The **dmesg** utility helps you see what happens at boot, including the processes started and hardware found.

```
[jdoe@frazz jdoe]$ dmesg | more
x98 ptys configured
Serial driver version 5.05c (2001-07-08) with HUB-6 MANY_PORTS MULTIPORT SHARE_IRQ SERIA
L_PCI ISAPNP enabled
ttyS00 at 0x03f8 (irq = 4) is a 16550A
Uniform Multi-Platform E-IDE driver Revision: 7.00alpha2
ide: Assuming 33MHz system bus speed for PIO modes; override with idebus=xx
PIIX4: IDE controller on PCI bus 00 dev 39
PIIX4: chipset revision 1
PIIX4: not 100% native mode: will probe irqs later
    ide0: BM-DMA at 0x1440-0x1447, BIOS settings: hda:pio, hdb:DMA
    ide1: BM-DMA at 0x1448-0x144f, BIOS settings: hdc:DMA, hdd:pio
hda: QUANTUM FIREBALLP LM30.0, ATA DISK drive
hdb: Maxtor 32049H2, ATA DISK drive
hdc: SAMSUNG DVD-ROM SD-612, ATAPI CD/DVD-ROM drive
ide0 at 0x1f0-0x1f7,0x3f6 on irq 14
ide1 at 0x170-0x177,0x376 on irq 15
hda: 58633344 sectors (30020 MB) w/1900KiB Cache, CHS=3649/255/63, UDMA(33)
hdb: 40021632 sectors (20491 MB) w/2048KiB Cache, CHS=2491/255/63, UDMA(33)
Partition check:
 /dev/ide/host0/bus0/target0/lun0: p1 p4 < p5 p6 >
 /dev/ide/host0/bus0/target1/lun0:<6> [EZD] [remap 0->1] [2491/255/63] p1
 p1: <solaris: [s0] p5 [s1] p6 [s2] p7 [s3] p8 [s4] p9 [s5] p10 [s6] p11 [s7] p12 >
RAMDISK driver initialized: 16 RAM disks of 32000K size 1024 blocksize
md: md driver 0.90.0 MAX_MD_DEVS=256, MD_SB_DISKS=27
md: Autodetecting RAID arrays.
md: autorun ...
 ...
Mounted devfs on /dev
Freeing unused kernel memory: 136k freed
Real Time Clock Driver v1.10e
usb.c: registered new driver usbdevfs
usb.c: registered new driver hub
usb-uhci.c: $Revision: 1.275 $ time 18:49:04 Sep 20 2002
usb-uhci.c: High bandwidth mode enabled
PCI: Found IRQ 9 for device 00:07.2
PCI: Sharing IRQ 9 with 00:10.0
usb-uhci.c: USB UHCI at I/O 0x1400, IRQ 9
usb-uhci.c: Detected 2 ports
usb.c: new USB bus registered, assigned bus number 1
hub.c: USB hub found
hub.c: 2 ports detected
-More-
```

# Setting the Date and Time

Setting the date and time is very important for a system administrator. Why? Because if you find something inappropriate or possibly problematic in your log files (for example, repeated unsuccessful login attempts from a specific location), you want to be able to accurately cross-reference your log files with the log files of your colleagues at the other location. That can happen only if the time on both hosts is pretty close to accurate.

## To set the time with `ntpdate`:

- **sudo /usr/sbin/ntpdate pool.ntp.org**

  Use **ntpdate** with the name of a time server (currently available servers are listed at **www.ntp.org**) to update your system clock to the current, accurate time (**Code Listing 15.7**). If you get an error message about the socket being in use, type **ps -ef | grep ntp** to find the **ntp** daemon that's running to keep your time synchronized. (If this happens, your time is probably OK and doesn't need to be set.)

  *or*

- **sudo date -s "Tues Jan 27 5:30:23 2015"**

  If your system doesn't have **ntpdate**, you'll have to set the time manually. Use **sudo**, **date** with the **-s** option, and all the rest of the needed information. (If you need to change, say, only the time, you can just provide the time, as in **sudo date -s 5:45**).

> **TIP** It's much better to use **ntpdate** or have the **ntpd** daemon run to keep your time up to date at all times. Using **date** manually is a poor second choice.

**A** Unix and Linux dates are measured in seconds since January 1, 1970, which is useful to know for understanding the creative use shown at the top right of this figure.

**Code Listing 15.7** Setting the date (and making sure it stays up to date) is an important **root** user responsibility.

```
unixvqs@LinuxMint ~ $ sudo date -s 5:30
Sat Mar 29 05:30:00 MDT 2014
unixvqs@LinuxMint ~ $ sudo date -s
→ "Sat Mar 29 05:30:21"
Sat Mar 29 05:30:21 MDT 2014
unixvqs@LinuxMint ~ $ sudo date -s
→ "Sat Mar 29 05:30:21 2014"
Sat Mar 29 05:30:21 MDT 2014
unixvqs@LinuxMint ~ $ sudo date -s
→ "Tue Apr 1 05:30:21 2014"
Tue Apr  1 05:30:21 MDT 2014
unixvqs@LinuxMint ~ $ date
Sat Mar 29 09:25:23 MDT 2014
unixvqs@LinuxMint ~ $ sudo
→ /usr/sbin/ntpdate pool.ntp.org
29 Mar 09:25:41 ntpdate[2596]: step time
→ server 50.116.55.65 offset 1.081716 sec
unixvqs@LinuxMint ~ $
```

> **TIP** All Unix and Linux dates are measured in seconds since the epoch, which is January 1, 1970. Use **date +%s** to see how many seconds it's been, or **date -d @1406104838** to see what that number of seconds translates to. You'd need to do this calculation to, for example, find out when upcoming Flobots concerts are scheduled **A**.

# 16

# Sensational Unix Tricks

Throughout this book, we've given you Unix building blocks—individual Unix commands, scripting techniques, and other insights that you can use individually or combine. In this chapter, we'll show you some clever things to do with Unix. You might consider this an "advanced" chapter, but most of the things we'll show you here are simply combinations of things you've already learned about in earlier chapters.

## In This Chapter

# Cleaning Up HTML Documents with tidy

If you ever have to develop HTML documents—when developing personal websites, completing a class project, or creating webpages on the job—the **tidy** utility can be a handy resource for you. If you're creating HTML pages by hand, you'll likely make occasional errors. These errors probably won't cause significant problems with using the pages, but they might make the pages harder to read, harder to maintain, and harder to subject to the scrutiny of your peers. Not to worry; **tidy** can help!

## To clean up HTML documents with tidy:

1. **vi sampledoc.html**

   Use the editor of your choice to create an HTML document. Our sample document is named, well, **sampledoc.html** Ⓐ. Don't worry about getting the tagging or syntax exactly right; **tidy** will take care of the details. Save and close your document.

2. **tidy sampledoc.html**

   The **tidy** utility will apply HTML formatting rules and then output a massaged version of your document that is technically correct (**Code Listing 16.1**). Cool, huh?

3. **tidy sampledoc.html >**
   **⇢ fixedupdoc.html**

   If you like the results, redirect the document to a new filename, as shown here, or use **tidy -m sampledoc.html** to replace the original document.

Ⓐ Even a flawed HTML document, like this one, can be fixed by **tidy**.

**Code Listing 16.1** The `tidy` command is handy for cleaning up HTML documents.

```
unixvqs@LinuxMint $ tidy sampledoc.html
line 1 column 1 - Warning: missing <!DOCTYPE> declaration
line 4 column 1 - Warning: inserting implicit <body>
line 12 column 14 - Warning: discarding unexpected </ul>
Info: Document content looks like HTML 3.2
3 warnings, 0 errors were found!

<!DOCTYPE html PUBLIC "-//W3C//DTD HTML 3.2//EN">
<html>
<head>
<meta name="generator" content=
"HTML Tidy for Linux (vers 25 March 2009), see www.w3.org">
<title>UnixVQS Home Page</title>
</head>
<body>
<h1>Making Unix and Linux Work, One Day at a Time</h1>
<p>Read these tips, when I get around to writing them, and
weep.</p>
<ul>
<li>To be written</li>
<li>To be written later</li>
<li>To be written next week</li>
<li>To be written next summer, if at all</li>
</ul>
<address>unixvqs@raycomm.com</address>
</body>
</html>
To learn more about HTML Tidy see http://tidy.sourceforge.net
Please fill bug reports and queries using the "tracker" on the Tidy website.
Additionally, questions can be sent to html-tidy@w3.org
HTML and CSS specifications are available from http://www.w3.org/
Lobby your company to join W3C, see http://www.w3.org/Consortium
unixvqs@LinuxMint $
```

**TIP** For even spiffier results, we like using `tidy -indent -quiet --doctype loose -modify sampledoc.html`, which suppresses the informative messages from `tidy`, makes the output an HTML 4 document, tidily indents the output, and replaces the original with the modified file (Code Listing 16.2). All that, and only one command.

**TIP** Consider using `tidy` with the `sed` script (described in the next section) to do a lot of cleanup at once.

Code Listing 16.2 The `tidy` command, with the appropriate flags, performs miracles—almost.

```
unixvqs@LinuxMint $ tidy -indent -quiet --doctype loose sampledoc.html
line 1 column 1 - Warning: missing <!DOCTYPE> declaration
line 4 column 1 - Warning: inserting implicit <body>
line 12 column 14 - Warning: discarding unexpected </ul>
<!DOCTYPE html PUBLIC "-//W3C//DTD HTML 4.01 Transitional//EN">

<html>
<head>
  <meta name="generator" content=
  "HTML Tidy for Linux (vers 25 March 2009), see www.w3.org">

  <title>UnixVQS Home Page</title>
</head>
<body>
  <h1>Making Unix and Linux Work, One Day at a Time</h1>
  <p>Read these tips, when I get around to writing them, and
  weep.</p>
  <ul>
    <li>To be written</li>
    <li>To be written later</li>
    <li>To be written next week</li>
    <li>To be written next summer, if at all</li>
  </ul>
  <address>
    unixvqs@raycomm.com
  </address>
</body>
</html>
unixvqs@LinuxMint $
```

```
#!/bin/bash
for i in `ls -l *.htm*`
  do
  cp $i $i.bak
  sed ""s/<\/*BLINK>//g"" $i > $i.new
  mv $i.new $i
  echo "$i is done!"
done
```

"thestinkinblinkintag" 9 lines, 143 characters

**A** Create a script to search and replace in multiple documents.

# Searching and Replacing Throughout Multiple Documents with sed

Back in Chapter 6, we talked about **sed** and how to use it to search and replace throughout files, one file at a time. Although we're sure you're still coming down off the power rush from doing that, we'll now show you how to combine **sed** with shell scripts and loops. In doing this, you can take your search-and-replace criteria and apply them to multiple documents. For example, you can search through all the **.html** documents in a directory and make the same change to all of them. In this example **A**, we strip out all the **<BLINK>** tags, which are offensive to all HTML purists as well as to right-minded individuals everywhere. Fortunately, they're also not supported by most browsers now.

Before you get started, you might want to take a look at Chapter 6 for a review of **sed** basics and Chapter 10 for a review of scripts and loops.

## To search and replace throughout multiple documents:

1. **vi thestinkinblinkintag**

   Use the editor of your choice to create a new script. Name the file whatever you want.

2. **#!/bin/bash**

   Start the shell script with the name of the program that should run the script.

*continues on next page*

3. **for i in `ls -1 *.htm*`**

   Start a loop. In this case, the loop will process all the **.htm** or **.html** documents in the current directory.

4. **do**

   Indicate the beginning of the loop content.

5. **cp $i $i.bak**

   Make a backup copy of each file before you change it. Remember, Murphy is watching you.

6. **sed "s/<\/*BLINK>//g" $i > $i.new**

   Specify your search criteria and replacement text. A lot is happening in this line, but don't panic. From the left, this command contains **sed** followed by

   ▸ ", which starts the command.

   ▸ **s/**, which tells **sed** to search for something.

   ▸ **<**, which is the first character to be searched for.

   ▸ **\/**, which allows you to search for the **/**. (The **\** escapes the **/** so the **/** can be used in the search.)

   ▸ **\***, which specifies zero or more of the previous characters (**/**), which takes care of both the opening and closing tags (with and without a **/** at the beginning).

   ▸ **BLINK>**, which indicates the rest of the text to search for. Note that this searches only for capital letters.

   ▸ If you are searching for **<BLINK>** tags to delete and don't know if they might be uppercase, lowercase, or both, try adding the **i** (for case-insensitive) option to your **sed** command, like this: **sed "s/<\/*BLINK>//ig"**.

```
[unixvqs@LinuxMint scripting]$
→ more ›thestinkinblinkintag
#! /bin/bash
for i in `ls -1 *.htm*`
do
cp $i $i.bak
sed "s/<\/*BLINK>//g" $i > $i.new
mv $i.new $i
echo "$i is done!"
done
[unixvqs@LinuxMint scripting]$
→ chmod u+x thestinkinblinkintag
[unixvqs@LinuxMint scripting]$
→ ./thestinkinblinkintag
above.htm is done!
file1.htm is done!
file2.htm is done!
html.htm is done!
temp.htm is done!
[unixvqs@LinuxMint scripting]$
```

- **//**, which ends the search section and the replace section (there's nothing in the replace section because the tag will be replaced with nothing).

- **g**, which tells **sed** to make the change in all occurrences (globally), not just in the first occurrence on each line.

- **"**, which closes the command.

- **$i**, which is replaced with each file-name in turn as the loop runs.

- **> $i.new**, which indicates that the output is redirected to a new file-name. (See **Code Listing 16.3**.)

**7. mv $i.new $i**

Move the new file back over the old file.

**8. echo "$i is done!"**

Optionally, print a status message onscreen, which can be reassuring if there are a lot of files to process.

**9. done**

Indicate the end of the loop.

**10.** Save and close your script.

**11.** Try it out.

Remember to make your script executable with **chmod u+x** and the filename, and then run it with **./thestinkinblinkintag**. In our example, we'll see the "success reports" for each of the HTML documents processed (Code Listing 16.3).

> **TIP** You could perform any number of other operations on the files within the loop. For example, you could strip out other codes, use tidy as shown in the previous section, replace a former webmaster's address with your own, or automatically insert comments and last-update dates.

# Generating Reports with awk

Back in Chapter 6, we showed you how to edit delimited files with **awk**, which is cool because it lets you extract specific pieces of information, such as names and phone numbers, from delimited files. As shown in **Code Listing 16.4**, you can also use **awk** to generate reports. We start with the information from an `ls -la` command, and then use **awk** to generate a report about who owns what.

## To generate reports with awk:

```
ls -la | awk '{print $9 " owned by "
→ $3 } END { print NR " Total Files" }'
```

Whew! In general, pipe `ls -la` to the long-winded **awk** command. (Yes, this is the origin of awkward.) **awk** then prints the ninth field (**$9**), the words "owned by," then the third field (**$3**), and at the end of the output, the total number of records processed (**print NR " Total Files"**). Code Listing 16.4 shows the printed report.

> **TIP** Remember that you could embed awk scripts in a shell script, as with the previous sed example, if they're something you'll use frequently.

**Code Listing 16.4** Use **awk** to generate quick reports.

```
[unixvqs@LinuxMint /home]$
→ ls -la | awk '{print  $9 " owned by "
→ $3 } END { print NR "  Total Files" }'
 owned by
. owned by root
.. owned by root
admin owned by admin
anyone owned by anyone
asr owned by asr
awr owned by awr
bash owned by bash
csh owned by csh
deb owned by deb
debray owned by debray
ejr owned by ejr
ejray owned by ejray
ftp owned by root
httpd owned by httpd
lost+found owned by root
merrilee owned by merrilee
oldstuff owned by 1000
pcguest owned by pcguest
raycomm owned by pcguest
samba owned by root
shared owned by root
22 Total Files
[unixvqs@LinuxMint /home]$
```

```
fi

# set PATH so it includes user's private bin if it exists
if [ -d "$HOME/bin" ] ; then
    PATH="$HOME/bin:$PATH"
fi

echo -e "Which editor do you want as the default? (vi or nano)"
read choice
if [ $choice = "vi" ]
    then EDITOR=/usr/bin/vi ; export EDITOR ; echo "You chose vi!"
    elif [ $choice = "nano" ]
    then EDITOR=/usr/bin/pico nano ; export EDITOR ; echo ""You chose nano!"
    else echo "Editor unchanged"
fi

"~/.profile" [Modified] line 34 of 34 --100%-- col 1
```

Ⓐ Add this mini-script to your **.zprofile**, **.bash_profile**, or **.profile** configuration file, right at the end.

**Code Listing 16.5** When the system asks your preferences, you know you're on top.

```
[unixvqs@LinuxMint ejr]$ su - ejr
Password:
Which editor do you want as the default?
→ (vi or nano)
vi
You chose vi!
[unixvqs@LinuxMint ejr]$
```

# Using Input to Customize Your Environment

Way back in Chapter 8, we talked about setting up your environment variables by customizing the configuration files that run upon login. You can further customize your environment variables by requiring input whenever a startup script runs. For example, you can set your configuration files (which are actually scripts) so that they request that you specify the default editor for the session (**Code Listing 16.5**).

## To use input to customize your environment:

1. **vi ~/.profile**

   Use your favorite editor to edit your script, and move to the end of the file.

2. **echo -e "Which editor do you want as → the default? (vi or nano)"**

   Using **echo -e**, specify the text that will prompt you to input information Ⓐ.

3. **read choice**

   On the next line, add **read** followed by the name of the variable to read in. We chose **choice** because we're using this input to set the preferred **EDITOR** environment variable.

4. **if [ $choice = "vi" ]**

   Start an **if** statement—in this case, one that tests for the **vi** option.

   *continues on next page*

**5.** `then EDITOR=/usr/bin/vi ; export`
`→ EDITOR ; echo "You chose vi!"`

Here, the **then** clause sets the **EDITOR** environment variable to **vi**, exports the environment variable, and announces your choice.

**6.** `elif [ $choice = "nano" ]`

Check for your other option with **elif** (else if). This statement covers the **nano** option.

**7.** `then EDITOR=/usr/bin/nano ; export`
`→ EDITOR ; echo "You chose nano!"`

This **then** clause sets the **EDITOR** environment variable to **nano**, exports the environment variable, and announces your choice.

**8.** `else echo "Editor unchanged"`

Set up an **else** statement, which will be used if neither option was entered at the **read** prompt. In this example, if neither **vi** nor **nano** was entered, it'll just say that the editor was unchanged.

**9.** `fi`

End the **if** statement.

**10.** Save and exit.

**11.** `su - yourid`

At the shell prompt, type **su -** followed by your userid to log in again and test the revised login script (Code Listing 16.5).

**TIP** This technique is very useful for setting the TERM(inal) environment variable if you access the system from different remote systems with different capabilities.

# Using ROT13 Encoding with sed

In various places on the Internet, text is often encoded with something called ROT13, which is an abbreviation for "rotate (the alphabet by) 13." That is, A becomes N, B becomes O, and so forth. If text is encoded, people have to take extra steps to decode the message. For example, if the message is a movie review, people who don't want to know the ending won't have the surprise spoiled. Instead, the message encoded with ROT13 might look like this:

```
Tbbq sbe lbh--lbh svtherq vg bhg!
→ Naq ab,

gurer'f ab chapuyvar. Ubcr lbh
→ rawblrq

gur obbx! Qrobenu naq Revp
```

A great way to use ROT13 encoding (and decoding) is with **sed**, which will let you easily manipulate text.

## To use ROT13 encoding with sed:

1. `vi script.sed`

   Use the editor of your choice to create a file named **script.sed**. Because the command we're using will be reused, we'll create a **sed** script instead of just typing in everything at the shell prompt.

2. `y/abcdefghijklmnopqrstuvwxyz`
   `→ ABCDEFGHIJKLMNOPQRSTUVWXYZ/`

   Start with a **y** at the beginning of the command. **y** is the **sed** command to translate characters (capital to lowercase or whatever you specify).

   After **y**, type a slash (/), the original characters to look for (all lowercase and uppercase characters), and another slash.

**3.** `y/abcdefghijklmnopqrstuvwxyz`
   `→ ABCDEFGH IJKLMNOPQRSTUVWXYZ/`
   `→ nopqrstuvwxyz abcdefghijklm`
   `→ NOPQRSTUVWXYZABCDEFGHIJKLM/`

After the second slash, add the translation characters (the lowercase alphabet, starting with **n** and continuing around to **m**, then uppercase from **N** to **M**), followed by a slash to conclude the replace string.

**4.** Save the script and exit the editor.

**5.** `sed -f script.sed limerick |`

Test the ROT13 encoding by applying it to a file. Here we apply it to the **limerick** file, and then pipe the output to **more** for your inspection. You'll see that all you get is gibberish. To test it more thoroughly, use **sed -f script.sed limerick | sed -f script.sed |** to run it through the processor twice. You should end up with normal text at the end of this pipeline (**Code Listing 16.6**).

**TIP** Text is rotated by 13 simply because there are 26 letters in the alphabet, so you can use the same program to encode or decode. If you rotate by a different number, you'll need to have separate programs to encode and decode.

**TIP** Check out the next section to see how to turn this lengthy process into a shell script and make it even easier to reuse over and over.

**TIP** Consider that you can use this same process not only to use ROT13 encoding on files, but to encode in other ways, which might somewhat obfuscate your secrets. Do note that ROT13 is by no means actual encryption.

**Code Listing 16.6** A spiffy **sed** command can ROT13 encode and decode messages.

```
[unixvqs@LinuxMint creative]$ sed -f script.sed limerick
Bhe snibevgr yvzrevpx
1.
Gurer bapr jnf n zna sebz Anaghpxrg,
Jub pneevrq uvf yhapu va n ohpxrg,
Fnvq ur jvgu n fvtu,
Nf ur ngr n jubyr cvr,
Vs V whfg unq n qbahg V'q qhax vg.
[unixvqs@LinuxMint creative]$ sed -f script.sed limerick | sed -f script.sed
Our favorite limerick
1.
There once was a man from Nantucket,
Who carried his lunch in a bucket,
Said he with a sigh,
As he ate a whole pie,
If I just had a donut I'd dunk it.
[unixvqs@LinuxMint creative]$
```

```
Terminal
#! /bin/bash
/bin/sed y/abcdefghijklmnopqrstuvwxyzABCDEFGHIJKLMNOPQRSTUVWXYZ/nopqrstuvwxyzabc
defghijklmNOPQRSTUVWXYZABCDEFGHIJKLM/ "$1"




"rot13" 4 lines, 143 characters
```

**A** A brief shell script makes ROT13 as easy as, well, EBG13.

# Embedding ROT13 Encoding in a Shell Script

If you completed the steps in the previous section, you might have noticed that you did a lot of typing. And, goodness, if you made it through steps 3 and 5, your fingers are probably on strike right about now. If you plan to encode or decode with ROT13 frequently, consider embedding the **sed** commands in a shell script to avoid retyping them each time you encode or decode text, as shown in **A**. You might refer back to Chapter 10 for details on shell scripts before you get started here.

## To create a ROT13 shell script:

1. **vi rot13**

   Start a new shell script to process your commands.

2. **#! /bin/bash**

   Add the obligatory shell specification, as shown in **A**.

3. **/bin/sed y/abcdefghijklmnopqrstu
   → vwxy zABCDEFGHIJKLMNOPQRSTU
   → VWXYZ/nopqr stuvwxyzabcdefghi
   → jklmNOPQRSTUVWXYZABCDEFGHIJKLM/**

   Specify the **sed** program (using the full path to make the program a little more flexible) and the command that encodes and decodes ROT13 text. It's better to make the shell script self-contained, so instead of referencing an external file with the **sed** script, we'll just put it in the command line here.

*continues on next page*

**4.** **/bin/sed y/abcdefghijklmnopqrstu**
   ↪**vwxy zABCDEFGHIJKLMNOPQRSTU**
   ↪**VWXYZ/nopqr stuvwxyzabcdefghi**
   ↪**jklmNOPQRSTUVWXYZABCDEFGHIJKLM/**
   ↪**"$1"**

Here, we added **$1** to pass the filename from the command line (as in **rot13 thisfile**) to **sed**.

**5.** **/bin/sed y/abcdefghijklmnopqrstu**
   ↪**vwxy zABCDEFGHIJKLMNOPQRSTU**
   ↪**VWXYZ/nopqr stuvwxyzabcdefghi**
   ↪**jklmNOPQRSTUVWXYZABCDEFGHIJKLM/**
   **"$1" | more**

Next, pipe the output to **more** so you see the file one screen at a time.

**6.** Save and close the file.

**7.** **chmod u+x rot13**

Make the shell script executable, so you can just enter the name **rot13** rather than **sh rot13**.

**8.** **./rot13 limerick**

Test the script. Because we developed this script in a directory that's not in the path, we have to execute the script with **./rot13**. If you develop the script in a directory in your path, you should just be able to type **rot13**.

---

**TIP** You can also build in an option to redirect the output of the script to a file and save it for later. Basically, all you do is create an if-then statement and give yourself the option of automatically redirecting the output to a filename, as Code Listing 16.7 shows. Check out Chapter 10 for more information about scripts and if-then statements.

**TIP** If you really insist on doing things in alternative ways, ROT13 can also be done with the **tr** utility, like this: **tr '[A-Za-z]' '[N-ZA-Mn-za-m]'** Or if you want to get yet fancier, hark back to **alias** in Chapter 8 and use **alias rot13="tr '[A-Za-z]' '[N-ZA-Mn-za-m]'"**.

---

**Code Listing 16.7** If you want to get really fancy with the script, you can bring together some of the handiest bits of other chapters to make a masterpiece.

```
[unixvqs@LinuxMint creative]$ more rot13
#! /bin/bash
#    If the first item (after the script name) on the command
#    line is save or s, and the second item is a readable file
#    then do the first case.
if [ \( "$1" = "save" -o "$1" = "s" \) -a \( -r "$2" \) ]
then
#    This case saves the ROT13 output under the same filename with
#    a rot13 extension.
/bin/sed y/abcdefghijklmnopqrstuvwxyzABCDEFGHIJKLMNOPQRSTUVWXYZ/nopqrstuvwxyzabcdefghijklm
 ↪ NOPQRSTUVWXYZABCDEFGHIJKLM/ "$2" > "$2.rot13"
else
#    This case pipes the ROT13 output to more, because a save
#    wasn't specified.
/bin/sed y/abcdefghijklmnopqrstuvwxyzABCDEFGHIJKLMNOPQRSTUVWXYZ/nopqrstuvwxyzabcdefghijklm
 ↪ NOPQRSTUVWXYZABCDEFGHIJKLM/ "$1" | more
fi
[unixvqs@LinuxMint creative]$
```

# Making Backups with `rsync`

The **rsync** utility is a fancy way to synchronize files and directories, either locally or across a network. We like to use it to make backups so we don't have to worry when we mess something up. Yes, we could use **cp** or something equally boring, but we like the speed and flexibility of **rsync**. In this example, we're copying files locally, but we could as easily be making remote backups to another server somewhere else.

## To make backups with `rsync`:

1. `mkdir ~/.BACKUPDIR`

   Create a directory to house your backups. Ideally, you'll create the directory on a different physical disk from the stuff you're backing up, but do what you can. We're creating a backup directory that's a subdirectory of the home directory, which will help protect us against self-inflicted damages but not against a disk failure. (We trust the system administrator for protecting against disk failures...er, Eric, you are up to date on our backups, aren't you?)

2. `rsync -v -a /home/jdoe/data`
   `→ ~/.BACKUPDIR`

   Specify the **rsync** command, **-v** (for verbose), and **-a** (for archive) options, as well as the source and destination directories (**Code Listing 16.8**).

   Wait while it does the initial backup (showing you each file as it gets copied). The first backup takes a while but no longer than using **cp** would.

**TIP** When you subsequently run **rsync**, you'll discover that it's far faster because it copies only the files that have changed. Handy, huh?

**TIP** You can gain huge benefits from **rsync** if you start making backups across a network. For example, you can synchronize your web server content with your friend's content located on a different server. Check the **rsync** man page (man **rsync**) for the specifics.

**Code Listing 16.8** The `rsync` utility is a handy tool for making backups. Note that it takes much less time for all updates after the first one.

```
[jdoe@frazz bin]$ rsync -v -a /home/jdoe/data ~/.BACKUPDIR
building file list ... done
data/
data/#*scratch*#
data/#all.programs#
data/#local.programs.txt#
data/*scratch*
data/1
data/2
data/Mail/
data/News/
data/Project/
data/Project/keep
data/Project/keeper.jpg
data/Project/kept
data/Project/kidder.txt
data/Project/kiddo
data/Project/kidnews
data/Project/kidneypie
data/Project/kids
data/Project/kidupdate
data/address.book
data/address.book~
data/all.programs
data/b
data/backup-files/
data/backup-files/.Xauthority
data/backup-files/.bash_history
data/backup-files/.bash_logout
data/backup-files/.bash_profile
data/backup-files/.bashrc
data/backup-files/.mailcap
data/backup-files/.screenrc
data/backup-files/.ssh/
   ...
wrote 24841142 bytes read 14708 bytes 741965.67 bytes/sec
total size is 24779055 speedup is 1.00
[jdoe@frazz bin]$
[jdoe@frazz jdoe]$ rsync -v -a /home/jdoe/data ~/.BACKUPDIR
building file list ... done
data/newer.programs.txt
wrote 30149 bytes read 36 bytes 20123.33 bytes/sec
total size is 24765461 speedup is 820.46
[jdoe@frazz jdoe]$
```

# Using Advanced Redirection with `stderr`

Throughout this book, we've been redirecting input to output, piping the output of one command to the input of another, and generally getting fairly fancy. Can you believe that there's even more you can do with redirection?

Unix provides three channels (technically known as file descriptors) for communication between the user and the system:

- **Standard input (`stdin`)**, which refers to providing information at the shell prompt or accepting information from a different program.

- **Standard output (`stdout`)**, which refers to the output you see whirring by on your screen after you issue a command—for example, if you issue the command **find / -name test**.

- **Standard error (`stderr`)**, which includes error messages you might see whir by on your screen after you issue a command. You might think of this channel as the "second" output channel.

Until now, you've been redirecting **stdin** and **stdout** with **<**, **>**, **|**, **>>**, and sometimes **tee**. Everything on **stderr** has just accompanied **stdout**. Adding separate redirection of **stderr** to your arsenal can make your Unix experience even more flexible.

## To redirect **stderr** in **zsh**, **bash**, and similar shells:

1. **time -p ls**

   Use the **time** utility, covered in Chapter 9, and note that you get both the output of **ls** and the output of **time**. As it happens, the output of **time** is on the **stderr** channel, although you can't see that (all the output just shows up on the screen).

2. **time -p ls 2> time-results.txt**

   Where you'd usually put a **>** to redirect everything to a file, use **2>** to redirect the second output channel to a file. Now you'll get the output of **ls** on **stdout** on your screen, and the output of **time**, sent to **stderr**, in **time-results.txt** (Code Listing 16.9).

*continues on next page*

Code Listing 16.9 Redirecting standard output and standard error separately can be handy.

```
[jdoe@sulley Project]$ ls
keep keeper.jpg kept kidder.txt kiddo kidnews kidneypie kids kidupdate
[jdoe@sulley Project]$ time -p ls
keep keeper.jpg kept kidder.txt kiddo kidnews kidneypie kids kidupdate
real 0.00
user 0.00
sys 0.01
[jdoe@sulley Project]$ time -p ls 2> time-results.txt
keep     kept     kiddo  kidneypie       kidupdate
keeper.jpg     kidder.txt  kidnews   kids  time-results.txt
[jdoe@sulley Project]$ time -p ls 1> /dev/null
real 0.00
user 0.00
sys 0.00
[jdoe@sulley Project]$ time -p ls >/dev/null 2>&1
[jdoe@sulley Project]
```

3. **`time -p ls 1> /dev/null`**

   Or you can send the **stdout** to oblivion (**/dev/null**, which just throws it away) and get **stderr** on your screen.

4. **`time -p ls >/dev/null 2>&1`**

   Or you can send the **stderr** to **stdout** and **stdout** to oblivion. It's apparently pointless, but it's useful in shell scripts if you care only to know whether something succeeded or failed. (Note that, technically, **1>** and the old standby **>** are the same—but this example makes more sense if you regard redirecting **stdout** [1] and **stderr** [2] explicitly.)

**TIP** If you're using **zsh**, you'll need to specify the full path to **time** (**/usr/bin/time**). **time** is a special **zsh** built-in command, so it works a bit differently from the other shells.

**TIP** Redirecting **stdout** and **stderr** separately in **csh** is more challenging, but you can accomplish the same thing with **time -p ls >& /dev/null**. This also works in **bash** and **zsh**.

**TIP** You can **echo $?** to find out whether your command succeeded. You'll get bonus points for being the first person who emails a valid original example of the value of this operation to unixvqs@raycomm.com.

# Unix and Linux Reference

In this appendix, you'll find a fairly thorough reference on Unix and Linux commands and flags as well as examples and descriptions of each. We organized this appendix to generally parallel the book so that you can easily reference key commands and related flags without being overwhelmed with long lists of commands.

**Tables A.1–A.14** contain commands and flags that relate to the topics covered by the similarly numbered or are otherwise grouped with similar commands. In addition to the commands and flags discussed in the chapters, you'll also find related commands and options that you might find useful in your Unix or Linux adventures, reference information that will jog your memory, and ideas to help you get off and running on additional projects. If you're looking for a thorough command line argument and flag reference, check out Appendix C.

**TABLE A.1  Getting Started with Unix and Linux: Survival Skills**

| Command | Function |
| --- | --- |
| apropos *keyword* | Find appropriate **man** pages for *keyword*. |
| cat *file* | Display *file* contents onscreen or provide *file* contents to standard output. |
| cat *file1 file2* | Display *file1* and *file2*. |
| cd | Return to your home directory from anywhere in the Unix or Linux system. |
| cd .. | Move up one level in the directory tree. |
| cd /etc | Change to the */etc* directory relative to the system root. |
| cd ~/subdir | Use a tilde (~) as a handy shortcut for your home directory. |
| cd Projects | Move to the **Projects** directory relative to the current directory. |
| col -b | Filter backspaces and reverse line feeds out of input. Use to make **man** pages editable without odd formatting. |
| Ctrl+D | Close your current process (often a shell) and your Unix or Linux session if you close the login shell. |
| exit | Close your current shell and your Unix or Linux session if you're in the login shell. |
| less *file* | Use to view *file* screen by screen. |
| logout | Close your Unix or Linux session. |
| ls | List files and directories. |
| ls / | List the files and directories in the root directory. |
| ls *directory* | List the files and directories in *directory*. |
| ls -a | List all files and directories, including hidden ones. |
| ls -c (or ls -t) | List files and directories by modification date. |
| ls -l | List files and directories in long format, with extra information. |
| ls -lh | List files and directories in long format, with extra information and human readable sizes. |
| man 5 *command* | View the specified section (5) of the **man** pages for *command*. Sometimes used as **man -s 5** *command*. |
| man *command* | View the manual (help) pages for *command*. |
| man -k *keyword* | Find appropriate **man** pages for *keyword*. |
| more *filetoview* | View *filetoview* screen by screen. |
| passwd | Change your password. |
| pwd | Display the path and name of the directory you are currently in. |
| reset | Reset the shell to fix display problems. |
| stty sane | Try to fix unexpected, sudden, and strange display problems. |
| su - *yourid* | Relog in without having to log out. |
| su | Become the root user. |
| sudo *command* | Run *command* with the authority of the root user. |

## TABLE A.2 Using Directories and Files

| Command | Function |
|---|---|
| cp *existingfile newfile* | Copy *existingfile* to a file named *newfile*. |
| cp -i *existingfile newfile* | Copy *existingfile* to a file named *newfile*, prompting you before overwriting existing files. |
| cp -r /Projects /shared/Projects | Copy the directory **/Projects** to the new name **/shared/Projects**, specifying recursive copy. |
| find . -name lostfile -print | Find a file or directory in the current directory or subdirectories named **lostfile**. |
| find /home -name "pending*" -print | Find all files or directories with names starting with "pending" in the home directory or subdirectories. |
| find /home/shared -mtime -3 -print | Find all files or directories in the **shared** directory that were modified within the past three days. |
| find ~ -name '*.backup' -exec → compress {} \; | Compress all files in the home directory and its subdirectories whose names end with ".backup", without confirmation. |
| find ~ -name '*.backup' -ok rm {} \; | Find and remove, with confirmation, all files in the home directory and its subdirectories whose names end with ".backup". |
| ln /home/a/* /home/b | Hard link all of the files in the **a** directory to the files in the **b** directory. |
| ln *afile alink* | Link *afile* and *alink*, making the same file essentially exist in two different directories. |
| ln -s /home/deb/Projects /home/helper/Project | Create a soft link from **/home/deb/Projects** to **/home/helper/Project**. |
| locate *string* | Locate files with *string* in their names. |
| mkdir *Newdirectory* | Make a new directory named *Newdirectory*. |
| mv *existingfile newfile* | Rename *existingfile* to *newfile*. |
| mv -i *oldfile newfile* | Rename *oldfile* to *newfile*, requiring the system to prompt you before overwriting (destroying) existing files. |
| rm *badfile* | Remove *badfile*. |
| rm -i * | Delete interactively, with prompting before deletion. Good for files with problematic names that Unix or Linux thinks are command flags. |
| rm -i *badfile* | Remove *badfile* interactively. |
| rm -ir dan* | Interactively remove all the directories or files that start with "dan" in the current directory and all of the files and subdirectories in the subdirectories starting with "dan". |
| rmdir *Yourdirectory* | Remove the empty directory *Yourdirectory*. |
| touch *newfile* | Create a file named *newfile* with no content. |
| touch -t *201512312359 oldfile* | Update file date for *oldfile* to December 31, 23 hours, and 59 minutes in 2015. |
| which *command* | Find out the full path to *command*. This is valuable for seeing which of multiple commands with the same name would be executed. |
| whereis *file* | Find out the full path to *file* and related files. |

## TABLE A.3 Working with Your Shell

| Command | Function |
| --- | --- |
| !10 | Rerun command 10 from the history list in **bash**, **csh**, or **zsh**. |
| bash | Start a **bash** subshell or run a **bash** script. |
| chsh | Change your login shell. |
| csh | Start a **csh** (C) subshell or run a **csh** shell script. |
| echo $SHELL | Display the value of the **$SHELL** environment variable. |
| exit | Leave the current shell and return to the previous one, or log out of the login shell. |
| history | View a numbered list of previous commands. |
| sh | Start an **sh** (Bourne) subshell or run an **sh** shell script. |
| stty erase '^?' | Make ⌷Delete⌷ erase characters to the left of the cursor. |
| stty erase '^H' | Make ⌷Backspace⌷ (⌷Ctrl⌷+⌷H⌷) erase characters to the left of the cursor. |
| su | Switch user to root. |
| su - | Start a new login shell as root. |
| su - *yourid* | Start a new login shell as *yourid*. |
| su *user* | Switch user to *user*. |
| tcsh | Start a **tcsh** subshell or run a **tcsh** shell script. |
| zsh | Start a **zsh** subshell or run a **zsh** shell script. |

## TABLE A.4 Creating and Editing Files

| Command | Function |
| --- | --- |
| ed | Choose a line-oriented text editor. |
| emacs | Choose a tremendously powerful, somewhat easy to use text editor. |
| emacs -n | Open **emacs** and force a terminal-window-oriented session. |
| emacs *filename* | Open **emacs** and edit *filename*. |
| nano | Choose for menu-oriented, user-friendly text editing. |
| nano *filename* | Open and edit *filename* in **nano**. |
| nano -w *filename* | Disable word wrapping for *filename* in **nano**. This is particularly useful for configuration files. |
| pico | Choose for menu-oriented, user-friendly text editing. |
| pico *filename* | Open and edit *filename* in **pico**. |
| pico -w *filename* | Disable word wrapping for *filename* in **pico**. This is particularly useful for configuration files. |
| vi | Choose a powerful but complex editor. |
| vi *filename* | Open and edit *filename* in **vi**. |

**TABLE A.5** Controlling File Ownership and Permissions

| Command | Function |
|---|---|
| chgrp | Change the group association of files or directories. |
| chgrp *groupname filename* | Change the group association of *filename* to *groupname*. |
| chgrp -R *group directory* | Recursively change the group association of *directory* and all subdirectories and files within it to *group*. |
| chmod | Change the permissions for a file or directory. |
| chmod a-w *file* | Remove write permission for *file* for all (everyone). |
| chmod g+w *file* | Add write permission for *file* for the owning group. |
| chmod -R go-rwx * | Revoke all permissions from everyone except the user for all files in the current directory and all subdirectories and their contents. |
| chmod u=rwx,g=rx,o=r *file* | Set the permissions on *file* to user read, write, and execute, group read and execute, and others read. |
| chmod ugo= * | Revoke all permissions for everything in the current directory from everyone. |
| chown | Change the ownership of files or directories. |
| chown -R *user Directory* | Recursively change the ownership of *Directory* and all contents to *user*. |
| chown *user file* | Change the ownership of *file* to *user*. |
| umask *033* | Specify the default permissions for all created files. |

### TABLE A.6 Manipulating Files

| Command | Function |
| --- | --- |
| awk | Manipulate a file as a database. |
| awk /CA/'{ print $2 $1 $7 }' *file* | Select (and display) three fields in each record in *file* on lines that contain "CA". |
| awk '{ print $1 }' *file* | Select (and display) the first field in each record in *file*. |
| awk -f script.awk *file* | Run an **awk** command from a script called **script.awk** on *file*. |
| awk -F, '{ print $1 }' *file* > → *newfile* | Select the first field in each record in *file*, specifying that a "," delimits fields, and redirect the output to *newfile*. |
| awk -F: '{ print $2 " " $1 → " in " $7 }' *file* | Select (and display) several fields and some text for each record in *file*, using a colon (:) as a field delimiter. |
| basename | Remove the path from a filename, leaving only the name proper. Good to use in scripts to display just a filename. |
| cmp *newfile oldfile* | Compare *newfile* to *oldfile*. |
| crypt | Encrypt a password-protected file. |
| csplit | Divide files based on line number or other characteristics. |
| diff -b *newfile oldfile* | Find differences (ignoring white space) between *newfile* and *oldfile*. |
| diff *Directory Newdirectory* | Find differences between *Directory* and *Newdirectory*. |
| diff -i *newfile oldfile* | Find differences (except in case) between *newfile* and *oldfile*. |
| diff -iBw *file1 file2* | Find all differences between *file1* and *file2* except those involving blank lines, spaces, tabs, or lowercase/uppercase letters. |
| diff *newfile oldfile* | Find the differences between *newfile* and *oldfile*. |
| diff -w *newfile oldfile* | Find differences (ignoring spaces) between *newfile* and *oldfile*. |
| fmt *file* | Reformat *file* so it has even lines and a nice appearance. |
| fold -w 60 *file* | Reformat *file* so no lines exceed a specified length (60 characters here). |
| grep *expression file* | Find *expression* in *file* and view the lines containing *expression*. |
| grep -c *expression file* | Count how many times *expression* appears in *file*. |
| grep -i *expression file* | Find all lines containing *expression* in *file*, using any capitalization (case-insensitive). |
| grep -n *expression file* | Display each found line and a line number. |
| grep 'Nantucket$' *limerick** | Find the lines in the *limerick* files that end with "Nantucket". |
| grep -v *expression file* | Find all lines in *file* that do not contain *expression*. |
| grep '^[A-Za-z]' *limerick* | Find all the lines in *limerick* that start with any letter, but not with a number or symbol. |
| grep '^[A-Z]' *limerick* | Find all the lines in *limerick* that start with a capital letter. |
| grep '^There' *limerick** | Find all the lines in the *limerick* files that start with "There". |
| grep -5 'word[1234]' *file* | Find *word1*, *word2*, *word3*, or *word4* in *file* and view the surrounding five lines as well as the lines containing the words. |
| head -20 *file* | View the first 20 lines of *file*. |

*table continues on next page*

**TABLE A.6** *continued*

| Command | Function |
|---------|----------|
| head *file* | View the first 10 lines of *file*. |
| pr *file* | Reformat *file* for printing, complete with headers and footers. |
| pr --columns=2 *file* | Reformat *file* for printing, complete with headers and footers and two columns. |
| sdiff *newfile oldfile* | View the differences between *newfile* and *oldfile*. |
| sdiff -s *newfile oldfile* | View the differences between *newfile* and *oldfile*, without showing identical lines. |
| sed | Make changes throughout a file according to command-line input or a **sed** script. |
| sed '/old/new/g' *file.htm* | Search through *file.htm* and replace every occurrence of "old" with "new". |
| sed -f script.sed *file* > *file.new*; mv *file.new file* | Run the commands in **script.sed**, apply them to *file*, and replace *file* with the manipulated content. |
| split -b 500k *file* | Split *file* into 500 KB chunks. |
| sort *file* \| uniq | Sort *file* and send it to **uniq** to eliminate duplicates. |
| sort *file* > *sortedfile* | Sort the lines in *file* alphabetically and present the sorted results in *sortedfile*. |
| sort *file1* \| tee *sorted* \| mail *boss@raycomm.com* | Sort *file1* and, with **tee**, send it both to the file *sorted* and to standard output, where it gets mailed to the boss. |
| sort *file1 file2* \| uniq -d | Sort *file1* and *file2* together and find all the lines that are duplicated. |
| sort *file1 file2 file3* > *bigfile* | Sort and combine the contents of *file1*, *file2*, and *file3* and put the sorted output in *bigfile*. |
| sort -n *file* | Sort *file* numerically. |
| sort -t, *file* | Sort fields in the comma-delimited *file*; the character following **-t** (**,**) indicates the delimiter. |
| sort -t, +2 *file* | Sort on the third (really) field in the comma-delimited *file*. |
| spell *file* | Check the spelling of all words in *file*. Returns a list of possibly misspelled words. |
| tail -15 *file* | View the last 15 lines of *file*. |
| tail *file* | View the last 10 lines of *file*. |
| tidy *file.html* | Clean *file.html* to make it "good" HTML, and optionally also easier to read and maintain. |
| tr A-Za-z a-zA-Z < file | Change uppercase to lowercase and lowercase to uppercase. |
| uniq | Use with sorted files to eliminate duplicate lines. |
| wc -b *file* | Count the bytes in *file*. |
| wc *file* | Count the lines, words, and bytes in *file*. |
| wc -l *file* | Count the lines in *file*. |
| wc -w *file* | Count the words in *file*. |

## TABLE A.7 Getting Information About Your System

| Command | Function |
| --- | --- |
| df | See what file systems are mounted where, and how much space is used and available. |
| df /usr/local/src | Find out where **/usr/local/src** is mounted and how much space is available on it. |
| df -k /home | View the file system for **/home** with the usage reported in 1 KB, not 512-byte, blocks. |
| df -h /home | View the file system for **/home** with the usage reported in human-readable terms. |
| du | Get information about disk usage in the current directory as well as in all subdirectories. |
| du /home | Get information about disk usage in the **/home** directory. |
| du -k | Get information about disk usage, measured in 1 KB blocks. |
| du -h | Get information about disk usage, displayed in human-readable terms. |
| file */usr/bin/pico* | Find out the file type of */usr/bin/pico*. |
| finger | See who else is logged in to the system and get a little information about them. |
| finger *@example.org* | Find out who is logged in to the *example.org* system. |
| finger *ejr* | Get information about user *ejr* on your system. |
| finger *ejray@example.com* | Get information about user *ejray@example.com*. |
| id | Find out the numeric value of your userid and what groups (by name and numeric userid value) you belong to. |
| id *otheruser* | Check someone else's status to find out what groups they're in. |
| quota | Find out if you're over quota. |
| quota -v | View your current quota settings and space usage. |
| uname | Use to find out what kind of Unix or Linux system you're using. |
| uname -a | Print all system information, including the Unix or Linux system type, host name, version, and hardware. |
| uname -sr | Find both the system type and release level. |
| watch | Monitor a file or other data for changes. |
| w | Get information about other users on the system and what they're doing. |
| who | Get information about the other users on the system. |
| whoami | Find out your current login userid. |

### TABLE A.8 Configuring Your Unix or Linux Environment

| Command | Function |
|---|---|
| `alias ourterm="longhonking command` <br> `→ -w -many -flags arguments"` | Create the alias **ourterm** to substitute for the command **longhonking command -w -many -flags arguments**. |
| `set` | Find out what environment variables are set and their current values in **zsh** and **bash**. |
| `set VARIABLE="long value"` | Use in **csh** to set the value of *VARIABLE* with spaces or special characters in it. |
| `set VARIABLE=value` | Use in **csh** to set *VARIABLE* to *value*. |
| `setenv` | Use in **csh** to find out what environment variables are set and their current values. |
| `setenv VARIABLE value` | Use in **csh** to make the *VARIABLE* available to other scripts in the current shell. |
| `VARIABLE="long value"` | Use in **zsh** and **bash** to set the value of *VARIABLE* with spaces or special characters in it. |
| `VARIABLE=value` | Use in **zsh** and **bash** to set the *VARIABLE* to *value*. |
| `export VARIABLE` | Use in **zsh** and **bash** to make the value of *VARIABLE* available to other scripts. |

## TABLE A.9 Running Scripts and Programs

| Command | Function |
| --- | --- |
| `at 01:01 1 Jan 2015` | Schedule a job or jobs to run at 01:01 on January 1, 2015. |
| `at 01/01/15` | Schedule a job to run on 1/1/15. |
| `at 3:42am` | Schedule a job to run at 3:42 a.m. |
| `at noon tomorrow` | Schedule a job to run at noon tomorrow. |
| `at now + 3 weeks` | Schedule a job to run in three weeks. |
| `at teatime` | Schedule a job to run at 4 p.m. |
| `atq` | Review jobs in the **at** queue. |
| `atrm 3` | Remove the specified queued job (3, in this case). |
| `batch` | Schedule jobs to run when system load permits. |
| `bg` | Run the most recently suspended or controlled job in the background. |
| `bg %2` | Run job 2 in the background. |
| `crontab -e` | Edit your **crontab** in the default editor to schedule regular processes or jobs. |
| `Ctrl`+`Z` | Suspend a running job, program, or process. |
| `fg` | Run the most recently suspended or controlled job in the foreground. |
| `fg 1` | Run job 1 in the foreground. |
| `jobs` | See a list of the currently controlled jobs. |
| `kill %ftp` | Kill a job by name or job number. |
| `kill 16217` | Kill process number 16217. |
| `kill -9 16217` | Kill process 16217; the -9 flag lets you kill processes that a regular **kill** won't affect. |
| `nice` | Run a job "nicely"—slower and with less of an impact on the system and other users. Bigger numbers are nicer, up to 19. 10 is the default. |
| `nice -n 19 slowscript` | Run *slowscript* nicely with a priority of 19. |
| `pkill badjob` | Kill the process called *badjob*. |
| `ps` | View the list of current processes that you're running. |
| `ps e` | View all processes, including those from other users. |
| `ps f` | View processes and their interrelationships (the forest view). |
| `ps x` | View the processes that the system itself is running (also called daemons). |
| `renice 19 processid-of-slowscript` | Run *slowscript* more nicely (change the niceness of *slowscript* to a priority of 19). |
| `time script` | Time how long it takes (in real time and system time) to run *script*. |
| `top` | Monitor system load and processes in real time. |

## TABLE A.10  Writing Basic Scripts

| Command | Function |
| --- | --- |
| `break` | Use in a shell script to skip the rest of the commands in the loop and restart at the beginning of the loop. |
| `case ... in ... esac` | Use in a shell script to perform separate actions for a variety of cases. |
| `clear` | Clear the screen. |
| `continue` | Use in a **for**, **while**, **until**, or **select** loop to stop the current iteration and start the next one. |
| `echo` | Display a statement or the value of an environment variable onscreen. |
| `echo "Your shell is $SHELL"` | Display "Your shell is" and the name of your shell onscreen. |
| `echo -e "\tA Tab Stop"` | Move one tab stop to the right and print "A Tab Stop" on the screen. |
| `for ... do ... done` | Use in a shell script with conditions and commands to specify a loop to occur repeatedly. |
| `getopts` | Use in a shell script to read flags from the command line. |
| `if ... then ... else ... fi` | Use in a script (with conditions and commands) to set a conditional process. |
| `read variable` | Use in a script to get input (the variable) from the terminal. |
| `sh -x script` | Execute *script* and require the script to display each command line as it is executed. |
| `sleep 4h 5m 25s` | Pause for 4 hours, 5 minutes, and 25 seconds here. |
| `sleep 5s` | Pause for 5 seconds. |
| `test` | Use in a script to check to see if a given statement is true. |
| `test expression` | See if *expression* is true or false—usually used with conditional statements. |
| `while ... do ... done` | Use in a shell script to perform a loop only while the condition is true. |

**TABLE A.11  Sending and Reading Email**

| Command | Function |
| --- | --- |
| `alpine` | Start the **alpine** mail program and read, respond to, or send email. |
| `alpine books@raycomm.com,info@raycomm.com` | Start an **alpine** mail message to *books@raycomm.com* and *info@raycomm.com*. |
| `alpine user@raycomm.com` | Start an **alpine** mail message to *user@raycomm.com*. |
| `mail` | Start the **mail** program. (Use **pine** or **mutt** rather than **mail** if possible.) |
| `mail books@raycomm.com < file` | Send *file* to *books@raycomm.com*. |
| `mail -s "For you!" books@raycomm.com < file` | Send *file* to *books@raycomm.com* with the subject "For you!". |
| `mail books@raycomm.com` | Start a simple email message to *books@raycomm.com*. |
| `mail books@raycomm.com info@raycomm.com` | Start a simple email message to *books@raycomm.com* and *info@raycomm.com*. |
| `mutt` | Start the **mutt** mail program and read, respond to, or send email. |
| `mutt books@raycomm.com` | Start a new **mutt** mail message to *books@raycomm.com*. |
| `mutt books@raycomm.com -a file.tgz` | Start a new **mutt** mail message to *books@raycomm.com* and attach *file.tgz*. |
| `mutt books@raycomm.com,info@raycomm.com` | Start a new **mutt** mail message to *books@raycomm.com* and *info@raycomm.com*. |
| `pine` | Start the **pine** mail program and read, respond to, or send email. |
| `pine books@raycomm.com,info@raycomm.com` | Start a **pine** mail message to *books@raycomm.com* and *info@raycomm.com*. |
| `pine user@raycomm.com` | Start a **pine** mail message to *user@raycomm.com*. |
| `procmail` | Filter and sort mail according to a "recipe." Run from the **.forward** file or automatically by the system. |
| `vacation` | Initialize **vacation** and edit the message template. |
| `vacation -I` | Start **vacation** and tell it to respond to incoming messages. |
| `vacation -j` | Start **vacation** and automatically respond to all messages. |

### TABLE A.12 Accessing the Internet

| Command | Function |
| --- | --- |
| dig *www.raycomm.com* | Look up the IP address for the host name *www.raycomm.com*. |
| dig *@nameserver.some.net*<br>⤏ *www.raycomm.com* | Look up the name *www.raycomm.com* from the name server *nameserver.some.net*. |
| dig -x *192.168.12.52* | Look up the name corresponding to the IP address *192.168.12.52*. |
| ftp *ftp.raycomm.com* | Transfer files to or from *ftp.raycomm.com* using the FTP protocol. |
| irc *wazoo irc.netcom.com* | Connect to the irc server at *irc.netcom.com* and use the nickname *wazoo*. |
| links | Start the **links** web browser. |
| links *http://www.google.com/* | Start the **links** web browser at *http://www.google.com/*. |
| lynx -dump *http://url.com > newname.txt* | Get a spiffy plain text file named *newname.txt* out of an HTML document from *http://url.com*. |
| lynx | Start the **lynx** web browser. |
| lynx *http://www.yahoo.com/* | Start the **lynx** web browser on *http://www.yahoo.com/*. |
| mesg n | Refuse **talk** and **write** messages. |
| mesg y | Accept **talk** and **write** messages. |
| nslookup *www.raycomm.com*<br>⤏ *nameserver.some.net* | Look up the name *www.raycomm.com* from the name server *nameserver.some.net*. |
| nslookup *www.raycomm.com* | Look up the IP address for the host *www.raycomm.com*. |
| ping *www.raycomm.com* | Test the connection to the host *www.raycomm.com*. |
| ssh *somewhere.com* | Securely connect to and use a computer on the Internet named *somewhere.com*. |
| talk *deb* | Talk interactively with the owner of the ID *deb*. |
| talk *id@wherever.com* | Talk interactively with a user **id** on the system *wherever.com*. |
| telnet *somewhere.com* | Connect to and use a computer on the Internet named *somewhere.com*. |
| tn3270 *library.wherever.edu* | Connect to a host computer named *library.wherever.edu* that uses an IBM-mainframe-type operating system, like many library card catalogs. |
| traceroute *www.yahoo.com* | Identify the computers and other devices between you and the host *www.yahoo.com*. |
| traceroute -n *hostname* | Check the path to *hostname* without resolving the intervening host names for faster results. |
| wall | Send a **write**-type message to all users on the system. |
| wget *http://www.example.com/* | Download the file found at *http://www.example.com/*. |
| wget -r -l 2 *http://www.example.com/* | Download the files found at *http://www.example.com/* for two levels down in the web structure. |
| write *otherid* | Send a message to the user *otherid* on the same system. |

## TABLE A.13 Working with Encoded and Compressed Files

| Command | Function |
|---|---|
| `bzip2 file.tar` | Compress *file.tar*. The named file will be replaced with a file of the same name ending with **.bz2**. |
| `bzip2 -c filetozip > compressed.bz2` | Compress *filetozip* and keep a copy of the original, uncompressed file. |
| `bzip2 -d archive.tar.bz2` | Uncompress (un-bzip) a file. |
| `compress -c file.tar > file.tar.Z` | Compress *file.tar* under the same name with a **.Z** ending while retaining the original file. |
| `compress file.tar` | Compress *file.tar*. The named file will be replaced with a file of same name ending with **.Z**. |
| `gunzip archive.tar.gz` | Uncompress (un-gzip) *archive.tar.gz*. Including **.gz** on the end of the filename is optional. |
| `gzip archive.tar` | Compress *archive.tar*. The zipped file will replace the unzipped version and will have a new **.gz** extension. |
| `gzip -c filetogzip > compressed.gz` | Compress *filetogzip* and keep a copy of the original, unzipped file. |
| `gzip -d archive.tar.gz` | Uncompress (un-gzip) a file. Including **.gz** on the end of the filename is optional. |
| `tar -cf newfile.tar Directory` | Create a new **tar** archive containing all of the files and directories in *Directory*. |
| `tar -czf newfile.tgz Directory` | Create a new gzipped **tar** archive containing all of the files and directories in *Directory*. |
| `tar -v` | Add the **-v** flag to **tar** for a verbose description of what is happening. |
| `tar -xf archive.tar --wildcards "*file*"` | Extract the files with names containing "file" from the **tar** archive. |
| `tar -xf archive.tar` | Extract the contents of *archive.tar*. |
| `tar -xzf archive.tgz` | Uncompress and extract the contents of *archive.tgz*. |
| `uncompress archive.tar.Z` | Uncompress *archive.tar.Z*, resulting in a file of the same name but without the **.Z** ending. |
| `uncompress -c archive.tar.Z > archive.tar` | Uncompress *archive.tar.Z* and retain the original file. |
| `unzip zipped` | Unzip *zipped* without specifying the extension. |
| `uudecode file.uue` | Uudecode *file.uue*. |
| `uuencode afile.jpg a.jpg > tosend.uue` | Uuencode *afile.jpg* with the decode name *a.jpg* and save the encoded output as *tosend.uue*. |
| `uuencode -m` | Specify base64 encoding, if your version of **uuencode** supports it. |
| `gzcat archive.gz \| more` | Uncompress (on the fly without deleting the original) *archive.gz* to read the contents. |
| `zip zipped file` | Create a new zip file named *zipped*.zip from *file*. |
| `yencode file` | Create a new yencoded file from *file*. |

**TABLE A.14  Using Handy Utilities**

| Command | Function |
| --- | --- |
| bc | Use a calculator to add, subtract, multiply, divide, and more. |
| expr | Evaluate mathematical or logical expressions. |
| cal | View the current month's calendar. |
| cal 12 1941 | View the calendar for December 1941. |
| cal 2015 | View the calendar for 2015. |
| cal -j | View the Julian calendar. |
| calendar | View reminders for the current date, read from the file *~/calendar*. |
| fortune | Display a fortune, saying, quotation, or whatever happens to come up. |
| look | Look up a word in the system dictionary. |
| lp | Print a file. |
| rsync *file backupfile* | Remotely synchronize (copy) *file* to *backupfile*. |
| script | Record your actions in a file called *typescript* in the current directory. |
| script *covermybutt* | Record your actions in the file *covermybutt*. |
| units | Convert from one kind of unit to another. |

# What's What and What's Where

As you're using Unix or Linux, you'll undoubtedly encounter files that look important or directories that look interesting, but it's often hard to know what files belong to which programs and even harder to figure out what some directories are for. Therefore, we're trying to help out a little with the information in this appendix.

**Table B.1** lists important Unix and Linux files and directories.

**Table B.2** lists the contents of common Unix and Linux directories. In practice, the contents of these directories (and their existence) vary greatly by system, but the configuration described here is fairly standard.

## TABLE B.1 Key Files in Your Unix or Linux Environment

| File Name | Description |
|---|---|
| / | The root directory of the whole system. Note that this differs from /root, which is the home directory for the root user. |
| ~/ | Your home directory. |
| ~/.forward | Address(es) to forward mail to, or redirects mail to a vacation program or to procmail. |
| ~/.procmailrc | Configuration information for procmail. |
| ~/.pinerc | Configuration information for pine and alpine. |
| ~/.muttrc | Configuration information for mutt. |
| ~/.signature | Your signature, which is appended to your messages by email programs. |
| /etc/bashrc | Systemwide bash resource file shared by all bash users. |
| /etc/csh.cshrc | Systemwide csh resource file. |
| /etc/group | System group records. |
| /etc/ksh.kshrc | Systemwide configuration files for ksh users. |
| /etc/passwd | System passwords and user records. |
| /etc/profile | Systemwide configuration file used by bash and ksh. |
| /etc/skel | Original configuration files placed into the home directory of new users. |
| ~/.bash_profile | Primary personal configuration file for bash users. |
| ~/.cshrc | Resource file for csh users. |
| ~/.kshrc | Configuration file for ksh users. |
| ~/.login | Configuration file for csh users in a login shell. |
| ~/.profile | Primary configuration file for ksh users; used by bash if .bash_profile isn't available. |
| ~/.tcshrc | Configuration file for tcsh. |
| ~/.vimrc | Configuration information for vim. |
| ~/.zlogin | Configuration file for zsh users in a login shell. |
| ~/.zshrc | Resource file for zsh users. |
| ~/.zprofile | Configuration file for zsh users. |
| ~/.zshenv | Environment file for zsh users. |
| ~/mail | Mail directory customarily used by pine. |
| ~/Mail | Mail directory customarily used by system mailer and mutt. |
| Makefile | Configuration information used by make to compile and install new software. |
| README | Important information, usually distributed with a new program or script, about installation or usage. |

## TABLE B.2 Common Unix and Linux Directories and Their Contents

| Directory | Contents |
|---|---|
| /bin | Essential programs and commands for use by all users. |
| /boot | Files that the system boot loader uses. |
| /dev | Devices (CD-ROM, serial ports, etc.) and special files. |
| /etc | System configuration files and global settings. |
| /etc/skel | Template configuration files for individual users. |
| /etc/X11 | Configuration files and information for the X Window System. |
| /home | Home directories for users. |
| /lib | Essential shared libraries and kernel modules. |
| /lost+found | Mount point for temporarily mounted file systems, including CDs or DVDs, as well as other file systems. |
| /media | Directory that contains fragments of files found when the operating system checked the file system. These fragments may provide the content of missing files after a system crash or panic. |
| /mnt | Mount point for temporarily mounted file systems. |
| /opt | Directory for add-on application software packages. |
| /proc | Location of kernel and process information (virtual file system). |
| /root | Home directory for the root user/system administrator. |
| /sbin | Essential programs and commands for system boot. |
| /tmp | Temporary files. |
| /usr/bin | Commands and programs that are less essential for basic Unix or Linux system functionality than those in **/bin** but that were installed with the system. |
| /usr/include | Standard include files and header files for C programs. |
| /usr/lib | Libraries for programming and for installed packages. |
| /usr/local | Most files and data that were developed or customized on the system. |
| /usr/local/bin | Locally developed or installed programs. |
| /usr/local/man | Help (manual) pages for local programs. |
| /usr/local/src | Source code for locally developed or installed programs. |
| /usr/sbin | Additional nonessential standard system binaries. |
| /usr/share | Shared (system-independent) data files. |
| /usr/share/dict | Word lists. |
| /usr/share/man | Help (manual) pages for standard programs. |
| /usr/share/misc | Miscellaneous shared system-independent data. |
| /usr/src | Source code for standard programs. |
| /usr/X11R6 | X Window System, Version 11 Release 6. |
| /usr/X386 | X Window System, Version 11 Release 5, on x86 platforms. |

*table continues on next page*

**TABLE B.2** *continued*

| Directory | Contents |
| --- | --- |
| /var | Changeable data, including system logs, temporary data from programs, and user mail storage. |
| /var/account | Accounting logs, if applicable. |
| /var/adm | Administrative log files and directories. |
| /var/cache | Application-specific cache data. |
| /var/cache/fonts | Locally generated fonts. |
| /var/cache/man | Formatted versions of help (manual) pages. |
| /var/crash | Information stored from system crashes, if applicable. |
| /var/games | Variable game data. |
| /var/lock | Lock files created by various programs. |
| /var/log | Log files and directories. |
| /var/mail | User mailbox files. |
| /var/run | Run-time variable files. |
| /var/spool | General application spool data. |
| /var/spool/cron | **cron** and **at** job schedules. |
| /var/spool/cups | Cups-printer daemon print queues. |
| /var/spool/lpd | Line-printer daemon print queues. |
| /var/spool/mail | Incoming mail for users. |
| /var/state | Variable state information for the system. |
| /var/state/*editorname* | Editor backup files and state information. |
| /var/state/misc | Miscellaneous variable data. |
| /var/tmp | Temporary files that the system keeps through reboots. |
| /var/yp | Database files that the Network Information Service (NIS) uses. |

# Commands, Flags, and Arguments

This appendix provides a list of many (but certainly not all) Unix and Linux commands and programs as well as many of the related command-line flags.

In general, flags and arguments offer a thorough selection of options for programs that operate exclusively from command line input, as well as an overview of the functionality for many other programs. Please keep in mind, however, that command-line options only touch the surface of the capabilities of interactive programs (like **nano**, **vi**, **links**, or **alpine**) or particularly complex programs that rely on special expressions (such as **grep** or **tr**) or that use multiple files or sources for information (such as **procmail**).

**Table C.1** provides you with a brief reminder and starting point for learning more about these Unix and Linux commands. While the options we've included here work on our systems, they will likely vary somewhat on different systems or different Unix or Linux versions, or with different shells. Check your local **man** pages for specifics.

Note that multiple equivalent commands or options all appear on the same line, separated by commas. Additionally, multiple options (unless contradictory) can be used with all commands. The brackets [] indicate that one of the options enclosed may be used.

## TABLE C.1 Commands, Flags, and Arguments

| Command/Flag | Function and Action |
|---|---|
| `alias` | Use to create command aliases. |
| `alpine` | Use to read news and email. |
|   `-d` *debug-level* | Displays diagnostic information at levels from **0** (none) to **9** (complete). |
|   `-f` *folder* | Specifies to open *folder* instead of inbox. |
|   `-F` *file* | Opens specified file with **alpine**. |
|   `-h` | Displays brief help message. |
|   `-i` | Specifies to start in folder index. |
|   `-I` *keystrokes* | Specifies initial set of comma-separated keystrokes to execute on startup. |
|   `-k` | Specifies to use function keys for commands. |
|   `-n` *number* | Specifies to start with given message number. |
|   `-o` | Opens first folder as read-only. |
|   `-p` *config-file* | Specifies configuration file to use instead of default personal configuration file. |
|   `-P` *config-file* | Specifies configuration file to use instead of systemwide configuration file. |
|   `-r` | Requires demo mode. |
|   `-z` | Allows eventual suspension of **alpine** process. |
|   `-conf` | Outputs a new copy of systemwide configuration file. |
|   `-pinerc` *file* | Outputs new **alpinerc** configuration file. |
|   `-sort` *order* | Specifies sort order in folders as **arrival**, **subject**, **from**, **date**, **size**, **orderedsubj**, **thread**, **score**, **to**, **cc**, or **reverse**. |
| `at` | Use to schedule, examine, or delete jobs for queued execution. |
|   `-V` | Displays version information. |
|   `-q` *queue* | Specifies queue to use (as a letter). Higher letters are nicer. |
|   `-m` | Specifies mail notification to user when job has completed. |
|   `-f` *file* | Reads job from *file*. |
|   `-l` | Lists queues, just like **atq**. |
|   `-d` | Deletes scheduled jobs, just like **atrm**. |
| `atq` | Use to show queues of scheduled jobs. |
|   `-q` *queue* | Specifies queue to use (as a letter). |
| `atrm` | Use to remove a job from the queue. |
| `awk` | Use to manipulate files as databases. |
|   `-F`*fieldseparator* | Specifies field separator. |
|   `-v` *variable=value* | Sets *variable* to *value*. |

*table continues on next page*

**TABLE C.1** *continued*

| Command/Flag | Description |
|---|---|
| -f *program-file* | Specifies file or files containing **awk** program source. |
| --help | Prints help information. |
| --version | Prints version information. |
| -- | Specifies end of option list. |
| bash | Use the efficient, user-friendly shell **bash**. |
| -c *string* | Reads commands from *string*. |
| -i | Makes the shell interactive, as opposed to noninteractive, as in a shell script. |
| -s | Specifies that additional options, beyond those given, should be read from standard input. |
| -, -- | Indicates the end of options and stops further option processing. |
| --norc | Specifies not to read ~/.bashrc. |
| --noprofile | Specifies not to read systemwide or individual configuration files. |
| --rcfile *file* | Specifies alternative configuration file. |
| --version | Displays **bash** version number. |
| --login | Specifies to start **bash** as a login shell. |
| --posix | Specifies Posix compliance, which helps make anything more portable from system to system. |
| batch | Use to schedule jobs for low system loads. |
| bg | Use to move a job to the background. |
| cal | Use to display a calendar. |
| -j | Displays Julian dates with days numbered through the year from January 1. |
| -y | Displays the current year's calendar. |
| *month year* | Specifies month (1 to 12) and year (1 to 9999). |
| cat | Use to send text to standard output, usually the screen. |
| -b, --number-nonblank | Specifies to number all nonblank output lines. |
| -n, --number | Specifies to number all output lines. |
| -s, --squeeze-blank | Specifies to replace adjacent blank lines with a single blank line. |
| -v, --show-nonprinting | Specifies to display control characters with "^" preceding them. |
| -A, --show-all | Specifies to show all control characters. |
| -E, --show-ends | Specifies to display a "$" at the end of each line. |
| -T, --show-tabs | Specifies to display tab characters as "^I". |
| --help | Displays a help message. |
| --version | Displays the version number. |

*table continues on next page*

**TABLE C.1** *continued*

| Command/Flag | Description |
|---|---|
| cd | Use to change the working directory. |
| chgrp | Use to change the group ownership of files. |
|   -c, --changes | Specifies to list files whose ownership actually changes. |
|   -f, --silent, --quiet | Suppresses error messages for files that cannot be changed. |
|   -v, --verbose | Specifies to describe changed ownership. |
|   -R, --recursive | Specifies to recursively change ownership of directories and contents. |
|   --help | Displays help message. |
|   --version | Displays version information. |
| chmod | Use to change the access permissions of files. |
|   -c, --changes | Specifies to list files whose permissions actually change. |
|   -f, --silent, --quiet | Suppresses error messages. |
|   -v, --verbose | Specifies to describe changed permissions. |
|   -R, --recursive | Specifies to recursively change permissions of directories and contents. |
|   --help | Displays help message. |
|   --version | Displays version information. |
| chown | Use to change the user and group ownership of files. |
|   -c, --changes | Specifies to list files whose ownership actually changes. |
|   -f, --silent, --quiet | Suppresses error messages for files that cannot be changed. |
|   -v, --verbose | Specifies to describe changed ownership. |
|   -R, --recursive | Specifies to recursively change ownership of directories and contents. |
|   --help | Displays help message. |
|   --version | Displays version information. |
| chsh | Use to change your login shell. |
|   -s, --shell | Specifies the new login shell. |
|   -l, --list-shells | Displays the shells in **/etc/shells**. |
|   -u, --help | Prints a help message. |
|   --version | Prints version information. |
| cmp | Use to compare two files. |
|   -l | Displays the byte number (which starting byte in the file) in decimal and the differing bytes in octal for each difference. |
|   -s | Displays nothing for differing files except exit status. |

*table continues on next page*

**TABLE C.1** *continued*

| Command/Flag | Description |
|---|---|
| `compress` | Use to compress and expand archives. |
| `-c` | Specifies that **compress/uncompress** write to standard output (usually your screen) and leave files unchanged. |
| `-r` | Specifies to recursively process directories. |
| `-V` | Displays version information. |
| `cp` | Use to copy files or directories. |
| `-a, --archive` | Specifies to preserve file structure and attributes. |
| `-b, --backup` | Specifies to make backups of files before overwriting. |
| `-d, --no-dereference` | Specifies to copy symbolic links as symbolic links rather than the files that they point to. |
| `-f, --force` | Specifies to overwrite all existing destination files. |
| `-i, --interactive` | Requires prompting before overwriting. |
| `-l, --link` | Specifies to make hard links instead of copies of files. |
| `-P, --parents` | Completes destination filenames by appending the source filename to the target directory name. |
| `-p, --preserve` | Specifies to preserve the original file characteristics, including permissions and ownership. |
| `-r, -R, --recursive` | Specifies to copy directories recursively. |
| `-s, --symbolic-link` | Specifies to make symbolic links instead of copies of files. |
| `-u, --update` | Specifies not to overwrite newer files. |
| `-v, --verbose` | Displays filenames before copying. |
| `-x, --one-file-system` | Restricts action to a single file system. |
| `--help` | Prints a help message. |
| `--version` | Prints version information. |
| `-S suffix, --suffix=suffix` | Specifies a suffix for backup files. |
| `crontab` | Use to maintain **crontab** files. |
| `-l` | Displays current **crontab**. |
| `-r` | Removes current **crontab**. |
| `-e` | Opens **crontab** in default editor. |
| `curl` | Use to download files from or upload files to a remote server. |
| `-o` | Specifies local file to which to save the remote content. |
| `-C` | Specifies to resume an interrupted download. |
| `-O` | Specifies the remote URL to download from, and to use the remote name as the local name when saving. |
| `-z 9-Nov-2015` | Specifies date, and requires that only files modified after that data will be downloaded. |

*table continues on next page*

TABLE C.1 *continued*

| Command/Flag | Description |
| --- | --- |
| `df` | Use to display information about free disk space. |
| `-a, --all` | Specifies that all file systems, including special ones (for example, CDROM, MSDOS), should be processed. |
| `-i, --inodes` | Displays inode (disk element) usage information. |
| `-k, --block-size=1K` | Displays sizes in 1 KB blocks instead of 512-byte blocks. |
| `-h` | Provides file sizes in human-readable format. |
| `-P, --portability` | Uses Posix standard output format. |
| `-T, --print-type` | Displays type of each file system. |
| `-t, --type=`*fstype* | Displays only named file system types. |
| `-x, --exclude-type=`*fstype* | Displays only non-named file system types. |
| `--help` | Prints help information. |
| `--version` | Prints version information. |
| `diff` | Use to display differences between text files. |
| `-b` | Specifies to ignore trailing blanks (spaces and tabs) and consider other blanks equivalent. |
| `-i` | Specifies case-insensitive comparisons. |
| `-t` | Specifies to expand tab characters to spaces in output. |
| `-w` | Specifies to ignore all blanks. |
| `-c` | Specifies a listing of differences with three lines of context. |
| `-C` *number* | Specifies a listing of differences with *number* lines of context. |
| `-e` | Specifies output of a script for the **ed** editor to re-create the second file from the first. |
| `-f` | Specifies output of a script to create the first file from the second. |
| `-h` | Specifies fast and not necessarily complete comparison. |
| `-n` | Specifies output of a script to create the first file from the second along with a total of changed lines for each command. |
| `-D` *string* | Outputs combined version of first and second files with C preprocessor controls to compile as the first or the second file. |
| `-r` | Specifies that **diff** should recursively process subdirectories common to both given directories. |
| `-s` | Outputs names of identical (not different) files. |
| `-S` *name* | Begins comparison within a directory with the specified filename. |
| `dig` | Use to look up IP numbers or domain names. |
| `-b` *ip-address* | Specifies to set the source IP address of the query. |
| `-f` *filename* | Specifies to read lookup requests from a file (*filename*). |
| `-p` *portnumber* | Specifies a port number to use instead of the standard 53. |
| `-t` *type* | Specifies the query type. |
| `-x` *address* | Specifies reverse lookups (addresses to names). |

*table continues on next page*

**TABLE C.1** *continued*

| Command/Flag | Description |
| --- | --- |
| du | Use to display disk usage information. |
|   -a, --all | Displays information for all files. |
|   -b, --bytes | Displays sizes in bytes. |
|   -c, --total | Displays totals for all arguments. |
|   -k, --block-size=1K | Displays sizes in kilobytes. |
|   -h, --human-readable | Provides file sizes in human-readable format. |
|   -l, --count-links | Displays sizes of all files, including linked files counted elsewhere. |
|   -s, --summarize | Displays only totals for each argument. |
|   -x, --one-file-system | Specifies not to process directories on other file systems. |
|   -L, --dereference | Displays space used by linked file or directory, not just space used by link. |
|   -S, --separate-dirs | Counts directories separately. |
|   --help | Prints help information. |
|   --version | Prints version information. |
| emacs | Use to edit files. |
|   *file* | Specifies name of file to edit. |
|   *+number* | Specifies to go to the specified line number. |
|   -q | Specifies not to load an initialization file. |
|   -u *user* | Specifies to load *user*'s initialization file. |
|   -t *file* | Specifies to use *file* as the terminal. |
| expr | Use to evaluate expressions. |
|   --help | Specifies to display help information. |
|   --version | Specifies to display version information. |
| fg | Use to move a job to the foreground. |
| file | Use to determine file type. |
|   -m *list* | Specifies alternative list of files with magic numbers (helping to indicate file type). |
|   -z | Attempts to look into compressed files. |
|   -b | Specifies brief output mode. |
|   -c | Checks magic file. |
|   -f *file* | Specifies to read names of the files to be examined from *file*. |
|   -L | Specifies to follow symbolic links. |

*table continues on next page*

**TABLE C.1** *continued*

| Command/Flag | Description |
| --- | --- |
| `find` | Use to find files in the Unix or Linux system. |
| `-daystart` | Specifies to measure all times starting today, not 24 hours ago. |
| `-depth` | Specifies to process directory contents before the directory. |
| `-help, --help` | Prints a help message. |
| `-maxdepth levels` | Specifies how many *levels* below starting directory level to descend. |
| `-mindepth levels` | Specifies how many *levels* below starting directory level to start processing. |
| `-mount, -xdev` | Specifies not to descend directories on other file systems. |
| `-noleaf` | Specifies not to optimize for Unix or Linux systems, which is needed for CD-ROM directories, for example. |
| `-version, --version` | Prints version information. |
| `-amin n` | Finds files accessed *n* minutes ago. |
| `-anewer file` | Finds file accessed more recently than *file* was modified. |
| `-atime n` | Finds files accessed *n* days ago. |
| `-cmin n` | Finds files whose status was changed *n* minutes ago. |
| `-cnewer file` | Finds files whose status was changed more recently than *file* was modified. |
| `-ctime n` | Finds files whose status was changed *n* days ago. |
| `-empty` | Finds files and directories that are empty. |
| `-fstype type` | Finds files on file systems of specified *type*. |
| `-gid n` | Finds files with numeric group ID of *n*. |
| `-group gname` | Finds files with group name of *gname* or corresponding group ID. |
| `-ilname pattern` | Finds files that are symbolic links with *pattern* text in the name, case-insensitive. |
| `-iname pattern` | Finds files with *pattern* in the name, case-insensitive. |
| `-inum n` | Finds files with inode number *n*. |
| `-ipath pattern` | Finds files with *pattern* in the path, case-insensitive. |
| `-iregex pattern` | Finds files whose full paths are matched by the regular expression *pattern*, case-insensitive. |
| `-links n` | Finds files with *n* links. |
| `-lname pattern` | Finds files that are symbolic links with *pattern* in the name. |
| `-mmin n` | Finds files last modified *n* minutes ago. |
| `-mtime n` | Finds files last modified *n* days ago. |
| `-name pattern` | Finds files with name of *pattern*. |

*table continues on next page*

**TABLE C.1** *continued*

| Command/Flag | Description |
|---|---|
| `-newer` *file* | Finds files modified more recently than *file*. |
| `-nouser` | Finds files with no user name corresponding to the numeric userid. |
| `-nogroup` | Finds files with no group name corresponding to the numeric group ID. |
| `-path` *pattern* | Finds files with paths matching *pattern*. |
| `-regex` *pattern* | Finds files with regular expression *pattern* in name, case-sensitive. |
| `-size` *n*[cwbkMG] | Finds files using *n* bytes, words, 512-byte blocks, kilobytes, megabytes, or gigabytes, respectively, of space. |
| `-type` *type* | Finds files of type **type**, where **b** is block (buffered) special, **c** is character (unbuffered) special, **d** is directory, **p** is named pipe (FIFO), **f** is regular file, **l** is symbolic link, or **s** is socket. |
| `-uid` *n* | Finds files with numeric userid of *n*. |
| `-used` *n* | Finds files last accessed *n* days after status changed. |
| `-user` *uname* | Finds files owned by userid or numeric id user ID. |
| `-exec` *command* \; | Executes *command* for each found file. |
| `-fprint` *file* | Prints full filename into *file*. |
| `-ok` *command* \; | Executes *command* with confirmation for each found file. |
| `-print` | Prints results to standard output. |
| `finger` | Use to display information about users. |
| `-s` | Displays the login name, real name, terminal name and write status, idle time, login time, office location, and office phone number. |
| `-l` | Specifies multiple-line format with information from **-s** option plus user's home directory, home phone number, login shell, mail status, and the contents of the `.plan`, `.project`, and `.forward` files. |
| `-p` | Prevents **-l** from displaying contents of `.plan` and `.project` files. |
| `-m` | Disables matching user names. |
| `fmt` | Use to format files. |
| `-c, --crown-margin` | Specifies to preserve indent of first two lines. |
| `-p, --prefix=`*chars* | Specifies to combine lines with *chars* at the beginning. |
| `-s, --split-only` | Specifies to split long lines, but not to combine short ones. |
| `-t, --tagged-paragraph` | Specifies that the indent of the first line differs from the next. |
| `-u, --uniform-spacing` | Specifies to ensure one space between words, two after sentences. |
| `-w, --width=`*n* | Specifies a maximum line width (default of 75 chars). |
| `--help` | Specifies to display a usage message. |
| `--version` | Specifies to display version information. |

*table continues on next page*

**TABLE C.1** *continued*

| Command/Flag | Description |
| --- | --- |
| `ftp` | Use to put files in or get files from FTP (File Transfer Protocol) archives. |
| `-v` | Specifies verbose output of responses and statistics. |
| `-n` | Restricts automatic login. |
| `-i` | Turns off interactive prompting during multiple file transfers. |
| `-d` | Enables debugging output. |
| `-g` | Disables wildcards ("globbing"). |
| `git` | Use to manage files, copy remote collections of files (repositories) and keep valuable files safe. |
| `grep` | Use to display lines matching a given pattern. |
| `-n` | Displays matches with *n* lines before and after matching lines. |
| `-A n, --after-context=n` | Displays matches with *n* lines after matching lines. |
| `-B n, --before-context=n` | Displays matches with *n* lines before matching lines. |
| `-C n, --context=n` | Displays matches with *n* lines of surrounding context. |
| `--version` | Displays version information. |
| `-c, --count` | Displays count of matches for each file. |
| `-e pattern, --regexp=pattern` | Specifies pattern explicitly. |
| `-f file, --file=file` | Reads patterns from *file*. |
| `-h, --no-filename` | Specifies not to display filenames in output. |
| `-i, --ignore-case` | Searches without regard to case. |
| `-L, --files-without-match` | Prints the names of all non-matching files. |
| `-l, --files-with-matches` | Prints the names of all matching files. |
| `-n, --line-number` | Displays output line numbers. |
| `-q, --quiet` | Suppresses output and stops scanning on first match. |
| `-s, --no-messages` | Suppresses error messages. |
| `-v, --invert-match` | Inverts matching to select non-matching lines. |
| `-w, --word-regexp` | Finds only matches for whole words. |
| `-x, --line-regexp` | Finds only matches for the whole line. |
| `gzip` | Use to compress (gzip) or expand files. |
| `-a, --ascii` | Specifies to convert ends of lines in ASCII text mode to conform to Unix and Linux conventions. |
| `-c, --stdout, --to-stdout` | Sends output to standard output while maintaining original files unchanged. |
| `-d, --decompress, --uncompress` | Uncompresses files. |
| `-f, --force` | Forces compression or decompression. |
| `-h, --help` | Displays help message. |
| `-l, --list` | Lists information about compressed files. |

*table continues on next page*

**TABLE C.1** *continued*

| Command/Flag | Description |
|---|---|
| --verbose | Displays additional information about archive files. |
| -L, license | Displays the **gzip** license. |
| -n, --no-name | Specifies not to save the original filename and time. |
| -N, --name | Specifies to always save the original filename and time-stamp information when compressing. |
| -q, --quiet | Suppresses all warnings. |
| -r, --recursive | Specifies to descend subdirectories. |
| -S .*suf*, --suffix .*suf* | Specifies alternative suffixes. |
| -t, --test | Tests compressed-file integrity. |
| -v, --verbose | Displays name and percentage reductions for each file processed. |
| -V, --version | Displays version information. |
| head | Use to output the first part of files. |
| -c, --bytes *n[b,k,m]* | Displays first *n* bytes of file, in **b** (512-byte blocks), **k** (1 KB blocks), or **m** (1 MB blocks). |
| -n *n*, --lines=*n* | Displays first *n* lines of a file. |
| -q, --quiet, silent | Specifies not to display filenames. |
| -v, --verbose | Displays filename. |
| --help | Displays help message. |
| --version | Displays version information. |
| info | Use to read online documentation for commands and utilities. |
| --apropos=*termtosearchfor* | Specifies to look up *termtosearchfor* in documentation. |
| -d, --directory=*yourdirectory* | Specifies to add *yourdirectory* to the list of directories that contain info files. |
| -f, --file=*yourinfofile* | Specifies to use info to open and present the content in *yourinfofile*. |
| -h, --help | Displays help message. |
| -o, --output=*localfilecopy* | Specifies to copy selected content to file called *localfilecopy*. |
| -O, --show-options, --usage | Specifies to show usage options. |
| --vi-keys | Specifies to use keys for navigation that resemble **vi** or less commands. |
| --version | Displays version information. |
| id | Use to display real and effective userids and group IDs. |
| -g, --group | Displays only group ID. |
| -G, --groups | Displays only supplementary groups. |
| --help | Displays help message. |
| -n, --name | Displays user or group name, not number. |
| -r, --real | Displays real, not effective, userid or group ID. |
| -u, --user | Displays only userid. |
| --version | Displays version information. |

*table continues on next page*

**TABLE C.1** *continued*

| Command/Flag | Description |
| --- | --- |
| `jobs` | Use to display list of jobs under control. |
| `-l` | Displays additional information (long listing) for jobs. |
| `-p` | Displays job process IDs. |
| `-n` | Displays jobs that have stopped or exited since notification. Only in **ksh**. |
| `kill` | Use to terminate a process. |
| `-s signal, -signal` | Specifies kill signal to send. |
| `-l` | Displays a list of signal names. |
| `less` | Use to page through files; similar to **more**. |
| `-?, --help` | Displays a command summary. |
| `-a` | Specifies to start searches below visible display. |
| `-bn` | Specifies the amount of buffer space to use for each file, in kilobytes. |
| `-B` | Specifies automatic buffer allocation. |
| `-c` | Specifies not to scroll, but rather to paint each screen from the top. |
| `-C` | Specifies not to scroll, but rather to clear and display new text. |
| `-d` | Suppresses error messages for dumb terminals. |
| `-e` | Specifies to automatically exit if you move down after hitting the end of the file. |
| `-E` | Specifies to automatically exit when you hit the end of the file. |
| `-f` | Forces all files to be opened. |
| `-g` | Specifies to highlight only last found string. |
| `-G` | Specifies no highlighting of found strings. |
| `-hn` | Specifies maximum number (*n*) of lines to scroll backward. |
| `-i` | Specifies case-insensitive searches except when search string contains capital letters. |
| `-I` | Specifies case-insensitive searches always. |
| `-jn` | Specifies a line on the screen where a target line should be located. |
| `-k filename` | Specifies to open and interpret *filename* as a lesskey file. |
| `-m` | Specifies verbose prompting, displaying percentage into the file viewed. |
| `-M` | Specifies even more verbose prompting. |
| `-n` | Suppresses line numbers. |
| `-N` | Specifies line number for each displayed line. |
| `-ofilename` | Tells **less** to copy input to *filename* as it is viewed. |
| `-Ofilename` | Tells **less** to copy input to *filename* as it is viewed and overwrite without confirmation. |
| `-ppattern` | Specifies to start display at first occurrence of *pattern*. |
| `-q` | Specifies quiet operation and only rings bell on certain errors. |

*table continues on next page*

**TABLE C.1** *continued*

| Command/Flag | Description |
|---|---|
| -Q | Specifies totally quiet operation and never rings bell. |
| -r | Specifies to display control characters directly, even if display problems result. |
| -s | Compresses consecutive blank lines into a single blank line. |
| -S | Specifies that long lines should be chopped off, not wrapped. |
| -u | Specifies that backspaces and carriage returns should be sent to the terminal. |
| -U | Specifies that backspaces, tabs, and carriage returns should be treated as control characters. |
| -V, --version | Displays the version number. |
| -w | Specifies that blank lines, not tilde (~), represent lines after the end of the file. |
| -x*n* | Sets tab stops every *n* columns. |
| -X | Disables termcap initialization strings. |
| -y*n* | Specifies maximum number of lines to scroll. |
| -*n* | Specifies the scrolling window size as *n*. |
| -" | Specifies filename quoting character. |
| -- | Indicates end of options. |
| links | Use to browse the web in character-only mode, but with tables and frames. |
| -g | Specifies to run in graphics mode, on an appropriate terminal. |
| -async-dns *n* | Specifies to look up domain names as needed (0) or preemptively (1). |
| -max-connections *n* | Specifies the maximum number of concurrent Web connections. |
| -max-connections-to-host *n* | Specifies the maximum number of concurrent connections to a specific host. |
| -retries *n* | Specifies the number of retries to retrieve a webpage. |
| -receive-timeout *n* | Specifies the length (in seconds) of the timeout when retrieving a webpage. |
| -unrestartable-receive-timeout *n* | Specifies the timeout on nonrestartable connections. |
| -format-cache-size *n* | Specifies the number of webpages to cache for quicker retrieval. |
| -memory-cache-size *n* | Specifies the amount of cache memory in kilobytes. |
| -http-proxy *name:n* | Specifies the name and port number of the HTTP proxy, if needed. |
| -ftp-proxy *name:n* | Specifies the name and port number of the FTP proxy, if needed. |
| -download-dir *path* | Specifies the default download directory. |
| -anonymous | Specifies to restrict capabilities to run in an anonymous account. |
| -no-connect | Specifies to run links as a separate process instead of within an existing process. |
| -version | Specifies to display the version number. |
| -help | Specifies to print help information. |

*table continues on next page*

**TABLE C.1** *continued*

| Command/Flag | Description |
|---|---|
| `ln` | Use to make links between files. |
| `-b, --backup` | Backs up files before removing them. |
| `-f, --force` | Overwrites destination files. |
| `-i, --interactive` | Prompts before overwriting files. |
| `-n, --no-dereference` | Attempts to replace symbolic links. |
| `-s, --symbolic` | Specifies to make symbolic links when possible. |
| `-v, --verbose` | Specifies to display filenames before linking. |
| `--help` | Prints a help message. |
| `--version` | Prints version information. |
| `-S suffix, --suffix=suffix` | Specifies *suffix* for backup files. |
| `locate` | Use to find files with a specific string in their names or paths. |
| `-u` | Specifies to create **locate** database starting at the root directory. |
| `-U path` | Specifies to create **locate** database starting at *path*. |
| `-e dir,dir,...` | Specifies to exclude directories from the **locate** database. |
| `-f fstype` | Specifies to exclude files on named file system types from the database. |
| `-c` | Specifies to process **/etc/updatedb.conf** file when updating the database. |
| `-l n` | Specifies the security level as 0 (no checking, faster) or 1 (checking, slower). |
| `-i` | Specifies to do a case-insensitive search. |
| `-q` | Specifies to use quiet mode and suppress all error messages. |
| `-n n` | Specifies to limit the number of results shown to *n*. |
| `-r regex, --regexp=regex` | Specifies to search the database using a regular expression. |
| `-o name, --output=name` | Specifies the database to create. |
| `-d path, --database=path` | Specifies the *path* of databases to search in. |
| `-h, --help` | Specifies to print help information. |
| `-v, --verbose` | Specifies to use verbose mode when creating database. |
| `-V, --version` | Specifies to display the version number. |
| `look` | Use to look up words in the system dictionary. |
| `-d` | Specifies to use dictionary (alphanumeric) character set and order. |
| `-f` | Specifies to use case-insensitive search. |
| `-a` | Specifies to use the alternate dictionary **/usr/share/dict/web2** |
| `-t` | Specifies the end of the string to compare. |

*table continues on next page*

**TABLE C.1** *continued*

| Command/Flag | Description |
| --- | --- |
| `lp` | Use to print files. |
| `-c` | Specifies to copy file to spool directory before printing. |
| `-d name` | Specifies to print files to the printer *name*. |
| `-i n` | Specifies an existing job number *n* to modify. |
| `-m` | Specifies to send email when the job is completed. |
| `-n copies` | Specifies the number of copies to print. |
| `-q priority` | Specifies the job priority from 1 to 50 (highest). |
| `-s` | Specifies not to report the resulting job IDs. |
| `-t name` | Specifies the *name* for the job being submitted. |
| `-H handling` | Specifies immediate, hold, resume, or *hh:mm* to determine when the job will be printed. |
| `-P page-list` | Specifies which pages to print. |
| `ls` | Use to list directory contents. |
| `-a, --all` | Lists all files. |
| `-b, --escape` | Prints octal codes for nongraphic characters using backslash sequences. |
| `-c, --time=ctime, --time=status` | Sorts according to status change time, not modification time. |
| `-d, --directory` | Lists directory names, not contents. |
| `-f` | Does not sort directory contents. |
| `--full-time` | Provides full, not abbreviated, time listings. |
| `-g` | Displays filename, file permissions, number of hard links, group, size, and time. |
| `-h` | Provides file sizes in human-readable format. |
| `-i, --inode` | Displays index number of each file. |
| `-k, --block-size=1K` | Displays file sizes in kilobytes. |
| `-l, --format=long, --format=`<br>`→ verbose` | Displays filename, file permissions, number of hard links, owner, group, size in bytes, and time. |
| `-m, --format=commas` | Displays names separated by commas. |
| `-n, --numeric-uid-gid` | Displays numeric userid and group ID. |
| `-p, -F` | Displays extra character for each filename to show the file type. |
| `-q, --hide-control-chars` | Displays question marks rather than nongraphic characters. |
| `-r, --reverse` | Sorts names in reverse order. |
| `-s, --size` | Displays file sizes in 1 KB blocks. |
| `-t, --sort=time` | Sorts directory contents by modification time, newest first. |
| `-u, --time=atime, --time=access,`<br>`→ --time=use` | Sorts names by last access time instead of the modification time. |
| `-x, --format=across, --format=`<br>`→ horizontal` | Displays names in columns, sorted horizontally. |

*table continues on next page*

**TABLE C.1** *continued*

| Command/Flag | Description |
|---|---|
| -A, --almost-all | Lists all names except for "." and "..". |
| -B, --ignore-backups | Does not display names that end with "~". |
| -C, --format=vertical | Displays names in columns, sorted vertically. |
| -G, --no-group | Does not display group information. |
| -L, --dereference | Lists names of symbolic links instead of the link contents. |
| -N, --literal | Does not quote names. |
| -Q, --quote-name | Quotes names in double quotes and nongraphic characters in C syntax. |
| -R, --recursive | Displays the contents of all directories recursively. |
| -S, --sort=size | Sorts names by file size, largest first. |
| -U, --sort=none | Does not sort names. |
| -X, --sort=extension | Sorts names alphabetically by file extension. |
| -1, --format=single-column | Lists one file per line. |
| -w, --width *n* | Sets display to *n* columns wide. |
| -T, --tabsize *n* | Sets tabs to *n* columns wide. |
| -I, --ignore *pattern* | Does not display names matching *pattern*. |
| --color, --colour, --color=yes, → --colour=yes | Displays the names in color depending on the type of file and terminal characteristics. |
| --color=tty, --colour=tty | Displays names in color only if standard output is a terminal. |
| --color=no, --colour=no | Disables color display of names. |
| --help | Displays help message. |
| --version | Displays version information. |
| lynx | Use to browse the web. |
| - | Specifies to take arguments from standard input. |
| -anonymous | Specifes anonymous account. |
| -assume_charset=*MIMEname* | Specifies default character set. |
| -assume_local_charset=*MIMEname* | Specifies character set for local files. |
| -assume_unrec_charset=*MIMEname* | Specifies character set to use if remote character set is not recognizable. |
| -auth=*ID:PASSWD* | Specifies authorization ID and password for protected documents. |
| -base | Specifies HTML BASE tag to use when dumping source code. |
| -blink | Specifies high-intensity background colors for color mode if possible. |
| -book | Specifies bookmark page as initial file. |
| -buried_news | Specifies automatic conversion of embedded URLs to links in Netnews. |
| -cache=*n* | Specifies to cache *n* documents in memory. |
| -case | Specifies case-sensitive searching within pages. |
| -cfg=*file* | Specifies alternative **lynx** configuration file. |

*table continues on next page*

**TABLE C.1** *continued*

| Command/Flag | Description |
|---|---|
| -child | Specifies no save to disk and quick exit with ⏎ in first document. |
| -color | Specifies color mode, if possible. |
| -cookies | Toggles handling of cookies. |
| -core | Toggles core dumps on crashes. |
| -crawl -traversal | Specifies to output each browsed page to a file. |
| -dump | Specifies to dump formatted output of specified page to standard output. |
| -editor=*editor* | Enables editing with specified *editor*. |
| -emacskeys | Enables **emacs**-style key movement. |
| -enable_scrollback | Toggles scrollback when supported by communications programs. |
| -error_file=*FILE* | Specifies where to save error code. |
| -force_html | Specifies that the start document be considered HTML. |
| -force_secure | Toggles security flag for SSL cookies. |
| -from | Toggles use of From headers. |
| -ftp | Specifies no FTP access. |
| -get_data | Retrieves form data from standard input and dumps results. |
| -head | Requests MIME headers. |
| -help | Displays help message. |
| -hiddenlinks=[*merge,listonly, ignore*] | Specifies handling of hidden links. |
| -historical | Toggles use of > or --> as comment terminator. |
| -homepage=*URL* | Sets home page URL for session. |
| -image_links | Toggles display of links for all images. |
| -index=*URL* | Sets the default index file to the specified URL. |
| -ismap | Toggles presentation of links for client-side image maps. |
| -link=*NUMBER* | Specifies starting number for files crawled. |
| -localhost | Specifies browsing only on local host. |
| -locexec | Enables local program execution from local files. |
| -mime_header | Displays MIME header with document source. |
| -minimal | Toggles minimal or valid comment parsing. |
| -newschunksize=*n* | Specifies *n* articles in chunked news listings. |
| -newsmaxchunk=*n* | Specifies maximum number of news articles before chunking. |
| -nobrowse | Disables directory browsing. |
| -nocc | Disables prompts for user copies of sent mail. |
| -nocolor | Disables color mode. |
| -noexec | Disables local program execution. |
| -nofilereferer | Disables Referrer headers for file URLs. |
| -nolist | Disables link listings in formatted text output (dumps). |

*table continues on next page*

**TABLE C.1** *continued*

| Command/Flag | Description |
|---|---|
| `-nolog` | Disables mailing error messages to document owners. |
| `-nopause` | Disables pauses on status messages. |
| `-noprint` | Disables printing. |
| `-noredir` | Disables automatic redirection. |
| `-noreferer` | Disables Referrer headers for all URLs. |
| `-nosocks` | Disables SOCKS proxy use. |
| `-nostatus` | Disables retrieval status messages. |
| `-number_links` | Numbers links. |
| `-pauth=ID:PASSWD` | Sets ID and password for a protected proxy server. |
| `-popup` | Toggles handling of single-choice SELECT options as pop-up windows or as lists of radio buttons. |
| `-post_data` | Sends form data from standard input with POST dump results. |
| `-preparsed` | Specifies that HTML source be preparsed and reformatted when viewed. |
| `-print` | Enables printing. |
| `-pseudo_inlines` | Toggles pseudo-ALT text for inline images with no ALT string. |
| `-raw` | Toggles default setting of 8-bit character translations or CJK mode for the initial character set. |
| `-realm` | Specifies access only to URLs in initial domain. |
| `-reload` | Specifies to empty proxy server cache and reload document. |
| `-resubmit_posts` | Toggles forced resubmissions of forms when the documents they returned are revisited. |
| `-rlogin` | Disables **rlogin** commands. |
| `-selective` | Restricts directory browsing to those specified with `.www_browsable`. |
| `-show_cursor` | Specifies cursor to be shown at start of current link. |
| `-source` | Sends output as HTML source to standard output. |
| `-telnet` | Disables Telnet commands. |
| `-term=TERM` | Specifies terminal type for **lynx**. |
| `-tlog` | Toggles **lynx** tracing log. |
| `-trace` | Enables **WWW** trace mode. |
| `-traversal` | Follows links from start file. |
| `-underscore` | Toggles use of underline in dumps. |
| `-useragent=Name` | Specifies alternative **lynx** User-Agent header name. |
| `-validate` | Accepts only HTTP URLs for validation. |
| `-version` | Displays version information. |
| `-vikeys` | Enables **vi**-like key movement. |
| `-width=n` | Specifies number of columns for dump formatting. |

*table continues on next page*

**TABLE C.1** *continued*

| Command/Flag | Description |
|---|---|
| `man` | Use to display online manual (Help) pages. |
|   `-M` *path* | Specifies the directories to search for `man` pages. |
|   `-P` *pager* | Specifies which pager (`more` or `less`) to use. |
|   `-S` *section_list* | Specifies list (colon-separated) of manual sections to search. |
|   `-a` | Specifies to display all matching `man` pages, not just the default first one. |
|   `-d` | Specifies not to display `man` page; rather, display debugging information. |
|   `-f` | Provides `whatis` information. |
|   `-h` | Prints help message. |
|   `-k` | Searches for string in all `man` pages. |
|   `-m` *system* | Specifies alternate `man` pages for *system*. |
|   *section*, `-s` *section* | Specifies to display `man` page from the given section. |
|   `-w` | Specifies not to display `man` pages; rather, print the path of the files. |
|   `-W` | Specifies not to display `man` pages; rather, print the filenames without additional information. |
| `mail` | Use to send and receive mail. |
|   `-v` | Specifies verbose mode and displays delivery details. |
|   `-i` | Specifies to ignore interrupt signals. |
|   `-I` | Specifies interactive mode even if input is not from a terminal. |
|   `-n` | Disables `mail.rc` reading when starting. |
|   `-N` | Disables initial display of message headers when reading mail. |
|   `-s` *subject* | Specifies subject on command line. |
|   `-b` *addresses* | Specifies a blind-carbon-copy (BCC) recipient. |
|   `-c` *addresses* | Specifies a carbon-copy (CC) recipient. |
|   `-f` *file* | Reads contents of file for processing and returns undeleted messages to this file. |
| `mkdir` | Use to make directories. |
|   `-m` *mode*, `--mode=`*mode* | Sets the mode of created directories as with `chmod`. |
|   `-p`, `--parents` | Makes directories and any necessary parent directories. |
|   `--help` | Displays help message. |
|   `--version` | Displays version information. |
| `more` | Use to view files a screen at a time. |
|   `-`*num* | Specifies number of lines onscreen. |
|   `-d` | Specifies prompting and no bell on errors. |
|   `-l` | Specifies not to pause after a Ctrl L in the file. |
|   `-f` | Specifies to count logical lines rather than screen lines. |

*table continues on next page*

**TABLE C.1** *continued*

| Command/Flag | Description |
|---|---|
| -p | Specifies not to scroll, but rather to clear and display new text. |
| -c | Specifies not to scroll, but rather to paint each screen from the top. |
| -s | Specifies to squeeze multiple blank lines together. |
| -u | Specifies to suppress underlining. |
| */string* | Specifies a string to find and start at for displaying the file. |
| *+num* | Specifies to start at line number *num*. |
| mutt | Use a small but very powerful text-based program for email. |
| -a *file* | Specifies to attach a file to your message. |
| -b *address* | Specifies a blind-carbon-copy (BCC) recipient. |
| -c *address* | Specifies a carbon-copy (CC) recipient. |
| -e *command* | Specifies a configuration command to be run after initialization files. |
| -f *mailbox* | Specifies which mailbox to load. |
| -F *muttrc* | Specifies an initialization file to read instead of **~/.muttrc**. |
| -h | Specifies to display help information. |
| -H *draft* | Specifies a draft file to use for creating a message. |
| -i *include* | Specifies a file to include in a message. |
| -m *type* | Specifies a default mailbox type. |
| -n | Specifies to ignore the system configuration file. |
| -p | Specifies to resume a postponed message. |
| -R | Specifies to open a mailbox in read-only mode. |
| -s *subject* | Specifies the subject of the message. |
| -v | Specifies to display version information. |
| -x | Specifies to emulate **mailx** compose mode. |
| -y | Specifies to start with a listing of all mailboxes specified. |
| -z | Specifies not to start if there are no messages, when used with **-f**. |
| -Z | Specifies to open the first mailbox specified that contains new mail. |
| mv | Use to rename or move files. |
| -b, --backup | Specifies to make backups of files before removal. |
| -f, --force | Specifies to overwrite all existing destination files. |
| -i, --interactive | Requires prompting before overwriting. |
| -v, --verbose | Displays filenames before moving. |
| --help | Prints a help message. |
| --version | Prints version information. |
| -S *suffix*, --suffix=*suffix* | Specifies suffix for backup files. |

*table continues on next page*

**TABLE C.1** *continued*

| Command/Flag | Description |
|---|---|
| `nano` | Use for user-friendly text editing. |
| `+n` | Starts **nano** with the cursor located *n* lines into the file. |
| `-d` | Specifies that the Delete key rubs out the character the cursor is on rather than the character to its left. |
| `-k` | Specifies that "Cut Text" removes characters from the cursor position to the end of the line. |
| `-o dir` | Specifies operating directory. |
| `-rn` | Wraps lines at *n* columns. |
| `-t` | Specifies that a changed buffer will always be saved without prompting. |
| `-v` | Specifies view-only. |
| `-w` | Disables word wrap. |
| `-x` | Disables menu. |
| `-z` | Allows Ctrl+Z suspension of **nano**. |
| `nice` | Use to run a program with a different priority. |
| `-n adjustment, -adjustment, --adjustment=adjustment` | Adds *adjustment* number to initial priority. |
| `--help` | Displays help message. |
| `--version` | Displays version information. |
| `passwd` | Use to set a password for the system. |
| `pico` | Use for user-friendly text editing. |
| `+n` | Starts **pico** with the cursor located *n* lines into the file. |
| `-d` | Specifies that the Delete key rubs out the character the cursor is on rather than the character to its left. |
| `-e` | Enables filename completion. |
| `-f` | Specifies to use function keys for commands. |
| `-j` | Specifies that goto commands to indicate directories are allowed. |
| `-k` | Specifies that "Cut Text" removes characters from the cursor position to the end of the line. |
| `-nn` | Enables mail notification every *n* seconds. |
| `-o dir` | Specifies operating directory. |
| `-rn` | Specifies column *n* for right margin of justify command. |
| `-t` | Sets tool mode for when **pico** is the default editor in other programs. |
| `-v` | Specifies view-only. |
| `-w` | Disables word wrap. |
| `-x` | Disables menu. |
| `-z` | Allows Ctrl+Z suspension of **pico**. |

*table continues on next page*

**TABLE C.1** *continued*

| Command/Flag | Description |
|---|---|
| `pine` | Use to read news and email. Choose **alpine** instead of **pine** if available. |
| `-d debug-level` | Displays diagnostic information at levels from **0** (none) to **9** (complete). |
| `-f folder` | Specifies to open *folder* instead of inbox. |
| `-F file` | Opens specified file with **pine**. |
| `-h` | Displays brief help message. |
| `-i` | Specifies to start in folder index. |
| `-I keystrokes` | Specifies initial set of keystrokes to execute on startup. |
| `-k` | Specifies to use function keys for commands. |
| `-n number` | Specifies to start with given message number. |
| `-o` | Opens first folder as read-only. |
| `-p config-file` | Specifies configuration file to use instead of default personal configuration file. |
| `-P config-file` | Specifies configuration file to use instead of systemwide configuration file. |
| `-r` | Requires demo mode. |
| `-z` | Allows eventual suspension of **pine** process. |
| `-conf` | Outputs a new copy of systemwide configuration file. |
| `-pinerc file` | Outputs new **pinerc** configuration file. |
| `-sort order` | Specifies sort order in folders as **arrival**, **subject**, **from**, **date**, **size**, **orderedsubj**, **thread**, **score**, **to**, **cc**, or **reverse**. |
| `ping` | Use to see if a specific host is reachable. |
| `-c count` | Specifies number of responses to receive before stopping. |
| `-d` | Specifies SO_DEBUG option. |
| `-f` | Specifies flood **ping** (for system administrators only). |
| `-i wait` | Specifies how many seconds to wait between packets. |
| `-l preload` | Specifies initial flurry of packets before reverting to normal behavior; for system administrators only. |
| `-n` | Specifies not to look up domain names. |
| `-p pattern` | Specifies content for packets to diagnose data-dependent problems. |
| `-q` | Specifies quiet output with only initial and ending summary information displayed. |
| `-r` | Specifies to ignore routing and send directly to host on attached network. |
| `-s packetsize` | Specifies size of packet to send in bytes. |
| `-v` | Specifies verbose output and lists all received packets. |

*table continues on next page*

**TABLE C.1** *continued*

| Command/Flag | Description |
|---|---|
| `pgrep` | Use to look up processes based on name or other characteristics. |
| -d *string* | Specifies the string used to delimit each process ID output. |
| -f | Specifies to match against full path. |
| -g *pgrp,...* | Specifies to match only processes under the specified process group IDs. |
| -G *gid,...* | Specifies to match only processes whose real group ID is listed. |
| -l | Specifies to list the process name as well as the process ID. |
| -n | Specifies to list only the newest matching process. |
| -P *ppid,...* | Specifies to match only processes whose parent process ID is listed. |
| -s *sid,...* | Specifies to match only processes whose process session ID is listed. |
| -t *term,...* | Specifies to match only processes whose controlling terminal is listed. |
| -u *euid,...* | Specifies to match only processes whose effective user ID is listed. |
| -U *uid,...* | Specifies to match only processes whose real user ID is listed. |
| -v | Specifies to match the opposite of the characteristics given. |
| -x | Specifies to match only exactly. |
| `pkill` | Use to send a kill signal to processes based on name or other characteristics. |
| -f | Specifies to match against full path. |
| -g *pgrp,...* | Specifies to match only processes under the specified process group IDs. |
| -G *gid,...* | Specifies to match only processes whose real group ID is listed. |
| -n | Specifies to list only the newest matching process. |
| -P *ppid,...* | Specifies to match only processes whose parent process ID is listed. |
| -s *sid,...* | Specifies to match only processes whose process session ID is listed. |
| -t *term,...* | Specifies to match only processes whose controlling terminal is listed. |
| -u *euid,...* | Specifies to match only processes whose effective user ID is listed. |
| -U *uid,...* | Specifies to match only processes whose real user ID is listed. |
| -v | Specifies to match the opposite of the characteristics given. |
| -x | Specifies to match only exactly. |
| -*signal* | Specifies the signal (numeric or by name) to send to each matched process. |

*table continues on next page*

**TABLE C.1** *continued*

| Command/Flag | Description |
|---|---|
| `procmail` | Use to process incoming email. |
| `-v` | Specifies to display version information. |
| `-p` | Specifies to preserve existing environment. |
| `-t` | Specifies to retry failed deliveries later. |
| `-f` *name* | Specifies to regenerate the From line that separates messages with *name*. |
| `-o` | Specifies to override fake From lines. |
| `-Y` | Specifies to ignore any **Content-Length:** fields. |
| `-a` *argument* | Specifies arguments to pass to **procmail**. |
| `-d` *recipient* ... | Specifies delivery mode. |
| `-m` | Specifies that **procmail** should act as a general-purpose mail filter. |
| `ps` | Use to report process status (note that *ps* arguments work with or without a -, and warn you not to use - in the future). |
| `-e` | Specifies to show every process on system. |
| `-l` | Specifies long format. |
| `-j` | Specifies jobs format. |
| `-o s` | Specifies signal format. |
| `-o v` | Specifies vm (virtual memory) format. |
| `-m` | Displays thread information. |
| `-H` | Specifies "forest" tree format. |
| `-f` | Shows full listing. |
| `-a` | Displays processes of other users on the same terminal. |
| `-x` | Displays processes without controlling terminal (daemons). |
| `-S` | Displays add child CPU time and page faults. |
| `-w` | Specifies wide output and does not truncate command lines. |
| `-h` | Disables header display. |
| `-r` | Shows running processes only. |
| `-n` | Specifies numeric output for user and wchan fields. |
| `-t--x` | Specifies only processes with controlling **tty** *x*. |
| *pids* | Lists only specified processes. |
| `--help` | Displays help message. |
| `--version` | Displays version information. |
| `pr` | Use to convert and reformat files for printing or display. |
| `-n, --columns=`*n* | Specifies to create *n* columns across the page. |
| `-c, --show-control-chars` | Specifies to use hat notation (^G) and octal backslash notation. |
| `-d, --double-space` | Specifies to double space the output. |
| `-D, --date-format=`*FORMAT* | Specifies to use *FORMAT* for the header date. |

*table continues on next page*

**TABLE C.1** *continued*

| Command/Flag | Description |
|---|---|
| -F, -f, --form-feed | Specifies to use form feeds instead of newlines to separate pages. |
| -h *header*, --header=*header* | Specifies to use a centered header instead of filename in page header. |
| -t, --omit-header | Specifies to omit page headers and footers. |
| -T, --omit-pagination | Specifies to omit page headers, footers, and all pagination. |
| -v, --show-nonprinting | Specifies to use octal backslash notation to display nonprinting characters. |
| -W *w*, --page-width=*w* | Specifies that page width be *w* (72 default) characters. |
| --help | Specifies to display help message. |
| --version | Specifies to display version information. |
| pwd | Use to display name of current working directory. |
| --help | Displays help message. |
| --version | Displays version information. |
| quota | Use to display disk usage and limits. |
| -g | Displays group quotas for the executing user's group. |
| -v | Displays quotas on file systems where no storage is allocated. |
| -q | Displays only information for file systems over quota. |
| renice | Use to change the priority (niceness) of jobs. |
| -g | Specifies to force parameters to be interpreted as process group IDs. |
| -u | Specifies to force parameters to be interpreted as user names. |
| -p | Specifies to require parameters to be process IDs. |
| rm | Use to remove files. |
| -f, --force | Specifies to overwrite all existing destination files. |
| -i, --interactive | Requires prompting before overwriting. |
| -R, --recursive | Specifies to copy directories recursively. |
| -v, --verbose | Displays filenames before moving. |
| --help | Displays a help message. |
| --version | Displays version information. |
| reset | Use to reset a terminal session to normal behavior. |
| -q | Specifies to display the terminal type only. |
| -e *a* | Specifies to set the erase character to the given character. |
| -I | Specifies not to send initialization strings to the terminal. |
| -Q | Specifies not to display values for erase, interrupt, and line kill characters. |
| -V | Specifies to display the version number. |
| -i *a* | Specifies to set the interrupt character to the given character. |
| -k *a* | Specifies to set the line kill character to the given character. |

*table continues on next page*

**TABLE C.1** *continued*

| Command/Flag | Description |
| --- | --- |
| -m | Specifies to map a port type to a terminal type. |
| -r | Specifies to display the terminal type to standard error. |
| -s | Specifies to display the initialization commands. |
| rmdir | Use to remove empty directories. |
| -p, --parents | Specifies to remove any parent directories listed, if they are empty after the specified files are removed. |
| --help | Displays a help message. |
| --version | Displays version information. |
| rsync | Use to copy files and synchronize directories. |
| -v, --verbose | Specifies to increase verbosity. |
| -q, --quiet | Specifies to decrease verbosity. |
| -c, --checksum | Specifies to calculate a checksum for files, not just check dates. |
| -a, --archive | Specifies to use archive mode. |
| -r, --recursive | Specifies to recursively copy. |
| -R, --relative | Specifies to use relative path names. |
| -b, --backup | Specifies to make backups with the default ~ suffix. |
| --backup-dir | Specifies to use this backup directory. |
| --suffix=*string* | Specifies to change backup suffix to *string*. |
| -u, --update | Specifies to update only and not overwrite newer files. |
| -l, --links | Specifies to copy symlinks as symlinks. |
| -L, --copy-links | Specifies to copy the associated file for symlinks. |
| --copy-unsafe-links | Specifies to copy links outside the source directory tree. |
| --safe-links | Specifies to ignore links outside the destination directory tree. |
| -H, --hard-links | Specifies to preserve hard links. |
| -p, --perms | Specifies to preserve permissions. |
| -o, --owner | Specifies to preserve owner, for use by root only. |
| -g, --group | Specifies to preserve group. |
| -D, --devices | Specifies to preserve devices, for use by root only. |
| -t, --times | Specifies to preserve times. |
| -S, --sparse | Specifies to handle sparse files efficiently. |
| -n, --dry-run | Specifies to show what would have been transferred, but not actually transfer. |
| -W, --whole-file | Specifies to copy whole files without making incremental checks. |
| --no-whole-file | Specifies not to copy whole files without checking. |
| -x, --one-file-system | Specifies not to cross file system boundaries. |
| -B *size*, --block-size=*size* | Specifies the checksum block size (default 700). |

*table continues on next page*

**TABLE C.1** *continued*

| Command/Flag | Description |
|---|---|
| -e *command*, --rsh=*command* | Specifies the **rsh** replacement command (probably **ssh**). |
| --rsync-path=*PATH* | Specifies the path to **rsync** on the remote machine. |
| -C, --cvs-exclude | Specifies to autoignore files in the same way CVS does. |
| --existing | Specifies to update only files that already exist. |
| --ignore-existing | Specifies to ignore files that already exist on the receiving side. |
| --delete | Specifies to delete files that don't exist on the sending side. |
| --delete-excluded | Specifies to also delete excluded files on the receiving side. |
| --delete-after | Specifies to delete after transferring, not before. |
| --ignore-errors | Specifies to delete even if there are I/O errors. |
| --max-delete=*NUM* | Specifies not to delete more than *NUM* files. |
| --partial | Specifies to keep partially transferred files. |
| --force | Specifies to force deletion of directories even if not empty. |
| --numeric-ids | Specifies to set permissions with numeric IDs on target. |
| --timeout=*n* | Specifies to set I/O timeout in seconds. |
| -I, --ignore-times | Specifies to copy even files that match in length and time. |
| --size-only | Specifies to copy files only if file sizes differ. |
| --modify-window=*n* | Specifies range of time (*n* seconds) to consider equivalent. |
| -T, --temp-dir=*path* | Specifies to create temporary files in directory path. |
| --compare-dest=*DIR* | Specifies to compare destination files relative to path. |
| -z, --compress | Specifies to compress files when transferring. |
| --exclude=*string* | Specifies to exclude files matching *string*. |
| --exclude-from=*file* | Specifies to exclude patterns listed in *file*. |
| --include=*string* | Specifies to include files matching *string*. |
| --include-from=*file* | Specifies to include patterns listed in *file*. |
| --version | Specifies to display version number. |
| --daemon | Specifies to run as an rsync daemon. |
| --no-detach | Specifies not to detach from the parent. |
| --address=*ADDRESS* | Specifies to bind to the specified address. |
| --config=*file* | Specifies an alternate **rsyncd.conf** file. |
| --port=*PORT* | Specifies an alternate **rsyncd** port number. |
| --blocking-io | Specifies to use blocking I/O for the remote shell. |
| --no-blocking-io | Specifies to turn off **--blocking-io**. |
| --stats | Specifies to show some file transfer statistics. |
| --progress | Specifies to show progress during transfer. |
| --log-format=*format* | Specifies to log file transfers using specified format. |
| --password-file=*file* | Specifies to get password from *file*. |

*table continues on next page*

**TABLE C.1** *continued*

| Command/Flag | Description |
| --- | --- |
| `--bwlimit=n` | Specifies to limit I/O bandwidth to *n* KBps. |
| `--read-batch=string` | Specifies to read batch fileset starting with *string*. |
| `--write-batch=string` | Specifies to write batch fileset starting with *string*. |
| `-h, --help` | Specifies to display help information. |
| `sed` | Use for processing and editing files in batch mode. |
| `-e` | Specifies edit commands to follow as the next argument. |
| `-f` | Specifies edit commands to be taken from named file or files. |
| `-n` | Suppresses default output. |
| `set` | Use to set or view the values of variables. |
| `setenv` | Use to change or view the value of an environment variable (**csh**). |
| `screen` | Use to manage multiple virtual screens in a physical window. |
| `-a` | Specifies to include all capabilities in each window. |
| `-A` | Specifies to adapt the sizes of all windows to the size of the current terminal. |
| `-c file` | Specifies to override the default configuration file (**~/.screenrc**) with *file*. |
| `-d, -D` | Specifies to detach another running screen from the controlling terminal. |
| `-d -r` | Specifies to reattach a session, after detaching it if necessary. |
| `-d -R` | Specifies to reattach a session, after detaching or creating it first if necessary. |
| `-d -RR` | Specifies to reattach a session, after detaching or creating it if necessary, and to use the first session if multiple sessions are available. |
| `-D -r` | Specifies to reattach a session, after detaching and logging out remotely if necessary. |
| `-D -R` | Specifies to attach immediately, after notifying other users. |
| `-D -RR` | Specifies to attach immediately, after doing anything necessary to other sessions. |
| `-e xy` | Specifies the command character (default is cAa), specified as ^Aa. |
| `-f, -fn, -fa` | Specifies flow-control settings to off, on, or automatic. |
| `-h n` | Specifies the size of the history as *n* lines. |
| `-l, -ln` | Specifies to turn login mode on or off. |
| `-ls, -list` | Specifies to display list of existing screen sessions. |
| `-m` | Specifies to force creation of a new session. |
| `-d -m` | Specifies to start screen in detached mode. |
| `-D -m` | Specifies to start screen in detached mode, in existing process. |
| `-q` | Specifies to suppress display error messages and exit codes. |

*table continues on next page*

**TABLE C.1** *continued*

| Command/Flag | Description |
|---|---|
| -r | Specifies to resume a detached screen session. |
| -R | Specifies to attempt to resume the first available detached screen session it finds. |
| -s *string* | Specifies the default shell as *string*. |
| -S *name* | Specifies to use *name* as the name for the new session. |
| -t *name* | Specifies the title for the default shell or specified program. |
| -v | Specifies to display the version number. |
| -wipe | Specifies to remove destroyed sessions. |
| -x | Specifies to attach to a session in multidisplay mode. |
| -X | Specifies to send the specified command to a running screen session. |
| ssh | Use to securely log in to and run commands on a remote system. |
| -a | Specifies not to forward the authentication agent connection. |
| -A | Specifies to forward the authentication agent connection. |
| -b *bind_address* | Specifies the interface to transmit from if multiple interfaces are available. |
| -c *blowfish*\|*3des*\|*des* | Specifies the encryption method to use. |
| -e *ch*\|*^ch*\|*none* | Specifies the escape character for sessions with a pty (default: ~). |
| -f | Specifies for **ssh** to go to the background before the command runs. |
| -g | Specifies that remote hosts can connect to local forwarded ports. |
| -i *identity_file* | Specifies the file from which to read the identify key. |
| -l *login_name* | Specifies the user name to log in as on the remote machine. |
| -n | Specifies to ignore standard input. |
| -N | Specifies not to execute a remote command. |
| -o *option* | Specifies to give options as presented in configuration file. |
| -p *port* | Specifies the port to connect to on the remote host. |
| -P | Specifies a nonprivileged port (>1024) for outgoing connections. |
| -q | Specifies that warning and diagnostic messages should be suppressed. |
| -s | Specifies to request invocation of a subsystem on the remote system. |
| -t | Specifies to allocate a pseudo-tty. |
| -T | Specifies not to allocate a pseudo-tty. |
| -v | Specifies to provide verbose output. |
| -x | Specifies to disable X11 forwarding. |
| -X | Specifies to enable X11 forwarding. |
| -C | Specifies to compress all data for transmission. |

*table continues on next page*

**TABLE C.1** *continued*

| Command/Flag | Description |
|---|---|
| -F *configfile* | Specifies an alternative configuration file. |
| -L *port:host:hostport* | Specifies port forwarding from local to remote sides. |
| -R *port:host:hostport* | Specifies port forwarding from remote to local sides. |
| -D *port* | Specifies dynamic port forwarding from local to remote sides. |
| -1 | Specifies to use only protocol version 1. |
| -2 | Specifies to use only protocol version 2. |
| -4 | Specifies to use only IPv4 addresses. |
| -6 | Specifies to use only IPv6 addresses. |
| split | Use to split files into smaller parts. |
| -b, --bytes=*n* | Specifies to put *n* bytes in each output file (use **k** for kilobytes, **m** for megabytes). |
| -C, --line-bytes=*n* | Specifies to put no more than *n* bytes of lines in each output file. |
| -l, --lines=*n* | Specifies to put *n* lines into each output file. |
| --verbose | Specifies to provide verbose output. |
| --help | Specifies to display help information. |
| --version | Specifies to display version information. |
| sort | Use to sort text files by line. |
| -c | Checks to see if file is already sorted. |
| -m | Merges sorted files together. |
| -b | Ignores extra spaces at the beginning of each line. |
| -d | Sorts by ignoring everything but letters, digits, and blanks. |
| -f | Sorts without case sensitivity. |
| -M | Sorts by month, recognizing three-character month abbreviations. |
| -n | Sorts numerically. |
| -r | Reverses result order. |
| -o *output-file* | Sends output to specified file instead of standard output. |
| -t *separator* | Uses indicated character as field separator. |
| -u | Displays only one of the matching lines. |
| --help | Displays help information. |
| --version | Displays version information. |

*table continues on next page*

**TABLE C.1** *continued*

| Command/Flag | Description |
|---|---|
| su *otherid* | Use to substitute *otherid* for current userid. |
| -c *command*, --command=*command* | Runs specified command as other user. |
| --help | Displays help information. |
| -, -l, --login | Specifies to start as login shell. |
| -m, -p, --preserve-environment | Specifies not to change environment variables from current settings. |
| -s *shell*, --shell=*shell* | Uses the specified shell instead of the default. |
| --version | Displays program version. |
| sudo | Use to execute a command as another user. |
| -V | Specifies to display the version number. |
| -l | Specifies to list the available and forbidden commands for the issuing user. |
| -L | Specifies to list configurable default parameters. |
| -h | Specifies to display a help message. |
| -v | Specifies to update the timestamp and extend the timeout. |
| -k | Specifies to set the timeout to a past time, forcing revalidation. |
| -K | Specifies to remove the timestamp for a current user. |
| -b | Specifies to run the specified command in the background. |
| -p *prompt* | Specifies to replace the default password prompt with a custom prompt. |
| -u *user* | Specifies user under whose ID the command will run. |
| -s | Specifies to use the specified (default) shell. |
| -H | Specifies to change the $HOME environment variable to the target user. |
| -P | Specifies to preserve the user's group ID when running the command. |
| -S | Specifies to read password from standard input. |
| -- | Specifies to stop processing command-line options. |
| - | Specifies to force a login shell. |
| tail | Use to output the last part of a file. |
| -c, --bytes *n[b,k,m]* | Displays last *n* bytes of file, in **b** (512-byte), **k** (1 KB), or **m** (1 MB) blocks. |
| -f, --follow | Specifies to keep running and trying to read more from end of file. |
| -l, -n *N*, --lines *N* | Displays last *N* lines of file. |
| -q, --quiet, --silent | Specifies not to display filenames. |
| -v, --verbose | Specifies to always display filenames. |
| --help | Displays help message. |
| --version | Displays version information. |

*table continues on next page*

**TABLE C.1** *continued*

| Command/Flag | Description |
|---|---|
| `talk` | Use to talk to another user. |
| `tar` | Use to create **tar** archives. |
| `-A, --catenate, --concatenate` | Specifies to append **tar** files to an archive. |
| `-c, --create` | Creates a new archive. |
| `-d, --diff, --compare` | Identifies differences between archive and file system. |
| `--delete` | Removes files from the archive. |
| `-r, --append` | Appends files to the archive. |
| `-t, --list` | Lists contents of the archive. |
| `-u, --update` | Updates archive with newer files. |
| `-x, --extract, --get` | Extracts files from archives. |
| `--atime-preserve` | Specifies not to change access times. |
| `-b n, --block-size=n` | Specifies block size of *n* x 512 bytes. |
| `-C dir, --directory=dir` | Changes to specified directory. |
| `--checkpoint` | Displays directory names while processing. |
| `-f, --file` | Uses specified file or device. |
| `--force-local` | Forces local archive file regardless of filename. |
| `-h, --dereference` | Processes linked files, not symbolic links. |
| `-i, --ignore-zeros` | Specifies to ignore zeros in archives (and not to interpret as EOF). |
| `-k, --keep-old-files` | Specifies that old files should be retained, not overwritten. |
| `-K file, --starting-file=file` | Starts at file *file* in the archive. |
| `-l, --one-file-system` | Specifies to remain in current file system. |
| `-m, --modification-time` | Specifies not to extract the file modification time. |
| `-M, --multi-volume` | Specifies to process as multivolume archive. |
| `-N date, --after-date=date,`<br>`--newer date` | Stores files newer than *date*. |
| `-o, --old-archive, --portability` | Specifies old archive format. |
| `-O, --to-stdout` | Specifies to extract files to standard output. |
| `-p, --same-permissions,`<br>`--preserve-permissions` | Specifies to extract all permissions data. |
| `-P, --absolute-paths` | Specifies to maintain absolute paths. |
| `--remove-files` | Specifies to remove files that have been added to archive. |
| `-s, --same-order, --preserve-`<br>`order` | Specifies list of filenames to match archive. |
| `--same-owner` | Specifies to extract files with same ownership. |
| `-T file, --files-from=file` | Retrieves names of files to extract or create from file *file*. |
| `--totals` | Displays total bytes of created files. |
| `-v, --verbose` | Displays verbose information about processed files. |

*table continues on next page*

**TABLE C.1** *continued*

| Command/Flag | Description |
|---|---|
| -V *name*, --label=*name* | Creates archive with volume name of *name*. |
| --version | Displays version information. |
| -w, --interactive, --confirmation | Requires confirmation for actions. |
| -W, --verify | Verifies information in archive after creating archive. |
| --exclude=*file* | Specifies to exclude *file* from archive. |
| -X *file*, --exclude-from=*file* | Specifies to exclude files listed in *file* from archive. |
| -Z, --compress, --uncompress | Specifies to compress or uncompress the archive. |
| -z, --gzip, --ungzip | Specifies to process the archive with **gzip**. |
| --use-compress-program=*program* | Specifies name of compression program as *program*. |
| tee | Use to read from standard input and write to standard output and files. |
| -a, --append | Appends to specified files instead of overwriting. |
| --help | Prints help information. |
| -i, --ignore-interrupts | Specifies to ignore interrupt signals. |
| --version | Prints version information. |
| telnet | Use to connect to and use remote computers. |
| -8 | Specifies 8-bit operation, which is not the **telnet** default. |
| -E | Disables the escape character. |
| -L | Specifies 8-bit operation on output. |
| -a | Attempts automatic login with the current user name. |
| -d | Enables debugging output. |
| -r | Specifies rlogin emulation. |
| -e *character* | Specifies the escape character to control command-mode access. |
| -l *user* | Specifies the user for remote login. |
| -n *tracefile* | Starts tracing connection to *tracefile*. |
| tidy | Use to validate, correct, and clean up HTML files. |
| -config *file* | Specifies to set options from *file*. |
| -indent, -i | Specifies to indent contents of elements. |
| -omit, -o | Specifies to omit optional endtags. |
| -wrap *n* | Specifies to wrap output at column *n*. |
| -upper, -u | Specifies to output tags in uppercase. |
| -clean, -c | Specifies to replace formatting tags with CSS-style properties. |
| -raw | Specifies to output characters with values higher than 127 unchanged. |
| -ascii | Specifies to use Latin-1 (ISO 8859-1) character set for input, and US ASCII character set for output. |
| -latin1 | Specifies to use Latin-1 (ISO 8859-1) character set for both input and output. |

*table continues on next page*

**TABLE C.1** *continued*

| Command/Flag | Description |
|---|---|
| -iso2022 | Specifies to use ISO 2022 character set for both input and output. |
| -utf8 | Specifies to use UTF-8 character set for both input and output. |
| -mac | Specifies to use MacRoman character set for input. |
| -numeric, -n | Specifies to output numeric rather than named entities. |
| -modify, -m | Specifies to modify original files in place. |
| -errors, -e | Specifies to only show errors without modifying the original file. |
| -quiet, -q | Specifies to suppress extra output. |
| -f *file* | Specifies to write errors to *file*. |
| -xml | Specifies that input is well-formed XML. |
| -asxml | Specifies to convert HTML to well-formed XML. |
| -help, -h | Specifies to display a help message. |
| time | Use to time a job. |
| touch | Use to change file times and create empty files. |
| -a, --time=atime, --time=access, ↪ --time=use | Changes access time only. |
| -c, --no-create | Specifies not to create files that do not already exist. |
| -d, --date *time* | Updates files with given (not current) time. |
| -m, --time=mtime, --time=modify | Changes modification time only. |
| -r, --reference *file* | Updates files with time of reference *file*. |
| -t [[CC]YY]MMDDhhmm[.ss] | Specifies time argument for setting time. |
| --help | Displays help message. |
| --version | Displays version information. |
| tr | Use to translate or delete characters. |
| --help | Specifies to display help message. |
| --version | Specifies to display version information. |
| traceroute | Use to identify the route that packets take to a network host. |
| -f *first_hop* | Specifies initial time-to-live used in the first probe. |
| -F | Specifies "don't fragment" setting for probes. |
| -d | Enables socket-level debugging. |
| -g *gateway* | Specifies the source route gateway. |
| -i *interface* | Specifies the network interface to use for probes. |
| -I | Specifies ICMP ECHO instead of UDP datagrams. |
| -m *max_hop* | Specifies maximum number of hops to use. |
| -n | Specifies not to look up domain names for addresses. |
| -p *port* | Sets base UDP port number for probes. |
| -r | Specifies to ignore routing and send directly to host on attached network. |

*table continues on next page*

**TABLE C.1** *continued*

| Command/Flag | Description |
|---|---|
| -s *addr* | Specifies IP address as source for probe. |
| -v | Specifies verbose output and lists all received packets. |
| -w *seconds* | Specifies the number of seconds to wait for a response to a probe. |
| umask | Use to set the file creation mask. |
| unalias | Use to remove aliases from the list. |
| -a | Removes all alias definitions. |
| uname | Use to display system information. |
| -m, --machine | Displays the machine or hardware type. |
| -n, --nodename | Displays the node or host name. |
| -r, --kernel-release | Displays the operating system release number. |
| -s, --kernel-name | Displays the operating system name. |
| -v, --kernel-version | Displays the operating system version. |
| -a, --all | Displays all the above information. |
| --help | Displays help information. |
| --version | Displays version information. |
| uniq | Use to remove duplicate lines from a sorted list. |
| -u, --unique | Outputs only unique lines. |
| -d, --repeated | Outputs only duplicate lines. |
| -c, --count | Outputs number of occurences of each line followed by the text of each line. |
| -*number*, -f *number*, --skip-fields=*number* | Specifies number of fields to ignore before checking for uniqueness. |
| +*number*, -s *number*, --skip-chars=*number* | Specifies number of characters to skip before checking for uniqueness. |
| -w *number*, --check-chars=*number* | Specifies number of characters to compare. |
| --help | Prints help information. |
| --version | Prints version information. |
| units | Use to convert from one kind of unit to another. |
| -c, --check | Specifies to check that the units data file is valid. |
| --check-verbose | Specifies to check that the units data file is valid, with verbose output. |
| -o *format*, --output-format=*format* | Specifies the format for numeric output (in **printf** syntax). |
| -f *filename*, --file=*filename* | Specifies to use *filename* as the units data file. |
| -h, --help | Specifies to display a help message. |
| -q, --quiet, --silent | Specifies quiet output and suppression of prompts. |
| -s, --strict | Specifies not to convert to reciprocal units. |
| -v, --verbose | Specifies more verbose output. |
| -V, --version | Specifies to display version number. |

*table continues on next page*

**TABLE C.1** *continued*

| Command/Flag | Description |
| --- | --- |
| `unzip` | Use to manipulate and extract compressed files in a zip file. |
| `-f` | Specifies to extract only files newer than those on disk. |
| `-l` | Lists archive files in short format. |
| `-p` | Extracts files to standard output. |
| `-t` | Tests archive files for accuracy and completeness. |
| `-T` | Sets the timestamp to the same as the newest file in the archive. |
| `-u` | Updates existing files from the archive and creates new files as needed. |
| `-v` | Displays verbose or diagnostic version information. |
| `-z` | Displays archive comments. |
| `-j` | Junks paths and puts all files in the current directory. |
| `-n` | Specifies never to overwrite existing files. |
| `-o` | Overwrites existing files without prompting. |
| `-P password` | Requires password to decrypt zip file entries. |
| `-q` | Performs operations quietly, without displaying most status information. |
| `-qq` | Performs operations even more quietly. |
| `uudecode` | Use to decode a file created by **uuencode**. |
| `-o file` | Directs output to *file*. |
| `uuencode` | Use to encode a binary file. |
| `-m` | Specifies MIME (Base 64) encoding. |
| `vacation` | Use to reply to mail automatically. |
| `-I` | Initializes **.vacation.db** file and starts **vacation**. |
| `-a alias` | Specifies alias for vacation user, so that mail sent to that alias generates a reply. |
| `-j` | Specifies to always reply, regardless of To: or CC: addressing. |
| `-tn` | Specifies the number of days between repeat replies to the same sender. |
| `-r` | Specifies to use the "Reply-To:" header if available. |
| `-?` | Displays a short help message. |
| `vi` | Use for powerful text editing. |
| `-s` | Specifies no interactive feedback. |
| `-l` | Specifies LISP program editing setup. |
| `-L` | Lists names of files saved after crashes. |
| `-R` | Forces read-only mode. |
| `-r filename` | Recovers *filename* and edit file saved after a crash. |

*table continues on next page*

**TABLE C.1** *continued*

| Command/Flag | Description |
|---|---|
| -t *tag* | Starts editor with cursor at tag position. |
| -V | Specifies verbose output with input echoed to standard error. |
| -x | Specifies encryption option like that of **ex** and prompts for a key. |
| -w*n* | Specifies default window size. |
| +*command*, -c *command* | Starts editor and executes specified command. |
| w | Use to show who is logged on and what they are doing. |
| -h | Disables header. |
| -s | Specifies short format, omitting login, JCPU, and PCPU times. |
| -f | Toggles display of remote host name. |
| -V | Displays version information. |
| watch | Use to execute a program repeatedly with full-screen output. |
| -h, --help | Specifies to display a help message. |
| -v, --version | Specifies to display version number. |
| -n *n*, --interval=*n* | Specifies to override the default 2-second interval with *n*. |
| -d, --differences | Specifies to display differences between successive updates. |
| --cumulative | Specifies to keep all changes highlighted. |
| wc | Use to count the number of bytes, words, and lines in a file. |
| -c, --bytes | Displays the byte counts. |
| -m, --chars | Displays the character counts. |
| -w, --words | Displays only word counts. |
| -l, --lines | Displays only newline counts. |
| --help | Displays help message. |
| --version | Displays version information. |
| wget | Use to download files or entire websites. |
| -V, --version | Specifies to display the version number. |
| -h, --help | Specifies to display a help message. |
| -b, --background | Specifies to start as a background process. |
| -e *command*, --execute=*command* | Specifies to execute *command* at end of startup process. |
| -o *logfile*, --output-file=<br>→ *logfile* | Specifies to log all messages to the specified file. |
| -a *logfile*, --append-output=<br>→ *logfile* | Specifies to append all messages to the specified file. |
| -d, --debug | Specifies to display debugging information. |
| -q, --quiet | Specifies to suppress output. |
| -v, --verbose | Specifies to provide verbose output (the default setting). |
| -nv, --non-verbose | Specifies to provide nonverbose, nonquiet output. |

*table continues on next page*

**TABLE C.1** *continued*

| Command/Flag | Description |
|---|---|
| -i *file*, --input-file=*file* | Specifies to read URLs from the file given. |
| -F, --force-html | Specifies to force input to be treated as an HTML file. |
| -B *URL*, --base=*URL* | Specifies to prepend URL to relative links in specified file. |
| -t *n*, --tries=*n* | Specifies number of retries. Use 0 for infinite. |
| -O *file*, --output-document=*file* | Specifies to concatenate all documents as *file*. |
| -nc, --no-clobber | Specifies to not destroy a file of the same name as the file being downloaded. |
| -c, --continue | Specifies to continue getting a partially downloaded file. |
| --progress=*type* | Specifies type of the progress indicator as "dot" or "bar". |
| -N, --timestamping | Specifies to enable time stamps. |
| -S, --server-response | Specifies to print the headers and responses sent by servers. |
| --spider | Specifies to verify pages but not download them. |
| -T *seconds*, --timeout=*seconds* | Specifies length of the read timeout in seconds. |
| --limit-rate=*n* | Specifies to limit the download speed to *n* bytes (or kilobytes with **k**, or megabytes with **m**) per second. |
| -w *n*, --wait=*n* | Specifies to wait the specified number (*n*) of seconds between retrievals. |
| --waitretry=*n* | Specifies interval to wait before retrying failed downloads. |
| --random-wait | Specifies to wait random intervals between requests. |
| -Y *on/off*, --proxy=*on/off* | Specifies to turn proxy support on or off. |
| -Q *quota*, --quota=*quota* | Specifies the download quota (in **b**, **k**, or **m**) for automatic retrieval. |
| -nd, --no-directories | Specifies not to create a hierarchy of directories on recursive retrieval. |
| -x, --force-directories | Specifies always to create a hierarchy of directories on recursive retrieval. |
| -nH, --no-host-directories | Specifies not to create host name–prefixed directories. |
| --cut-dirs=*number* | Specifies to ignore (flatten) specific numbers of directory levels. |
| -P *prefix*, --directory-prefix=*prefix* | Specifies directory prefix to use. |
| -E, --html-extension | Specifies to append .html to filenames. |
| --http-user=*user*, --http-passwd=*password* | Specifies the user name *user* and password *password* for an HTTP server. |
| -C *on/off*, --cache=*on/off* | Specifies to avoid or use server-side caching. |
| --cookies=*on/off* | Specifies to use or disable cookies. |
| --load-cookies *file* | Specifies to load cookies from *file* before the first retrieval. |
| --save-cookies *file* | Specifies to save cookies to *file* at the end of the session. |
| --ignore-length | Specifies to ignore "Content-Length" headers. |
| --header=*additional-header* | Specifies to define an additional header to be passed to the HTTP servers. |

*table continues on next page*

**TABLE C.1** *continued*

| Command/Flag | Description |
|---|---|
| `--proxy-user=user, proxy-↪passwd=password` | Specifies the user name *user* and password *password* for authentication on a proxy server. |
| `--referer=url` | Specifies to include "Referer: url" header in HTTP request. |
| `-s, --save-headers` | Specifies to save the headers sent by the HTTP server to the file. |
| `-U agent-string, --user-agent=↪agent-string` | Specifies *agent-string* to send to the HTTP server. |
| `-nr, --dont-remove-listing` | Specifies not to remove the temporary listing files generated by FTP retrievals. |
| `-g on/off, --glob=on/off` | Specifies to turn FTP globbing (wildcard use) on or off. |
| `--passive-ftp` | Specifies to use the passive FTP retrieval method for use behind firewalls. |
| `--retr-symlinks` | Specifies to retrieve files pointed to by symbolic links. |
| `-r, --recursive` | Specifies to turn on recursive retrieving. |
| `-l depth, --level=depth` | Specifies the maximum depth for recursive retrieval. |
| `--delete-after` | Specifies to delete files downloaded as soon as they're retrieved. |
| `-k, --convert-links` | Specifies to convert the links in the document for local viewing. |
| `-K, --backup-converted` | Specifies to back up the original version with a .orig suffix. |
| `-m, --mirror` | Specifies to turn on options suitable for mirroring. |
| `-p, --page-requisites` | Specifies to download all required files to display a page. |
| `-A acclist, --accept acclist, -R rejlist --reject rejlist` | Specifies lists of filename patterns to accept or reject. |
| `-D domain-list, --domains=domain-list` | Specifies domains to be followed. |
| `--exclude-domains domain-list` | Specifies the domains that are not to be followed. |
| `--follow-ftp` | Specifies to follow FTP links from HTML documents. |
| `--follow-tags=list` | Specifies to use *list* for tags that indicate links. |
| `-G list, --ignore-tags=list` | Specifies to ignore listed tags for indication of links. |
| `-H, --span-hosts` | Specifies to recursively retrieve from multiple hosts. |
| `-L, --relative` | Specifies to follow relative links only. |
| `-I list, --include-directories=↪list` | Specifies a list (with wildcards) of directories to follow when downloading. |
| `-X list, --exclude-directories=↪list` | Specifies a list (with wildcards) of directories to exclude when downloading. |
| `-np, --no-parent` | Specifies not to download from the parent directory. |
| `whereis` | Use to find information about the specified file. |
| `-b` | Specifies to search only for binary files. |
| `-m` | Specifies to search only for **man** pages. |
| `-s` | Specifies to search only for source files. |

*table continues on next page*

**TABLE C.1** *continued*

| Command/Flag | Description |
|---|---|
| -u | Specifies to search for unusual entries, which are files with fewer than one binary, man, and source entry. |
| -B *directory* | Specifies to change or limit where **whereis** searches for binaries. |
| -M *directory* | Specifies to change or limit where **whereis** searches for **man** pages. |
| -S *directory* | Specifies to change or limit where **whereis** searches for source files. |
| -f | Specifies to end the directory list and start the filename list; for use with the **-B**, **-M**, or **-S** options. |
| who | Use to display information about who is logged on to the system. |
| -m | Specifies "me", as in "who am I?" |
| -q, --count | Displays login names and total number of logged on users. |
| -u, --users | Lists the users who are currently logged in. |
| -H, --heading | Displays column headings. |
| -T, -w, --mesg, --writable, → --message | Displays user message status. |
| --help | Displays a help message. |
| --version | Displays version information. |
| write | Use to send a message to another user. |
| ydecode | Use to decode yencoded files. |
| yencode | Use to encode files with the yEnc algorithm. |
| zsh | Use the flexible, powerful Z-shell. |
| -c | Specifies to take the first argument as a command to execute. |
| -i | Specifies to force an interactive shell. |
| -s | Specifies to force shell to read commands on standard input. |
| --version | Specifies to print the version number. |
| --help | Specifies to print help information. |
| zip | Use to create a zip-format file archive. |
| -A | Accommodates a self-extracting executable archive. |
| -b *path* | Specifies a path for the temporary files. |
| -c | Provides one-line comments for each file in the archive. |
| -d | Deletes entries from an archive. |
| -D | Specifies not to create entries in the zip archive for directories. |
| -e | Encrypts the contents of the zip archive using a password. |
| -f | Freshens an existing entry in the archive if the new file has been modified more recently than the version in the zip archive. |
| -F | Fixes the zip archive. |
| -g | Appends file to the specified archive. |

*table continues on next page*

**TABLE C.1** *continued*

| Command/Flag | Description |
|---|---|
| -h | Displays help information. |
| -i *files* | Includes only specified files. |
| -j | Junks path name and stores only filename. |
| -J | Junks prepended data (for self-extracting archives) from the archive. |
| -l | Translates Unix or Linux text files to MS-DOS text files. |
| -ll | Translates MS-DOS text files to Unix or Linux text files. |
| -L | Displays the zip license. |
| -m | Moves specified files into the archive and deletes originals. |
| -n *suffixes* | Specifies not to compress files with the given suffixes. |
| -o | Sets the modification time of the zip archive to that of oldest of the files in the archive. |
| -q | Specifies quiet mode to eliminate messages and prompts. |
| -r | Includes files and directories recursively. |
| -t *mmddyyyy* | Ignores files modified before the given date. |
| -T | Tests the new archive and reverts to the old archive if errors are found. |
| -u | Updates an existing entry in the archive only if the existing file has been changed more recently than the copy in the archive. |
| -v | Specifies verbose mode to print diagnostic and version information. |
| -x *files* | Excludes the specified files. |
| -z | Requires a multiline comment for the entire archive. |
| -@ | Gets a list of input files from standard input. |

# Index